DEVELOPMENT AND SECURITY IN SOUTHEAST ASIA

The International Political Economy of New Regionalisms Series

The *International Political Economy of New Regionalisms Series* presents innovative analyses of a range of novel regional relations and institutions. Going beyond established, formal interstate economic organizations, this essential series provides informed interdisciplinary and international research and debate about myriad heterogeneous intermediate level interactions.

Reflective of its cosmopolitan and creative orientation, this series is developed by an international editorial team of established and emerging scholars in both the South and North. It reinforces ongoing networks of analysts in both academia and think-tanks as well as international agencies concerned with micro-, meso- and macro-level regionalisms.

Other Titles in the Series

Global Turbulence
Edited by Marjorie Griffin Cohen and Stephen McBride

Reconstituting Sovereignty
Rory Keane

Japan and South Africa in a Globalising World
Edited by Chris Alden and Katsumi Hirano

Development and Security in Southeast Asia

Volume II: The People

Edited by

DAVID B. DEWITT
York University, Canada
CAROLINA G. HERNANDEZ
University of the Philippines, Philippines

Routledge
Taylor & Francis Group
LONDON AND NEW YORK

First published 2003 by Ashgate Publishing

Reissued 2019 by Routledge
2 Park Square, Milton Park, Abingdon, Oxon, OXl 4 4RN
52 Vanderbilt Avenue, New York, NY 10017

Routledge is an imprint of the Taylor & Francis Group, an informa business

A Library of Congress record exists under LC control number:

ISBN 13: 978-1-138-72583-6 (hbk)
ISBN 13: 978-1-315-19170-6 (ebk)

Contents

VOLUME I: THE ENVIRONMENT

VOLUME III: GLOBALIZATION

PART I: INTRODUCTION

PART II: REGIONAL CASE STUDIES

List of Figures and Map

Figures

Map

List of Tables

List of Contributors

EDITORS

David B. Dewitt is Professor of Political Science and since 1988, Director of the Centre for International and Security Studies, York University, Toronto.

Carolina G. Hernandez is President, Institute for Strategic and Development Studies, Inc. (ISDS) and Professor, Department of Political Science, University of the Philippines, Diliman, Quezon City.

AUTHORS

Jacques Bertrand is Assistant Professor of Political Science at the University of Toronto.

Tubagus Feridhanusetyawan is Senior Economist and Head of the Department of Economics at the Centre for Strategic and International Studies (CSIS Jakarta), lecturer in the graduate program, Faculty of Economics, University of Indonesia, Jakarta.

Muhammad AS Hikam is a Senior Research Fellow at the Indonesian Institute of Sciences (LIPI), Jakarta. He is also teaching at the Graduate School for Government Studies, Satya Gama University, Jakarta. He has written three books on democracy and civil society in Indonesia. He served as the Minister of State for Research and Technology, Chairman of the Agency for the Assessment and Application of Technology (BPPT), Chairman of the Indonesian National Research Council (DRN), and Chairman of the East Indonesian Development Council (DKTI) during Abdurrahman Wahid's administration.

Ruth R. Lusterio is Fellow at the Institute for Strategic and Development Studies, Inc. (ISDS), Philippines and Assistant Professor at the Department of Political Science, University of the Philippines, Diliman, Quezon City.

Jorge V. Tigno is the Director for Local Governance and National Development at the Institute for Strategic and Development Studies, Inc. (ISDS), Assistant Professor at the Department of Political Science, University of the Philippines, and a doctoral candidate in public administration at the University of the Philippines, Diliman, Quezon City.

Gisèle Yasmeen was a researcher, educator and consultant in the area of development and food-security for several years before taking on her current position as Director (BC-Yukon) of the Centre for Research and Information on Canada, a program of the Council for Canadian Unity. She has undertaken work for the United Nations Food and Agriculture Organization, and the International Development Research Centre among other clients. In addition, she serves as a columnist for the Canadian Broadcasting Corporation's English and French Radio.

Acknowledgements

It is a pleasure to acknowledge the institutions that provided the support so essential to undertaking a somewhat unusual multifaceted research program. The Canadian International Development Agency (CIDA) reached beyond its traditional focus when it agreed to explore in what ways the expanded discourse on security in the post-cold war world might be relevant to their primary mandate of development. In cooperation with the Ottawa-based International Development Research Centre (IDRC), funding was received to bring together experts from throughout Southeast Asia (SEA) and from Canada to undertake some exploratory work. We are most thankful to Ann Bernard, then of IDRC, and Norm Macdonnell of CIDA, who shepherded us through the early stages and provided guidance and advice along the way.

CIDA generously agreed to fund the program, and we are grateful to the Asia Branch and to Jean-Marc Metevier, then Vice-President Asia and to Susan Davies, then Regional Director, for their support. Brian Hunter, Senior Economist did much more than serve as our principal contact and project manager. He offered sustained intellectual support, took an individual interest in each and every researcher, and never failed to challenge and to provoke. Indeed, had either of us encountered economists like Brian when we were students it is quite likely that we would now be in his, rather than our profession.

The Canadian embassies in Manila and in Jakarta provided in-country support throughout the program. We are particularly thankful to Ambassador Stephen Heeney and Mr Stewart Henderson, both in Manila during the start and early part of the Development and Security in Southeast Asia (DSSEA) Program, and to Ambassador Gary Smith, then in Jakarta, for their assistance. We would be remiss if we did not acknowledge the intellectual encouragement offered by General Jose T. Almonte, ret., then National Security Adviser to Philippine President Fidel V. Ramos, who insisted that we were exploring questions that to him, were fundamental to a better understanding of the challenges facing the nations of SEA. Since leaving government many of his public statements continue to reflect his unique sense of obligation to humanist values, the obligation of government to its people, and the necessity for the peoples of SEA to forge a new consensus in its common fight against poverty and injustice.

Three research centers carried the bulk of the administrative and organizational responsibilities for the DSSEA program. Our colleagues at the Centre for International and Strategic Studies (CSIS) in Jakarta, especially Hadi Soesastro and Clara Joewono who managed all the field research, conferences, and echo seminars which took place in Indonesia. Hadi served both as the Chair of the Task Force on Globalization for the DSSEA program and as the Indonesia country coordinator. A man of remarkable intellect and kindness, it is always a pleasure and honor to work with him. Clara provides all of us with a model of humility, modesty, and graciousness even in the face of extremely trying and, at times, dangerous circumstances. She is a remarkable stabilizing force, and has an exceptional knowledge of the politics of Indonesia and, more generally, SEA. It is a pleasure to acknowledge, with thanks, our good friend and colleague, Jusuf Wanandi, who ensured that CSIS Jakarta was always available to assist us throughout the life of the program.

The Institute of Strategic and Development Studies, Inc. (ISDS), Manila, served not only as the coordinating center for all the Philippine-based DSSEA activities, but also took on the primary responsibility for the *DSSEA Update*, a publication which emerged as an unanticipated major aspect of our program. It is a pleasure to acknowledge the devotion and extraordinary efforts that Crisline Torres, Josefina Manuel, Maria Ela Atienza, and Rowena Layador have brought to this program. Their unflagging support and commitment made the complications and challenges of running a multiyear, international program manageable, even during the most trying political circumstances. We also wish to note the important help received in the final stages of preparing the manuscript for publication: Myla Tugade who did the layout, Dona Dolina who assisted with transforming the materials into the Ashgate format, and Amado Mendoza, Jr. and Ruth Lusterio-Rico who assisted the final editing of the second and third volumes, respectively.

The Centre for International and Security Studies (CISS), York University (Toronto) assumed the lead role in handling all the administrative and financial details of the program, from negotiating the contracts first with CIDA and IDRC and then with each of the researchers, through to providing the accounting and preparing the annual reports. Heather Chestnutt and Joan Broussard not only managed all these technical details with their characteristic combination of efficiency, effectiveness, and accuracy, but also monitored the quality of the DSSEA activities, provided advice to the program co-directors, and often served as the first lifeline to the researchers as they each faced what often would seem as unique challenges in undertaking field work. Without fail Joan and Heather would solve whatever problems occurred and thereby ensured that each scholar was able to pursue his or her research unencumbered by administrative or other problems. Their skills and knowledge make directing this complex research and outreach program much easier and more pleasant than it otherwise would have been.

Our final thanks must go to those colleagues who provided the intellectual guidance and strength of this program. Paul Evans, now of the University of British Columbia, but formerly a colleague at York University, was a principal motivator behind launching this effort, and together with us and Amitav Acharya engaged CIDA and the IDRC in the initial ideas of linking development with security. Tim Shaw of Dalhousie University not only was a participant in the pilot study, but also convinced us that we should transform a difficult and eclectic set of research papers into a somewhat more coherent book project. We thank him for his unfailing encouragement and his personal commitment to these volumes. And of course, the last word goes to our colleagues, those whose chapters you are about to read and to those many scholars, policy makers, and members of non-government organizations who joined us in this endeavor. The authors of the following chapters are a remarkable group of scholars, some senior and with deserved international reputations, others just starting off on what we are certain will be important careers. This was an unusual program that each of them agreed to join, and we are thankful and appreciative of their contributions. We also must point out the special roles played by Jennifer Clapp, Peter Dauvergne, Hadi Soesastro, and Jorge V. Tigno, each of whom served as principal guide to their colleagues on their respective task forces. Without their participation, our task as co-directors would have been much more difficult and far less pleasant. We thank them.

David B. Dewitt and Carolina G. Hernandez
Toronto and Manila

List of Abbreviations

ADB	Asian Development Bank
AKAN	Center for Overseas Employment
AMC	Asian Migrant Center
APEC	Asia Pacific Economic Cooperation
APMMF	Asia Pacific Mission for Migrant Filipinos
APMRN	Asia Pacific Migration Research Network
APPEND	Alliance of Philippine Partners in Enterprise Development, Inc. Network
APR	Asia Pacific Roundtable
ARF	ASEAN Regional Forum
ARMM	Autonomous Region in Muslim Mindanao
ASEAN	Association of Southeast Asian Nations
ASEM	Asia-Europe Meeting
BAPPENAS	National Development Planning Agency of Indonesia
BPS	Badan Pusat Statistik or the Indonesian Central Bureau of Statistics
BSP	Bangko Sentral ng Pilipinas or the Central Bank of the Philippines
CBOs	Community-based organizations
CCUVA	Cebu City United Vendors Association
CIDA	Canadian International Development Agency
CLEAR	Cebu Labor Education, Advocacy and Research Center
DFA	Philippine Department of Foreign Affairs
DOLE	Department of Labor and Employment – Philippines
DPPD	Dewan Penelitian Pengupahan Daerah or the Regional Council for Wage Studies
DPPN	Dewan Penelitian Pengupahan Nasional or the National Council for Wage Studies
DSSEA	Development and Security in Southeast Asia
EOI	Export-Oriented Industrialization
FAO	Food and Agriculture Organization
FBSI	Federasi Buruh Seluruh Indonesia or the All Indonesian Labor Federation
FGD	Focus Group Discussions
FSPSI	Federasi Serikat Pekerja Seluruh Indonesia or the All Indonesian Labor Union Federation
GBHN	Garis-garis Besar Haluan Negara or the State's Broad Guidelines
GDI	Gender-Related Development Index
HDI	Human Development Index
HIP	Pancasila Industrial Relations
ICMI	Ikatan Cendekiawan Muslimin Indonesia

IFLS	Indonesian Family Life Survey
ILO	International Labor Organization
IMF	International Monetary Fund
IOM	International Organization for Migration
ISI	Import Substitution Industrialization
KFM	Kebutuhan Fisik Minimum or the Minimum Physical Needs
KHM	Kebutuhan Hidup Minimum or the Minimum Living Needs
L/C	Letter of Credit
LFPR	Labor Force Participation Rate
LNG	Liquified Natural Gas
MFMW	Mission for Filipino Migrant Workers
M1	Currency and Demand Deposits
M2	Currency and Demand Deposits, and Time Deposits
MILF	Moro Islamic Liberation Front
MNLF	Moro National Liberation Front
MPPHI	Majelis Penyelesaian Perselisihan Industrial or the Board of Industrial Conflict Resolution
MTUC	Malaysian Trade Union Congress
NGOs	Non-governmental Organizations
NSB	National Seamen Board
NU	Nahdlatul Ulama
OCWs	Overseas Contract Workers
ODA	Official Development Assistance
OECD	Organization for Economic Cooperation and Development
OEDB	Overseas Employment Development Board
OWWA	Overseas Workers Welfare Administration
PBSP	Philippine Business for Social Progress
PDOS	Pre-Departure Orientation Seminar
PEOS	Pre-Employment Orientation Seminar
PMRN	Philippine Migration Research Network
PO	People's Organizations
POEA	Philippine Overseas Employment Administration
PPSW	Center for Women's Resources Development
PUK	Local Unit
PVO	Private Voluntary Organizations
RIA	Research Institute of ASEAN
Rp	Rupiah
SBMSK	Serikat Buruh Merdeka Setiakawan or the Independent and Solidarity Labor Union
SBSI	Serikat Buruh Sejahtera Indonesia or the Indonesian Prosperity Labor Union
SMEC	Small and Medium Enterprise Credit
SPCPD	Southern Philippine Council for Peace and Development
SPTSK	Serikat Pekerja Tingkat Satuan Kerja or the Unit-based Labor Union
TKI	Tenaga Kerja Indonesia

TSKI	Taytay sa Kauswagan, Inc.
UMR	Upah Minimum Regional or the Minimum Wage Standard
UNDP	United Nations Development Programme
UNIFEM	United Nations Development Fund for Women
UNSFIR	United Nation Support Facility for Indonesian Recovery
UNWCED	United Nations World Commission on Environment and Development
UNWFP	United Nations World Food Program
VICTU	Visayan Cooperative Federation

Map Showing Location of Study Area

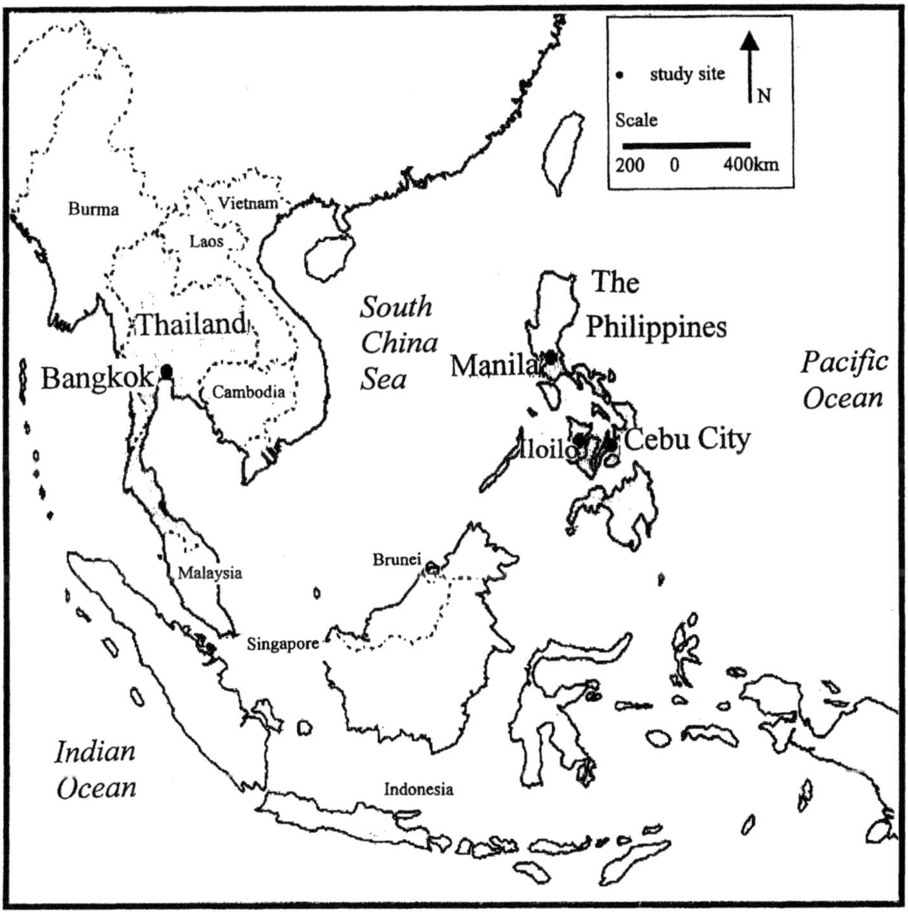

PART I
INTRODUCTION

Chapter 1

Defining the Problem and Managing the Uncertainty

David B. Dewitt and Carolina G. Hernandez

Introduction

Development and Security in Southeast Asia (DSSEA) has as its core the question of the relationship between government and civil society in their efforts to define and to pursue security, broadly defined. Thus, the DSSEA research program at the outset posits a tension between how government and its instruments understand and pursue security and how people and the communities that they comprise understand and seek their own particular security interests. It is based on the premise that the process of development is, essentially, a partnership between official agencies, the private sector, and people, and that the issue of security is found across levels of social, economic, and political organization and is intimately entwined with the challenges posed by the dynamics of (mis)managing development. Moreover, our approach to development and security explicitly acknowledges the potential importance of the tensions between local and external factors across levels of authority, production, and distribution.

Governance, whether in terms of an explicit 'social contract' or implicitly as the control, management, and allocation of public resources (including goods and services) and, in some cases, intruding into and distorting the relationship between the public and the private, is at the heart of the overarching challenges linking development with security in SEA. A subset of this focus is the underlying realization of the importance of human resource development. Consequently, the concept of social capital runs throughout all the specific projects pursued within this research program and reported in these three volumes.

The DSSEA program is concerned with the attainment of three goals: (1) identifying and understanding the linkages between security and development through conducting case studies across levels of state-society relations, as well as comparatively within the region; (2) developing enhanced theoretical and conceptual understanding of these complex linkages both to further our knowledge and to improve our abilities to develop practical instruments in support of improved human well being; and (3) using the acquired knowledge and information for empowerment and change. This volume, along with the accompanying other two, reports the results of empirical research conducted primarily in Indonesia and the Philippines by scholars from these two countries and Canada.

The three volumes represent research organized around the complementary themes of environment and resources, globalization, and people and communities, with each connected through the common concern on the linkages between the dynamics of development and the challenges to security.[1] The approach is based on two underlying assumptions: (1) that the model of development on which the rapid economic expansion of SEA has been articulated is not sustainable because it involves dynamics of social and political inequality bound to cause its demise over the long term; and (2) that the language of security provides the best vocabulary through which these problems can be delineated, debated, and resolved. Supporting these two assumptions are the ideas of human security and social capital, the former, while acknowledging the primacy of the state, focuses on the well being of the individual and her community, and the latter referring to the extent to which community-based organizations and civil society more generally are engaged participants in forms of local and national political and economic decision-making.[2]

Defining the Problem

In the post-cold war era, the concepts of both development and security have been transformed to meet new strategic realities. Development has long been recognized as a non-linear process often accompanied by unintended consequences; it also is no longer presumed to be either benign or necessarily a public good. On the other hand, development is increasingly argued to be inherently linked with freedom, as 'a process of expanding the real freedoms that people [ought to] enjoy'.[3] Within this broader understanding, the economic, social, and political are entwined into a composite which provides the foundation for such personal and community freedom and, hence, also enhanced security.

Security no longer is defined simply as defense of one's national territory by armed forces against military threat. Neither threat nor risk to the state or its people come only from military forces or groups prepared to engage in violence but also from many other factors which cross boundaries, penetrate society, and challenge the capacity of the state to regulate entry and exit. Further, security is more than protecting the state or even the governing regime as important as both of those may be. Today, security also is viewed as a descriptor of community and individual life; that the authorities have a responsibility to ensure personal safety and well being, just as the integrity of communities and their sense of their own future needs confirmation. The question of agency – the instruments responsible for the security of people and institutions – therefore, likely involves more than only the military and the police, and as such also becomes entwined with the concerns about the agents for development.[4]

Neither development nor security as policies can be achieved through unilateral means. Both are dependent on a mix of short-, medium-, and long-term factors located in the interstices between the individual, the society, the state, and the inter-state systems. Yet relatively little is understood about the linkages, never mind casual relations, which bind these two core components of national expression. The DSSEA program addresses aspects of these linkages. Most concretely, our interest is to locate the strong and weak links between some of the complex dynamics of development and the challenges of security. We situate this effort initially within the paradigm of the nation-state, but explicitly acknowledge that many non-state and sub-state actors, as well as the attendant social forces, may turn out to be the defining variables in this exercise. Indeed, as it turns out almost all of the case studies in this project explore the linkages between government, the private sector, and civil society.

Non-military threats to security seem to be crowding the policy agenda of nations throughout the world. Particularly after the attacks against the United States on 11 September 2001, the rise of terrorism, whether domestic or international, has hugged the headlines of national and international media and assumed the status of a major security concern in countries the world over. The alarming global spread of the devastating disease acquired immunodeficiency syndrome (AIDS) threatens the security of individuals as well as entire nations. The rate of ecological damage rapid economic development creates is wreaking havoc of immense proportions with devastating consequences for our collective futures whether in terms of biodiversity or simply making less land either habitable or productive. Non-renewable resources have been exploited to the point of making them a focal point of international competition and even war, while individuals and their communities become increasingly vulnerable and insecure to the globalized forces of extraction, production, and distribution. Access to and management of 'strategic resources' including water continues to command bilateral and multilateral attention. Disputes over fish stocks have brought allies and partners to the point of diplomatic brinkmanship, while communities at home suffer from resulting massive unemployment and its consequent social dislocation.

Markedly different from the Western concept of security based essentially and primarily on the state's military and defense capability, East Asian concepts view security in a comprehensive, multidimensional, and holistic manner. The five non-communist states of Indonesia, Malaysia, the Philippines, Singapore, and Thailand which together formed the original core of the Association of Southeast Asian Nations (ASEAN), have viewed security in these terms since the Association's founding in August 1967.[5] Believing that a nation's security begins from within, Indonesia stressed the primacy of domestic security by solving internal sources of security threats such as communist insurgency, ethnic tensions, economic malaise, and social divisions within its far-flung archipelago, creating in the process a condition of national resilience.[6] According to the Indonesian view, one subsequently and implicitly supported by the rest in ASEAN, when all the states in the region achieve national resilience, there would be no security problems they could export to their neighbors. The result would be a community of confident and secure nation-states, resilient to extra-regional threats, and hence, better able to promote and to sustain regional stability and security.[7]

The Malaysian concept of comprehensive security emphasized non-military sources of security threats. It was seen as 'inseparable from political stability, economic success, and social harmony'.[8] As with national resilience, security threats were seen as originating primarily from within the state. This conception was in large measure due to the presence of domestic insurgencies and the problems engendered by the task of nation building in multiethnic societies with great disparities in wealth and income among their constituent ethnic communities. While the inter-ethnic violence of 30 years ago has not reappeared, the 1997 Asian financial crisis and the controversy surrounding Prime Minister Mahathir Mohamed's continuing efforts to retain political dominance have introduced a level of domestic tension and unease not witnessed for a number of decades. The vulnerability of developing states and their governments to the fortunes of 'performance legitimacy' can be seen throughout the region, though Malaysia, as well as Thailand and Singapore, has been sufficiently resilient to withstand the havoc experienced in Indonesia.

Singapore developed a similar notion of security. Viewed in terms of 'total defense', it is also multidimensional, holistic, comprehensive, and begins from within. The Philippines and Thailand also adopted similar conceptions of security making for an ASEAN-wide acceptance of comprehensive security in SEA by the 1980s, though this is now under severe strain since the expansion to the ASEAN-10 coming almost simultaneously with the shock of the 1997-98 Asian financial meltdown.

While security in the cold war era focused an external threats to states and relied primarily on military means, including the establishment of a network of bilateral and multilateral military alliances focused on nuclear deterrence, a new concept of security mechanism launched by former Canadian Secretary of State for External Affairs, Joe Clark, emphasized an evolving inclusive regionalism and multilateralism as a complement to bilateralism, mutual reassurance instead of nuclear deterrence, and the use of both military and non-military means to promote security in recognition of the multifaceted nature of threats to security. Cooperative security as the notion came to be known, is a complementary mechanism to comprehensive security in dealing with a post-cold war environment increasingly challenged by non-military threats to the security of individuals, communities, societies, and nation-states as well as the international system.[9]

This Canadian contribution has been complemented by the more recent articulation of human security. Initially given wide attention as a result of the United Nations Development Programme (UNDP) *Report on Human Development*,[10] it was adapted by then Canadian Foreign Minister Lloyd Axworthy to frame Canada's articulation of how, when, where, and why Canada and like-minded countries should be prepared to intervene to protect and make safe individuals and communities from the ravages of war, whether domestic or international, the threats to their safety and well being from systemic challenges, as well as to enhance their security in the face of man-made or natural calamities. In Axworthy's language, 'human security entails taking preventive measures to reduce vulnerability and minimize risk, and taking remedial action where prevention fails'.[11] One of the critical aspects of this approach is the acknowledgement that security not only is multifaceted but that it is both a process and an objective which calls on responsible actions by both governments and others. In this construction, security is no longer a state-centric phenomenon; nor can it be achieved merely by employing the traditional instruments of the state. Indeed, in many situations it is its very reliance on the state and its dominance in defining the meaning of security that renders people, communities, and other states insecure.[12]

Most of the regimes in Southeast Asia (SEA) are – or were until recently – authoritarian; their legitimacy has been sustained either by force or by remarkable levels of economic development. Failure, as dramatically witnessed by the 1997 financial crisis and the ensuing upheaval in Indonesia, severe economic downturn in Thailand and South Korea along with the tensions experienced by Malaysia and the Philippines, has eroded support, even among elites, and challenged the foundations of some governing regimes. The stark alteration in the economic well being of these countries and the capacity of the governments to distribute, even minimally, the benefits that previously accrued through economic expansion, has shaken their political and social structures. Though the general resilience of the political, military, and economic classes to such pressures has been notable in spite of the precipitous decline of specific families, the inter-ethnic domestic tensions released have threatened the security of the state as well as many of its communities. Moreover, the precarious raw materials and resource-based economic system, laid vulnerable to the financial upheavals combined with the impact of the globalization of production and marketing which affects commodity pricing, has exacerbated the already uncertain situation faced by poorly educated workers and migrant labor, creating both domestic and cross-border tensions.

Sustainable development is not possible in an unstable domestic environment. Ironically, however, economic development has unleashed a set of dynamics generating social, economic, and political change, including increasing popular participation in the economy and in the society, increasing access to education and information, increasing mobility of peoples, along with the rise of a middle class. If the experiences of Taiwan and South Korea in Northeast Asia and more recently Thailand and the Philippines in SEA are relevant in this discussion, demands for greater political participation, liberalization, and democratization are likely to occur in other parts of Eastern Asia. Resistance on the part of governing elites to accommodate these demands, whether dramatically as in Indonesia or more cautiously in Malaysia, can lead to political instability of the sort that undermines sustainable development and domestic security itself. In this context, sustainable development also encompasses the creation of domestic and inter-state institutions that have the specialized knowledge and skills to regulate, to manage, and to facilitate stable political pluralism, economic development, and social equity. Thus, sustainable development is more than merely attaching specific conditions to economic change; it is also the evolution of a responsible civil society in which there exists a consensus concerning the benefits that accrue from institutionalizing good governance, resource management, and social equity. It provides an approach to achieving 'development as freedom' enunciated so passionately by Amartya Sen.

Since well before the UN-sponsored World Commision on Environment and Development (Brundtland Commission) published their 1987 report, *Our Common Future*, scholars, journalists, and non-governmental organizations had been raising serious concerns over the relationship between economic development, environmental consequences, and security. However, it was the Brundtland report that finally gave political meaning to the range of implications that were becoming ever more apparent, thereby moving ecology from the esoteric to center stage. The core concept around which the analysis and recommendations evolved was sustainable development, defined as the ability 'to ensure that [development] meets the needs of the present without compromising the ability of future generations to meet their own needs'. For this to be achieved, policy, behavior, and analysis among all sectors of society – government, industry, individuals – would have to come to terms with the implications of the nature of the 'interlocking crises' to be faced.[13]

Although some wrote on the probable connections between economic development, environmental degradation, and politics, few explored these linkages with any scientific rigor, and fewer with questions of security explicitly in mind.[14] While the ending of the cold war has not had a marked affect on the realities of this complex set of issues – if anything the 'facts on the ground' may be worse – it has led to an increased awareness of and concern with development and security. The 1992 Earth Summit and its adoption of *Agenda 21* gives some indication that political leaders are becoming more aware of the core significance of the environmental-economic-political linkages for their own countries if not the globe, although this does not mean that a consensus has been achieved concerning appropriate action.[15] Indeed, recent environmental summits in Kyoto and The Hague have underlined the extent to which state and private sector interests continue to coalesce in ways which impede significant progress on global environmental norms and regulations. Undoubtedly, while much of this has to do with the domestic politics of participating countries, it also is a reflection of the pervasive impact of the forces of globalization and the uncertainties attendant among the public, the private sector, and governments about how to address this market phenomenon which, in so many ways, impacts upon environmental and ecological issues.

The linkage between sustainable development and the environment is relatively well-known and has formed the basis of much discussion since the Brundtland Commission, as well as efforts at encouraging both standards and policy since the United Nations 1992 Conference on Environment and Development (UNCED). Over the last few years, the relationship between sustainable development (or aspects of it) and security has become a focus for research, for it encapsulates the tensions between the demands for economic growth, political stability, and individual and collective rights. Depending upon the context and the mix of choices, some scholars have pointed to the causal linkages between environmental degradation – often caused by resource depletion, improperly managed industrial development, and human displacement – and conflict. The scale of conflict can vary from interpersonal violence to challenges to governmental authority, from internal disturbances to regime repression, from revolution to interstate violence. Unsustainable and mismanaged economic activities which degrade the environment, aggravate human relations, and exacerbate intra-state as well as inter-state relations can lead to social upheaval, challenging the security of the individual, of the community, of the country, and potentially of the region.

Both problems and opportunities abound. Over the three decades prior to the 1997 financial crisis, SEA had been the locus of remarkable economic development. The stability of governing regimes was tied to performance legitimacy. The costs, however, were profound, including depletion of scarce resources, deterioration of marine and land environments, population migrations, and inadequately controlled rapid urbanization. Domestic as well as territorial problems, including current secessionist efforts, can be linked to policies fostering specific forms of economic growth in a vacuum of political representation, a fundamental political unwillingness to redress the inequitable redistribution of economic benefits, and the presence of an emerging and demanding civil society. Due to accompanying environmental scarcities and degradation, already difficult domestic situations carried the potential to exacerbate points of tension with neighboring states.[16]

What was evident from both the research literature as well as the regular and reputable journalistic accounts well before the 1997 financial crisis was a sense that the then current economic developments, especially those viewed as evidence of the mismanagement of development, could compromise if not severely undermine the security of these states, where security is understood as being 'essentially concerned with the maintenance of society's basic values; and with the institutions, such as legitimate political or legal system, which enable a country to sustain and defend the values its nationals regard as central to its independent existence'.[17] As the decade of the 1990s evolved, it also became clear that the growing insecurity of individuals and their communities could be ignored only at the peril of governing institutions. The previous decades of development strategies, as inequitable and incomplete as they might have been, had created sufficient awareness and heightened expectations that the authorities no longer could assume their citizens' compliance, especially as their own performance-based legitimacy was under threat.

The economy and the environment are separate but intertwined – and in some cases, integrated – systems. Though the causal relations are complex, and even more so when linking them to politics and to security, it is evident that to separate them in an arbitrary manner, as if decisions about one can be taken in isolation and with impunity concerning the others, is both wrong and foolhardy. 'Threats to the peace and security of nations and regions [and individuals] from environmental breakdown are potentially greater than any foreseeable military threat from conventional arms'.[18] There are no significant parts of the globe which have not suffered from environmental degradation, though not all are affected equally nor are all equally culpable. Nevertheless, almost without exception the causes are political and economic choices, at times made from afar and even with the best of intentions given the available options. The results are a combination of resource depletion, uneven distribution of benefits, displacement, debt, and often political instability, conflict, and violence, as well as the intensification of 'poor governance'.[19] SEA is repository of all these factors.

Local political, economic, and commercial decisions have environmental consequences that, as with acid rain and deforestation, have not only regional but global ecological impact. As MacNeill notes, 'If nations are to stop depleting their basic stocks of ecological capital, governments will need to reform those public policies that now actively encourage the infamous *de's*: *de*forestation, *de*sertification, *de*struction of habitat and species, *de*cline of air and water quality'.[20] In many places, these second-order phenomena aggravate already contentious resource-based contexts, where two or more countries draw on the same river system, fish from the same sea, or claim under-sea and under-seabed rights from the same location at a time when each has increased needs driven by, among other things, demography, development, and rapid unplanned and unmanaged urbanization.[21] Much the same occurs with agricultural and grazing lands as well as with timber stands and mineral and ore deposits, though these usually are less state boundary questions initially and more likely to be tribal, clan, and other sub-state boundary problems.

Hence, for the DSSEA program, development makes sense only when understood in terms of sustainable development, a comprehensive concept with ecological, economic, social, and political dimensions. To be sustainable, economic development must be sensitive to its excessive demands on natural resources and its negative impact on the physical environment. Development, broadly defined, must also take into account the social dimension which includes the competing requirements of economic development and the preservation of social structures and cultural norms and values without which the survival of communities would be at risk. These include rights to ancestral lands without access to which tribal communities are likely to perish, and the capacity of both rural and urban dwellers to maintain their primary identities seriously diminished. The fruits of economic development need to be shared more equitably within the state's regions and peoples as well as across regions beyond the nation-state. The alternative would be economic deprivation for the powerless, a phenomenon that has often led to social tension and division within the society, and ultimately insecurity, conflict, and violence.

There is also a political dimension to sustainable development. Erosion of the ecological balance, uneven distribution of the economic pie, neglect or destruction of the rights of peoples, and other negative outcomes of the (mis)management of development results in eventual political decay, contributing to social tension and political turmoil that ties up the resources of the state as it reacts defensively to such challenges, dissipating state resources, fraying the social fabric, undermining the political legitimacy of ruling elites, and leading to violence. That this is at least partially a snapshot of what became the Asian financial crisis, the mirror image of the Asian economic miracle, is generally condeded. What remains in dispute are the appropriate responses more immediately as well as over the longer term.

The emergence of human rights, democratization, and the environment, in addition to economic development and market reforms, as issues in contemporary international relations that challenge the traditions of the inviolability of the sovereign state raises their potentials for engendering tensions and conflict between and among states. Examples within SEA are all too plentiful, not least of course the recent conflict and intervention in East Timor or the earlier hesitant involvement of ASEAN in the putative coup in Cambodia. The diplomatic tensions between the Philippines and Singapore in the mid-1990s must be seen not only in terms of uneven economic development within ASEAN but also in terms of divergences in their conceptions about human rights and democracy, about which Singapore ardently advocates a set of Asian values distinct from those in the West.[22] The protracted multilateral disputes around, in, and under the South China Sea are more than an issue of Chinese-ASEAN relations or bilateral security and defense politics. It is a set of issues that range from classic questions of boundary legitimacy to fundamental concerns about access to and control over the management of fish, mineral, and energy resources, and all the economic, social, and political factors linked with these productive and extractive sectors. Forest fires in Indonesia continue to undermine sustainable development and create threats to the well being of individuals both at home and abroad, thereby creating political demands which require governmental response with the potential for exacerbating relations between states in both bilateral as well as regional terms. Even the seemingly benign decision to allow Taiwanese entrepreneurs to introduce a non-Asian snail into Vietnam for commercial harvesting and sales is evolving into a serious threat to Vietnam's capacity to produce sufficient rice to feed its people. How that will play into the emerging regional interdependencies and competition, including the Mekong River project, remains uncertain but is at least instructive concerning the unintended consequences of economically driven decisions. Furthermore, both these examples (forest fires and snails), depending upon how they are handled, could undermine movement towards democratic and market reforms in various states in the region. Thus, understanding the complex linkages between the processes of development and their implications for the security of individuals at various levels of governance is an urgent imperative of our time, particularly where state-society relations remain biased in favor of the state.

DSSEA: The Research Program

The research was organized around three task force themes – environment, globalization, and people – that had been identified as principal factors in the development-security nexus. Our preference to understand these phenomena at least partially through human security and social capital concepts as a means to balance the privileged position of the state in both the security and development literature informed the selection of specific research projects, with the results of each task force presented in three volumes. The most significant findings and their policy implications are stated in each volume's overview chapter immediately following this one.

The program involved two additional activities beyond the conventional empirical research: echo seminars and a broader outreach effort. Echo seminars were designed to engage member of civil society (including other researchers), and the private sector, as well as local and national officials and politicians. The purpose was both to inform them of our work and to involve them, when possible, as participants. These meetings took place both in capital cities as well as in regional centers in the Philippines and Indonesia, at times drawing in excess of 150 local experts to a single session. Although the impact of these meetings on this initial research phase is difficult to measure, it is evident that the discussions and the ensuing contacts among interested parties has heightened awareness of the issues, stimulated opportunities for more intensive collaboration on future research, and in some locales invigorated policy development and political action. These meetings also made clear the extent to which, in both Indonesia and the Philippines, local activists and researchers have intensive knowledge and intuitive understanding of the security-development linkages, and a strong desire to have a role in policy formulation. Equally clear is the absence of positive dialogue between civil society and both the government and the private sector. The solitudes are striking given the profound long-term consequences and the fact that to address the security-development nexus requires involvement of all the principal stakeholders. Further outreach was undertaken through the regular publication and wide distribution of the *DSSEA Update*, designed to inform the various participants in the program, to engage the wider governmental audience throughout SEA and within ASEAN, and to encourage as well as to facilitate the involvement of civil society.

While both the *DSSEA Update* and our echo seminars were very well received, our three-year program confirmed what conventional wisdom has long asserted: that the differences in perceptions as well as policy preferences and priorities between researchers from universities and the institutions of civil society in Manila and Jakarta and the elites from the political and private sector are striking; and even more so from non-governmental experts and locals from provincial arenas. Although echo seminars often provided very positive encounters between researchers, activists, private sector representatives and government officials, our research tended to confirm the embedded nature of the dilemma: that development as defined by some combination of government policy and private sector interests undermined security as defined by individuals and their communities.

Much of the discourse of disagreement revolved around the different points of departure and of purpose: a government-defined security of national well being and the capacity to deal with threat focused on the harnessing of state capacity, whether in terms of military security or economic security, in support of regime stability. This became increasingly evident in the shadow of the 1997 financial crisis, where domestic political, communal, and economic matters and the importance of regional interstate political and economic relations highlighted the inside/outside duality of managing national security. Security was threatened both by domestic instabilities and by external factors at times beyond the control of the government. On the other hand, locally-defined security was premised on the capacity individuals, families, and communities to ensure well being, to be free of fear and of want, and to find ways to better manage the personal and inter-communal consequences of the intervention of government and the private sector in their daily lives. Whether the issue was the availability of food at fair and constant prices or protection from environmental degradation or the challenges introduced through the phenomenon of globalization, locals understood the multi-layered nature of security even as they were alienated from the process. Their extraordinary vulnerability was exacerbated and highlighted by the incapacity of the government to address the national-level security challenges in the wake of the 1997 financial crisis.

The DSSEA Research Program, begun before the financial crisis, found itself caught up in the spiral of events precipitated by the financial meltdown throughout much of SEA. Though requiring some adjustment by a number of the researchers, what the crisis did offer was a sudden opportunity for fieldwork that could track the local and regional impacts of the ensuing events. The chapters offered in these three volumes present insights into how different sectors of society weathered not only the chronic challenges of development and their impact on facets of security, but how the unanticipated acute changes were managed. To what extent were the local-through-national forces of security able to respond? How did this dramatic economic dislocation that posed fundamental challenges to the political integrity of the governing regimes affect the processes of development, and to what extent did any of this heighten insecurity? How resilient were the political, social, and economic forces that underpin much of the development ethos and are the building blocks of government policy and are reflected in the criteria of performance legitimacy? Do we now know something new about the linkages between development and security because this research program was able, by chance, to factor in the crash of 1997?

Managing the Uncertainty

Even before the 1997 financial crisis, it was evident to scholars and practitioners alike the SEA was in the midst of some profound transformations in state-society relations. Although still struggling with the extremes of wealth and poverty while encumbered by the twin scourges of authoritarian politics and corruption, civil society was increasingly a force for social, economic, and political change, at times challenging but also often in partnership with government and the private sector. Moreover, the forces of globalization along with the actions of regional and global organizations, especially financial institutions, had an ever growing impact on the range of policy options available, while introducing new issues around productive competitiveness and market vulnerability. For most of SEA, this period of economic growth, although not equitably distributed, did usher in a period of heightened expectations and confirmed the model of 'performance legitimacy' as one of the templates by which regime success was assessed.

Yet even at this time the uncertainty of what dramatic economic change could bring was evident in the inability of most governments to address the social dislocations and political discord fostered by the all too often mismanagement of development strategies. From the individual to community through to the state levels, the basic issue should have been how to manage the uncertain outcomes brought forth by the actions of interventionist governments, the role of medium-and large-scale private enterprise, the pervasive results of globalization, and the profound impact of the international financial markets on local conditions. As challenging as all these would have been in more cohesive, well off and structurally-integrated societies, when imposed upon polities which were divided by ethnicity, religion, language, loyalties, and wealth differentials, and already under stress from profound environmentally induced dislocations, the only certainty was insecurity.

The research reported in these three volumes attests to the intimate relationship between the process of development and the perceived sense of well being and security, whether of the individual or the nation. Further, this scholarship identifies the importance of governments recognizing that in their pursuit of wealth (especially if it is linked with more equitable distribution of well being), power, and political stability, taking seriously their obligations to view civil society as partners in development is essential for overall security and even to regime survival, unless the preference is a return to authoritarian or totalitarian rule. To ensure that security is a positive outcome of economic development requires that other aspects of development, including social and political freedoms, were strengthened. Our research testifies to the centrality of this assertion. Whether in land management, agricultural production or resource practices, or the challenges faced by labor in response to the changing nature of globalized competition, development cannot occur solely as an economic phenomenon blind to the issue of its two-sided impact on the individual, the community, or the nation. The improvement of economic well being, as Amartya Sen declared, is not the sole criterion of development; it need not nor should it occur at the cost of individual or community security. Indeed, it should be synonymous with enhancing the security of the nation and its government through the process of empowering citizens and ensuring their well being.

The chapters in these three volumes report on original research undertaken in an effort to better understand the intricate relationship between the human desire for security and, concomitantly, its expression through seeking an improved standard of living. Too often we uncovered examples where the pursuit of economic change as the dominant and clearly too narrow expression of development policies compromised the desire for security. The overview chapters that begin each of these volumes offer a number of insights and policy recommendations which attempt, in a very modest way, to address this tension between the dynamics of development and the desire for security. Though we began this project with an overriding sense of wanting to explore how development intersected with inter-state security, what has emerged from this research is a profound refocusing on the sub-state levels of security as the engine of change. From this perspective, inter-state and regional security can only be strengthened when each national community is secure in its place and its sense of a welcome future. Ironically, this harkens back to the earliest thinking within ASEAN when the ideas of comprehensive security and national resilience as the guides for national development strategies provided a rationale also for arguing the need for each country to pursue these twin goals and, out of that would emerge a secure, stable, and increasingly prosperous region. In some interesting and unanticipated ways, this research project tends to confirm that early intuitive position. Although it is too early to suggest that regional security in fact would be a natural derivative of successful country-by-country development (in the fuller Amartya Sen terms), it is likely that it would allow the dynamics of cooperative security arrangements to emerge as an effective approach to the management of inter-state and inter-regional relations.[23]

Notes

1 The two project co-directors authored a draft paper which set out the assumptions and the conceptual direction of the project. This was revised and published as Acharya, A., Dewitt, D. B., and Hernandez, C. G. (1995), 'Sustainable Development and Security in Southeast Asia: A Concept Paper', *CANCAPS Papier Number 6*, August. Much of the conceptual discussion in this chapter is drawn from this paper though informed by the results of the ensuing research program. In this regard it is a pleasure to acknowledge the ongoing

contributions to our thinking by our academic colleagues in the DSSEA program, and to Brian Hunter, Senior Economist, Asia Pacific Branch, Canadian International Development Agency, who, while supporting our work, actively confronted and challenged us throughout this effort.

2 This language is partially paraphrased from an undated Fall 1999 discussion brief, *Development, Security, and Post-Crisis Reconstruction in Southeast Asia*, prepared by Pierre Lizee as he responded to our request for DSSEA researchers to reflect on this project.

3 Sen, A. (1999), *Development as Freedom*, Alfred A. Knopf, New York, pp.3.

4 Amartya Sen explores these issues in much detail. See his *Development as Freedom*.

5 These five were joined by the admission of Brunei Darussalam in 1984 and then in 1995 Vietnam was admitted and in 1997 Laos and Myanmar, followed in 1998 by Cambodia. See Acharya, A. (2001), *Constructing a Security Community in Southeast Asia*, Routledge, London.

6 While useful as political rhetoric and ideological orthodoxy in Indonesia's and ASEAN's formative years of nation-building and regional consolidation, comprehensive security and resilience clearly fell to the forces of revisionism, fundamentalism, corruption, mismanagement of development, and economic inequities most recently and cruelly seen both in the East Timor struggle and the protracted domestic violence and ongoing expressions of secessionism or autonomy. Nevertheless, in principle these ideas of comprehensive security and national resilience so widely shared among the original five ASEAN partners afford a clear and well-reasoned statement about the inherent linkages between economic progress, well being, governance, regional cooperation, and security.

7 We are not offering any judgement on the validity of these assertions, nor on any causal connections these might have with the political, social, or economic realities which are the histories of the countries and communities of contemporary Southeast Asia. Rather, the point here is to identify the security-relevant doctrines and ideologies which have been articulated and employed by the leaders of these countries as they faced the challenges of nation-building and regime survival.

8 Malaysian Prime Minister Mahathir Mohamad as cited in Acharya, *Constructing a Security Community in Southeast Asia*, 2001, pp.4.

9 For an overview of these ideas see Dewitt, D. B. (1994), 'Common, Comprehensive, and Cooperative Security in Asia Pacific', *The Pacific Review*, vol. 7, no.1.

10 United Nations Development Program (UNDP) (1994), *Human Development Report 1994*, Oxford University Press, New York.

11 Department of Foreign Affairs and International Trade (1999), *Human Security: Safety for People in a Changing World*, Government of Canada, April, pp.5.

12 For a most interesting statement on human security, see Almonte, J. T. (2000), *A Human Agenda for ASEAN*, remarks drawn from his presentation at the 'Inaugural Meeting of the ASEAN People's Assembly', Batam Island, Indonesia, 24-26 November 2000, distributed as *PacNet 1*, 5 January 2001, CISIS/Pacific Forum, Honolulu.

13 The World Commission on Environment and Development (1987), *Our Common Future*, Oxford University Press, Oxford, chapter 1.

14 *Ibid.*, chapter 11, did address aspects of the relationship between development, peace, conflict, and security. A more recent statement by the principal author of the Brundtland Report is MacNeill, J. (1989), 'Strategies for Sustainable Economic Development', *Scientific American* 261, September; also in still more developed form, see MacNeill, J., Winsemius, P., and Yakushiji, T. (1991), *Beyond Interdependence: The Meshing of the World's Economy and the Earth's Ecology*, Oxford University Press, New York. See also Holmberg, J., Bass, S., and Timberlake, L. (1991), *Defending the Future: A Guide to Sustainable Development*, International Institute for Environment and Development,

London. Among the earlier pieces which challenged the cold war definition of security, see Ullman, R. H. (1983), 'Redefining Security', *World Politics*, vol.8, no.1; and Mathews J. T. (1989), 'Redefining National Security', *Foreign Affairs*, vol.68, no.2, Spring. An important contribution to this literature was an article which provided the first public report of a large and ongoing research program exploring the causal connections between environment and conflict; see Homer-Dixon, T. (1991), 'On the Threshold: Environmental Changes as Causes of Acute Conflict', *International Security*, vol.16, no.2, Fall.

15 For a view which clearly challenges the now orthodox view of sustainable development as expressed in *Our Common Future* as well as *Agenda 21*, see Crovitz, L. G. (1994), *The Asian Manager: Asian Imperatives and Western Perspectives in Sustainable Development*, a paper presented at the 'Asian Institute of Management Conference', Manila, Philippines, 17 February 1994.

16 For relatively early statements which foreshadowed much of this, see Lonergan, S. (1994), *Environmental Change and Regional Security in Southeast Asia*, Project Report No. PR 659, Directorate of Strategic Analysis, Ottawa, March; and Myers, N. (1993), *Ultimate Security: The Environmental Basis of Political Stability*, W. W. Norton, New York; and MacNeill, *et. al.*, (1991), 'Environmental refugees' has become a significant factor of both cross-border and internal tensions and conflict in many parts of Eastern Asia, both north and south.

17 Harris, S. (1994), 'Enhancing Security: Non-Military Means and Measures II', in B. Nagara and K.S. Balakrishnan (eds), *The Making of A Security Community in the Asia-Pacific*, ISIS Malaysia, Kuala Lumpur, pp.191.

18 MacNeill, J. (1991), 'Strategies for Sustainable Economic Development', chapter 10.

19 See a superbly focussed discussion on this issue by Jones, S. 'Promoting Human Rights', in Nagara and Balakrishnan (eds), *The Making of a Security Community*, 1994, pp.344-46.

20 MacNeill, *et. al.*, *Beyond Interdependence: The Meshing of the World's Economy and the Earth's Ecology*, 1991, pp.23.

21 There is a growing literature, some anecdotal but much increasingly scientific, which describes and begins the difficult process of explaining the causal relationships between environment, ecology, economic development, land tenure, social construction, displacement, violence, etc. In addition to the previous citations, see for example, Homer-Dixon, T. F. (1999), *Environment, Scarcity, and Violence*, Princeton University Press, Princeton, N.J.; Kaplan, R. (1994), 'The Coming Anarchy', *The Atlantic*, February; Homer-Dixon, T. F., Boutwell, J. H. and Rathjens, G. W. (1993), 'Environmental Change and Violent Conflict', *Scientific American*, February; Homer-Dixon, T. F. (1994), 'Across the Threshold: Empirical Evidence on Environmental Scarcities as Causes of Violent Conflict', *International Security*, Summer; Homer-Dixon, T. F. (1994), 'The Ingenuity Gap: Can Poor Countries Adapt to Resource Scarcity?', University of Toronto ms., April; Ruckelshaus, W. D. (1989), 'Toward a Sustainable World', *Scientific American* 261, September; and Westing, A.H. (ed.) (1986), *Global Resources and International Conflict: Environmental Factors in Strategic Policy and Action*, Oxford University Press, New York. On the important issue of maritime environments, see, for example, Townsend-Gault, I. (1994), 'Testing the Waters: Making Progress in the South China Sea', *Harvard International Review*, Spring; and his *Ocean Diplomacy, International Law, and the South China Sea*, preliminary draft paper presented at the 'Eighth Asia Pacific Roundtable', Kuala Lumpur, June 1994; and 'Part IV: SLOCs and Maritime Security', in Nagara and Balakrishnan (eds) (1994), *The Making of a Security Community*.

22 Hernandez, C. G. (1995), *ASEAN Perspectives on Human Rights and Democracy in International Relations: Divergencies, Commonalities, Problems, and Prospects*, Center for Integrative and Development Studies, University of the Philippines, Quezon City.

23 One can consider the difficulties which the expanded ASEAN-10 now faces as evidence of what continued national asymmetries coupled with substantial domestic underdevelopment and insecurity within a number of Southeast Asian countries can do to any efforts to create an improved sense of security or consolidate a more effective regional mechanism to manage uncertainty.

References

Acharya, A. (2001), *Constructing a Security Community in Southeast Asia*, Routledge, London.

Acharya, A., Dewitt, D. B., and Hernandez, C. G. (1995), 'Sustainable Development and Security in Southeast Asia: A Concept Paper', *CANCAPS Papier Number 6*, August.

Almonte, J. T. (2000), *A Human Agenda for ASEAN*, paper presented at the 'Inaugural Meeting of the ASEAN People's Assembly', Batam Island, Indonesia, 24-26 November 2000, distributed as *PacNet 1*, 5 January 2001, CSIS/Pacific Forum, Honolulu.

Crovitz, L. G. (1994), *The Asian Manager: Asian Imperatives and Western Perspectives in Sustainable Development*, paper presented at the 'Asian Institute of Management Conference', Manila, Philippines, 17 February 1994.

Department of Foreign Affairs and International Trade (1999), *Human Security: Safety for People in a Changing World*, Department of Foreign Affairs and International Trade, Government of Canada, April, pp.5.

Dewitt, D. B. (1994), 'Common, Comprehensive, and Cooperative Security in Asia Pacific', *The Pacific Review*, vol. 7, no. 1.

Harris, S. (1994), 'Enhancing Security: Non-Military Means and Measures II', in B. Nagara and K.S. Balakrishnan (eds), *The Making of A Security Community in the Asia-Pacific*, ISIS Malaysia, Kuala Lumpur, pp. 191.

Hernandez, C. G. (1995), *ASEAN Perspectives on Human Rights and Democracy in International Relations: Divergencies, Commonalities, Problems, and Prospects*, Center for Integrative and Development Studies, University of the Philippines, Quezon City.

Holmberg, J., Bass, S., and Timberlake, L. (1991), *Defending the Future: A Guide to Sustainable Development*, International Institute for Environment and Development, London.

Homer-Dixon, T. F. (1999a), *Environment, Scarcity, and Violence*, Princeton University Press, Princeton.

Homer-Dixon, T. F. (1994b), 'Across the Threshold: Empirical Evidence on Environmental Scarcities as Causes of Violent Conflict', *International Security*, Summer.

Homer-Dixon, T.F. (1994c), *The Ingenuity Gap: Can Poor Countries Adapt to Resource Scarcity?*, University of Toronto ms., April.

Homer-Dixon, T. F. (1991d), 'On the Threshold: Environmental Changes as Causes of Acute Conflict', *International Security*, vol. 16, no. 2, Fall.

Homer-Dixon, T. F., Boutwell, J. H. and Rathjens, G. W. (1993), 'Environmental Change and Violent Conflict', *Scientific American*, February.

Jones, S. 'Promoting Human Rights', in B. Nagara and K.S. Balakrishnan (eds), *The Making of A Security Community in the Asia-Pacific*, ISIS Malaysia, Kuala Lumpur, pp.344-46.

Lonergan, S. (1994), *Environmental Change and Regional Security in Southeast Asia*, Project Report No. PR 659, Directorate of Strategic Analysis, Ottawa, March.

MacNeill, J. (1989), 'Strategies for Sustainable Economic Development', *Scientific American*, no. 261, September.

MacNeill, J., Winsemius, P., and Yakushiji, T. (1991), *Beyond Interdependence: The Meshing of the World's Economy and the Earth's Ecology*, Oxford University Press, New York.
Mathews J. T. (1989), 'Redefining National Security', *Foreign Affairs*, vol. 68, no. 2, Spring.
Myers, N. (1993), *Ultimate Security: The Environmental Basis of Political Stability*, W.W. Norton, New York.
Ruckelshaus, W. D. (1989), 'Toward a Sustainable World', *Scientific American*, no. 261, September.
Sen, A. (1999), *Development as Freedom*, Alfred A. Knopf, New York, pp.3.
The World Commission on Environment and Development (1987), *Our Common Future*, Oxford University Press, Oxford.
Townsend-Gault, I. (1994a), *Ocean Diplomacy, International Law, and the South China Sea*, preliminary draft paper presented at the 'Eighth Asia Pacific Roundtable', Kuala Lumpur, June 1994.
Townsend-Gault, I. (1994b), 'Part IV: SLOCs and Maritime Security', in B. Nagara and K.S. Balakrishnan (eds), *The Making of A Security Community in the Asia-Pacific*, ISIS Malaysia, Kuala Lumpur.
Ullman, R. H. (1983), 'Redefining Security', *World Politics*, vol. 8, no. 1.
United Nations Development Programme (UNDP) (1994), *Human Development Report 1994*, Oxford University Press, New York.
Westing, A. H. (ed.) (1986), *Global Resources and International Conflict: Environmental Factors in Strategic Policy and Action*, Oxford University Press, New York.

Chapter 2

Development and Security for the Peoples of Southeast Asia: Dealing with the Dynamics of Growth and Crisis

Jorge V. Tigno

Introduction

It is not an exaggeration to claim that Southeast Asia (SEA) has become the *sine qua non* for phenomenal dynamism and divergence: growth and decline, prosperity and misery, cohesion and conflict. Within the last two decades at least, the region has confronted a gamut of such upheavals and transformations from the economic to the cultural as well as the political. Unprecedented change and contrasts have entailed unprecedented costs. The sea of change that has swept much of SEA has caused the price of development to run terribly high for individuals and communities in the region.

This volume seeks to outline the phenomenal social, economic, and cultural issues in the dynamic interplay between development and security for the peoples of SEA. More importantly this volume is about how peoples have responded to the constantly shifting nexus between development and security situations in SEA. It is about groups and individuals affected by and adapting to a changed and continuously changing social, political, and economic environment that is SEA. Specifically, it is about those costs as perceived, felt, and confronted by selected peoples in SEA. In all the research findings, there is a concern for the subjectivity and inter-subjectivity (as well as negotiated objectivity) of views and conceptions as these views alternate between the individual and the group and between image and reality.

The studies in this volume attempt to investigate a variety of active and potent situations in four Southeast Asian countries—Indonesia, Malaysia, the Philippines, and Thailand. The studies emphasize how peoples or collectivities and organizations of human beings and networks of interactions have been subjected and have responded to radically altered realities. The groups of peoples studied are ethno-religious groups, migrants, workers, women, and small entrepreneurs. Although not exhaustive of peoples in the region, the contributors consider these groups to be vital in the security-development drama that is unfolding in the region. First and most obviously, they comprise a significant portion of the region's growing population. SEA is host to hundreds of diverse ethno-linguistic groups. Indeed, the region can be defined almost entirely in terms of ethnic and religious characteristics. Moreover, globalization and rapid industrialization have induced an exceptional increase in the urban population and in the industrial workforce. Migrant flows across borders are constantly on the rise due to often contiguous and sometimes disputed national boundaries as well as disparities in national economic capacities.

Second, these groups of peoples play a crucial role in bringing about the critical security and development nexus being investigated by this volume's contributors. Migrant labor in SEA accounts for a substantial portion of the economic growth that has taken place in the region. But while they may account for much of the economic expansion that has occurred in both sending and receiving areas, they are also seen as recurring security threats. Small-scale entrepreneurs contribute extensively (albeit, mostly unofficially) to the gross domestic product (GDP) of economies in the region. Throughout SEA, while the economically active population may be high (that is, between 60 to 70 per cent), there is also much to be said about the 'inactive' population who can be typically assumed to be involved in informal self-employed occupations and enterprises. Moreover, globalization and technological evolution have caused the increasing feminization of the work force of practically all the major Southeast Asian economies. In 1975, the percentage of women in the economically active population in the five Association of Southeast Asian Nations (ASEAN) countries of Indonesia, Malaysia, the Philippines, Singapore, and Thailand was 44.5 per cent. By 1996, it had increased to more than 49 per cent. Likewise, since the end of the cold war there has been a remarkable resurgence in movements for self-determination initiated on political and religious grounds by indigenous ethnic groups in Asia.

Third, these various groups, by their sheer numbers and capacities (with the exception of the agricultural sector), are the ones who will either benefit from the successes or endure the failures of development planners and technocrats. Since the 1960s, the state in SEA has become an exceptional catalyst for rapid economic growth and radical social and political disparities in the region. State action as well as inaction and mismanagement become major concerns for these peoples inasmuch as states provide for their basic human needs. Peoples; perceptions matter when it comes to establishing certain observations about the effectiveness (or ineffectiveness) of state initiatives and interventions.

And fourth, while these groups represent a significant portion of the productive and human resource capacities of the region, they are rarely involved in political decision making and other relevant social processes and institutions. Existing formal mechanisms and processes in SEA rarely possess the ability to peacefully confront (much less address) and accommodate marginal interests. At best, their participation has been nominal and piecemeal bordering on tokenism. Although not all-embracing, the groups included in this volume typically represent sectors and segments of the general population who continue to live in the margins of the society and the polity.

What are the things worth knowing about the studies in this volume? In general, they collectively and individually examine peoples' perceptions and perspectives of as well as responses to persistent and new security threats including the uncertainties and inequities brought about by rapid and unchecked (or mismanaged) socio-economic development in a region where such perceptions have become politically vital. Increasing democratization and the popularization of issues (that traditionally have been monopolized by so-called 'experts' and technocrats) have allowed for the greater and more profound importance of previously 'silent' and 'neglected' social sectors such as those studied in this volume. Technology has given these formerly disenfranchised groups the opportunity to become involved and to be influential politically.

Development and Security

The studies in this volume treat development matters as those pertaining to activities that (1) nurture and enlarge labor resource productivity; (2) enhance and intensify collective as well as individual self-esteem; (3) promote tolerance and cooperation in the midst of diversity characterized by contrasted and often conflicting or competing interests and identities; and (4) politically and economically empower marginal sectors and groups.

Likewise, the notion of security refers to a reduction or outright elimination and prevention of anxieties and vulnerabilities encountered by individuals and social groups that invariably result from the inequitable distribution of material benefits and other dividends of development. It includes generally the closing of the social, political, and economic divide between the haves and the have-nots. Security also refers to human security.

Political empowerment in the context of pluralism and diversity becomes a key aspect of comprehensive human security used in this volume. Moreover, human security issues and concerns must deal with maintaining ethnic dignity and identity as well as religious freedom in the midst of diversity and pluralism. It also means income and job security as well as continued human productivity, dignity, and competitiveness. Finally, it also seeks to address the question of migrants' and workers' rights and welfare. In the final analysis, security must bring about a significant reduction of disparities in income, and a corresponding growth in self-esteem, social identities, employment, and productivity of peoples achievable through their participation in the making of decisions on matters that affect their lives.

Actors in the Security-Development Drama

Numerous actors play significant roles in the linkage between development and security, comprehensively defined. For simplicity, two entities are discussed below that figure most prominently in the studies included in this volume. These are government and civil society.

Government

What role do governments play in bringing the costs of development up or down? The question of maintaining ethnic cohesion and homogeneity is a matter typically raised by national governments when confronted with increasing ethnic diversity due largely to transmigration and globalization as well as a growing middle class. This issue of maintaining or strengthening ethnic cohesion becomes a security problem when one ethnic identity is forced to submit to a dominant one by virtue of official government fiat. In this regard, one group at the expense of the rest of society enjoys the fruits of development. By being insensitive to certain sectoral demands and interests, governments may actually be conforming to particularistic claims and interests at the expense of other relevant groups.

People

Inappropriate and mismanaged development strategies can cause a great deal of insecurity for all concerned sectors and communities. Different peoples respond to immediate and perceived security threats differently. Workers laid off due to economic decline can respond by way of insisting on strengthened collective bargaining organizations such as labor unions. Others, especially women, may respond to crisis by engaging in small-scale (and informal) but independent enterprises.

Countless individuals dismissed from the formal macro-economic system due to the financial crisis are now engaged in informal micro-entrepreneurship. Micro-enterprises offer more security and stability in the face of unpredictable macro-economic events and reversals (not to mention greater convenience for the consuming public provided by small variety stores, restaurants, and sidewalk food stalls offering services during odd hours). Increasingly, people laid off in the formal job market are opening their own micro-enterprises and small-scale food chains. Still others resort to out-migration to areas where better economic prospects are foreseen often at tremendous costs to themselves as well as to their families.

These costs in turn affect governments. Authorities and bureaucratic institutions need to respond to them in several ways but mainly by managing already meager resources to continue to provide for essential human needs.

This volume does not seek to explain all types of behavioral responses to change. Its main intent is to describe a range of responses undertaken by peoples when confronted with rapidly changing circumstances such as in the immediate aftermath of a serious economic downturn or in the context of long-running ethnic and gender disparities.

Some Thematic Propositions

For the most part, the studies seek to highlight at least three thematic arguments or propositions in relation to development and security for people. The first is that current official development strategies (as carried out by governments in the region) are inadequate and can actually be insensitive to communities, classes, and sectors either in addressing the problems of threatened employment, reduced income and productivity, unresolved ethnic identity and homogeneity, or exploited/abused gender stereotypes. Such inadequacies and insensitivities can lead to intolerance by a dominant social group that is often puntuated by suspicion, bigotry, and even violence against the subordinate group. Subsequently, the vulnerabilities and uncertainties of peoples are magnified. Either by accident or by design, development programs and policies cause greater inequities that subsequently lead to human anxieties that are the chief cause of social and political insecurities among peoples and instabilities within and between social and economic groups.

Greater empowerment of sub-national units and entities can also be another cause of concern insofar as magnifying local intolerance is concerned. The group that is empowered may come only from a particular sector or ethnic community. This can actually widen the socio-economic gap rather than reduce it by schemes such as decentralization. Administrative subsidiarity (including those undertaken through increasing market deregulation can create new issues that highlight disparities between peoples.

The growing prosperity and affluence of an increasing number of people in SEA has given an increasing number of people more leisure time and opportunities to explore and go beyond their immediate environment. In terms of intra-Asian travel and tourism, the number traveling to SEA as tourists in 1996 are more than 21 million or one-fourth of the world's total.

SEA is a region of considerable diversity not only in tastes and preferences but also of ethnicity, religions, levels of economic development, types of political systems, and essential social values among peoples and communities. The diversity of values and norms has likewise led to a divergence among polities and societies in the region in their approaches to numerous social and political issues such as human rights protection and promotion, sexual harassment, elections, ethnic claims, among others. This divergence in values is brought to the fore by rapid developments in information technology and mainly by the expansion of the points of social contacts and activities including an increase in the number of social venues other than those initiated or established by the state such as non-governmental and people's organizations (NGOs and POs).

Second, while domestic conflicts and ethnically-defined tensions and turmoil may threaten the integrity, stability, and primordial character of the nation-state, it may take more than official national legislation and action to minimize and prevent such tensions because the state is seen as part of the problem. Unofficial or informal but 'real' concerns of peoples ought to be taken into more serious account. The concept of social capital, although still in its formative cognitive stage can eventually provide an alternative framework to the state-centered development and security perspectives of the previous cold war era. Efforts need to be sustained towards nurturing non-formal and non-state (decentralized and empowering) mechanisms that can be as effective (or even more effective) than formal state interventions.

Allowing active citizens' participation in defining their own role in society and in drafting political choices that directly affect their lives both in the short-and long-terms have increasingly become the regional standard of political development in SEA. The public sphere is presently no longer limited to what governments can do and know but incorporates (indeed, in some cases requires) the participation of individuals and groups beyond what is understood to be 'official' matters. In many ways, the meaning of the term 'public' has shifted away from those that concern the state towards that which is 'social' or within the realm of civil society.[1] Subsequently, the work of government has now come to broadly mean a more dynamic and complex process of governance.[2]

The official and the public have in turn given way to the 'popular' as peoples assert their critical importance in governance. Governance from a popular standpoint proposes that official government structures and policies reflect an inherently redistributive and integrative character in the context of increasing social, economic, and political diversity. Current conditions have induced changes in the expectations of peoples about what constitute the public and private spheres. Indeed, the distinction is no longer between the public and the private but between the public (or official) and the popular. The private perspective has now become a distinct object of the security and development discourse on the part of any sensible and sensitive government in that the way people perceive a security issue and/or a development strategy can eventually determine its attainment. When a certain group or sector is unable to identify with a specific security issue as defined by the state, this may reflect a divergence between the 'official' and the 'real' security and development issue. When the official view differs from the grassroots perspective, such a divergence may have serious implications for popular mobilization that can eventually affect the achievement of security and development.

The third thematic proposition is that a sustainable development and security strategy must also incorporate a multilateral approach and that no single community must be made to bear the entire costs of development in the same way that no single social group must benefit from the dividends of development at the expense of others. This is especially so for a region as dense and yet as diverse as SEA. In order to enhance the sustainability of a response, it must be undertaken on a broad and coordinated level either on a regional platform or higher, given the comprehensive and complex nature of the problems of development and security. This can also include the possibility of involving third (multilateral) parties and even international development agencies such as the International Labor Organization (ILO) in the case of labor issues, in resolving tensions and disparities.

Over the last decade at least, there has been an unraveling of the weaknesses of the state (as well as the state-centric development model). Authoritarianism and development technocracies have been increasingly criticized as being inappropriate, irrelevant, and inhuman in their development strategies. A multilateral and 'softer' (that is, more transparent, responsible, and accountable) administrative approach to sustainable development and durable social and economic security is essential to any development program.

Options for Policy Advocacy and Action

What follows are some of the major points and issues highlighted in the different studies that have to do with broad policy advocacy guidelines. They are directed not only to governments but also to non-governmental and intergovernmental agencies.

Improve Social Protection for Marginalized Peoples

The contributors all underscore the critical significance of establishing mechanisms for social safety nets in the face of the uncertainties brought about by regional integration and interdependence. The regional financial crisis brought home the point that there are very few certainties in a region as dynamic and complex as SEA. Rising unemployment brought about by the fluidity of capital flows and government mismanagement compel authorities in the region to place more emphasis on 'non-market' concerns such as unemployment insurance, food subsidies, state-subsidized education, and relevant occupational re-training. Clearly, the market in itself is neither the sole nor the best purveyor of progress. A normatively 'pro-poor' policy, although costly over the short-term, may in the long-run mean tremendous savings for governments in the areas of health care and housing services.

Promote Responsible Entrepreneurship

In relation to establishing better and more appropriate safety nets to previously unprotected economic sectors, there is a need for both governments and non-governmental agencies to nurture an entrepreneurial vitality among peoples most affected by economic short falls and crises. This entrepreneurial approach cannot go empty-handed. Government must be prepared to provide more resources through appropriate micro-lending facilities. Moreover, governments and private agencies can cooperate in providing more relevant training and guidance to small investors so that their small capital may not be wasted by the next economic crisis.

Support Managed and Responsible Movement of Human Resources

Multilateral institutions need to be considered in coordinating and managing the flows of peoples across borders. The studies in this volume also acknowledge the proximate and porous borders (often arbitrarily set by colonialism) that exist between countries in the region as well as the need to sustain the dynamism of these different economies through the dynamism of their peoples. There is a need for a more effective mechanism for resolving migration-related problems of individuals so that they do not cause a serious security problem for individuals, for societies, and for states. Authorities need to recognize the substantial contribution and savings that migrant workers make to their respective national economies over the long-term.

Encourage Tolerance in Diversity

Recognizing the multiethnic and multi-religious character of SEA, more serious attention needs to be given in the direction of instituting better ways for the equitable administration of basic social services without resorting to ethnic or religious biases. Government institutions should promote ethnic and religious freedoms and identities but not at the expense of minority groups. As the studies argue, the state can contribute towards enhancing the disparities and differences that exist across ethno-religious groups and, thus, worsen ethnic conflicts. Tolerance is essential to civility. Intolerance can come from ignorance and misinformation. An appropriate national educational policy may serve to diminish the level of intolerance that exists between ethnic communities in certain areas.

Establish More Institutions of Good Governance

Institutions and mechanisms for promoting good governance (for example, accountable, transparent, representative, responsible, and effective social and political governing structures) ought to be strengthened and increased. Intolerance, inequities, and conflicts occur when governments are unable or unwilling to acknowledge the claims and interests of previously and extensively marginalized peoples. Good governance creates the conditions for the non-violent resolution of conflicts through open dialogue and competition. Moreover, there ought to be further public demands and efforts for greater transparency and public accountability in government. Good governance can lead to a reduction in government inefficiencies especially through graft and corruption leading to increased savings that can then be directed towards the provision of more and better social services. Public consultations essentially through elections have now become the norm in any government structure, program, or initiative. Decentralized governance is another. Good governance eventually creates the conditions for the convergence of perspectives between the 'official' and the 'real' in terms of understanding what security and development issues and concerns are and what are not. Needless to say, good governance needs to be extended to the public, private, and civil society sectors.

Look for Exemplars

From an academic standpoint, studies should be encouraged that will examine and dissect best practices in the areas of good governance and provisions for social protection to marginalized groups. These exemplars can then be used as models or benchmarks for other Asian countries and eventually replicated or emulated in these areas. In addition to official initiatives by governments, non-governmental initiatives and models should also be examined and encouraged. International development agencies working in the region must pay closer attention to such peoples' initiatives in light of the continued and inherent limitations of official development plans and strategies. Likewise, there should be more serious attention given to nurturing regional mechanisms and institutions leading to a convergence of official and non-official security perspectives and perceptions at the international level. Existing forums and venues for the discussion of contemporary security issues appear to accommodate only the official governmental perspectives. Efforts should be initiated to encourage greater popular participation in such forums at both the national and regional levels.

Redirect the Work of Development Agencies and Non-Governmental Initiatives in Reevaluating the Value of Administrative Subsidiary

In the wake of the ousting of the Marcos dictatorship in the Philippines in 1986, international development agencies diverted their assistance from the non-governmental sector to the official channels of government. This is partly because the new regime that emerged out of the rubble of authoritarianism had sought a more meaningful level of popular legitimacy. Other countries in the region are also in the same situation. While some of the official development assistance has achieved a measure of success, more funds appear to be relatively underutilized and even used for counter-productive purposes. In light of their experience in the at least last decade, international development agencies should reevaluate their current strategies for providing support to either government or non-governmental initiatives especially in light of the increasingly popular trend towards administrative and political decentralization. At the same time, non-governmental undertakings need to be encouraged short of creating a condition of discord among them, as this can also be counter-productive. Different peoples' initiatives should manifest a strong degree of coherence, cooperation, and complementation to be most effective at the local levels. Here, the process of open and interactive dialogue between and among social sectors is crucial. This is one way of nurturing and forming social capital towards effectively mobilizing these local communities.

Notes

1 For details, at least in terms of how this change in terminology has affected Japanese society, see Yamamoto, T. (1999), *Deciding the Public Good; Governance and Civil Society in Japan*, Japan Center for International Exchange, Tokyo.

2 For details on the changing notion of government in the United States, see Osborne, D. and Gaebler, T. (1992), *Reinventing Government; How the Entrepreneurial Spirit is Transforming the Public Sector*, Addison-Wesley Publishing Company, Inc., Massachussetts.

References

Osborne, D. and Gaebler, T. (1992), *Reinventing Government; How the Entrepreneurial Spirit is Transforming the Public Sector*, Addison-Wesley Publishing Company, Inc., Massachusetts.

Yamamoto, T. (1999), *Deciding the Public Good; Governance and Civil Society in Japan*, Japan Center for International Exchange, Tokyo.

PART II
CASE STUDIES

Chapter 3

Migration, Security, and Development: The Politics of Undocumented Labor Migration in Southeast Asia

Jorge V. Tigno

Introduction: Understanding Perceptions of 'Undocumentedness'

This chapter highlights the linkage between security/insecurity and people's perceptions of their social and political environment in the context of rapid socioeconomic development and changes manifested in transborder migratory flows. It argues that insecurity is caused by a people's ability to distinguish their identity from others (that is, the migrant, newcomer, immigrant settler, others) that in this case is the foreigner. Such distinction between the 'national self' and the 'other' is based on semi-fixed preferences and is reinforced or transformed by social agents of public opinion (for example, government, media, religion, class, ethnic group, others). It also argues that people feel insecure primarily because of their inability to comprehend and capture the infinite array of actions and consequences they expect from themselves and from others. This eventually leads firms, communities, and especially policymakers, politicians, and bureaucrats to rationalize the immigration question by initiating action that can very well compound the problem (for example, the 'commodification' of human labor or the 'criminalization' of the migrant) rather than resolve it.

The study focuses on the clandestine movement of generally low-skilled labor in Southeast Asia (SEA) and excludes other forms of population movements and movers, such as refugee migration and professional expatriates (who tend to move legally anyway). The countries to be examined are Indonesia, the Philippines, Malaysia, and Thailand. The study is an attempt to determine people's perceptions and expectations on issues and concerns related to undocumented flows of migrant labor. This issue is a distinct challenge in social research. The absence of more reliable and comparable information on undocumented migrant flows is also a major restraint to policy-making and implementation. However, in the absence of this information and given the urgent necessity to arrive at policy options and decisions, bureaucrats and politicians try to overcome this inadequacy by relying on a variety of personal (that is, social and psychological) anecdotes to render the necessary policy judgments.

Migration and the Post-Cold War World

It is almost an understatement to say that at present transnational migration is a phenomenon of increasing social, economic, and political significance for peoples as well as for nation-states. The end of the cold war has created new conditions for the rise in persistent, as well as new immigration issues and areas of concern from both the academic and policy perspectives.

One immediate and profound effect of these developments is a reconfiguration of the ways in which the security situation is understood. Security encompasses not just the political and military dimension but also the 'softer' aspects that include ethnic harmony, environmental sustainability, social (including gender and ethnic) equity, and sustainable economic growth, among many others. These aspects are now of strategic importance to any society and may even be seen as having primacy over the conventional notions of security.

Subsequent to the diffusion of the locus of power after the cold war, there occurred a dispersal of the sources of conflict, from presumably monolithic and powerful nation-states to disparate and previously powerless communities. The conflicts that arise now revolve around social issues (for example, gender, ethnicity, environment, and religion). States now see an urgent need to redefine their conventional notion of security and discard previously held assumptions especially in the context of the increasing importance of civil society groups such as non-governmental and people's organizations (NGOs and POs).

As a consequence, a second consequence of the end of the cold war is the emergence of new social, political, and economic pressures now confronting government. The policy debate surrounding these issues has proceeded with great difficulty often leading to serious and sometimes violent confrontations with people from the margins of society. Rapid and profound socioeconomic changes, especially in the Asia Pacific region, have prompted many not only to question their present situation but also to take steps to alter it. Economic prosperity and globalization have raised many peoples' social and political expectations. As a consequence, these heightened expectations have led to popular demands for social equity, creating conditions for political conflicts to arise between the people and their government.

A third consequence of the end of the cold war is the intensification of the process of globalization, a phenomenon directly linked to transnational migration. The global integration of societies and markets, facilitated largely by improvements in transportation and communications technologies has reinforced people's intentions to move. Such technologies provide people with a wider range of possible options in modes of transit and destinations from which they can choose.

The confluence of the three consequences discussed above occasioned a change in the attitudes of both the general public and political leaders. In the context of transnational migration, they see security as being compounded by the rise in the flows of people across national boundaries, especially of low-skilled undocumented labor. Limited resource capacities of receiving countries are further strained by immigration, including the capacity of their political and administrative agencies to deal with various problems associated with transnational migration.

Private firms recognize the direct economic gains from low-skilled migrants. However, receiving countries fear that they will add to the strain on the state's administrative capacities to deliver basic services. Sending countries benefit from labor outflows by relieving somewhat their domestic unemployment and underemployment problems and by receiving migrant savings through remittances. Moreover, they may be faced with the long-term problem of brain drain and the inability to productively utilize migrant's remittances for national development goals. This situation is further compounded by the 1997 Asian financial crisis where both sending and receiving countries have been adversely affected. An intensification of undocumented migration came in the wake of the crisis. In the final analysis, migration is both the cause and effect of the need of peoples to acquire some degree of stability and security for themselves and their families in social, political, and economic terms.

All of these have affected the behavior of state authorities and how they regard social identity. The immigration issue has become a highly politicized debate characterized by deepening government involvement and increasing public responsiveness. Both sending and receiving countries have become polarized in their effort to resolve the impacts and implications of transnational labor migration. As a result of state action, there is now a growing concern over how national political authorities have attempted to 'refine' or redefine immigration-related concepts (for example, citizenship, immigrants, refugees, others). Receiving countries now find it difficult to make the distinction between economic migrants, political refugees, and asylum seekers without attracting some measure of opposition from different social groups. This is true not only in many European countries (for example, France, Germany, and Britain) but, ironically, also in countries such as Australia, Canada, and the United States (US) that are made up of large immigrant communities.

The Problematique: Security in Identity

Over the last decade at least, there has been an increasing movement of goods and capital across borders. Unfortunately, the same cannot be said regarding the movement of human labor. Indeed, the trend in many countries is to resist the free flow of foreign migrant labor across borders and for governments to institutionalize 'protectionist' mechanisms against such flow.

This phenomenon underscores the tensions that exist between development, migration, and changing perceptions of regime and people's security. It also forms the undercurrent and dilemma of societies in the way they perceive themselves in relation to others. Why is there resistance to the freer flow of human resources and not to that of finance and capital goods? And why is it that in spite of the economic crisis there is a resounding call to further liberalize capital and trade in goods while the opposite is being argued for labor, at least as far as state policies are concerned? The answers to these questions may lie in understanding people's perceptions that may be different from or incompatible with those of government officials, bureaucrats, politicians, employers, and others.

A Conceptual Framework for Undocumented Migration

Definition of Terms

Although the emphasis of the study is on low-skilled foreign laborers, the terms labor migrant, migrant worker, foreigner, and newcomer are used interchangeably. A migrant worker, generally, is someone who is engaged in a compensated activity in foreign territory. This definition is adopted for purposes of simplicity and manageability.

This study also distinguishes labor receiving from labor sending countries. Since some countries in SEA are both senders and receivers (for example, Thailand and Malaysia), such a dichotomy may not suffice in explaining the real nature and dynamic character of transnational migration. These terms are used merely to distinguish the source from the destination of labor.

Undocumented (or clandestine) migration or undocumented/clandestine migrant are used rather than illegal or illegitimate migration/migrant – see Appendix A and B because the legal parameters for migration have yet to be resolved outside the policies being implemented by individual sending and receiving countries. People migrate legally as much as possible, but are compelled to take extra-legal actions and remedies often in the context of complex political or policy-related situations in both the sending and receiving countries.

Presently, there are three measures undertaken by governments to tackle undocumented migrant flows in Asia.[1] The first is active prevention from entry, overstaying, and violating the terms of the visa through stringent monitoring and examination of travel documents. The second is actual expulsion and/or deportation, at times subject to procedural safeguards. And the third is regularization or legalization of the status of undocumented migrants – see Appendix A. Ironically, it is possible for these policies to create the very condition of irregularity and 'clandestinity' that authorities seek to avoid.

As many academics and experts observe, aside from the economic and labor market conditions in both sending and receiving countries, geographical proximity, and cultural affinity, irregular migration is in fact also generated by the migration policy of the host country.[2] At the same time, however, while some receiving and sending countries in SEA have instituted their own guest-worker policies (for example, Malaysia, Thailand, the Philippines, and Singapore), others have yet to embark on their own foreign labor programs. In the latter case, unfortunately, it is the very absence of information and institutions that contributes to migrant 'clandestinity'. The economic crisis that hit the region compounds the situation further as discussed below.

Migration and Instability: Two Sides of the Same Coin?

It is commonly perceived that foreigners and immigrants cause crime, unemployment, social disharmony, economic backwardness, and disease. In the last 20 years, there has been a substantial increase among governments that believe that their country's immigration levels are too high. In 1976, about six per cent of those governments surveyed (covering developed countries) considered their immigration too high. By 1996 the number had increased to 21 per cent.[3]

Public opinion in the US and Australia, for instance, (two traditional destination countries) is now greatly affected by the immigration question. Prior to 1970, no less than 40 per cent of American respondents thought that US immigration levels should be reduced. By the 1980s, however, this had increased to about 60 per cent.[4] An opinion poll conducted by Time/CNN notes that almost 80 per cent of Americans surveyed favored stricter limits on immigration. Already, the US has taken a more hard line position in its official immigration policy. It has taken local illegal immigration initiatives and actually deported legal immigrants who have serious criminal records and convictions (this attitude is likely to harden in the light of the events of 11 September 2001).

While clandestine migration may bring occasional benefits in the form of increased income and savings for migrants, it also has implicated and exposed illegal migrants to exploitation by recruiters, brokers, and government authorities. In numerous instances, the bargaining position of the worker is weakened especially if the worker comes from poor countries such as Myanmar, Sri Lanka, or Pakistan where both poverty and illiteracy offer few employment opportunities to their nationals.

Undocumented migrants have been exposed to numerous insecurities both at the source and the destination. Governments and employers frequently marginalize and isolate them at the periphery of the economy and the society. At the same time, politicians, publics, and bureaucrats alike are also anxious about their migrant population in general or the undocumented (that is, the 'invisible') migrant workforce in particular. When perceptions of differences turn to perceptions of disparities, security problems arise.

Migration as a security issue has affected the thinking of the public and those within the bureaucracy. And 'once turned into a security problem, the migrant appears as the other who has entered (or who desires to enter) a harmonious world and, just by having entered it, has disturbed the harmony'.[5] Migration is now seen as a process of increasing the prospect of danger and uncertainty by allowing 'others' to be accepted and assimilated into a 'pure' and 'harmonious' social or ethnic context.

Very little has changed as far as policy pronouncements are concerned. In general, emigration policies and guidelines among countries in SEA are inclined to be reactive, incremental, and intractable. Sending country options are limited to what the external labor markets (the receivers) demand. Any policy to promote the emigration of nationals specifically for employment almost always takes the limits of the labor market into account. What this means is that country emigration policies tend to be deferential toward the demands and needs of the receiving country for fear of losing out in the market. For many Asian countries, the remittances sent by nationals abroad represent a substantial portion of their foreign currency earnings. They have also generated official development assistance (ODA).

Labor emigration programs have a strong stopgap orientation, that is, that labor migration is necessary to address current and persistent national economic and social concerns (for example, unemployment, balance of payments deficit, others). It is a common perception that once these fundamental problems are addressed, migration will no longer be an option nor a necessity. Labor migration guidelines have become more and more intractable, enforced by increasingly truncated government policies. In many cases, the foreign affairs, labor, finance, and justice ministries (not to mention the health and police agencies) of the sending countries have become deeply involved in the formulation as well as implementation of overlapping emigration guidelines. This has not only caused the deterioration in agency unity between bureaucracies but has actually institutionalized an ostensibly 'stopgap' policy.

Immigration policies among receiving countries tend to converge toward inchoate, ambivalent, and acrimonious guidelines that follow double standards. Countries in the Asia Pacific that follow such guidelines often fail to acknowledge the root causes of their immigration problems and concerns. They discriminate in favor of the more skilled expatriates as against the less skilled or unskilled laborers through their guest worker programs. Likewise, for the unskilled and semi-skilled workforce, there are quota restrictions imposed on the number that certain countries might admit within a given period.

In short, there appears to be a serious absence of certainty, predictability, and decisiveness in the policy framework. Instead of understanding the true nature of the policy challenge, receiving countries opt for the easier way out by criminalizing (and imposing corporal punishment in some cases) the undocumented labor migrants in spite of the fact that many governments recognize and benignly tolerate the presence of a largely clandestine foreign workforce.

Impressions That Last

The current scale of clandestine transnational labor flows across East and SEA is fast gaining notoriety within the region and beyond. One study estimates that 'in almost every host country, the number of illegal workers typically exceeds the number of legal workers by two to three times'.[6]

What are some of the common apprehensions in receiving areas associated with clandestine population flows of whatever variety in Asia? It has been argued that allowing the uncontrolled stream of foreigners especially those with little or no skills may depress domestic wage rates and worker benefits since local employers will presumably want to hire the more docile and less discriminating foreign nationals. This will have the overall effect of reducing the employment of the local working population as well as preempt the adoption of labor saving and technology intensive production methods and devices.

Receivers also fear the negative effects that foreigners will bring on the local society and culture. They argue that foreigners who are less educated tend to be less socially desirable and are inclined toward anti-social activities. In a closed or ethnically homogenous society, an increase in the foreigner population (of whatever kind) may lead to a disruption of that country's social and cultural homogeneity and harmony. In a multiethnic social context (for example, Singapore and Malaysia), an increase in the influx of foreign nationals is feared to jeopardize the fragile ethno-political balance that already exists.

Available statistical data especially in developing country situations on the stocks and flows of foreign workers are inadequate for continued and comparable macro-level analyses. Whatever data are available tend to be limited and disparate, making comparisons over time difficult if not impossible.[7] Speculations on the presumed number of undocumented migrants have been and are often shrouded in a mist of exaggerated perceptions that often incline toward exaggerated estimates.[8]

In summary, given that real difficulties exist and persist in obtaining accurate statistical data, certain compromises occur in the utilization of labor market as well as immigration information. Mainly in the absence of more reliable information (and partly because of the difficulty in generating more reliable data sets), policymakers are thus more likely to base their judgments on less problematique, but equally troublesome perceptions of reality. The complexity of the migration situation also promotes 'a systematic tendency toward temporal illusion even in so-called open, democratic societies where the policy discourse is less constrained and the flow and exchange of information less influenced by state authorities'.[9] In some cases, a measure of social construction, ethnic stereotyping, and a cultural as well as occupational niche is both the cause and effect of the absence of more reliable and accurate quantitative data.[10]

It is, therefore, not surprising to observe that studies on the effects of immigration are often controversial and contentious – a virtual Pandora's box. This is even more so when such studies deal with undocumented and irregular flows of primarily unskilled foreign labor.

Ideological, class, and cultural prejudices serve to intensify and polarize the debates on whether or not to restrict the entry of foreign workers and whether or not to regularize the residence and employment of undocumented, unskilled foreigners. In fact, it is the ideological factor more than anything else that can underpin the policy on undocumented migration.

Why Prefer Undocumented Migrants?

Foreign migrant labor is a significant part of human resource capacities of many receiving countries in SEA. What follows are some of the more common views and perceptions of the major sectors involved in undocumented migrant labor. These are the employer, the labor contractor/broker, and the migrant.

A survey of the views of employers hiring foreign workers in Malaysia[11] found that almost all (97 per cent) said that the reason they hire foreigners is because it is difficult to hire local workers. Moreover, those that can be hired locally are either more costly or less productive (that is, they work less hours) or do not intend to stay long in their jobs altogether. Others say that it is simply too difficult to hire local workers and only foreigners are willing to accept the working conditions and lower wages that they offer. In addition, foreigners are seen to be more cooperative, docile, and easier to manage.[12] Meanwhile, the foreign workers surveyed say that they prefer to work in

Malaysia even as they are unlikely to get the full benefits due them under Malaysian law. This is because Malaysian employers and contractors offer relatively higher pay.

In Thailand, employers also prefer to hire foreign workers. The shortage of local workers is cited as a main reason for hiring foreigners. Thai workers prefer to work in less difficult and higher paying jobs mostly in the cities or urban areas. Also, some employers say that Thai workers are undisciplined or lazy in their work habits.[13] On the other hand, foreign migrants prefer to work for foreign employers and contractors because they have already incurred substantial cash advances that can only be repaid through regular salary deductions.

Foreigners also prefer to go abroad, not only because of the higher salaries being offered by employers (relative to local wage rates), but also as a result of on going military and political campaigns in their areas. Those from Myanmar, for instance, are actually forced to leave due to the unsafe and uncertain social, political, and economic conditions at home. The same conditions generally prevailed in Mindanao, the southern part of the Philippines during the 1970s and early 1980s when the Muslim secessionist campaign was at its strongest.[14] Many of these mostly Muslim Filipinos fled across to Sabah and Borneo.

Of Counts, Costs, and Contribution of Migrant Labor

As already noted, estimates about the number of foreigners and migrant workers that arrive, leave, and stay are usually varied and are somewhat clouded by preexisting attitudes and perceptions. In Thailand, for instance, a government survey estimates the number of foreign workers in the Kingdom to be more than 733,000 as of February 1996. A substantial number of these migrants are found within the Bangkok Metropolitan Area and outlying areas as well as the northern provinces – see Table 3.1. On the other hand, official sources from the Myanmar government say there are only 78,000 Burmese abroad from 1990 to 1997.[15]

Mahidol University puts the figure at 400,000 undocumented Burmese migrants out of an estimated total of 750,000 undocumented foreigners in Thailand.[16] The Thai Labor Ministry puts the figure at 740,000,[17] while another estimate puts the figure at 986,000.[18] The International Organization for Migration (IOM) estimates the number of undocumented migrants in Thailand to be around 943,000,[19] while the Thai National Security Council estimates that there are from 700,000 to one million undocumented foreigners now in the Kingdom.[20]

According to Indonesian Embassy authorities in Malaysia, on the one hand, the number of Indonesian migrants in that country is around 1.6 million of which about 900,000 are undocumented. On the other hand, official sources in Indonesia, say there are only some 317,000 documented Indonesian migrant workers in Malaysia,[21] while a Malaysian NGO puts the number of undocumented Indonesian migrants in Malaysia at about 1.5 million.[22] In other sources, the total number of foreign workers in Malaysia are close to two million of whom about 800,000 are undocumented.[23] A Malaysian newspaper estimates there are 1.5 million foreigners in Malaysia half of whom are undocumented.[24] The highest estimate so far is around three million, most of whom are Indonesians.[25]

Table 3.1 Estimated Number of Undocumented Foreign Workers in Thailand by Region (Province) and by Type of Employment

Region	Number of Provinces	Number of Foreign Workers	Types of Employment Sector
Southern Thailand	14	99,176	agricultural workers
Northern Thailand	17	167,822	agriculture, construction
Central Thailand	6	14,016	agriculture, construction
Northeast Thailand	19	5,838	transportation, construction, industry, retail trade
Greater Bangkok	5	83,843	construction, industry
Eastern Thailand	8	38,875	agriculture
Western Thailand	6	48,730	agriculture
Bangkok	-	275,340	construction, industry
Total	75	733,640	

Source: Department of Employment, Ministry of Labor and Social Welfare (February 1996 survey), from Chalaemwong, Y. (1996), *An Estimated [sic] of Undocumented Migrant Workers in Thailand*, Thailand Development Research Institute, Bangkok, [in Thai].

In 1995, the Overseas Workers Welfare Administration (OWWA) under the Philippine Department of Labor estimates that there are about 4.2 million Filipino migrants throughout the world, 42.7 per cent of whom are undocumented. And in Asia, the Filipino migrant stock is around 1.3 million, about half of which are undocumented.[26] About 100,000 undocumented Filipino migrants are said to be in parts of SEA, most of whom are in Sabah, Malaysia.[27] Overall, the estimates of undocumented Filipinos worldwide can run from a 'low' of 1.9 million to a 'high' of four to six million.

These many, and at times conflicting estimates point to the need to improve the ways in which immigration authorities monitor and regulate migrant worker flows across their borders. The conservative estimate that can be made so far for SEA is that every one regular or documented migrant has as many as three to four undocumented equivalents. Every month about 1,700 Indonesians are said to enter Malaysia from Sarawak with an additional 6,000 cross the Malacca Strait.[28] Likewise, an estimated 100 to 300 Burmese workers are smuggled into Thailand each day.[29]

The estimated figures on their contribution to and the cost/benefits they incur for the receiving countries in general and for employers in particular are quite significant. About 70 per cent of the 1.2 million registered alien population in Malaysia are employed in the construction industry.[30] Another estimate says that 80 per cent of the

700,000 construction workers are foreigners with another 350,000 as foreign maids.[31] Another report says the proportion of construction workers to the outstanding number of foreigners in Malaysia is closer to 60 per cent.[32]

Low-skilled expatriate workers (mostly Indonesians) in Malaysia are said to cause a significant outflow of funds with more than US$1.14 billion sent by foreign workers as annual home-bound remittances.[33] Burmese workers in Thailand sent home around B3.45 million (around US$76,000), according to a study by Mahidol University in 1997.[34] The amount is not substantial and may be more indicative of the low wages paid to Burmese migrants by Thai firms. Another government estimate, however, puts the amount of total outflows by all foreign workers at up to B6 billion (more than US$1.4 million) per year.[35] In the case of the Philippines, remittances by overseas Filipino migrants (both documented and undocumented) amounted to more than US$3.869 billion in 1995. In 1996, these increased to more than US$4.306 billion, representing roughly five per cent of the country's gross national product (GNP).

Employers derive substantial savings from hiring low-skilled foreign workers especially in labor-intensive enterprises. It is estimated that employers in Thailand who hire migrants from Myanmar, Laos, and Cambodia are able to save some US$500 million a year in labor costs by hiring undocumented foreigners.[36] Another estimate puts the savings of Thai firms at B20 billion per year (around US$440 million).

In addition to remittance earnings, Indonesian migrant workers also generate a large income for governments in sending and receiving countries through levies, processing, and recruitment fees. Indonesian workers seeking employment in Malaysia are charged some US$80 each for services and insurance costs.[37] They pay around US$130-235 to be able to cross the Strait of Malacca, enter Peninsular Malaysia, and eventually work in plantation and construction sites there.

For those Indonesians intending to work outside the region where the returns may be higher, the broker's fees are much higher. Indonesians seeking to work in Taiwan, for instance, pay as much as Rp8 million to Rp18 million (around US$900 to US$1,000 at 1998 exchange rates) to brokers.

A local survey conducted among Filipino workers in Taiwan observed that the actual placement fees paid by a majority (83 per cent) of the respondents is between P50,000 to P80,000 (around US$1,500 to US$1,800 at 1998 exchange rates).[38] South Asian and Burmese migrants intending to work in Thailand need to pay from B50,000 to B70,000 (US$1,100 to US$1,600) and B2,000 to B5,000 (US$50 to US$110), respectively. For Thai workers intending to work in Japan and elsewhere, the recruitment costs can go as high as B400,000 (US$9,000-10,000).

These activities generate huge earnings for organized criminal syndicates, labor brokers, and recruitment/employment agencies, including corrupt government personnel who may choose to close their eyes to such unscrupulous trafficking activities. Migrant trafficking is a multi-billion dollar industry in many regions of the world today, especially during times of economic uncertainty. Chinese smuggling to the US is said to cost about US$3 billion annually.[39]

SEA and the rest of the world are definitely no different. It is estimated that the 'industry' is able to generate some US$5 billion to US$7 billion annually.[40] A Burmese migrant is usually charged B6,000 to B8,000 (US$180-200) by brokers and traffickers to enter Thailand.[41]

In the first three months of 1998, Thai overseas migrant workers were reported to have lost some B27 million (more than US$480,000) to unscrupulous brokers compared to B27 million (US$600,000) for the whole of 1997.[42] Table 3.2 shows estimates that between April 1996 and March 1998 Thai overseas migrants were cheated by illegal recruiters by more than B140 million (US$3.5 billion). It is difficult to assess the actual earnings of these syndicates and brokers because the clandestine nature of their work inhibits many migrants from filing official reports or complaints either for fear of reprisal and concern for the stigma that goes with clandestinity, or they are simply afraid that this will reduce their chances of working abroad.

Table 3.2 Thai Overseas Job Seekers Cheated by Labor Brokers in Thailand, April 1996 to March 1998

Country	Number of Persons	Monetary Losses (in Baht)
Japan	422	73,126,900.00
Singapore	25	1,229,900.00
Brunei	32	1,736,000.00
S. Korea	428	16,239,400.00
Taiwan	185	11,612,332.00
Israel	20	1,389,000.00
Laos	44	838,000.00
Denmark	10	200,000.00
Britain	6	560,000.00
Slovak Rp.	22	5,395,000.00
US	784	25,418,000.00
Finland	1	139,000.00
Hong Kong	8	225,000.00
France	3	300,000.00
NZ	13	1,780,000.00
Macao	3	150,000.00
Total	2006	140,338,532.00

Source: Inspection and Job Seekers Protection Division, Ministry of Labor and Social Welfare, Thailand; Charoensuthiphan, P. (1998), 'Slump a Boom to Cheats', *Bangkok Post*, 14 April.

Foreign labor migrants are high performing assets wherever they may be. There is notable consensus that foreign workers are able to contribute substantially to the economies of both source and destination countries. For instance, while not much official empirical evidence can be cited due to the fact that most of the workers concerned are undocumented, Indonesian migrant workers have been said to contribute about 25 to 30 per cent to Malaysia's GDP[43] and anywhere from 25 to 50 per cent to its GNP.[44] These 'subsidies' are broken down according to different economic sectors. It is estimated that the growth in Malaysia's construction sector would be five to eight per cent less without foreign workers, one to two per cent less in the manufacturing sector;[45] and as much as 60 per cent less in the agricultural sector.[46] Indeed, in the area of property development altogether, the estimate can go as high as 80 to 100 per cent.[47]

Migration and the Tenuous Border Security Situation

The sheer length of the borders that divide the countries of SEA represents a definite strain on the resources of any government, whether developed or developing, large or small. Mainland SEA has no less than 15,500 kilometers of land borders to guard and monitor – see Table 3.3 Moreover, much of these land borders are defined by tenuous river systems that change course ever so often, frequently altering the political borders in the process. In SEA, interstate borders can be generally described as porous and highly tentative as far as population movements are concerned and often complicated by competing territorial claims. In effect, these national boundaries are merely symbolic of effective territorial sovereignty.

Table 3.3 Length of Land Borders in Selected Mainland Southeast Asian Countries

Border	Length (kms)
Burma-China (Yunnan)	2,185
Lao-Vietnam	2,130
Thai-Myanmar	1,800
Indonesia-Malaysia	1,782
Thai-Lao	1,754
Vietnam-China	1,281
Cambodia-Vietnam	1,228
Indonesia-PNG	820
Lao-Cambodia	541
Thai-Malaysia	506
Thai-Cambodia	503
Malaysia-Brunei	381
Lao-China (Yunnan)	423
Lao-Burma	235
Total	15,569

Compiled from Stern, A. and Crissman, L. (1998), *Maps of International Borders Between Mainland Southeast Asian Countries and Background Information Concerning Population Movements at These Borders,* Asian Research Center for Migration, Bangkok, February. Figures for Indonesia are taken from *www.studyweb.com/geo/geograph* by American Computer Resources, Incorporated.

Countries with some of the longest borders in the sub-region include those that continue to face problems with undocumented migrants. These are Thailand (with Myanmar and Laos), Vietnam (with Laos, Cambodia, and China), and Laos (with Thailand and Vietnam). Efforts to curb undocumented movements have been initiated mainly through the establishment of official border crossing points that in mainland SEA currently stands at 41 – see Table 3.4.

Table 3.4 Official Border Crossing Points in Selected Mainland Southeast Asian Countries

Borders	Crossing Points	Number
Thai-Lao	Chiang Saen, Chiang Kong, Ta Li, Chiang Khan, Nong Khai, Beung Kan, Nakin Phanom, Mukdahan, Khemmarat, Chong Mek	10
Thai-Cambodia	Nam Yeun, Kap Choeng, Ta Praya, Klong Leuk, Ban Pakkard, Klong Yai	6
Thai-Myanmar	Mae Sai, Maw Sot, Ranong	3
Thai-Malaysia	Padang Besar, Sadao, Betong, Su-ngai Kolok, Tak Bai	5
Cambodia-Vietnam	Moc Bai, Kaom Samor, Phnom Den	3
Lao-Vietnam	None	0
Lao-Cambodia	None	0
Lao-China (Yunnan)	Mohan, Jiangcheng	2
Burma-China (Yunnan)	Lushui, Namkham, Muse, Kyukok, Kunlong-Hopang, Cangyuan, Daluo	7
Vietnam-China	Nam Cum, Lao Cai, Ha Giang, Tianpeng, Dong Dang	5
Total		41

Compiled from Stern, A. and Crissman, L. (1998), *Maps of International Borders Between Mainland Southeast Asian Countries and Background Information Concerning Population Movements at These Borders*, Asian Research Center for Migration, Bangkok, February.

Each day, thousands of persons pass through these official checkpoints making the sub-region one of the most traveled areas in the world – see Table 3.5. Still much of this traffic is not officially monitored. In the Myanmar-Southern China (specifically Yunnan Province) borders, no less than one million official border crossings took place in 1995 in one checkpoint alone.

In other areas, mechanisms to control land border traffic have yet to be institutionalized, partly because of on going border disputes caused either by post-colonial factors or by changing environmental landscapes (such as the diversion of the Salween/Moei River system that runs along the Thai-Burma border caused by natural erosion/siltation). The tenuous river systems in these areas have historically been used to define borders. This creates problems for long-standing communities that have developed close ties (often in the form of blood relations) with people across the 'border' such as in the great Mekong River.

For countries that do not have hard land borders, there is that equally daunting task of monitoring boundaries drawn across the water. Archipelagic systems, such as those of the Philippines and Indonesia suffer from the additional difficulty of inadequate capacities to undertake border patrols due to the long coastlines surrounding these countries. Moreover, the Philippines has yet to demarcate its archipelagic boundaries as required by the UN Convention on the Law of the Sea (UNCLOS). Indonesia is composed of over 13,500 islands while the Philippines is made up of over 7,100 islands – see Table 3.6. Indonesia, Malaysia, and Thailand have both land boundaries and coastlines.

Table 3.5 Estimated Official Human Two-Way Traffic Across Selected Mainland Southeast Asian and Neighboring Countries

Border	Estimated Number
Thai-Lao	830,194[a]
Thai-Burma	90,000[b]
Lao-China	144,000[c]
Myanmar-China	1,090,000[d]
China-Vietnam	124,000[e]

[a]1996.
[b]per month during 1997 in Mae Sai only.
[c]1995.
[d]1995 in Wanding-Kyukok only. At Ruili-Muse there were 2,737,000 crossings in 1995.
[e]1995 in Jinshuihe-Nam Cum only. At Tianbao-Ha Giang there were 97,000 crossings.

Source: Compiled from Stern, A. and Crissman, L. (1998), *Maps of International Borders Between Mainland Southeast Asian Countries and Background Information Concerning Population Movements at these Borders*, Asian Research Center for Migration, Bangkok, February.

Table 3.6 Length of Coastlines in Selected Southeast Asian Countries

Country	Coastline (kms)
Indonesia	54,716
Malaysia	4,675
Philippines	36,289
Thailand	3,219

Source: Compiled from *www.studyweb.com/geo/geograph* by American Computer Resources, Incorporated. The total for Malaysia is divided into Peninsular Malaysia (2,068 kms.) and East Malaysia (2,607).

With so many land and sea boundaries to cover and monitor and given the limited (and in many cases diminishing) government resources, states in the sub-region are finding it increasingly difficult to control not just the movement of goods but also the mobility of peoples. Long-standing historical (often pre-colonial) ties between communities that straddle modern and state-defined national boundaries compound the mobility of peoples.

In the Philippines, however, out-migrants typically leave the country by way of the international airports – one each in Manila, Laoag (north of Manila), Cebu (in the Visayas), and Davao (in Mindanao). All of these airports are able to accommodate aircraft for international destinations. As far as sea travel is concerned, there is the so-called Philippine southern 'backdoor' in Mindanao, part of the East Asia growth Area (EAGA) that includes parts of Brunei, Indonesia, Malaysia, and the Philippines. Filipinos may leave for Sabah, Malaysia and even parts of Indonesia (for example, Kalimantan) without leaving any record. This accounts for the paucity of official data on the number of Filipinos leaving through the Mindanao area.

At any rate, it is quite obvious that the border traffic in the sub-region is quite extensive, complex, and comprehensive. Migrants may decide to transit from one country to another before eventually settling (for example, acquiring stable but not regular employment) in another area. There have been numerous cases of Chinese from Yunnan Province in Southern China using Myanmar, Laos, or Vietnam as transit points for eventually establishing their residence either in Thailand, Cambodia, or Malaysia. Likewise, migrants from as far away as Pakistan and Bangladesh travel through Myanmar and Thailand and eventually settle in Malaysia where a large South Asian community already exists. In many cases, migrants are found in settlements just across or near the borders. These communities have been established by earlier inflows of people and now possess extensive networks for information, support, and employment that are used by newcomers.

Undocumented Migration and the Economic Crisis: The Contagion Effect

The migrant population is usually made the scapegoat when uncertainties occur. In the wake of the economic crisis that began in July 1997, receiving countries in SEA have openly and officially signified a strong resolve to curb the clandestine movement mainly of unskilled foreign labor into their borders. Malaysian and Thai authorities have expressed strong sentiments to tighten border controls as well as increase the surveillance of foreign workers in their territory.[48] The immediate impact of the crisis on employers is to visualize a grim future for the economy as a whole with massive retrenchments occurring across all sectors. Authorities in the region are now faced with the serious challenge to respond to the crisis to the extent that in arguing that their national security is at stake, they call on the local population 'to be their eyes and ears'.[49]

Many poor locals are convinced of the threat to their way of life posed particularly by unskilled and undocumented migrant workers and are quick to take up the challenge. Nationals of receiving countries actually perceive a kind of 'war' against the influx of foreigners. Immigration enforcement problems have subsequently convinced government authorities to mobilize army and police authorities who have been traditionally tapped in addressing traditional security threats.[50] In some exceptional cases, vigilante groups have been formed to guard against the illicit entry of foreigners.[51] Elsewhere, more draconian measures to curb illicit flows have been initiated such as imprisonment and even caning.[52]

In November 1997, several enterprises in Malaysia anticipated a direct reduction and slowdown in employment levels in certain sectors, particularly in construction and transportation immediately after the crisis struck.[53] Almost at the same time, a Thai government committee recommended that a million undocumented foreign workers, mostly from Myanmar be repatriated 'to prevent them from competing with Thais for jobs during the economic downturn'.[54]

Prior to the crisis, however, in June 1996, a Thai cabinet resolution allowed the registration of undocumented foreign workers in Thailand. This measure yielded some 323,100 applicants and over 293,600 were eventually granted work permits.[55] A policy reversal occurred in the wake of the perceived implications of the regional economic crisis. The Thai Labor Minister vowed in January 1998 to deport 300,000 undocumented foreigners within three months.[56] This statement came following an Asian Development Bank (ADB) report estimating that almost two million Thais would lose their jobs as a result of businesses collapsing from the financial crisis.[57] A succeeding Thai proposal suggested that repatriation centers and even manufacturing enterprises be established close to the borders, especially with Myanmar to prevent undocumented flows and settlements.[58]

Malaysian labor and immigration authorities began tightening their procedures for granting work permits (especially for construction companies) and even froze the entry of new unskilled foreign workers.[59] At the same time, authorities in Malaysia and other receiving areas in general stepped up efforts to prevent further unauthorized entries into their borders by mainly unskilled migrants. Moreover, these efforts have taken the form of actual deportation of undocumented migrants and those whose work permits had expired. In early 1998, Malaysia reiterated its intention to repatriate one million foreign workers coming mostly from Indonesia.[60] Very recently, however, authorities trimmed down such a target to 200,000.[61]

In response, authorities in sending countries have no choice but to accept their repatriated/deported nationals as Indonesia had done in the face of Malaysia's efforts to send back its Indonesian migrants.[62] From January to March 1998, some 26,000 Indonesians were deported from Malaysia and in April this figure increased to 30,000, which is still far below the quota set above.[63] Other governments have simply told their workers to look for jobs elsewhere in the world rather than face the grim prospect of being turned back. This is what the Ramos administration in the Philippines did.[64]

As a result of the regional financial crisis, the IOM estimated that up to 100,000 Filipino workers were going to be forced to return home, mostly those from Sabah.[65] A study commissioned by the United Nations Development Programme (UNDP) also arrived at a similar figure.[66] An informal survey by a migrant organization in the Philippines revealed that three out of five families of overseas contract workers felt their economic situation had worsened over the last 12 months since July 1997.[67] Remittances to the Philippines have also dropped over that year by 15 per cent.[68]

The policy of sending back undocumented migrants including those with expired or terminated work contracts has been both commended and criticized by all quarters in both Thailand and Malaysia. Those in favor of immigration control now argue that foreigners have served their purpose and in this crisis situation, 'it is time to get tough and show them the door'.[69] As indicated in the previous section, however, the borders that exist between these countries are so porous that it is difficult to actually control the movements of people. In fact, as one source argues in the case of Thailand, 'for every 20 people sent out, 50 new ones would come in'.[70]

In times of plenty, authorities in receiving countries have generally overlooked the legal or illegal status of their foreign workforces. When economic crises erupt, however, migrants are the first to be blamed. The recent Thai and Malaysian policy pronouncement to deport undocumented Burmese and Indonesian migrant does not acknowledge the contribution of foreign workers in strengthening their economies, at least over the last decade.

Also, it is unlikely that local workers would want to take on the jobs out of which foreign workers have moved. In January 1998, some 19,000 foreign workers in Thailand were deported presumably opening jobs for about 7,000 Thais.[71] It is not known how many Thais actually took over the jobs vacated by foreign workers. In many cases, local workers preferred not to take the jobs accepted by unskilled foreign workers. Locals usually do not wish to accept jobs that are in the agricultural, construction, and even certain manufacturing sectors. Most local workers in Malaysia and Singapore, for instance, no longer accept jobs as domestic helpers. At the same time, employers who suffer the most financially from the economic crisis are unable to increase the salaries of their workers, making their job offerings even less attractive to local laborers.

These efforts to conveniently ignore migrant contribution and to highlight instead their costs and liabilities during hard times are being duplicated in other areas, leading to a kind of contagion effect very much like the financial crisis that triggered it. Australian immigration authorities anticipated a stronger flood of economic migrants supposedly masquerading as asylum seekers and have taken measures to be more stringent in dealing with them.[72] Likewise, Singapore initiated a policy to discourage families from hiring foreign domestic helpers by raising the employer's levy from S$210 to S$220. This raised a debate about the importance of foreign workers in the city-state. Even Brunei has begun to initiate more stringent immigration rules and sanctions for offenses.[73] Such a trend against migrants now underlines much of the risks that accompany all unskilled foreign workers who have to contend with their limited usefulness during boom times and to confront accusations of having caused the economic crisis during bad times.

Already, a number of desperate foreign workers have sought political asylum in third country embassies in Malaysia even to the extent of using force.[74] A few Indonesian women have gone to the extent of offering marriage proposals to foreigners in order to escape the uncertainties in the home country.[75] Some have applied for permanent residence in the futile hope that this will allow them to stay longer in

Malaysia, only to be victimized by criminal syndicates.[76] Indeed, a number of South Asian and Chinese migrants have actually bought Malaysian passports on the black market for up to US$30,000.[77]

Despite this, however, employers – especially in construction, plantation, fisheries, and contractors in small- to medium sized enterprises – anticipate that companies already with a foreign workforce are unlikely to retrench these workers due mainly to the latter's willingness to accept lower wages and substandard working conditions.[78] Companies and employers are skeptical about efforts to replace foreign workers with locals. Immediately after the report of the planned deportations in Malaysia, Prime Minister Mahathir announced a relaxation of the policy to 'allow companies that are 100 per cent export-oriented to use foreign workers'.[79] Later, Malaysian authorities citing the continuing need for workers, especially in the plantation and manufacturing sectors assured the international community that it would not totally displace Malaysia's migrant workforce.[80] The same is true for other areas outside SEA, such as South Korea.[81]

Indeed, the initial plan to send home undocumented migrants in Malaysia was reversed by a plan to hire an additional 100,000 workers in the manufacturing and plantation sectors by July 1998.[82] In April 1998, owners of rice mills and rubber plantations in Thailand began to pressure the government not to push through with its intention to deport unskilled foreign workers.[83] Subsequently, some 1,700 enterprises asked the Ministry of Labor to allow them to hire over 93,800 foreign workers in 18 types of low-paying jobs deemed unacceptable to local workers.[84] In July 1998, Thai authorities announced a relaxation of its policy to deport all undocumented migrants in the Kingdom.[85] Such backtracking is common amidst the critical importance of foreign workers in these areas especially during periods of crisis.

Even before the crisis, however, there were other policy responses adopted by receiving countries to curb the flow of undocumented and low-skilled foreign workers. Beginning in the early 1990s, Malaysia conceived of a deportation program to complement its efforts to regularize the entry and stay of undocumented migrants mainly from Indonesia. From December 1991 to June 1992, Malaysia embarked on its OPS NYAH I campaign to deport undocumented Indonesian migrants back to their home country. The main goal of OPS NYAH I was to prevent the further entry of new and returning migrants into Malaysia by guarding the coastlines from indiscriminate and unauthorized entry, specifically along the beaches of Selangor, Johor, Negeri Sembilan, and Malacca. This campaign was later extended up to December 1995 with OPS NYAH II that started in July 1992. These two campaigns resulted in the arrest of more than 53,500 Indonesians (more than 3,500 of whom were caught landing in Peninsular Malaysia) with no less than 46,900 awaiting actual deportation.

In order to process the return of undocumented migrants (including those caught engaging in criminal activities), immigration authorities established detention centers within their areas close to the borders with source countries. Malaysia has ten such detention camps, some of which are Semenyih in Selangor, Machap Umbo in Malacca, Juru in Penang, Langgeng in Negeri Sembilan, Pekan Nanas in Johor, and Langkap in Perak.

Migrant Networks as Social Capital: Opening Pandora's Box

Migrant networks as part of social capital, refer to the complex system of services and agents that assist migrants and their families. On the whole, these networks provide an alternative mechanism to reduce the anxieties brought about by migrant clandestinity and as a source of support to cope with the insecurities and vulnerabilities brought about by migration in general and their undocumented status in particular. These alternative networks are indicative of the insufficiency or inappropriateness of current official mechanisms (whether from the sending or receiving side) to address the problems and causes of migration.

Initially, at least two types of such assistance can be identified. The first is well known and involves support systems in relation to seeking employment in another area. These are the networks that serve to promote the employment and deployment of foreign workers. Labor recruitment agents, brokers and, to some extent, close family members and neighbors may form part of this employment promotions network. Much of the work involved in this promotion scheme is basically for profit. All too often it is this network that is involved in the illicit trafficking of workers across borders. It is difficult to monitor and regulate this network primarily due to its extensive nature and also due to the fact that its activities are often illegal.

A second category involves non-profit entities that assist in absorbing the non-economic costs of migration. These non-profit agents provide social and psychological services to especially vulnerable migrants, such as women and undocumented foreigners. The extent and nature of these social service networks that provide much-needed assistance are also difficult officially to determine because government authorities do not acknowledge many of them. There are several dozens of prominent non-profit entities that operate in the Asian region. Quite a few function more as networks of networks or alliances that link together organizations across countries and across services in the region. In the area of policy and academic research, there are the Asia Pacific Migration Research Network (APMRN) being managed jointly by the University of Wollongong (Center for Multicultural Studies) in Australia and the Asian Research Center for Migration based at Chulalongkorn University in Bangkok. There is also the Institute for Population and Social Research based at Mahidol University in Nakhon Pathom, Thailand that conducts surveys pertinent to migrants in Thailand as well as Thai migrants in other Asian countries.

The Asia Pacific Mission for Migrant Filipinos (APMMF), the Mission for Filipino Migrant Workers (MFMW), and the Asian Migrant Center (AMC), all of which are based in Hong Kong are advocacy support groups and those that give direct assistance to migrants. While the first two offices cater mainly to Filipino migrants in the former British colony, they are also expanding to serve the basic needs of other foreign migrants, such as Bangladeshis, Indians, Thais, and Indonesians. These entities provide a range of services that seek to address the immediate felt needs of migrants in the areas of legal counseling, treatment for psychological and physical traumas, as well as policy advocacy.

Different areas are able to accommodate different types of social service networks. Hong Kong, for instance, may receive a greater variety of non-profit entities primarily because of its ideal location and also its liberal social environment (its return to Chinese control notwithstanding) despite being a receiving area for migrants. Other receiving countries, however, are not as conducive to non-governmental initiatives, partly because the authorities in these countries perceive migrants as a potential threat to national security and partly because they are yet unable to fully confront the social and cultural dilemmas of migration. These include Malaysia and Singapore. In Malaysia, the more prominent entities that both cater to migrants as clients and have become more vocal about foreign workers' issues are *Tenaganita* and the Malaysian Trade Union Congress (MTUC). Singapore is unable to sustain any visible non-governmental undertaking as those found in the rest of SEA. Thailand is able to sustain a few of these endeavors both as a sending and receiving country. Much of these initiatives are directed at foreign workers (especially from Myanmar but also from China) in Thailand. They include the Child Rights Asianet, the Jesuit Refugee Service as well as the Asian Forum for Human Rights and Development (Forum-Asia), and the Catholic Commission on Migration (Women's Desk).

Sending countries invariably nurture these sorts of initiatives primarily because there is an immediate felt need for the services they offer. Moreover, the governments in sending countries are more inclined to promote overseas employment and hence, are able to interface with employment promotions networks involving recruitment agents, brokers, and employers. In the Philippines, there are numerous institutional initiatives that service the needs of migrants and their families. There are also networks of initiatives, such as the Philippine Migration Research Network (PMRN), which is affiliated with the APMRN. In addition, there are several support, solidarity, and advocacy groups such as, *Gabriela, Pilipina*, and the *Kanlungan* Center Foundation, as well as *Unlad-Kabayan* (Migrant Services Foundation), among many others. In Indonesia, numerous non-governmental initiatives have also been undertaken and expanded over the last few years. Some of them are the *Solidaritas Perempuan* (Women's Solidarity for Human Rights) and the *Lembaga Bantuan Hukum Jakarta* (Jakarta Legal Aid Institute).

While some areas may have a heavier concentration of such social networks than others, it is nevertheless noteworthy that efforts to interface and link with different areas and diverse nationalities of migrants are being realized. These cooperative linkages are found not only at the non-governmental level but also between non-governmental and governmental as well as inter-governmental agencies. In areas where non-governmental initiatives cannot be sustained, there are cooperative mechanisms and linkages between governments. This is the case in Singapore and to some extent in Malaysia where workers' welfare centers are maintained by the Philippine embassies in these countries for Filipino migrants. These cooperative mechanisms take place on a bilateral basis and are facilitated in some cases by the existence of government-to-government agreements. Such cooperative mechanisms can be an effective way to reduce the anxieties of migration and for the migrants to better cope with the insecurities that are a consequence of their undocumented status.

The Interplay Among Conditioned Rationality, Identity, and Interests

As already noted, the response to the phenomenon of undocumented migration is generally conditioned by notions of desirability.[86] Perceptions of desirability or undesirability are in turn conditioned by effective and positive perceptions of the 'Self' in relation to the negative 'Other'. The national self is typically endowed with inherently positive traits and values (for example, law-abiding, healthy, normative, rational, others) while the foreigner is attributed with contrary traits and features (prone to dysfunctional behavior, unhealthy, irrational, others). It is this stereotyping of the migrant (underscored by economic uncertainties) that leads society to perceive migration as a security threat.

Such perceptions are neither fixed nor monolithic. They constitute part of the social constructs that are formed and created by social, economic, and political institutions, processes, and structures (including the mass media). Within each social construct there are certain differentials and nuances that arise and at times predominate. These variations may be along class, gender, political, and even (in multiethnic communities) ethnic and religious lines.

Threats on local culture and 'the way of life' are relative to perceived cultural standards. In dealing with immigration issues, the Chinese in Malaysia (especially those coming from the business sector), for instance, may highlight the threat of foreigners on businesses. The Indian community may underscore the entry of Pakistani migrants. The dominant Malays may feel some apprehensions about the entry of Indian or Indonesian migrants, who can easily blend with the general population. This multiethnic dimension becomes even more crucial in cases where authorities are confronted with severe resource inadequacies. Hence, the 'security threat' becomes more pronounced during periods of economic stagnation and decline but rarely during times of growth and prosperity.

There is also a persistent tension between social and economic sectors. Owners of agricultural (including fisheries) and manufacturing enterprises regard the phenomenon from the viewpoint of economic rationality and pragmatism. At the level of the firm, it makes sense to hire undocumented foreign workers rather than local laborers on the basis of labor productivity and costs that have a profound bearing on the comparative advantage and competitiveness of the enterprise. Employer surveys frequently reflect the pragmatic attitude of owners toward foreign workers. To them they are hardworking and are more productive relative to the wages they receive. In addition, employers are not as readily compelled by law to comply with social welfare and work safety regulations when hiring undocumented foreign workers than when local workers or even documented migrants are involved.

Then there are the obvious interests of recruitment agencies and labor brokers, including travel agents. Security concerns arise when such interests clash with the perspectives of other groups within civil society, particularly the welfare-oriented intentions of NGOs and POs that are more concerned about the social well being of migrants and their families. To these civil society groups, private and business sector interests have turned the human worker into a commodity and modern-day slave. Moreover, public authorities have done little to improve the safety nets available to displaced persons and migrants and have until now persisted with the view of criminalizing the foreigner. In contrast, the state perspective, although not entirely monolithic, views the migration question as an affront to the country's national integrity expressed mainly in territorial terms. This geopolitical (and to some extent cold war) perspective may not sit comfortably with the prevailing trend towards global economic and social integration. Too often, the responses that authorities adopt do not seem to directly address (and may even perpetuate and aggravate) the problem. In any complex system such as migration, 'the obvious and immediate effect might not be the dominant one'.[87] All these tensions are aggravated by the fact that very little empirical data on undocumented migration are available due to the clandestine nature of the phenomenon.

The strained relations between the local and foreign populations tend to be exaggerated and can even 'be manipulated for ulterior motives that have little to do with competition for resources or any real notion of a threat to culture, language or traditions'.[88] The migrant is typically the scapegoat for government inadequacies to cope with the increasing demands of citizens particularly in this age of democratization and globalization. The convenience of using the foreigner (particularly the silent and the vulnerable) is very clear to many politicians and bureaucrats. Afraid of losing popular support, leaders and elites easily point to foreigners as the cause of their society's problems and difficulties. This kind of xenophobia is not uncommon in SEA. Unfortunately, these responses do not really look at the heart of the issue and the fundamental causes of undocumented migration. In many cases, the response of authorities has been to address only the symptoms and not the causes of the illness.

Victimization and criminalization of the migrant have been the typical response even during times of economic expansion. They contribute to the increase in the number of undocumented migrants. These processes are complemented by a noticeable degree of militarization of the migration policy framework in that there is now an increasing reliance upon military and police forces by many governments confronted with the immigration problem.[89] As a result, the abused undocumented migrant dilemma of whether or not to report their mistreatment to the authorities. Police and immigration authorities typically require the immigration papers, documents, and work permits from the migrant-complainant. If none can be produced, either because the migrant does not have them in the first place or the defendant (the employer) has taken them from the, it is usually the foreign worker who is punished. The offense of the employer is often treated very lightly if at all.

The same situation can arise with migrants who suffer from serious illnesses. Afraid that the authorities might find out about their illegal status, migrants tend to suffer their illness in silence until it is too late and their condition becomes life threatening not only for themselves but also for the community in which they live. Hence, undocumented migrants constitute a threat to the well being and health of the receiving society. However, much of this situation is caused not by the fact that the people concerned are foreigners but by their condition of clandestinity that is not altogether their own doing. Indeed, in Malaysia, communicable diseases 'cannot be exactly attributable to [migrants], although their lifestyle and living conditions might have contributed to the spread'.[90] Migrants as much as possible would prefer to work in conditions of regularity and openness. But when this ideal situation is not present or is threatened by the unscrupulous actions of employers, brokers, and even state authorities, and the prospects for staying in the home country are not that bright, migrants are prepared to take extra-legal measures to be able to work abroad.

When migrants are detained, their conditions in the holding camps leave much to be desired.[91] Migrants frequently suffer from poor sanitary and living conditions that make it possible for diseases to spread. They also suffer inhuman treatment from detention officials. Deaths are not uncommon in many detention in camps in Malaysia, some with as high as four deaths per week from diseases such as typhoid diarrhea, and even beatings and torture reportedly inflicted by camp guards.[92]

Tentative Conclusions

The conclusions derived so far from this study are but tentative and indicative only of very general and broad conditions and perspectives. What the study has done so far is to examine the many dimensions that surround the phenomenon of undocumented migratory movements of low-skilled labor in selected countries in SEA. Part of the dimension that was examined is the social perceptions toward the migrant and the migration movement. In many cases, there is a certain social stigma associated with clandestine migration especially in terms of social, economic, and political security. Much of the insecurity associated with this form of migration can be a product of social construction.

The state has a role in establishing and shaping the society's mental construct of the foreigner-outsider. When the state is unable to encourage genuine debate on the real impacts (both positive as well as negative) of migration, there is a tendency in the destination country to develop apprehension initially, and later on, hostility. Local sentiments are framed and mobilized against migrants along these lines. At the same time, societies that have long-standing impressions of migrants may very well influence public authorities of the 'dangers' posed by migrants.

At any rate, because societies in the region have yet to arrive at a genuine consensus, there continues to be an expressed sense of ambivalence and uncertainty in both the formulation and conduct of immigration policy. This situation prevails in the governments of both sending and receiving countries. Authorities in sending countries, while acknowledging the dangers and social costs to the migrant, also realize the importance of migrants' earnings and the social benefits of overseas employment. While some countries have already instituted legal mechanisms to ensure the rights of undocumented migrants, most have done little to truly address the problem.

Some Proposals for Stakeholders

To be able to address the numerous issues and concerns raised above, this study offers some points for consideration by stakeholders both from the sending and receiving countries. These points cover the areas of (1) possible research directions; (2) alternative policy options; and (3) non-governmental initiatives. Likewise, they may be better appreciated in the context of the short-term (three to five years), medium-term (five to seven years), and long-term (seven to ten years) perspectives.

Research Directions

At the social research level, the issue of the tension that exists between globalization (manifested mainly through market integration) and immigration controls (specifically of unskilled labor) requires continued investigation as well as further debate. Further research on the specific conditions of undocumented migrants as well as their clandestine experiences can eventually lead to innovative as well as more responsive and effective policy perspectives and options. Over the short- and medium-terms, the research direction can be in the way of immediate social investigation of undocumented flows. In addition, there is a need to study how to convince the different stakeholders (employers, brokers, NGOs, communities at-large) of the need to address the root causes of undocumented migration and not merely its superficial symptoms. Likewise, further research needs to be undertaken on, and with civil society groups on the notion of social construction and social differentiation between foreigners and locals and between sectors of the local population. Better studies need to be undertaken that will look into the activities, strategies, and organization of criminal syndicates engaged in human trafficking and labor brokering. For the long-term, the research strategy needs to be in the direction of anticipating changes and problems that may arise both for migrants and for policymakers. It must also adequately respond to these changes and problems using more appropriate governmental (and to some extent non-governmental or multilateral) structures, mechanisms, and procedures.

Policy Options

There is an urgent need for government agencies and other concerned parties to exchange information on the systems and procedures for monitoring migratory flows of labor across the region and across national economies. In addition to procedures, there is a need to exchange accurate and actual (also statistical) information on the extent and direction of these flows including the changes that occur. Much of these efforts will go a long way towards eventually harmonizing the region's information systems and evolving new and better techniques for monitoring what once could not be tracked. Stricter enforcement of illegal recruitment regulations is required. This should be accompanied by more severe sanctions against illicit brokers and recruitment agents.

The typical policy response of deporting apprehended migrants who have gained unauthorized entry needs to be reexamined in order to devise long-term and more sustainable solutions to clandestine migration. The need to control is a distinguishing feature of any state. Immigration and police authorities, however, in their attempt to regain control of the migration situation may very well contribute to the problem's perpetuation. Many migrants after having been deported will immediately seek out ways to re-cross the borders even at risk to their lives. The experience in the region has shown that bolder and more stringent measures are met with even bolder border crossing techniques. Encouraging and agitating the local population to be more vigilant against the indiscriminate and illicit entry of foreigners (short of actually mobilizing hostility towards so-called 'illegal migrants') may be good in the short-term but can be problematique socially over the long-term. Moreover, there are serious questions that need to be raised involving multiethnic societies whose authorities encourage local people to wage this kind of dangerous anti-immigrant campaign that can lead to serious consequences such as racial violence and discrimination.

In the medium-term, there is a need to include migration problems, issues and concerns in the agenda of multilateral for a and arrangements within the affecting SEA, such as the Association of Southeast Asian Nations (ASEAN) Secretariat; the Research Institute of ASEAN (RIA); the ASEAN Regional Forum (ARF); the Asia Pacific Economic Cooperation (APEC) forum; the Asia-Europe Meeting (ASEM); and track two mechanisms like the Asia Pacific Roundtable (APR), among others. For instance, an ASEAN Forum Series on Transborder Flows can be initiated and institutionalized so that authorities in the sub-region can have a venue where experts can work out their difficulties as well as model their successes in the campaign to reduce undocumented flows and the trafficking of human beings.

Over the long-term, governments, especially in receiving countries, should explore the possibility of undertaking cooperative arrangements with authorities in sending countries. Moreover, a multilateral approach to undocumented migration issues is better than the more limited unilateral or bilateral initiatives. Not only will such multilateral approach be more effective but it will also be more efficient and sustainable over the long-term. They could include the establishment of mechanisms that would ease the pressures of migration. A reliable social security system can absorb the adverse costs of migration pressures. Such a system, however, cannot be possible without appropriate bureaucratic reforms, particularly those directed at curbing corruption and government inefficiency. A savings mobilization program that would tap the potential and collective earnings of migrants is also another helpful mechanism to generate much-needed resources for social safety nets.

Non-Governmental Initiatives

The development of social capital is important in helping authorities and societies deal with the complicated issue of undocumented migration in the Asia Pacific region. Civil society actors play an important role in sustaining migratory flows not only in SEA but in other regions as well. Their role in sustaining and generating new networks is one that authorities should take into account. Consequently, there is a need for governments in the sub-region to interface with civil society groups, especially private voluntary organizations (PVOs) or NGOs and POs and private research institutes to encourage greater transparency and accountability among bureaucrats, especially in the context of the campaign against corruption and human smuggling.

Appendix A

Understanding 'Clandestinity'

In general, the term undocumented migrant workers is defined under the United Nations International Population Conference as 'persons who do not fulfill the requirements established by the country of destination to enter, stay or exercise an economic activity'.[93] The latest UN Convention for the Protection of the Rights of All Migrant Workers and Members of Their Families (1990) extends the rights accorded by state parties to migrants to both documented and undocumented foreigners.[94]

Usually, numerous features can and do account for a migrant's 'clandestinity'. Conceivably, a person becomes undocumented in any of the following ways:

1. The person gains entry into another country without going through official inspection procedures and approval mechanisms;
2. The person gains entry through the use of (a) false; or (b) tampered travel documents;
3. The person gains entry through legitimate travel documents but either (a) performs activities (notably employment) which are not within the scope provided for upon legitimate entry and stay; or (b) extends the duration or the period of restrictions of residence and stay.

As a consequence, the 'clandestinity' of the migrant is neutralized in any of the following ways:

1. The undocumented migrant is deported prior to actual entry by state authorities upon detection of 'clandestinity' at the border or port of entry'
2. The migrant is immediately deported upon detection of undocumented entry after a period or duration of stay;
3. The migrant leaves without the knowledge of competent authorities (that is, either in the sending or receiving countries);
4. The undocumented migrant dies in the receiving country without documentation; and
5. The status of the migrant is regularized.

Regularization usually takes place in any of the following instances:[95]

1. The migrant is able to obtain an immigrant or non-immigrant or working visa.
2. The migrant qualifies for an amnesty, legalization, or quota program.

Edmonston, *et al.*, using literature available on US immigration distinguish between three general types of undocumented migration: 'settlers', 'sojourners', and 'commuters' which are actually not mutually exclusive categories.[96] Settlers are those who intend to or have actually established permanent residency in the receiving country. This type of immigration is more likely to include family members (especially spouses and children) and may, or may not involve countries which are contiguous to each other. Sojourners are persons who reside in another country presumably for employment. Such persons usually do not include family members and may involve only a fixed or impermanent duration. These may or may not include migrant workers employed in situations that are not bound by formal contractual obligations. Much of the work involved in this type of migration is seasonal and may or may not include countries that are contiguous to each other. Commuters are those who travel across contiguous borders for shorter periods of time (for example, on a daily, weekly, or monthly bases). Within SEA, there are settlers, sojourners, and commuters and a significant and growing number of these migrants are becoming undocumented.

Appendix B

Undocumented Migration and Trafficking

In Asia, undocumented as well as documented migrants are increasingly turning to human traffickers and smugglers for assistance in the absence of sufficient legal guidelines to facilitate the flows. Although it is not new in the region, migrant trafficking is considered to be so today when the following conditions become evident:[97]

1. **Money** (or another form of payment) changes hands.
2. A facilitator – the **trafficker** – is involved. This intermediary can provide any or all of the following forms of assistance: information, fraudulent or stolen travel/identity documents, formal (for example, scheduled flights) or informal (for example, hidden in a ship container) transportation, safe houses in transit points, guided border crossing, reception, and employment in the country of destination.
3. An **international border** is crossed.
4. Entry of **illegal**. The border crossing is effected by completely avoiding authorities or by presenting either fraudulent documents or genuine documents which have been stolen or altered.
5. The movement is **voluntary**. Determining true voluntariness is a complex task that requires understanding the interplay among available choices, motivations, likes and dislikes, resources, and others. Migrants are considered 'trafficked' so long as they have **chosen** to pay a trafficker for entry into another country, even if they would have preferred to stay at home'.

Some other countermeasures have been proposed or are actually applied against human trafficking and undocumented immigration. These include the creation of an international convention against human smuggling making it punishable in international criminal law; the further institutionalization (and subsequent regulation) of the operations of public and private immigration and labor recruitment agents; the criminalization of undocumented migration by applying corporal punishment on all parties concerned: the traffickers, employers, and workers.

Notes

1 See Bohning, W.R. (1996), *Employing Foreign Workers*, International Labor Office, Geneva.
2 Battistella, G. (1996), 'Migration and APEC: Issues for Discussion', *Asian Migrant Forum*, November, pp. 23.
3 This is according to the United Nations (1996), *World Population Monitoring 1996*, as cited in *Population Newsletter*, no. 62, December, pp. 12.
4 Espenshade, T. and Hempstead, K. (no date), 'Contemporary American Attitudes Toward US Immigration', *International Migration Review*, vol.30, no.2, pp. 536.
5 Huysmans, J. (1995), 'Migrants as a Security Problem: Dangers of "Securitizing" Societal Issues', in R. Miles and D. Thranhardt (eds), *Migration and European Integration; The Dynamics of Inclusion and Exclusion*, Pinter Publishers, London, pp. 59.
6 Smith, P. (1995), *Asia's Economic Transformation and Its Impact on Intraregional Labor Migration*, unpublished, Council on Foreign Relations Asia Project Working Paper, New York, March, pp. 5.
7 Nayyar, D. (1993), 'Statistics on International Labor Migration and Economic Analysis: Some Conceptual Issues', in ILO-ARTEP, *International Labor Migration Statistics and Information Networking in Asia*, International Labor Office, Geneva, pp.41.
8 For details, see Edmonston, B., Passel, J. and Bean, F. (1990), 'Perceptions and Estimates of Undocumented Migration to the United States', in F. Bean, B. Edmonston and J. Passel (eds), *Undocumented Migration to the United States: IRCA and the Experience of the 1980s*, The Rand Corporation, Santa Monica, pp.11-31.
9 Freeman, G. (1995), 'Modes of Immigration Politics in Liberal Democratic States', *International Migration Review*, no. 4, Winter, pp. 883.
10 For details, see Link, M. and Oldendick, R. (1996), 'Social Construction and White Attitudes Toward Equal Opportunity and Multiculturalism', *The Journal of Politics*, vol.58, no.1, February, pp. 149-168.
11 Lee, K. H. and Sivananthiran, A. (1996), 'Contract Labor in Malaysia: Perspectives of Principal Employers, Contractors, and Workers', *International Labor Review*, vol.135, no. 1, pp. 75-91.
12 The data comes from Lee, K. H. and Sivananthiran, A. (1996), 'Contract Labor in Malaysia: Perspectives of Principal Employers, Contractors and Workers', *International Labor Review*, vol.135, no.1, pp. 75-91.
13 For details, see Chintayananda, S., Risser, G. and Chantavanich, S. (1997), *The Monitoring of the Registration of Immigrant Workers From Myanmar, Cambodia and Laos in Thailand*, Institute of Asian Studies, Asian Research Center for Migration, Chulalongkorn University, Bangkok.
14 For instance, see the chapter by Jacques Bertrand in this volume.
15 Myint, N. (1998), *Myanmar Country Paper: Academic Aspects*, paper presented during the 'Regional Workshop on Transnational Migration and Development in ASEAN Countries', Institute for Population and Social Research, Mahidol University, International Organization for Migration, Bangkok and Hua Hin, 25-27 May 1998, pp.3, Table 4.
16 Hutasingh, O. (1997), 'Tough Fight Against Illegal Alien Workers; Two-Year Truce Helps Bring Temporary Peace', *Bangkok Post*, 15 December.
17 Hutasingh, O. (1997), 'Studies Show Who Benefits From Alien Workers Here', *Bangkok Post*, 25 May.
18 Charoensutthiphan, P. (1998), 'Plan to Let Aliens Work in Only 13 Provinces; Repatriation Centre Could be Established', *Bangkok Post*, 14 January.

19 *IOM News Release*, June 1998.
20 Hutasingh, O. (1998), 'How to Stem the Flow', *Bangkok Post*, 8 February; and Edwards, N. (1998), 'Fears Over Rising Illegal Immigration', *Bangkok Post*, 18 March.
21 *IOM News Release*, June 1998.
22 Krisnawaty, T. (1997), *The Role of Bilateral Agreements on Migrant Labor Issues: The Case of Indonesia and Malaysia*, paper presented at the 'Conference on Legal Protection for Women Migrant Workers: Strategy for Action', Manila, 8-12 September 1997, pp. 1.
23 Agence France Press (AFP) (1998), 'Malaysia Relaxes Labor Rules to Woo Investment', *Migration News*, 29 November; 'Southeast Asia: No Vacancy for Foreign Workers', *Inter Press Service (IPS)*, 2 December 1997; Edwards, 'Fears Over Rising Illegal Immigration', 1998.
24 'Malaysia "Alarmed" by Illegal Immigrant Surge', *Reuters*, 27 February 1998.
25 Tenaganita (1995), *A Memorandum on Abuse, Torture and Dehumanised Treatment of Migrant Workers at Detention Centres*, unpublished paper, August, pp. 1.
26 Cited by Go, S. (1998), 'Towards the 21st Century: Whither Philippine Labor Migration', in B. Carino (ed.), *Filipino Workers on the Move: Trends, Dilemmas and Policy Options*, Philippine Migration Research Network and Philippine Social Science Council, Quezon City, pp. 12.
27 IOM, June 1998.
28 See the chapter by Tubagus in this volume.
29 See 'Failed Policies Being Recycled; Buck-Passing Won't Solve Problem, Say Experts', *The Bangkok Post*, 19 July 1999; and Hutasing, O., *et al.* (1999), 'Life is Hard for Illegal Burmese Workers; Made to Suffer at the Hands of Job Brokers, Extortion Gangs, and Even Police', *The Bangkok Post*, 19 July.
30 According to an officer of the Construction Industry Development Board in Malaysia and 'Slowdown May Send Foreign Workers in Malaysia Packing', *The Straits Times*, 24 November 1997.
31 Ung, A. (1998), 'Malaysia May Expel One Million Workers', *The Straits Times*, 7 January.
32 Associated Press (AP) (1998), 'Malaysia Assures Neighbors It Won't Fire Foreign Workers', *Migration News*, 12 January.
33 AFP, 'Malaysia Relaxes Labor Rules to Woo Investment', 1998.
34 Hutasingh, 'Studies Show Who Benefits From Alien Workers Here', 1997.
35 'Rights and Wrongs of Repatriation', *Bangkok Post*, 1 March 1998.
36 Rungswasdisab, P. (1997), 'An Illegal Population Takes Root', *The Nation*, 2 June, pp. A9. The estimate is cited from a study by Voravit Chareoanlert and Bandit Ranachaisettawut entitled *Industrialization and Employment in Relation to Policy on Importation of Foreign Labor*. The figure in baht is actually 12.94 billion a year.
37 Based on interview with Ali Syarief, Executive Director, PT BIJAK, 2 April 1998, Jakarta.
38 Migrants Standing Committee (1996), *A Survey on Placement Fees Paid by Taiwan-Bound OFWs (Overseas Filipino Workers) to Philippine Agencies*, unpublished report by the St. Christopher's Parish Pastoral Council, October-December, Table 4, pp. 2.
39 Hugo, G. (1995), 'Illegal International Migration in Asia', in R. Cohen (ed.), *The Cambridge Survey of World Migration*, Cambridge University Press, Cambridge, pp. 398.
40 Tessier, K. (1995), 'The New Slave Trade: The International Crisis in Immigrant Smuggling', *Indiana Journal of Global Legal Studies*, vol. 3, no.1, Fall, pp. 1.
41 See 'Workers to be Classified; New Centre to Document Staff to Help Management of Labor Force', *The Bangkok Post*, 19 July 1999; and Hutasing, O., *et al.*, 'Life is Hard for Illegal Burmese Workers; Made to Suffer at the Hands of Job Brokers, Extortion Gangs, and Even Police', 1999.
42 Charoensuthiphan, P. (1998), 'Slump a Boom to Cheats', *Bangkok Post*, 14 April.

43 Based on interviews with Ali Syarief, Executive Manager, PT BIJAK, 2 April 1998, Jakarta; and Irene Fernandez, Director, Tenaganita, 18 March 1998, Kuala Lumpur.
44 Based on interviews with Premesh Chandran, Malaysian Trade Union Congress, 19 March 1998, Kuala Lumpur.
45 Based on interview with Premesh Chandran, Malaysian Trade Union Congress, 19 March 1998, Kuala Lumpur.
46 Based on interview with Irene Fernandez, Director, Tenaganita, 18 March 1998, Kuala Lumpur.
47 Based on interview with Irene Fernandez, Director, Tenaganita, 18 March 1998, Kuala Lumpur.
48 For details, see Abdullah, A. and Sooi, C. (1998), 'Security at Border Tightened to Stop Aliens', *New Straits Times*, 16 March, pp. 3.
49 Duff-Brown, B. (1998), 'Illegal Aliens to Enter Malaysia', *Migration News*, 30 March.
50 'Be on Lookout for Illegals, says Shahidan', *New Straits Times*, 17 March 1998, pp. 3.
51 Duff-Brown, B. (1998), 'Poverty Reaches Across Borders', *Bangkok Post*, 31 March, pp. 10.
52 Reuters (1998), 'Thais Among Immigrants Facing Cane', *Bangkok Post*, 23 March, pp. 1.
53 'Slowdown May Send Foreign Workers in Malaysia Packing', *The Straits Times*, 24 November 1997.
54 AFP (1997), 'Thai Labor Committee Wants to Send Back a Million Alien Workers', *Migration News*, 28 November.
55 Hutasingh, 'Tough Fight Against Illegal Alien Workers; Two-Year Truce Helps Bring Temporary Peace', 1997.
56 AP (1998), 'Thai Minister Vows to Deport Illegal Workers in Three Months', *Migration News*, 16 January 1998.
57 AP (1998), 'Jobless Rate Raises Fear of Social Unrest', *Bangkok Post*, 13 March, pp. 4.
58 Charoensutthiphan, P. (1998), 'Plan to Let Aliens Work in Only 13 Provinces; Repatriation Centre Could be Established', *Bangkok Post*, 14 January; and Vanaspong, C. (1997), 'Learning Lessons From a Neighbor', *Bangkok Post*, 9 March.
59 'Ministry of Labor Tightens Work Permit Procedures', *The Straits Times*, 20 November 1997.
60 AP-Dow Jones News Service (1998), 'Malaysia to Repatriate 1 Million Foreign Workers', *Migration News*, 2 January.
61 Vinesh, D. (1998), '200,000 Aliens to be Sent Back', *The Star*, 17 July.
62 AP (1998), 'Indonesian Navy to Bring Home Workers From Malaysia: Antara', *Migration News*, 6 January; AP (1998), 'Indonesian Navy to Take Illegal Workers From Malaysia', *Migration News*, 20 March.
63 Ahmad, R. (1998), 'Malaysia Dismisses Worries Over Indonesian Migrants', Reuters, April 1; AP (1998), 'Malaysia Deports Indonesians', *Migration News*, 29 May.
64 AFP (1998), 'Go Where Jobs Beckon, Ramos Tells Filipinos Abroad', *Migration News*, 7 January.
65 Kaban, E. (1998), 'Asia Set to Face Illegal Workers Crisis, Report', *Reuters*, 8 June.
66 Dancel, R. (1998), 'OFWs Unfazed by Low Pay, Shrinking Marts', *Philippine Daily Inquirer*, 18 August, pp. B1.
67 Dancel, R. (1998), 'Overseas Workers; Heroes in a Tragic Play', *Philippine Daily Inquirer*, 17 August, pp. B12.
68 *Ibid.*
69 Marukatat, S. (1998), 'Looking After Our Own in This Time of Crisis', *Bangkok Post*, 12 January, pp. 9.
70 Hutasingh, 'Tough Fight Against Illegal Alien Workers', 1997, pp. 2.

71 Tunyasiri, Y. and Charoenpo, A. (1998), 'Jobs Opened Up as 19,000 Foreign Workers Go Home', *Bangkok Post*, 17 February, pp. 1.
72 AFP (1998), 'Australia Sees Flood of Bogus Refugees', *Migration News*, 12 January.
73 Stephen, I. (1998), 'Tough Measures on Immigration Offenders', *Borneo Bulletin*, 1 April.
74 Gecker, J. (1998), 'Indonesians Ram Truck Into UN Base', *Migration News*, 30 March; Bernama (1998), 'Refugees' Free to go to Third Country', *The Star*, 6 May.
75 Wong, J. (1998), 'Ethnic-Chinese Women Seek to Wed to Flee Fear, Violence in Indonesia', *The Wall Street Journal*, 21 July.
76 'In a Desperate Bid to Avoid Being Sent Home...Foreign Workers Rush to Apply for Permanent Residence', *The Straits Times*, 7 January 1998.
77 Krishnamoorthy, M. (1998), 'Handsome Black Market Price for Our Passports', *The Star*, 28 July.
78 'Employers Still Hiring Illegals', *The Star*, 26 April 1998; Kyodo News Service, 'Illegal Workers Allowed to Work in Thai Fisheries', 6 May 1998.
79 AFP, 'Malaysia Relaxes Labor Rules to Woo Investment', 1998.
80 AP, 'Malaysia Assures Neighbors It Won't Fire Foreign Workers', 1998.
81 'Justice Ministry Postpones Plan to Expel Illegal Foreign Workers', *Korea Herald*, 8 January 1998.
82 Sadiq, J. (1998), 'Malaysia Hires Foreigners Despite Rising Jobless', *Reuters*, 9 July.
83 Unarat, S. (1998), 'Alien Workers Issue to be Reviewed; Concern Among Rice and Rubber Operators', *Bangkok Post*, 29 April, pp.3.
84 'Firms Want Rules on Hiring Immigrants to be Eased; Need to Fill Positions Shunned by Thais', *Bangkok Post*, 22 May 1998.
85 Charoensuthipan, P. (1998), 'Deadline on Aliens Put Off for Year; But Policy Will Not be Eased Further, Insists Bhichai', *Bangkok Post*, 16 July; 'Thailand Gives Reprieve to 95,000 Illegal Workers', *Reuters*, 21 July 1998.
86 Beare, M. (1998), 'Illegal Migration', in C. G. Hernandez and G. R. Pattugalan (eds), *Transnational Crime and Regional Security in the Asia Pacific*, Institute for Strategic and Development Studies, Inc. (ISDS), Quezon City, Manila, Philippines, pp. 252.
87 Jervis, R. (1997-98), 'Complexity and the Analysis of Political and Social Life', *Political Science Quarterly*, vol. 112, no. 4, pp. 569.
88 Beare, 'Illegal Migration', 1998, p. 256.
89 Smith, P. (1997), 'The Military's Increasing Role in Immigration Enforcement', article reproduced in *CISNEWS@cis.org* from *Immigration Review*, no. 29, Summer.
90 Shen-Li, L. (1998), 'Fighting to Keep Out Life-Threatening Ills', *New Sunday Times*, 18 January.
91 Tenaganita, *Memorandum on Abuse, Torture and Dehumanized Treatment of Migrant Workers at Detention Camps*, 1996.
92 *Ibid.*, pp. 7.
93 See United Nations (1994), *Report of the International Conference on Population and Development: Program of Action*, Cairo, 5-13 September.
94 For details, see Nafziger, J. and Bartel, B. (no date), 'The Migrant Workers Convention: Its Place in Human Rights Law', *International Migration Review*, vol. 25, no. 4; Bosniak, L. (no date), 'Human Rights, State Sovereignty and the Protection of Undocumented Migrants Under the International Migrant Workers Convention', *International Migration Review*, vol. 25, no. 4.
95 Edmonston, B., Passel, J. and Bean F. (1990), 'Perceptions and Estimates of Undocumented Migration to the United States', in F. Bean, B. Edmonston and J. Passel (eds), *Undocumented Migration to the United States: IRCA and the Experience of the 1980s*, The Rand Corporation, Santa Monica, pp. 11-31, 24-25.

96 Edmonston, *et al*, 'Perceptions and Estimates of Undocumented Migration to the United States', 1990, pp. 11-31.

97 International Organization for Migration (IOM) (1994), *Trafficking in Migrants: Characteristics and Trends in Different Regions of the World*, unpublished discussion paper presented at the '11th IOM Seminar on Migration', Geneva, 26-28 October 1994, pp. 2-3.

References

Abdullah, A. and Chor Sooi, C. (1998), 'Security at Border Tightened to Stop Aliens', *New Straits Times*, 16 March, pp. 3.

Agence France Press (AFP) (1998a), 'Malaysia Relaxes Labor Rules to Woo Investment', *Migration News*, 29 November.

Agence France Press (AFP) (1997b), 'Thai Labor Committee Wants to Send Back a Million Alien Workers', *Migration News*, 28 November.

Agence France Press (AFP) (1998c), 'Go Where Jobs Beckon, Ramos Tells Filipinos Abroad', *Migration News*, 7 January.

Ahmad, R. (1998), 'Malaysia Dismisses Worries Over Indonesian Migrants', *Reuters*, 1 April.

Associated Press (AP) (1998a), 'Malaysia Assures Neighbors It Won't Fire Foreign Workers', *Migration News*, 12 January.

AP (1998b), 'Thai Minister Vows to Deport Illegal Workers in Three Months', *Migration News*, 16 January.

AP (1998c), 'Jobless Rate Raises Fear of Social Unrest', *Bangkok Post*, 13 March, pp. 4.

AP (1998d), 'Indonesian Navy to Bring Home Workers From Malaysia: Antara', *Migration News*, 6 January 1998.

AP (1998e), 'Indonesian Navy to Take Illegal Workers From Malaysia', *Migration News*, 20 March 1998.

Battistella, G. (1996), 'Migration and APEC: Issues for Discussion', *Asian Migrant Forum*, November, pp. 23.

'Be on Lookout for Illegals, says Shahidan', *New Straits Times*, 17 March 1998, pp. 3.

Beare, M. (1998), 'Illegal Migration', in C. G. Hernandez and G. R. Pattugalan (eds), *Transnational Crime and Regional Security in the Asia Pacific*, Institute for Strategic and Development Studies, Inc. (ISDS), Quezon City, Manila, Philippines, pp. 252, 256.

Bernama (1998), 'Refugees' Free to go to Third Country', *The Star*, 6 May.

Bohning, W. R. (1996), *Employing Foreign Workers*, International Labor Office, Geneva.

Bosniak, L. (no date), 'Human Rights, State Sovereignty and the Protection of Undocumented Migrants Under the International Migrant Workers Convention', *International Migration Review*, vol. 25, no. 4.

Charoensutthipan, P. (1998a), 'Deadline on Aliens Put Off for Year; But Policy Will Not Be Eased Further, Insists Bhichai', *Bangkok Post*, 16 July.

Charoensutthipan, P. (1998b), 'Plan to Let Aliens Work in Only 13 Provinces; Repatriation Centre Could be Established', *Bangkok Post*, 14 January.

Charoensutthipan, P. (1998c), 'Slump a Boom to Cheats', *Bangkok Post*, 14 April.

Chintayananda, S., Risser, G. and Chantavanich, S. (1997), *The Monitoring of the Registration of Immigrant Workers From Myanmar, Cambodia and Laos in Thailand*, Institute of Asian Studies, Asian Research Center for Migration, Chulalongkorn University, Bangkok.

Dancel, R. (1998a), 'OFWs Unfazed by Low Pay, Shrinking Marts', *Philippine Daily Inquirer*, 18 August, pp. B1.

Dancel, R. (1998b), 'Overseas Workers; Heroes in a Tragic Play', *Philippine Daily Inquirer*, 17 August, pp. B12.

Duff-Brown, B. (1998a), 'Illegal Aliens to Enter Malaysia', *Migration News*, 30 March.

Duff-Brown, B. (1998b), 'Poverty Reaches Across Borders', *Bangkok Post*, 31 March, pp. 10.

Edwards, N. (1998), 'Fears Over Rising Illegal Immigration', *Bangkok Post*, 18 March.

Edmonston, B., Passel, J. and Bean, F. (1990), 'Perceptions and Estimates of Undocumented Migration to the United States', in F. Bean, B. Edmonston and J. Passel (eds), *Undocumented Migration to the United States; IRCA and the Experience of the 1980s*, The Rand Corporation, Santa Monica, pp. 11-31, 24-25.

Espenshade, T. and Hempstead, K. (no date), 'Contemporary American Attitudes Toward US Immigration', *International Migration Review*, vol. 30, no. 2, pp. 536.

'Failed Policies Being Recycled; Buck-Passing Won't Solve Problem, Say Experts', *The Bangkok Post*, 19 July 1999.

'Firms Want Rules on Hiring Immigrants to be Eased; Need to Fill Positions Shunned by Thais', *Bangkok Post*, 22 May 1998.

Freeman, G. (1995), 'Modes of Immigration Politics in Liberal Democratic States', *International Migration Review*, no. 4, Winter, pp. 883.

Gecker, J. (1998), 'Indonesians Ram Truck Into UN Base', *Migration News*, 30 March.

Go, S. (1998), 'Towards the 21st Century: Whither Philippine Labor Migration', in B. Carino (ed.), *Filipino Workers on the Move: Trends, Dilemmas and Policy Options*, Philippine Migration Research Network and Philippine Social Science Council, Quezon City, pp. 12.

Hugo, G. (1995), 'Illegal International Migration in Asia', in R. Cohen (ed.), *The Cambridge Survey of World Migration*, Cambridge University Press, Cambridge, pp. 398.

Hutasingh, O. (1997a), 'Tough Fight Against Illegal Alien Workers', *Bangkok Post*, 15 December, pp. 2.

Hutasingh, O. (1997b), 'Studies Show Who Benefits From Alien Workers Here', *Bangkok Post*, 25 May.

Hutasingh, O. (1998), 'How to Stem the Flow', *Bangkok Post*, 8 February.

Huysmans, J. (1995), 'Migrants as a Security Problem: Dangers of "Securitizing" Societal Issues', in R. Miles and D. Thranhardt (eds), *Migration and European Integration; The Dynamics of Inclusion and Exclusion*, Pinter Publishers, London, pp. 59.

'In a Desperate Bid to Avoid Being Sent Home...Foreign Workers Rush to Apply for Permanent Residence', *The Straits Times*, 7 January 1998.

International Organization for Migration (IOM) (1994), *Trafficking in Migrants: Characteristics and Trends in Different Regions of the World*, unpublished discussion paper presented at the '11th IOM Seminar on Migration', Geneva, 26-28 October, pp. 2-3.

Jervis, R. (1997-98), 'Complexity and the Analysis of Political and Social Life', *Political Science Quarterly*, vol. 112, no. 4, pp. 569.

'Justice Ministry Postpones Plan to Expel Illegal Foreign Workers', *Korea Herald*, 8 January 1998.

Krishnamoorthy, M. (1998), 'Handsome Black Market Price for Our Passports', *The Star*, 28 July.

Krisnawaty, T. (1997), *The Role of Bilateral Agreements on Migrant Labor Issues: The Case of Indonesia and Malaysia*, paper presented at the 'Conference on Legal Protection for Women Migrant Workers: Strategy for Action', Manila, 8-12 September 1997, pp. 1.

Lee, K. H. and Sivananthiran, A. (1996), 'Contract Labor in Malaysia: Perspectives of Principal Employers, Contractors, and Workers', *International Labor Review*, vol. 135, no. 1, pp 75-91.

Link, M. and Oldendick, R. (1996), 'Social Construction and White Attitudes Toward Equal Opportunity and Multiculturalism', *The Journal of Politics*, vol. 58, no. 1, February, pp.149-168.
Marukatat, S. (1998), 'Looking After Our Own in This Time of Crisis', *Bangkok Post*, 12 January, pp. 9.
Migrants Standing Committee (1996), *A Survey on Placement Fees Paid by Taiwan-Bound OFWs (Overseas Filipino Workers) to Philippine Agencies*, unpublished report by the St. Christopher's Parish Pastoral Council, October-December, Table 4, pp. 2.
'Ministry of Labor Tightens Work Permit Procedures', *The Straits Times*, 20 November 1997.
Myint, N. (1998), *Myanmar Country Paper: Academic Aspects*, paper presented during the 'Regional Workshop on Transnational Migration and Development in ASEAN Countries', Institute for Population and Social Research, Mahidol University, International Organization for Migration, Bangkok and Hua Hin, 25-27 May 1998, pp. 3, Table 4.
Nafziger, J. and Bartel, B. (no date), 'The Migrant Workers Convention: Its Place in Human Rights Law', and Bosniak, L., 'Human Rights, State Sovereignty and the Protection of Undocumented Migrants Under the International Migrant Workers Convention', *International Migration Review*, vol. 25, no. 4.
Nayyar, D. (1993), 'Statistics on International Labor Migration and Economic Analysis: Some Conceptual Issues', in ILO-ARTEP, *International Labor Migration Statistics and Information Networking in Asia*, International Labor Office, Geneva, pp. 41.
Population Newsletter, no. 62, December, pp. 12.
Reuters (1998), 'Thais Among Immigrants Facing Cane', *Bangkok Post*, 23 March, pp. 1.
Rungswasdisab, P. (1997), 'An Illegal Population Takes Root', *The Nation*, 2 June, pp. A9.
Shen-Li, L. (1998), 'Fighting to Keep Out Life-Threatening Ills', *New Sunday Times*, 18 January.
'Slowdown May Send Foreign Workers in Malaysia Packing', *The Straits Times*, 24 November 1997.
Smith, P. (1995), *Asia's Economic Transformation and Its Impact on Intraregional Labor Migration*, unpublished, Council on Foreign Relations Asia Project Working Paper, New York, March, pp. 5.
Smith, P. (1997), 'The Military's Increasing Role in Immigration Enforcement', article reproduced in *CISNEWS@cis.org* from *Immigration Review*, no. 29, Summer.
Stephen, I. (1998), 'Tough Measures on Immigration Offenders', *Borneo Bulletin*, 1 April.
Tenaganita (1995), *A Memorandum on Abuse, Torture and Dehumanised Treatment of Migrant Workers at Detention Centres*, unpublished paper, August, pp. 1.
Tessier, K. (1995), 'The New Slave Trade: The International Crisis in Immigrant Smuggling', *Indiana Journal of Global Legal Studies*, vol. 3, no. 1, Fall, pp. 1.
Tunyasiri, Y. and Charoenpo, A. (1998), 'Jobs Opened Up as 19,000 Foreign Workers Go Home', *Bangkok Post*, 17 February, pp. 1.
Unarat, S. (1998), 'Alien Workers Issue to be Reviewed', *Bangkok Post*, 29 April, pp. 3.
Unarat, S. (1998), 'Concern Among Rice and Rubber Operators', *Bangkok Post*, 29 April, pp. 3.
Ung, A. (1998), 'Malaysia May Expel One Million Workers', *The Straits Times*, 7 January.
United Nations (1994), *Report of the International Conference on Population and Development: Program of Action*, Cairo, 5-13 September.
Vanaspong, C. (1997), 'Learning Lessons From a Neighbor', *Bangkok Post*, 9 March.
Vinesh, D. (1998), '200,000 Aliens to be Sent Back', *The Star*, 17 July.
Wong, J. (1998), 'Ethnic-Chinese Women Seek to Wed to Flee Fear, Violence in Indonesia', *The Wall Street Journal*, 21 July.
'Workers to be Classified; New Centre to Document Staff to Help Management of Labor Force', *The Bangkok Post*, 19 July 1999.

Chapter 4

Perceptions of Women Migrant Workers from the Philippines and Indonesia

Ruth R. Lusterio

Introduction

During the past two decades, the international labor migration of women has grown both in volume and significance. The increase in participation of women in the global economy is attributed to the changing nature of labor markets that demand certain types of skills. In the early 1990s, some 1.4 million women workers were employed as foreign domestic workers in Asia and the Middle East.[1] The Philippines and Indonesia are among the major labor exporters to these regions.

In the Philippines, the feminization of the overseas employment profile has been observed since the 1980s. In 1996, women workers made up 54 per cent of the total number of newly deployed workers, up from 47 per cent in 1987[2] and 12 per cent in 1975.[3] Filipino women, mostly in their twenties and thirties are employed as service workers, mostly domestic helpers and entertainers, in countries like Japan, Singapore, and Hong Kong. Remittances from overseas employment contribute heavily to the Philippine economy. From 1982 to 1993, migrant workers have reportedly remitted a total of US$13.5 billion to the Philippines through bank channels.[4] In 1996 alone, a total of US$4.5 billion worth of worker's remittances through bank channels has also been recorded by the *Bangko Sentral ng Pilipinas* (BSP, Central Bank of the Philippines).[5] In spite of the growing number of cases of abused overseas contract workers (OCWs), especially women, Filipino workers continue to be pulled to places where better job opportunities exist. These trends are expected to continue due to the continuing effects of the economic crisis being experienced in Southeast Asia (SEA).

In Indonesia, the migration of its women has been traced 'to an increase in multinational activity, displacement of women from agriculture, rising levels of female education, and the breakdown of patriarchal systems'.[6] A great number of Indonesian migrant women are employed as domestic helpers in the Middle East and Malaysia. The Indonesian government's encouragement to send contract workers abroad since the 1980s must have facilitated this process. The flow of migrant workers from Indonesia is also expected to continue because of the economic difficulties faced by the country since the 1997 crisis.

This chapter seeks to provide some empirical referents for the conceptual linkages between development and security by determining the perceptions of women migrant workers about development, security, and the linkages between these two concepts.

The international labor migration of women has become a significant issue since the 1980s.[7] This is because of the phenomenon's implications for a country's economic development and for the security of its citizens, their families, as well as their communities. Overseas labor migration is generally perceived to bring about immediate economic benefits to individual migrant workers and their families. Hence, it is also believed that the development of the migrant workers and members of their families is enhanced. However, international labor migration also poses serious threats to the individual security of migrant workers. Poor working conditions and lack of familiarity with labor laws in another country affect the security of migrant workers as individuals. The security implications of this phenomenon, however, transcend that of the individual female migrant.

Objectives of the Study

The purpose of this study is to explore the meaning and linkages of development and security from the perspective of women migrant workers. As women are pushed from their countries to be employed as factory workers, domestic helpers, entertainers, and nurses in other countries, they have to deal with a number of realities that pose serious threats to their individual security. Yet, women continue to choose to work overseas. This study hopes to explain why this is so.

More specifically, it seeks to address the following questions: (1) How do women migrant workers define development and security? (2) What factors affect or influence women migrant workers' definitions of development and security? (3) How do women migrant workers perceive the linkages between development and security? (4) What are the implications of these perceptions for the broader meaning of development and security in terms of sources of insecurity? (5) How can the concerns of women migrant workers be effectively addressed by the state, the civil society, and even by the women migrant workers themselves?

The definition of development and security based on women's experiences in international labor migration has policy implications that governments of sending countries need to seriously consider. The long-term development and security implications of the overseas migration of a country's workforce, especially women, need to be acknowledged in the interest of addressing effectively society's development and security concerns. In the end, the study also looks at the attempts of the governments of the Philippines and Indonesia to address the issues and concerns of women migrant workers. In this regard, establishing networks and opportunities for cooperation with non-governmental organizations (NGOs) and other sectors of civil society is relevant in addressing the plight of women migrant workers.

Scope, Limitations, and Sources of Data

Understanding women migrant workers' definitions of development and security is crucial in determining the implications of such understanding for public policy, advocacy, and action – both for the state and civil society. The study basically focuses on the meaning of human development and human security at the level of the individual. However, it is recognized that the meaning of development and security at the individual level has significant implications for other levels, that is, family, community, and society.

The data for this study came from focus group discussions (FGDs) with Filipino and Indonesian women conducted from May to September 1998. The FGDs took place in migrant workers' training centers, in an NGO office, and the home of a former migrant worker. The FGD participants were contacted through NGOs advocating the rights and welfare of women migrant workers[8] and private recruitment agencies that send Indonesian workers abroad. The offices of these organizations are located in Quezon City, Philippines and Jakarta, Indonesia.

A Moderator's Topic Guide was constructed and used for all the FGDs. The questions were open-ended to elicit full responses from the participants and allow them to shape the responses themselves. The FGDs were conducted in the local languages, that is, Filipino and Bahasa Indonesia. Due to the researcher's lack of facility with Bahasa Indonesia, an Indonesian researcher facilitated the FGDs in Jakarta. The proceedings of the FGDs were tape recorded, then transcribed, and translated.

Admittedly, the findings of this study based on the data gathered from the FGDs cannot be generalized to a larger population. However, the perceptions of the FGD participants can be considered as representative of the perception of the larger population of women migrant workers from the two countries. In addition, determining the perceptions of a certain group of people through FGDs is valuable because of the quality of responses that can be generated. Other sources of data for this study include documents and statistics from government agencies and NGOs, as well as in-depth interviews and informal discussions with members of NGOs, researchers, selected government personnel, and academics.

Profile of FGD Participants

The participants consisted of women aged 15 to 40 who were either first time or returning migrant workers. The Filipino groups consisted of older women, the youngest being 26 years old while the oldest was 40. On the other hand, the youngest participant in the Indonesian groups was 15 years old while the oldest was 36.

Majority of the participants from both the Philippines and Indonesia are married. The others are either single or widowed. A few Filipina participants classified themselves as 'single parents'. The number of children of the participants ranged from two to five.

In terms of education, the Filipino participants received higher education most having finished high school, attended college, or had a college degree. Majority of the Indonesian participants, on the other hand, consisted of women who had received primary education only.

All the participants are employed or will be employed as domestic helpers. Most of the returning Indonesian migrant workers have come from the Middle East, particularly Saudi Arabia and the United Arab Emirates, and Malaysia. Meanwhile, most of the Filipino participants worked in Saudi Arabia, Malaysia, Singapore, Taiwan, and Hong Kong. Those who are going abroad for the first time are also bound for these countries.

A Conceptual Frame for Development and Security

Development is a concept with economic, social, political, and human dimensions.[9] Traditional theories on development have emphasized the importance of capital formation and economic growth. It is focused on the expansion of material resources available to people alone.[10] However, in the 1970s, the concept of human development began to emerge. This perspective views development as an improvement in the quality of human life and emphasizes the effects of the development process on human beings. In the 1990s, the United Nations Development Programme (UNDP) constructed the Human Development Index (HDI) and the Gender-Related Development Index (GDI) 'to serve as measures of (1) a country's performance in three aspects of human development namely, growth in real income per capita, level of skills and the state of health of its citizens, and of (2) the level of gender disparities in these areas'.[11] The UNDP defines human development as a process of expanding the range of people's choices and their capabilities.[12] Such notion of development indicates the direct relationship between development and security.

In its 1994 Human Development Report, the UNDP introduced the concept of human security which has two aspects: (1) safety from such chronic threats as hunger, disease and repression; and (2) protection from sudden and hurtful disruptions in the patterns of daily life.[13] According to the UNDP, 'human security is related to human development in the sense that it means that people can exercise their expanded choices (and develop their capabilities) safely and freely and can be relatively confident that the opportunities they have today are not totally lost tomorrow'.[14] The following have been identified as indicators of human security: (1) economic security; (2) food security; (3) health security; (4) environmental security; (5) personal security; (6) community security; and (7) political security.[15]

Like development, the definition of security, in general, has become more comprehensive, although the Association of Southeast Asian Nations (ASEAN) and Japan had earlier recognized this character of security – see Chapter 1 in this volume. Significant changes in the global environment consequently brought about a new perspective on security elsewhere in the world. The end of competition between the two superpowers subsequently altered the bipolar nature of international power structures and geoeconomics replaced geopolitics as the primary consideration in international relations.[16] At present, security is also seen as referring to defense against threats brought about by political, social, economic, and other causes.

The new perspective on security is seen 'from a multi-dimensional standpoint, where labor flows and markets play an important role'.[17] International labor migration has become part of the new security concerns because of the socio-cultural, economic, and political tensions it brings about which highlight the security sensitivities of both sending and receiving countries.[18] Hence, labor migration issues and concerns have gained significance as determinants of national security and stability.

The perspective on national security has likewise broadened. In the past, national security has been equated largely with the physical protection of the state from external threats. At present, national security concerns, especially of developing countries include economic development, human rights, environmental security, social modernization, and national integration.[19] The economic well being of the people is considered a core value of the national security of developing countries.[20] This is because 'persistent underdevelopment and deprivation of economic well being degrade national morale and precipitate social unrest, thus furthering internal fragmentation'.[21]

The broader concept of development and security provides the conceptual frame for this study. Concerned with the implications of international labor migration for the human development and human security of women migrant workers, the human dimension of the concepts of development and security are highlighted in this study.

Feminization of International Labor Migration and Human Security

One of the most striking economic and social phenomena that raises important policy issues and concerns is the feminization of international labor migration.[22] Women from the Philippines and Indonesia have been pushed to work in other countries because of the economic difficulties and lack of better job opportunities at home. Most often, women are employed in jobs that make them highly vulnerable to discrimination, abuse, and exploitation.

A number of studies have found out that the effects of labor migration are many and varied.[23] First, the nature and extent of the impact of migration bears directly on the migrant workers and their families. Although it generally contributes to the improvement of a family's living standards, overseas employment also has negative effects on family relationships.[24] Leaving one's family behind causes anxiety and loneliness on the part of the migrant workers, especially for the mothers. Some studies have also pointed out the negative effects and psychological costs of labor migration on the children of migrant workers.

Adaptation to a foreign culture is another problem that confronts migrant workers. While staying in a foreign country, they also need to feel secure about their work and working conditions. Not being familiar with laws covering labor and labor relations causes the feeling of insecurity on their part.

The problems and concerns facing women migrant workers arise both from their being migrants and their being women. Since they are most often involved in jobs most vulnerable to abuse, they have to contend with insecurity of employment, forced overtime, poor working and living conditions, absence of benefits, and even sexual harassment and rape. Yet, in spite of the number of factors that threaten their human security, there are still some of them who believe that the benefits of overseas employment outweigh its costs. In fact, according to a study made by Cruz and Paganoni migrant workers generally do not view labor migration as costly.[25]

How women migrant workers define development and security will eventually explain why they choose to work abroad in spite of the perceived threats to their personal security. Likewise, their perspectives on development and security are likely to have implications for the broader conceptualization of how development and security are linked.

The International Labor Migration of Women: Philippine and Indonesian Experiences

The Philippines and Indonesia are two of the major labor exporters in SEA. The deployment of women migrant workers from these two countries has continued to increase since the mid-eighties. This can be attributed mainly to two factors: (1) the increase in demand for female workers in countries which have experienced economic growth; and (2) the policies adopted by the government which encourage overseas employment. Both the Philippine and Indonesian governments have embarked on an overseas employment program to address the growing problem of unemployment and dwindling foreign currency reserves by establishing agencies that play an active role in promoting labor migration flows. These agencies are the Philippine Overseas Employment Administration (POEA) and AKAN (or Center for Overseas Employment) under the Department of Manpower in Indonesia.[26]

Women workers make up a large percentage of the total number of overseas workers from these two countries. In the Philippines, more than half of the total number of overseas workers deployed every year since 1992 consist of women – see Table 4.1. In the case of Indonesia, women migrant workers have outnumbered the men since 1994 – see Table 4.2. Likewise, a dramatic increase in the number of overseas workers, mostly women, can be observed during the period 1996-97. A total of 517,269 workers have left Indonesia during this period. Out of this number, 288,832 (or 56 per cent) were women.[27]

Table 4.1 Deployment of Overseas Filipino Workers 1992-96

	1992	1993	1994	1995	1996
Male	130,725	117,955	105,482	89,335	94,304
Female	129,869	138,242	153,504	124,822	111,487
Total	260,594	256,197	258,986	214,157	205,791

Source: Philippine Overseas Employment Administration, 1997.

Table 4.2 Deployment of Overseas Indonesian Workers 1994-98

	1994/95	1995/96	1996/97	1997/98
Male	42,833	39,102	228,437	15,624
Female	133,354	81,794	288,832	71,312
Total	176,187	120,896	517,269	86,936

Source: Department of Manpower, Indonesia, 1998.

Asia remains the top destination of women migrant workers from both countries. As of 1996, 67 per cent of the total number of female overseas workers from the

Philippines were employed in East Asia and the Middle East, more specifically in Hong Kong, Singapore, and Saudi Arabia – see Table 4.3.[28] Recently, Taiwan has also become a major destination of women overseas workers from the Philippines. Meanwhile, Indonesian women have preferred to be employed in the Middle East, especially in Saudi Arabia, although a substantial number also go to Malaysia – see Table 4.4. According to the records of the Directorate of Overseas Manpower Services, a total of 359,155 female Indonesian workers had been employed in Saudi Arabia while 200,935 were in Malaysia as of 1997.[29]

The labor migration of Filipino and Indonesian women is strongly characterized by the concentration in a very limited number of occupations found at the bottom of the occupational hierarchy. Such occupations include domestic work, service work in hotels and restaurants, as well as in assembly lines of labor-intensive manufacturing. Local women often shun these jobs because they offer low rewards, inferior working conditions, and limited job prospects or security.[30]

A great number of women migrant workers from the Philippines and Indonesia work in the service sector – see Tables 4.5 and 4.6. As of 1996, 95 per cent of women migrant workers from the Philippines were employed as service workers. During the same period, almost 65 per cent of the total number of documented migrant workers from Indonesia was employed in the service sector.[31]

A number of issues and policy concerns arise due to the concentration of Filipino and Indonesian women migrant workers in occupations that are most prone to abuse and exploitation, particularly domestic work. A female migrant worker who is employed as a domestic helper is especially vulnerable to abuse because she is in an individualized work situation where there is greater isolation and the establishment of networks of social support is less likely. In addition, as noted earlier, the problems that women migrant workers face are compounded by the fact that they are women and that they are migrants.

Women migrant workers encounter problems not only after they have reached their destination but also even before they depart for abroad. The problems that women migrant workers from Indonesia have to deal with can be grouped into three: (1) those that involve their agents or recruiters; (2) those that involve government personnel; and (3) those that involve their employers.[32] Before their departure, potential female migrant workers need to stay in training centers established by private recruitment firms accredited by the government. The Department of Manpower in Indonesia requires all applicants for overseas employment to submit a certification stating their qualification for the job so they need to stay in shelters provided by recruitment agencies where they receive training to learn to do housework using electronic appliances and other modern equipment.[33] Hence, a large number of them leave their homes months before their departure for their destination. They have to contend with the poor living conditions as well as the high cost of staying in the shelters/training centers prior to their departure. Some of the women also complain that sometimes, they need to wait for a long time before they can finally depart for abroad.

Table 4.3 Number of Female Migrant Workers from the Philippines by Place of Work (in thousands)

Place of Work	April-September 1995	April-September 1996
Africa	3	2
Libya	2	1
Other countries in Africa	1	1
Asia	328	331
East Asia	144	148
Hong Kong	105	100
Japan	15	16
Taiwan	23	26
South Korea	1	4
China	-	1
Other countries in East Asia	-	1
S East and S Central Asia	76	67
Singapore	54	37
Malaysia	17	20
Brunei	5	8
Other countries in SE/SC Asia	-	2
Middle East	105	118
Saudi Arabia	67	64
Kuwait	15	23
United Arab Emirates	10	10
Qatar	4	7
Bahrain	4	4
Oman	-	2
Jordan	1	2
Lebanon	2	4
Other countries in W Asia	2	2
Australia	-	1
Micronesia	3	4
Saipan	2	4
Guam	1	-
Europe	22	28
Greece	3	3
Italy	13	18
Norway	-	-
United Kingdom	1	1
Germany	-	1
France	-	-
Netherlands	1	-
Other countries in Europe	4	5
North and South America	22	26
United States of America	14	17
Canada	7	9
Other countries in the Americas	1	-
Country Not Specified	-	2

Source: National Statistics Office, *Survey of Overseas Filipinos*, 1996.

Table 4.4 Number of Female Migrant Workers from Indonesia by Place of Work (1994-98)

Place of Work	1994/95	1995/96	1996/97	1997/98
Asia Pacific	41,961	38,626	161,825	25,467
America	29	0	0	0
Europe	3	3	28	0
M East and Africa	91,361	43,165	126,979	45,845
Total	133,354	81,794	288,832	71,312

Source: Department of Manpower, Indonesia, 1998.

Table 4.5 Deployment of Newly Hired Overseas Filipino Workers (1996)

Skill Category	Female	Male	Total
Professional/Technical	24,238	11,817	36,055
Managerial Workers	64	241	305
Clerical	1,231	1,938	3,169
Sales	725	1,231	1,938
Service Workers	76,765	7,980	84,745
Agricultural	19	803	822
Production	8,174	67,509	75,683
Invalid	271	2,803	3,074
Total	111,487	94,304	205,791

Source: Philippine Overseas Employment Administration, 1996.

Table 4.6 Number of Indonesian Overseas Workers by Sector (1996)

Sector	Number
Agriculture	27,110
Mining	4
Processing/Industry	71,038
Electricity	1
Construction	586
Hotel/Restaurant/Retail	299
Transportation/Communication	50,326
Finance/Insurance	963
Services	265,035

Source: Institute of Agriculture, Bogor and Department of Manpower, Indonesia, 1996, p. 23.

Labor recruitment has become a lucrative business and has developed into an industry in both the Philippines and Indonesia.[34] Aside from the implementation of policies that promoted overseas employment the increase in number of private recruitment agencies has further facilitated both the legal and illegal labor migration of women. Undoubtedly, these agencies have also become the cause of the vulnerability of women migrant workers. The tendency of migrant workers to be dependent on their recruiters, both in the sending and receiving countries makes them more prone to, and can eventually lead to a series of exploitative practices.[35] Most of the time, women migrant workers do not have any other contact in their host countries. In the case of Indonesian migrant women, they become dependent even while they are still in their home country since they have already either spent or owed a lot of money either to the recruitment agencies or to their relatives while waiting for employment at the training centers. At times, the dependence is deliberately fostered by the recruitment agency through the widespread practice of withholding the migrants' passports.

Aside from the problems brought about by recruiters, female migrant workers also encounter problems that involve people from government agencies responsible for managing overseas employment. Some women from Indonesia have complained about the high cost of working abroad since they do not only have to pay for the services of the recruiters but also those of government bureaucrats. Oftentimes, too, they have to give money to what they call the '*oknum*', or those who prey on migrant workers.[36]

In the case of Filipino women, the most common problems they encounter are related to their working conditions, the restrictions imposed on them by their employers, their relationship with their employers (for instance, difficulty in communicating with them, being physically maltreated, verbally abused, others), violations in their contracts, and basic human rights issues.[37] Most of the time, the women who are employed as domestic helpers have very little understanding of the provisions of their contracts. This makes them dependent on their recruiters and employers and vulnerable to abuse. In some instances, even if they understand the terms of their contracts, they do not have enough information and knowledge as to how they would deal with the problems they encounter.

The characteristics of the labor migration of women from the Philippines and Indonesia as well as the problems and concerns of women migrant workers discussed above explain why the feminization of international labor migration is a security issue. As women are pushed to work in places where job opportunities exist, it is not only their personal security that is at stake. The decision to migrate temporarily in order to earn a living also impacts on the security of the family. While it is true that there are families of migrant workers that are not negatively affected by the absence of one parent, there are also cases that show that labor migration affects family relationships in a negative way.[38] Most often, the absence of one parent, especially the mother, impacts heavily on the psychological well being of the children. Migrant workers do not only have to deal with anxiety and homesickness. They also need to adapt to the laws and cultures of their host countries. They are often not familiar with the laws of foreign countries and because of this, they become victims of abuse, unfair labor practices, and human rights violations.

At the broader level, the migration of women also affects the security of the sending countries, more particularly their economic security. Governments of sending countries recognize the economic opportunities in exporting excess labor. Oftentimes, labor migration is viewed as the solution to the deteriorating unemployment situation at home. Remittances also constitute the biggest source of foreign exchange for many sending countries. However, there are a number of issues raised against the dependence of a government on an overseas employment program. There is the question of the sustainability of economic growth anchored on the export of labor. Another is the issue of channeling remittances into more productive uses than family consumption.[39] Finally, changes in the labor market of receiving countries definitely affect the economies of sending countries. For instance, the recent economic crisis in SEA has led Malaysia, which hosts a great number of Indonesian and Filipino migrant workers to implement its plan of deporting undocumented workers. This has become a serious concern for Indonesia since it has many migrant workers in Malaysia (most of them undocumented) and its own economy can no longer absorb its surplus labor. In the long run, the country's economic development and security are threatened.

Development and Security: Perceptions of Women Migrant Workers

From the focus group discussions with women migrant workers, it was established that the main reason why they decided to seek overseas employment is economic difficulties at home. The Indonesian participants in the FGDs identified the following reasons when asked why they have decided to seek employment in other countries:

1. to help their family by providing additional income;
2. to earn money to establish business;
3. to send their children to school;
4. to please their husbands;
5. for the experience and to see another place; and
6. to go to Mecca.

On the other hand, the Filipino participants cited the following as the main reasons why they decided to work abroad:

1. financial difficulties;
2. low salaries they received in their former jobs;
3. unemployment or lack of employment;
4. to augment the income of their family; and
5. to gain work experience.

When asked whether overseas employment changed their lifestyle (and those of their family), the Filipino and Indonesian participants said that they have experienced significant changes in their lifestyle. The changes identified by the Indonesian participants are:

1. an increase in income of the family which resulted in a change in their lifestyle because they already own their homes, a small piece of land, and are now able to buy the things that they want to buy like clothes and appliances;
2. they are now able to send their children to school;
3. they have become better equipped in doing housework; and
4. they have learned how to communicate better with others.

On the other hand, the Filipino participants cited the following changes in their lifestyle due to their overseas employment:

1. their children have to be raised by only one parent or by a relative;
2. they have to adjust to the culture of the countries where they are employed;
3. improved lifestyle or standard of living of both the migrant workers and their families as a consequence of an increase in income; and
4. being independent or learning how to deal with problems alone on the part of the migrant worker.

When asked to assess the overall impact of overseas employment on them, the responses of the Indonesian women were quite varied. Some of them considered that the benefits of overseas employment outweighed its costs because aside from the money they earned, they also feel more confident about making decisions and in dealing with their problems. However, there were some participants who said that they are really left with no alternative but to work in another country because they have to support their families. Others also said that they feel guilty about leaving their children behind but they realize that it is only temporary. In return, the children obtain education and have a better life. In general, the Indonesian participants did not say whether the impact of labor migration is positive or negative.

For their part, the Filipino participants basically share the same views as their Indonesian counterparts. They also believe that overseas employment has given them the benefit of earning an income that will enable them to provide for the needs of their families, especially the education of their children. The Filipino women, however, seemed to be more concerned about the impact of their absence on their children. Some said that because of their absence, their children have become 'spoiled' and 'irresponsible', while others pointed out that in some cases children have become more mature and responsible because they understand the kind of sacrifice their mothers are doing for their sake. The Filipino participants were also concerned about their children's lack of emotional attachment to them. They grow up under the care of their fathers, grandparents, or other relatives. Like the Indonesian participants, they did not say whether the impact of labor migration, on the whole, is positive or negative although they highlighted the negative impact of labor migration on their children.

In terms of the problems they encounter, the Filipinos identified the most common ones as poor working conditions, violations of employment contracts, maltreatment, long working hours, too many restrictions imposed on them (especially in the practice of their religion), difficulty in adjusting to different cultures, and difficulty in communicating with their employers. For their part, the Indonesians also identified long working hours and poor working conditions as their most common problems.

In summary, both the Filipino and Indonesian participants said that the main reason why they chose to work in another country is economic, that is, financial difficulties that they have experienced at home. They also said that their main goal is to increase the income of their families so that their living conditions would improve. However, some differences in the responses of the Filipino and Indonesian participants can be observed. The Filipino participants tended to be more concerned with the negative impact of their absence on their children. On the part of the Indonesians, most of them mentioned that part of the reason why they want to go to the Middle East to work is to pursue their religious belief or fulfill a religious obligation.

What Development Means

What does development mean? What are its indicators? Have the lives of women migrant workers and their families improved as a consequence of labor migration? Do the women migrant workers consider themselves to have been improved because of their experience in working abroad?

For the women migrant workers, development means two things: the improvement of their familys' economic well being and the improvement of their knowledge and skills. The FDG participants identified the following as indicators of development:[40]

1. increase in income;
2. better living conditions;
3. improved standard of living;
4. ability to provide the needs of their families;
5. ability to send their children to school;
6. having a permanent home; and
7. access to economic opportunities.

In terms of the improvement of their knowledge and skills, the Indonesian women said that this means learning how to do housework using modern appliances and learning to speak English. For the Filipino women, on the other hand, development means the enhancement of their well being as individuals, specifically being able to earn an income to help improve their family's well being. In addition, they said that acquiring the capacity to earn an income means empowerment for them since they now play a significant part in the decision-making in their household.

When asked if their employment abroad has resulted in the improvement of their lives, the women said that overseas employment has both positive and negative consequences. The participants generally agreed that the most important benefit is the money they have earned which enabled them to build their homes, send their children to school, and provide for the family's needs. Other benefits cited were: spiritual development (for the Indonesian women who were able to go to Mecca), gaining friends, travelling, learning to speak other languages, and learning how to deal with other peoples and cultures. On the other hand, their ability to live independently and to deal with various peoples and cultures were the result of working overseas according to the Filipino participants.

Among the negative consequences identified were: leaving their husband and family behind, being maltreated by their employers, and low self esteem for the migrant workers because they feel that people generally look down on them because of their jobs.

There were differences in the perspectives of the Filipino and Indonesian participants when asked if they considered themselves developed as individuals by overseas employment. The Indonesians generally considered themselves to have been developed or improved by their experience in overseas employment because they were able to earn an income. On the contrary, the Filipinos do not consider their personal well being to have been enhanced by their overseas employment. They said that this is because some of them already have a college education, and yet, they had to go to another country only to become domestic helpers. As one Filipino participant had put it: '...it (overseas employment) is not a promotion but rather a demotion (in her status).'

As a whole, the Filipino and Indonesian women think that the economic well being of their family has improved as a consequence of their employment abroad. Some of the Filipino participants expressed willingness to work in another country even if there are available jobs in their own country. They believe that incomes earned abroad are higher than those they would earn in the Philippines. They also said that a woman should maximize the economic opportunities while she is still young so that she can earn a lot of money and secure her own and her family's future.

What Security Means

What does security mean? What would determine the security of individuals? Has labor migration enhanced or threatened the security of migrant workers and their families?

For the FGD participants, security means being able to guarantee a better life for their families in the future. They identified the following as indicators of security:[41]

1. income;
2. permanent home;
3. education for the children;
4. peace and order;
5. low crime rates;
6. good family relations;
7. freedom; and
8. personal safety.

On the other hand, insecurity means:

1. unfamiliarity with the laws, language, and culture of their place of work;
2. uncertainty about their life while working abroad, such as the treatment by their employers; and
3. uncertainty about how their families would cope in their absence.

The majority of women said that their decision to work abroad was determined by their desire to secure a better life for their families, especially their children. They admitted that they chose to place their personal security at stake in exchange for their family's economic security. Most of the women also said that one's personal safety is guaranteed as long as you follow what your employers want and learn to adjust to the new environment.

When asked what contributes to their insecurity, many of the women said that they are uncertain about their future and what lies ahead for them and their family. A participant from Indonesia expressed the opinion that being economically endowed does not necessarily mean that one has already achieved security, especially when maltreated by her employers or if other people in society look down on her. In addition, some of the women said that what contributes to their insecurity is their guilt for having left their family behind. Some of the Indonesians said that some people even consider them as bad women.

In general, the women migrant workers believe that their personal security is not guaranteed because of the problems and concerns that they have to deal with once they are already abroad. However, the women still expressed their desire to work abroad in spite of the threats to their personal security. According to them, they have to give up something in exchange for the improvement of their family's economic well being.

Development and Security Linkages

The findings above show that the women migrant workers' definition of development and security focussed on the individual level and tended to emphasize the economic dimensions of the two concepts. More particularly, their definition of development emphasizes an improvement in the family's economic situation. However, most of the women also expressed the opinion that there is no development in a country where the people are pushed to go to another country to earn a living as domestic workers.

Although the women considered the positive effects of overseas employment on their personal abilities, they stressed that what overseas employment has really improved was the well being of the members of their family, particularly their economic condition. The Filipino women, in fact, feel that their own well being had deteriorated since many of them even have college education but they ended up working as domestic workers in other countries. They do not consider this as an improvement in their situation.

Nevertheless, they believe that the welfare of their family will improve because of the income that they can earn from overseas employment. With that, their children could go to school and get better education. In general, being able to provide education for their children is an assurance that their lives will improve since the children can find better jobs (if not in their own countries, then in other countries as well) when they get a college degree.

Moreover, the women migrant workers think that overseas employment has contributed significantly to the improvement of the national economy. Because of their earnings abroad, the problem of unemployment is eased (although temporarily), and the needs of the citizens are somewhat addressed. However, they believe that the government should devise a good program or a plan on how the problem of unemployment and lack of better job opportunities at home can be reduced and altogether eliminated. Hence, government should find a sustainable alternative.

As in their definition of development, the women migrant workers tend to focus on the economic dimension when asked to define security. Security is basically associated with economic relief, or more particularly, income stability. According to them their decision to work abroad is primarily due to the need to provide their family security of income to afford a suitable home and good education for the children. Being able to meet these needs would mean a better future for them.

The women have also associated security with their personal safety while they work in another country. They believe that their government must be able to guarantee the protection of their rights and welfare as human beings in order for them to have security.

However, they tend to disregard the insecurities arising from overseas employment because of the income that they can potentially earn abroad. It appears, therefore, that they would choose to place their lives at risk in pursuit of another value, in this case, economic security for the family. In addition, it is not only the life of the woman migrant worker that is at risk. Women migrant workers also gamble on the impact of their absence on their children and their husband. The incidence of having broken families resulting from the overseas employment of one parent has been observed in some studies.[42] Likewise, the FGD participants expressed this concern as one of the sources of their anxieties while they work in other countries.

Women migrant workers also believe that living in another country where one is unfamiliar with local laws, beliefs, and practices is already in itself a source of insecurity. Nevertheless, they tend to accept whatever condition is placed in their employment contracts, even if all its provisions are in favor of the employer. Worse, women migrant workers do not understand the terms and provisions of their contract. Most of the time, too, when employers violate the provisions of the contract, they are not considered as such by the laws of the host country.

Another indicator of security identified by the women migrant workers is peace and order in the communities where they came from. This view was more prevalent among the Filipino women. They believe that if there are acceptable economic opportunities for the citizens and if the young people are provided education, there would be fewer crimes and, therefore, greater security for the community. They believe that if there is economic development, security is also present in the society.

Although the women migrant workers cite other indicators or dimensions of development and security, it is quite evident that their tendency is to associate development and security with economic satisfaction. Why is this so? It may be inferred from the data discussed above that the perspectives of women migrant workers are shaped by their socioeconomic status and experiences as migrant workers. As already noted, when asked about the main reason why they chose to work in another country, most of the women said that lack of employment opportunities at home have pushed them to look for a job elsewhere.

The employment and poverty situation in the Philippines and Indonesia is an important factor that could explain why women from these two countries choose to work as domestic helpers in other countries. Domestic work, according to an International Labor Organization (ILO) report, is a job that is considered among those 'shunned by all nationals except the very poorest'.[43] The opportunity to earn an income, especially in a foreign currency has made overseas employment more attractive because it is seen as more lucrative.

Another important factor that could explain why women are encouraged to work in other countries are the social networks established among migrant workers. Many of these women have been motivated to work abroad because they have relatives and friends who are migrant workers in the same country who could provide them help and support when they need it. Hence, these women tend to disregard the uncertainties involved in labor migration.

On the whole, the women migrant workers' perspectives indicated the linkages of development and security at the individual level. The women believe that their development as human beings cannot be achieved unless their personal security is guaranteed. Their objective of attaining a better life for their family in the future cannot be realized if their lives would be at stake and if threats are present. Likewise, the women migrant workers expressed the idea that a society cannot be considered developed if threats on its people's security, whether personal, political, or economic continue to exist.

Although their definition of development and security focussed on the individual level, it is very important to consider the implications of these for other levels and institutions and how development and security are seen and addressed at these levels and institutions. The meaning of development and security at the individual level is related to what these mean for a state, or a society in general. The interest of the individual to have a better life, for instance, is not really contrary to the interest of the state to provide a good life for its citizens. In the area of international labor migration, both the individual and the state recognize the economic opportunities that can be gained from it. Hence, it is understandable that some people make the choice to leave and work in another country in spite of the insecurities this entails. Towards this economic end, it is expected that the governments of labor exporting countries would adopt policies and programs to manage labor migration flows that are eventually viewed as encouraging overseas employment.

Government policies, perceptions, and actions affect the achievement of development and security of individuals. There are times when the perspectives of the individual and the government come into conflict. As mentioned earlier, a government that wishes to attain economic growth may decide to adopt policies that would tend to promote labor migration in order to take advantage of prevailing economic opportunities. But, as previous studies have shown, the impact of labor migration on both the economy and the society in general has not been entirely favorable. The social costs have to be considered and these include the welfare of citizens and families. In addition, citizens expect the government to respond to their concerns and alleviate the threats to their personal security. But there are certain threats that are viewed by the government as unavoidable and sometimes, its capacity to address the concerns of its citizens can be limited.

Citizens naturally expect their government to protect their interests even while they work in other countries. In response to this need, the protection of the interests of migrant workers has been made part of the labor migration policies of labor exporting countries like the Philippines and Indonesia. However, efforts undertaken by the government are oftentimes viewed as inadequate. This is because the implementation of the policies of sending countries depends on a number of factors that include the perceptions and the policies adopted by the governments of receiving countries. For instance, sending countries recognize that concluding bilateral agreements with receiving countries is an important component in protecting the welfare of migrant workers. However, most of the major labor receiving countries do not want to enter into such agreements. This limits the capability of the government of sending countries to protect the welfare of their citizens who work abroad.

The implications of international labor migration for the development and security of human beings as well as of families, of communities, and of societies are indeed complex. Perhaps, this is the reason why it is difficult to find solutions that would fully address the issues and concerns that arise from this phenomenon. Preventing people to move to places where economic opportunities exist is unrealistic in that people will continue to make such choices whether government allows them or not. It is just up to the government, and perhaps other sectors in society to undertake efforts to address the concerns and alleviate the threats to the security of migrant workers and their families. Collaboration and cooperation among various groups in society must be undertaken to find means to address the complex development and security implications of the international labor migration for women and their families.

Addressing the Concerns of Women Migrant Workers

Addressing the issues and concerns arising from the international labor migration of women is indeed difficult. Oftentimes, efforts undertaken by the government to address these concerns are viewed as inadequate. However, although it is quite difficult to arrive at a sufficient solution or measure to address the issues, it is important to recognize the significance of people's attempts to cope with their situation.

The attempts to address the issues and concerns confronting women migrant workers can be considered as part of building social capital.[44] These attempts have been undertaken, either separately or jointly by the state, NGOs, and the migrant workers themselves. Although at times viewed as inadequate, efforts by these sectors are important in finding the most appropriate measures to address this complex phenomenon.

NGOs have been involved in the concerns of migrant workers primarily because of their recognition of the impact of labor migration on the well being of individuals, families, and communities. In the experience of the Philippines, the involvement of NGOs started during the late 1970s and early 1980s when the flow of migration increased significantly. The organizations were initially church-based groups and those that were organized by the migrant workers themselves. The increase in NGO involvement with labor migration issues can be attributed to the growing number of cases of abuse and contract violations that have been brought to the attention of government. NGOs provide an alternative whenever government effort is inadequate or in some cases, fails.

The Philippines and Indonesia have different experiences in the area of networking or cooperation in addressing the concerns of women migrant workers. For instance, the relationship between government agencies and NGOs concerned with migrant workers' issues in the Philippines has already been institutionalized while Indonesia is still behind in achieving such status. The experiences of the two countries are discussed below to draw out the important implications for the establishment of cooperation between the state and civil society actors in addressing the concerns and issues involving women migrant workers.

Philippine NGOs advocating the rights and welfare of migrant workers have been working with the POEA formally since 1993.[45] The involvement of NGOs in various programs of the POEA have been formalized through several memoranda of agreement between the POEA and the various NGOs. However, coordination with NGOs at the informal level has been going on for quite some time. The NGOs have been actively involved in bringing matters concerning distressed Filipino workers to the attention of POEA authorities.

The recognition of the NGOs' capabilities, especially in networking and advocacy work has led the government to open avenues for their participation. NGOs are actively involved in various areas in addressing the concerns of women migrant workers primarily through education and information dissemination. They are involved in the formulation and implementation of the gender-sensitive Workers' Education Program particularly special modules that address the needs and concerns of vulnerable sectors, that is, domestic helpers and entertainers. The POEA has likewise accredited five NGOs to conduct Pre-Departure Orientation Seminars (PDOS) for women who are going to be employed as domestic helpers.[46] In addition, NGOs have also been tapped to participate in developing modules for the Pre-Employment Orientation Seminars (PEOS) which the POEA intends to include as part of the documentary requirements for those who wish to work in other countries. The PEOS is targeted to be included in the curricula of elementary and high school students so that young people may be informed and eventually have an understanding of the consequences of overseas employment.

NGOs also participate in consultations, major policy deliberations, and program design and development.[47] Women migrant workers are represented in the governing board of the POEA. NGOs have also been active in the anti-illegal recruitment campaign because of their information and advocacy work. Legal assistance in filing complaints against recruitment agencies and employers has also been provided by NGOs.

On the whole, the Philippine government's policy towards NGOs is openness to encourage their active participation most especially in education and information campaigns. The government recognizes the special capabilities of the NGOs in the area of advocacy as well as their inherent advantage in establishing networks among NGOs that may be locally based or based in the migrant workers' place of work. Aside from these, NGOs also have contacts at the grassroots level with the families of migrant workers. These characteristics of NGOs had led the government to recognize their potential in becoming partners in the implementation of programs for women migrant workers.

In the case of Indonesia, openness and establishing cooperation between government and NGOs in addressing the concerns of women migrant workers is still considered as a major issue by the latter.[48] Generally, the government is viewed to have an entirely different perspective in looking at the phenomenon of international labor migration compared to the NGOs. The government is seen to be concerned only with the economic opportunities and not with the welfare of the citizens who work in other countries.[49]

Among the groups involved in issues concerning Indonesian women migrant workers include the Center for Indonesian Migrant Workers and the Center for Women's Resources Development (PPSW). These NGOs provide legal assistance, counselling, and training to women migrant workers. They are also involved in organizing potential and returning women migrant workers at the community level and in establishing networks with other local and international NGOs whether based in Indonesia or in the job sites. In 1998, some Indonesian NGO members visited the Philippines to observe and study how PDOS are conducted. Members of the Indonesian NGO sector hope that the Indonesian government would also adopt the policy of conducting PDOS and institutionalize cooperation with the NGO sector in order to address the problems and concerns of women migrant workers.[50]

The involvement of NGOs in addressing the development and security concerns of women migrant workers can be attributed to the opening up of democratic space and the willingness of the Philippine government to consider the NGOs as partners. Although the active involvement of Philippine NGOs in the issue of labor migration dates back to the time of the Marcos administration, the direct and formal involvement of NGOs traces its roots only in 1986 with redemocratization under the Aquino administration. In the case of Indonesia, although there are already a number of NGOs that undertake activities to alleviate the plight of women migrant workers, the prospects for cooperation with the government are still uncertain. The political and economic reforms being undertaken by the Indonesian government since 1998 could provide avenues for participation for the NGO sector in general.

Aside from the efforts of the government and the non-governmental sectors, women migrant workers themselves are involved in building social capital through the networks they establish while they are in their place of work or when they return to their countries. For instance, Filipina migrant workers organize social activities such as attending church services, shopping, and holding parties to celebrate Philippine holidays. NGOs operating in host countries also help organize Filipino migrant workers and put them in touch with each other. On the other hand, Indonesian women migrant workers begin their networking at the training centers since they stay there for quite some time before going to their destination countries. Indonesian NGOs also play an important part in organizing returning migrant workers at the community level. The effort to establish networks to help each other was made evident in one of the FGDs conducted for this study. Returning migrant workers met with this researcher and members of PPSW in one of the women's residences at Banen Village, Sukabumi, West Java. In that particular meeting, the women who have had work experience in another country gave advice to and discussed some important concerns with those who were working abroad for the first time.

The activities that women migrant workers do together cannot really be considered as direct attempts to alleviate their conditions or to solve their problems. However, these can be considered as first steps in establishing connections and networks that they could eventually draw upon in addressing their common problems and concerns.

Implications for Policy

Governments are generally expected to guarantee the welfare of their citizens especially as migrant workers in other countries. The efforts of the Philippine and Indonesian governments to protect migrant workers in general, and women migrant workers in particular are expressed in their policy pronouncements as well as the institutions they have put in place.

The Philippine government's policies on labor migration focus on the following thrusts: (1) the promotion of overseas employment; (2) the protection and promotion of the well being of overseas workers; and (3) the maximization of the developmental impact of labor migration. The Philippine government has adopted an overseas employment program since the passage of the Labor Code in 1974. The Code created the Overseas Employment Development Board (OEDB) and the National Seamen Board (NSB). These agencies were restructured in 1982 to become the POEA. The POEA spearheads the overall overseas employment promotional efforts of the industry in traditional and emerging markets.[51] Together with the Department of Foreign Affairs it also undertakes studies of foreign markets where Filipino workers can avail of employment opportunities.

In addition, the POEA is also mandated to protect the rights of overseas Filipino workers to fair and equitable employment practices and to promote their welfare. It implements this particular function by setting minimum wages and working conditions for overseas contract workers.

The continuous wave of labor migration from the Philippines in the 1970s has made the protection and welfare of overseas contract workers an important concern for the Philippine government. One of the earliest policies that aimed to address their welfare is Letter of Instruction (LOI) Number 537 issued on 1 May 1977 which created the Welfare Fund for Overseas Workers. In 1987, Executive Order Number 126 restructured the Welfare Fund and renamed it the Overseas Workers Welfare Administration (OWWA). The OWWA is the primary government entity concerned with the immediate welfare needs of overseas workers, before, during, and after overseas employment. This government agency is tasked to protect the interest and promote the well being of Filipino overseas workers, their families, and dependents.

The increase in the number of migrant workers has likewise added new complexities to the concerns of the Philippines' foreign service. It has become necessary for embassies, consulates, and other attached services abroad to attend to activities such as the resolution of labor related disputes, the provision of counselling services to distressed Filipino nationals as well as advice on remittances.

In addition, labor migration policies have also become an integral part of the Philippines' foreign policy. The government agencies concerned with labor migration – the Department of Labor and Employment (DOLE) (along with the POEA and OWWA) and the Department of Foreign Affairs (DFA) – pursue bilateral relations with host countries to promote and strengthen areas of cooperation in the field of labor, employment, and human resources development.

Aside from the welfare and protection of migrant workers, the Philippine government also adopted a policy on return migration. In 1995, the Philippine Congress passed the Migrant Workers and Overseas Filipinos Act (Republic Act 8042) that provided for an administrative machinery that would specifically deal with return migration. The implementation of this law is very important especially in the light of the financial crisis that has seriously hit the places of work and destination of Filipino migrant workers.

In the case of Indonesia, its government has also actively participated in the promotion of labor migration flows. In fact, its overseas employment program has been incorporated into Indonesia's national development plans. For instance, in its Fourth Five-Year Development Plan (1983-89), Indonesia targeted to send 225,000 women workers abroad. The target was increased to 500,000 in the Fifth Five-Year Development Plan (1989-94). Eighty per cent of these women were domestic helpers in the Middle East.[52]

The involvement of the government in labor migration has been institutionalized with the establishment of the AKAN under the Department of Manpower. This government agency was created primarily to encourage labor exports. Recently, the AKAN has been decentralized and the Directorate of Overseas Manpower Service under the Department of Manpower now performs its functions. In 1996, the Directorate General of Manpower adopted a set of regulations concerning the placement of workers in other countries. The regulations cover both workers who seek domestic and overseas employment as well as private placement or recruitment firms. Indonesian workers are required to register at the local offices of the Department of Manpower while placement agencies must obtain a permit from the Department of Manpower before they can operate. The regulations also contain the requirements for an Indonesian worker to work abroad, including skills training to be undertaken by migrant workers under a company accredited by the Department of Manpower.[53]

The complex issues arising from labor migration make collaboration between government and civil society groups critically important. The capabilities of each sector complement each other and efforts to address the concerns of women migrant workers were made more effective and successful. On the one hand, governments are not always fully equipped and capable in meeting the needs and demands of its citizens. The growth of the NGO sector in fact can be traced to the need to have an alternative mechanism to respond to the needs of citizens.

Although much has been achieved in the area of cooperation between the government and the NGOs in the Philippines, this does not necessarily mean that there are no longer issues that need to be addressed and challenges that need to be mastered in the future. Government and NGOs basically treat each other as competitors even if the government declares its willingness to collaborate with NGOs. There are certain areas in which NGOs can take part but there are also areas where the direct involvement of NGOs is not fully realized, for example, in policy-making. Aside from this, both the government and the NGOs have their own perceptions of what roles each of them must perform. There are inherent differences between these two sectors that cannot be easily reconciled and these can sometimes lead to conflict. Some government personnel often complain about the high expectations NGOs have from the government and this can become a source of tension between the two sectors. NGOs expect the government to be more aggressive in relating with host governments especially when the welfare of the women workers is concerned. However, there are instances when the government's capacity is limited due to inadequate resources and sometimes the need to maintain good diplomatic relations with the host government. For example, NGOs in the Philippines expect the government to be aggressive in concluding bilateral agreements with receiving countries, especially those that host Filipino domestic workers. Even while the government recognizes the need to forge bilateral labor agreements, these cannot be realized unless the governments of receiving countries are willing to enter into such agreements. As an alternative, the Philippine government has entered into bilateral agreements with the private sector, such as the agreement between the Association of Placement Agencies in Singapore and the Philippine Embassy.

The challenges that lie ahead both for the Philippine government and the NGO sector are: (1) the maintenance and enhancement of the cooperation between the government and NGOs in addressing the issues concerning women migrant workers; and (2) establishing networks with migrants as well as other groups, especially those that are directly in touch with the migrant workers.

On the part of Indonesia, greater challenges lie ahead for both government and the NGOs. The first one concerns the thrust of Indonesian labor migration policies that must incorporate the protection of women migrant workers through proper information and education. Although the Department of Manpower requires women migrant workers to attend skills training, a PDOS is useful especially in getting the women to be better prepared for overseas employment.

The Indonesian government must also consider the advantages of getting the NGO sector involved in addressing the concerns of women migrant workers. Like in the Philippines, the involvement of the NGO sector has been helpful in the campaign against illegal recruitment, thereby reducing the possibilities of illegal migration.[54] In addition, NGOs can also help in education and information campaigns. At present, this is already being done by some Indonesian NGOs but more migrant workers will be reached if the government would work with them. Indeed, Indonesian NGOs must confront a greater challenge since the government is not yet generally open to the idea of cooperating with NGOs or other civil society groups. Bridging the gap between the government and the NGOs is not at all an easy task since this requires a change in how one sector perceives the other.

The impact of the international labor migration of women on the development and security of the migrant workers and their families needs to be effectively addressed. Cooperation between the government, NGOs, and the private sector is necessary in order to find effective ways to alleviate the threats to migrant people's welfare and security.

Concluding Remarks

The perceptions of women migrant workers interviewed in this study about development and security indicated the direct relationship between the two concepts in their view. Development cannot be achieved without security, and *vice versa*. The women migrant workers' definitions of development and security also tended to focus on the economic dimensions of the two concepts.

The women basically associated development with the improvement of the family's economic well being and their improvement as individuals. Security for them also means being able to meet the family's needs in the future such as having a permanent home, a business, and sending their children to school. These considerations lead the women migrant workers to leave their homes and work in places where they are unfamiliar with the laws, culture, and practices of the host countries.

The definitions of development and security of women migrant workers have direct implications for policy. However, labor migration policy should not only be limited to the welfare and protection of women migrant workers. The thrust of government policies must also be geared towards long-term objectives such as addressing the factors that determine the decisions of women to work overseas as well as the implications of return migration for the economy, the society, and the migrant worker him/herself.

The problems and concerns arising from the international labor migration of women pertaining to the development and security of individuals, families, and communities can be properly addressed if cooperation among various sectors and groups in society is undertaken. Such cooperation can be an important component of policies that seek long-term solutions to the issues and concerns of women migrant workers.

Notes

1 Heyzer and Wee (1993), *Development*, vol.1, pp.37-40.
2 Philippine Overseas Employment Administration (POEA), 1996; see also Torres, C. I. (1995), 'The New Overseas Employment Program: Effectively Managing the Labor Migration Process', *Development Research News*, vol.XIII, no.3, May-June, pp.10.
3 Kanlungan Centre Foundation (1997), *Destination: Middle East (A Handbook for Filipino Women Domestic Workers)*, Kanlungan Centre Foundation, Quezon City, pp.9.
4 *Ibid*., pp.11.
5 *Ibid.*
6 Chant and Radcliffe (1992), 'Migration and Development: The Importance of Gender', in S. Chant (ed.), *Gender and Migration in Developing Countries*, Belhaven Press, London, pp.1-29.
7 Scalabrini Migration Center (1992), *Pre-Employment and Pre-Departure Services for Filipina Migrant Workers*, a report prepared by the Scalabrini Migration Center on behalf of the La Trobe University Regional Social Development Centre and International Social Service for Migrant Women Project for the International Labor Organization, April.

8 Friends of Filipino Migrant Workers (KAIBIGAN) in the Philippines and Center for Women's Resources Development (PPSW) in Indonesia.
9 Acharya, A., Dewitt, D., and Hernandez, C. (1995), 'Sustainable Development and Security in Southeast Asia: A Concept Paper', *CANCAPS Papier*, no.6, August.
10 Human Development Network (1997), *Philippine Human Development Report*, Human Development Network and the United Nations Development Programme, Philippines, pp.25.
11 *Ibid.*, pp.1.
12 O'Neill, H. (1997), 'Globalisation, Competitiveness and Human Security: Challenges for Development Policy and Institutional Change', *The European Journal of Development Research*, vol.9, no.1, June, pp.9.
13 *Ibid.*
14 *Ibid.*
15 *Ibid.*
16 Hernandez, C. G. (1995), 'Philippine Foreign Policy in the Post-Cold War Era: Challenges, Opportunities and Prospects', *Philippine Foreign Policy and Regional Politics*, University of the Philippines Center for Integrative and Development Studies, Quezon City, pp.40-41.
17 Hernandez, C. G. and Tigno, J. V. (1995), 'ASEAN Labor Migration: Implications for Regional Stability', *The Pacific Review*, vol.8, no.3, pp.545.
18 *Ibid.*
19 For a detailed discussion of this, see Azar, E. and Moon, C. (eds) (1991), *National Security in the Third World: The Management of Internal and External Threats*, Center for International Development and Conflict Management, Maryland.
20 Alaggapa, M. (1987), *National Security in Developing States*, Aubur House, Massachusetts, pp.2.
21 Azar and Moon, *National Security in the Third World: The Management of Internal and External Threats*, 1991, pp.281.
22 Lim, L. L. and Oishi, N. (1996), 'International Labor Migration of Asian Women: Distinctive Characteristics and Policy Concerns', *Asian and Pacific Migration Journal*, vol.5, no.1, pp.85.
23 For reference, see Perez, A. E. and Patacsil, P. C. (compilers) (1998), *Philippine Migration Studies: An Annotated Bibliography*, Philippine Migration Research Network, Quezon City.
24 See for example, Agano, M. E. (1995), 'Migrant Labor and the Filipino Family', in A. E. Perez (ed.), *The Filipino Family: A Spectrum of Views and Issues*, University of the Philippines Office of Research Coordination, Quezon City, Philippines, pp.79-96.
25 Cruz, V. P. and Paganoni, A. (1989), *Filipinas in Migration: Big Bills and Small Change*, Scalabrini Migration Center, Quezon City.
26 Recently, the AKAN has been decentralized and has been replaced by the Directorate of Overseas Manpower Service.
27 See also Institut Pertanian Bogor, 'Evaluasi Dampak Penempatan Tenaga Kerja Ke Luar Negeri' (Evaluation on the Impact of the Placement of Workers Abroad), 1996/1997, pp.19.
28 National Statistics Office (NSO), *Survey of Overseas Filipinos*, 1996.
29 Directorate of Overseas Manpower Services, 1997.
30 Lim and Oishi, 'International Labor Migration of Asian Women: Distinctive Characteristics and Policy Concerns', 1996, pp.91.
31 *Ibid.*, pp.23.
32 Interview with Dr. Rianto Adi, Atma Jaya Catholic University, Jakarta, Indonesia, 8 May 1998.
33 Similarly, Filipinos who seek to work abroad must also present a certification of attendance of a Pre-Departure Orientation Seminar (PDOS) conducted by accredited NGOs. In the case

of the Filipinos, however, they need not stay in training centers because the seminars are conducted in offices of NGOs.

34 Lim and Oishi, 'International Labor Migration of Asian Women: Distinctive Characteristics and Policy Concerns', 1996, pp.90. The authors noted that in Indonesia, labor recruiters have organized themselves into trade associations in order to lobby for policy changes which would be favorable for them. In the Philippines, the number of registered recruitment agencies reached 700 in 1991. Most of these agencies specialize in a specific industry or sector such as the employment of domestic workers and entertainers.

35 *Ibid.*

36 Based on the interview with Dr. Rianto Adi, and the discussions with women migrant workers.

37 Kanlungan Centre Foundation, *Destination: Middle East (A Handbook for Filipino Women Domestic Workers)*, 1997, pp.31-32.

38 For a more comprehensive discussion of the impact of labor migration of women on their families and marital relationships, see Agano, 'Migrant Labor and the Filipino Family', 1995; Beltran, R. P., Samonte, E. L. and Walker, Sr. L. (1996), 'Filipino Women Migrant Workers: Effect on Family Life and Challenges for Intervention', in R. P. Beltran and G. F. Rodriguez (eds), *Filipino Women Migrant Workers: At The Crossroads and Beyond Beijing*, Giraffe Books, Quezon City, Philippines, pp.15-45.

39 *Ibid.*

40 The items in this list are not arranged in any specific order or ranking.

41 The items in this list are not arranged in any specific order or ranking.

42 For reference, see Agano, 'Migrant Labor and the Filipino Family', 1995; and Beltran *et al.,* 'Filipino Women Migrant Workers: Effects on Family Life and Challenges for Intervention', 1996.

43 Bohning, W. R. (1998), *SEAPAT Working Paper 1: The Impact of the Asian Crisis on Filipino Employment Prospects Abroad*, International Labor Organization Southeast Asia Multi-Disciplinary Advisory Team, *http://www.ilo.org.*

44 The term 'social capital' is used to refer to those stocks of social trust, norms and networks that people can draw upon to solve common problems. For further reading on the concept of social capital see Robert Putnam's essays, 'The Prosperous Community: Social Capital and Public Life', *The American Prospect*, vol.13, Spring 1993, pp.35-42; 'Bowling Alone: America's Declining Social Capital' *Journal of Democracy*, vol.6, no.1, January 1995, pp.65-78; and 'The Strange Disappearance of Civic America', *The American Prospect*, vol.24, Winter 1996.

45 Interview with Ricardo Casco, Philippine Overseas Employment Administration (POEA), Ortigas Avenue, Pasig City, Philippines, 13 October 1998.

46 The five NGOs are as follows: Friends of Filipino Migrant Workers (KAIBIGAN), Women in Development Foundation, Center for Overseas Workers, Zonta Club of Quezon City and the National Greening Movement.

47 Interviews with Ricardo Casco, and Susan Cabreros, POEA, Ortigas Avenue, Pasig City, 13 October 1998.

48 Interview with Nelsy H., Center for Indonesian Migrant Workers, Jakarta, Indonesia, 13 May 1998.

49 These observations are based on the researcher's discussions with members of NGOs, women migrant workers, researchers and academics.

50 Interview with Yayah Subariah, Sukabumi, West Java, Indonesia, 9 May 1998.

51 Cabilao, M. I . (1995), *Labor Migration: Issues for DFA Personnel in Servicing Filipino Migrant Workers*, Foreign Service Institute, Pasay City.

52 Lim and Oishi, 'International Labor Migration of Asian Women: Distinctive Characteristics and Policy Concerns', 1996, pp.98-99.

53 For example, the Vocational Training Centre owned by the Indonesian Overseas and Domestic Employment Agency (PJTKI).

54 Interviews with R. Casco and S. Cabreros, 13 October 1998.

References

Acharya, A., Dewitt, D. and Hernandez, C. (1995), 'Sustainable Development and Security in Southeast Asia: A Concept Paper', *CANCAPS Papier*, no. 6, August.

Agano, M. E. (1995), 'Migrant Labor and the Filipino Family', in A. E. Perez (ed.), *The Filipino Family: A Spectrum of Views and Issues*, University of the Philippines Office of Research Coordination, Quezon City, Philippines, pp. 79-96.

Alaggapa, M. (1987), *National Security in Developing States*, Aubur House, Massachusetts, pp. 2.

Azar, E. and Moon, C. (eds) (1991), *National Security in the Third World: The Management of Internal and External Threats*, Center for International Development and Conflict Management, Maryland.

Beltran, R. P., Samonte, E. L. and Walker, Sr. L. (1996), 'Filipino Women Migrant Workers: Effect on Family Life and Challenges for Intervention', in R. P. Beltran and G. F. Rodriguez (eds), *Filipino Women Migrant Workers: At The Crossroads. Beyond Beijing*, Giraffe Books, Quezon City, Philippines, pp. 15-45.

Bohning, W. R. (1998), *SEAPAT Working Paper 1: The Impact of the Asian Crisis on Filipino Employment Prospects Abroad*, International Labor Organization Southeast Asia Multi-Disciplinary Advisory Team.

Cabilao, M. I . (1995), *Labor Migration: Issues for DFA Personnel in Servicing Filipino Migrant Workers*, Foreign Service Institute, Pasay City.

Chant and Radcliffe (1992), 'Migration and Development: The Importance of Gender', in S. Chant (ed.), *Gender and Migration in Developing Countries*, Belhaven Press, London, pp. 1-29.

Cruz, V. P. and Paganoni, A. (1989), *Filipinas in Migration: Big Bills and Small Change*, Scalabrini Migration Center, Quezon City.

Hernandez, C. G. (1995), 'Philippine Foreign Policy in the Post-Cold War Era: Challenges, Opportunities and Prospects', *Philippine Foreign Policy and Regional Politics*, University of the Philippines Center for Integrative and Development Studies, Quezon City, pp. 40-41.

Hernandez, C. G. and Tigno, J. V. (1995), 'ASEAN Labor Migration: Implications for Regional Stability', *The Pacific Review*, vol. 8, no. 3, pp. 545.

Heyzer and Wee (1993), *Development*, vol. 1, pp. 37-40.

Human Development Network (1997), *Philippine Human Development Report*, Human Development Network and the United Nations Development Programme, Philippines, pp. 25.

Kanlungan Centre Foundation (1997), *Destination: Middle East (A Handbook for Filipino Women Domestic Workers)*, Kanlungan Centre Foundation, Quezon City, pp. 9.

Lim, L. L. and Oishi, N. (1996), 'International Labor Migration of Asian Women: Distinctive Characteristics and Policy Concerns', *Asian and Pacific Migration Journal*, vol. 5, no. 1, pp. 85.

O'Neill, H. (1997), 'Globalisation, Competitiveness and Human Security: Challenges for Development Policy and Institutional Change', *The European Journal of Development Research*, vol. 9, no .1, June, pp. 9.

Perez, A. E. and Patacsil, P. C. (compilers) (1998), *Philippine Migration Studies: An Annotated*

Bibliography, Philippine Migration Research Network, Quezon City.

Putnam, R. (1993a), 'The Prosperous Community: Social Capital and Public Life', *The American Prospect*, vol.13, Spring, pp. 35-42.

Putnam, R. (1995b), 'Bowling Alone: America's Declining Social Capital' *Journal of Democracy*, vol.6, no.1, January, pp. 65-78.

Putnam, R. (1996c), 'The Strange Disappearance of Civic America', *The American Prospect*, vol. 24, Winter.

Scalabrini Migration Center (1992), *Pre-Employment and Pre-Departure Services for Filipina Migrant Workers*, La Trobe University Regional Social Development Centre and International Social Service for Migrant Women Project for the International Labor Organization, April.

Torres, C. I. (1995), 'The New Overseas Employment Program: Effectively Managing the Labor Migration Process', *Development Research News*, vol. XIII, no. 3, May-June, pp. 10.

Chapter 5

Security Implications of the Economic Crisis for Indonesian Workers

Tubagus Feridhanusetyawan

Introduction

We are fortunate to have an opportunity to see more clearly the linkage between development and security in a country that has been in a deep total – economic, social, and political – crisis. Indonesia has been in deep crisis and the security implications of various adjustments for the country can be easily seen everywhere on a daily basis. From the macro-perspective, for example, the fall in output and employment, combined with the sharp increase in inflation, led to the decrease in real income, and then to the increase in poverty. From the micro-perspective, declining employment and real income led to serious job and income insecurity at the household level, and a drastic decline of expenditure in terms of quality and quantity. Some families had to withdraw their children from school and sent them to the streets in order to seek additional family income. Combined with the political turmoil, the breakdown in law and order, the loss of public confidence in the military and the government, and other non-economic factors, the declining real income at the macro-aggregate and micro-individual levels led to various acts of crime and public violence. It comes as no surprise, therefore, that chaotic total crisis accompanied by massive rioting, looting, killing, and other forms of mass violence characterized the year 1998 in Indonesia.

Unfortunately, however, we are trying to shoot a moving target. Everything is changing very rapidly since the crisis so that it is difficult to identify the focus of development and security issues at a certain point in time. The relation between economic development and security is a dynamic concept that changes over time depending on the changes of the contributing factors – economic, social, and political – to security. Most everything has changed drastically in Indonesia during the last three years and many of the development and security issues that were crucial in the beginning of the crisis in mid-1997 are no longer relevant at present. Combined with great uncertainty, it is hard to provide a comprehensive picture of the linkage between development and security and even more difficult to predict what would happen in the future.

Given all of these constraints this chapter attempts to analyze the linkage between economic development, economic crisis, and security by looking at the employment and income of Indonesian workers. Its objective is to analyze the security implications of the economic crisis for Indonesian workers by focusing on employment and income adjustments both at the national and the individual level. The economic crisis led to various drastic and painful adjustments in the society, declining employment and real income, and combined with other factors such as political turmoil, the lack of social safety nets, and others, led to various security issues both at the individual and national levels. This study adopts a broad definition of human security, where security means freedom from any threat. On this basis, it analyzes how various adjustments due to the economic crisis have become security threats to Indonesian workers.

To analyze the impact of the crisis on worker's security, this study combines two approaches, the macro-aggregate or national level and the micro-individual or worker level. This dual approach is useful in understanding how the crisis has affected employment and income at the national level and changed the pattern of income and expenditure at the individual or family level. Furthermore, this two-level approach directly links the declining employment or income with workers' security at the national and personal levels. Consistent with this conceptual framework, this study utilizes two kinds of data: secondary data at the national level and primary data from field surveys at the individual level. This study used field surveys that consist of both in-depth interviews and questionnaire surveys to capture the changing patterns of income and expenditure and the perception of individual workers on security.

The first section of this chapter presents the conceptual framework of the linkage between economic crisis and security through employment and income adjustments both at the macro-national level and the micro-individual level. The second section presents the macro-perspective of the analysis by discussing macro-economic conditions during the crisis and then presents various adjustments in employment and income at the macro-national level and other problems that have some impact on the well being of Indonesian workers. Having discussed and analyzed how the economic crisis is transmitted to employment and income problems at the macro-level, the third section presents the security implications of the crisis at the level of the individual worker. Consistent with the general macro-micro approach adopted in this study, the security implications of the crisis for Indonesian workers are also viewed from the macro- and the micro-perspectives. It concludes with a summary and some policy implications.

From Economic Crisis to Security: The Framework

There are several clarifications to be made before we move to a further discussion on security. The first is the scope and the framework of the analysis where economic crisis is treated as the cause and security or insecurity as the effect. It should be realized that the relation between economic performance and security could not be narrowly viewed as a simple and one-way cause and effect relationship. They in fact affect one another through various processes, involving various agents and institutions, and taking place in different points in time. The Indonesian case clearly shows how deteriorating economic conditions during the economic crisis led to various social and economic problems, and eventually to various security problems. But security problems, such as riots, higher crime rate, and others reduced the confidence in the economy and led to deteriorating economic performance. Even at the micro-level, the loss of job security and increased uncertainty in the labor market could lead to declining personal consumption at the individual level that in turn could lead to lower aggregate demand at the national level. Therefore, to put the problem in a proper perspective, the analysis in this study should not be treated as a one-sided approach in analyzing security issues.

The second clarification is the definition of security adopted in this study. This study uses a broad definition of human security both at the personal or individual level and the state or national level. Mitchell *et. al*, explore contemporary definitions of security where the broadest definition of human security could be defined as 'the freedom from threat'.[1] The United Nations Development Programme (UNDP) Report provides a more specific definition where human security is defined as 'enabling people to exercise their choice safely and freely'—and that they can 'relatively be confident that the opportunities they have today are not totally lost tomorrow'.[2] Human security is broken down according to the following dimensions: people are assured of basic income, have economic security, food, health, environmental, personal, communal, and political security.[3] This study focuses more on the economic dimension of this broader definition of human security, by analyzing the decline in employment and income that affect Indonesian workers.

Another crucial dimension of security in the definition above is time, which means that security should be seen as a dynamic concept where the variables or factors affecting security change over time. Following this argument, the security of Indonesian workers would also be a dynamic concept. For example, on the one hand the decrease in income and employment opportunities would lead to a decrease in worker's security in the short run. But on the other hand, the increase in competitiveness of Indonesian labor because of the correction in real wages would increase worker's security in the longer run due to increasing exports.

In this regard, it is also worth noting that the security issues related to employment and income of Indonesian workers have changed rapidly because of the drastic changes in overall economic conditions. During the boom times, the tightening of the labor market where real wages increased faster than labor productivity was a major concern because it could lead to a deterioration in the competitiveness of Indonesian labor-intensive industries. Problems related to rapid urbanization were serious, and the provision of urban employment was crucial in absorbing labor from the rapidly shrinking agricultural sectors. Declining rural income was another major concern as the contribution of the agricultural sector in the economy diminished. But in less than two years, security concerns had changed. The rural and agricultural sectors had been considered as the natural safety net for the economy as people moved back to the rural areas. The tightening labor market suddenly became the loosening market, so that the real issue was no longer the rapid increase in real wage, but the sudden collapse of real wage and purchasing power.

To discuss security issues related to employment and income as a set of dynamic rather than static relationships and processes, there are several issues that need to be clarified. First, who is the stakeholder of security, or who is/are at stake in discussing security? Second, what form or what kind of security issues are covered, and what kinds of contributing variables or parameters are crucial? Third, what period of time is considered, and why does this time dimension matter? To cover all of those issues, the following discussion presents the transmission from the economic crisis to employment and income problems, and then to security. Figure 5.1 presents the conceptual framework used in this study to channel the transmission from the collapse of the economy, to various adjustments in the economy and society, to various labor-related problems at the individual or family level as well as the national level, and then to security issues.

The chart begins by showing several characteristics of the Indonesian economic crisis, namely, high inflation and sharp depreciation from the monetary side, falling government revenue from the fiscal side, and falling output and employment from the real side of the economy as a whole. These drastic changes in these macro-economic conditions are translated into declining employment and income through various channels of transmissions, both at the micro-household level and at the macro-aggregate or at the national level.[4]

The first channel of transmission is the process of adjustment in the output and the labor market. This process is characterized by falling employment in the formal, urban, and modern sector, and a sharp decline in overall real wages and labor productivity. The second transmission is through the adjustment in the household income and expenditure due to the sharp decline in family or individual real income. The third channel of transmission is through the drastic adjustments in government budgets or the changing patterns of government revenue and expenditure. The Indonesian case has shown that bad responses from the government in dealing with the crisis have led to further deterioration of economic conditions. In other words, the response to the crisis itself matters in characterizing the nature of the real impact of the crisis. In fact, factors that have contributed to the social impact of the crisis could also be classified into two groups: the economic crisis itself and the bad policies by the government in responding to the crisis.

Massive real sector contraction, high inflation, and excessive depreciation in the economy would lead to drastic changes in employment and income, both at the individual or family level and the aggregate or national level. At the national level, the adjustments take the form of massive layoffs, increase in unemployment, movement of labor between sectors, regions, and even countries, lower worker productivity, and others. It is important to note that the nature of the markets and the nature of the adjustments that take place matter in analyzing worker's security. For example, a flexible labor market, where adjustments take place in the form of a sharp reduction in real wages and a small increase in unemployment lead to different security issues compared with a sticky market that lead to a large increase in unemployment and a small decline in wages. At the individual level, adjustment in employment and income could be in the form of loss of jobs, declining family real income, adjustments in family expenditure, working longer hours for less purchasing power, and even forcing children to work to seek additional income. Workers might have to sell their assets to cope with increasing consumption, especially food.

But the transmission from these drastic adjustments in employment and income to various acts of public violence that took place in Indonesia in 1998 depended on the contribution of other non-economic factors. The economic factor seems to be a necessary but not sufficient condition for all of this violence to occur. It is a combination of economic deterioration, political turmoil and transition, fights among

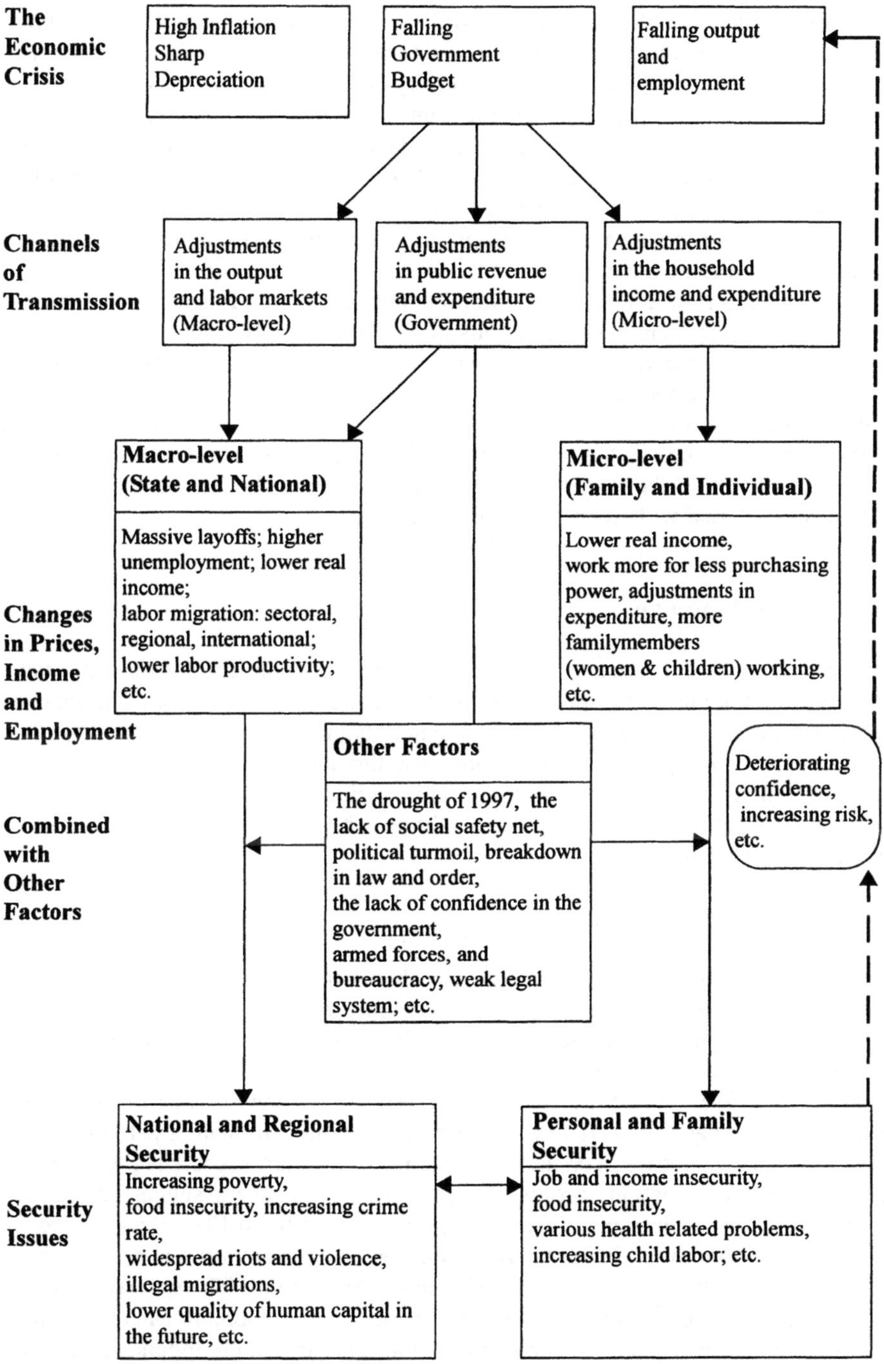

Figure 5.1 From Economic Crisis to Security Issues: The Conceptual Framework

the political elite, breakdown in law and order, loss of confidence in the government and the military, and other factors that mixed together and turned into mass violence. In this regard, the contributing factor of security is like a mix of various elements and processes that given a certain mixture, the right chemistry, and supportive temperature could explode like a bomb. The government in fact could play a crucial role in making or preventing some economic adjustments to become a threat or a security problem for the society. Serious security implications of massive layoffs, for example, could be prevented if the social safety net programs work effectively to provide a cushion for those who become unemployed.

With the contribution of various non-economic factors, drastic adjustments in income and employment become serious threats and security issues for Indonesian workers. At the individual level, lower real income leads to job and income insecurity. For the poor, it could turn into serious food insecurity. At the national level, the increase in poverty, food insecurity, riots and public violence become serious security issues in the short run. In the longer run, the security issues for Indonesian workers at the macro-level ranges from lower quality of human capital and problems associated with lower labor productivity.

The Macro-Perspective

This section analyzes the security implications of the economic crisis for Indonesian workers from the macro-perspective at the national or aggregate level. The focus is on the adjustment in the labor market at the national level, such as the employment, unemployment, underemployment, income, and the implication of these adjustments for the well being of Indonesian workers. This section also covers the implication of these employment and income adjustments for poverty, food security, labor migration, and other social issues.

Macro-economic Background

The course of the Indonesian economic crisis shows that the currency crisis in August 1997 soon turned into a serious financial and monetary crisis and then by December 1997, to a whole scale economic crisis. Combined with various political misfortunes, it finally led to the whole country's total – economic, political, and social – crisis by the middle of 1998. While the Indonesian crisis can be viewed as part of the Asian crisis in 1997, it has followed since 1998 a different and worsening path compared with other Asian countries in crisis. All economic indicators, especially the exchange rate depreciation, inflation, economic contraction, and others suggested that the Indonesian crisis has been much worse since January 1998. In 1997, the shock to the Indonesian economy was similar to what happened in other countries in crisis, namely a large capital flight out of the region. But since December 1997, especially January 1998 there was another specific domestic shock to the economy in the form of excessive monetary expansion. But one might also argue that the Indonesian crisis is in fact similar to or just an extreme case of the Asian crisis – where political misfortunes and loss of confidence found their way to create additional shocks to the economy. Bearing this in mind, the Indonesian crisis can be classified into three stages, based on the years when it took place: 1997, 1998, and 1999. The year 1997 was the time when the deteriorating Indonesian economic indicators suggested that Indonesia's crisis was part of the Asian crisis. The year 1998 was the year of the Indonesian total crisis and marked the difference between the Indonesian crisis and the crisis in other Asian countries. Finally, the year 1999 can be seen hopefully, as the starting year for economic recovery.

The economy plunged into deep recession in 1998 with the overall growth at minus 13.7 per cent that was very serious compared with less than five per cent contraction during the difficult times in the 1960s. The worst contraction was in the construction sector (-39.8 per cent), followed by the financial sector (-26.7 per cent), and trade, hotel, and restaurant (-18.9 per cent). Other sectors that experienced large contractions were manufacturing (-12.9 per cent) and transport and communication (-12.8 per cent). Mining and other services sectors experienced a contraction by around 4.5 per cent. The agricultural and utility sectors still experienced positive growth at around 0.2 and 3.7 per cent, respectively. The more robust performance of resource-based sectors also meant that the share of agriculture in the total gross domestic product (GDP) rose for the first time after 30 years from 16.1 per cent in 1997 to close to 18 per cent in 1998. The share of the mining sector also increased from 9.5 per cent in 1997, to 11.4 per cent in 1998. The share of industry continued to increase from 25.6 per cent in 1997, to 27 per cent in 1998 due to the growth from oil refining (which increases as increased refining is done domestically to save foreign exchange) and Liquified Natural Gas (LNG).

The sharp depreciation of the exchange rate obviously led to the collapse of the non-traded, import-dependent, and modern sectors. Those export oriented, natural resource-based, and labor-intensive sectors seemed to survive the crisis, even though their export performance has been disappointing so far. The crisis has moved resources from the non-traded such as construction, to the traded sectors, and from modern and highly import-dependent sectors to the traditional ones such as agriculture, mining, and forestry.

If one looks at the expenditure side of growth, the contraction has been mostly caused by a collapse in demand with a severe contraction experienced by consumer demand and investment. It is estimated that per capita national income (based on 1999 prices) declined from around US$1,055 in 1997 to around US$460 in 1998 (based on 13 per cent economic contraction and the average exchange rate of Rp10,000/US$). While GDP per capita decreased by more than 50 per cent, the decline in private consumption was only around 2.9 per cent, smaller than the decrease in government expenditure at more than 14 per cent. This suggests that people were consuming their savings and maintaining their expenditures during the crisis.

The effect of the economic crisis on inflation has been dramatic. Prior to the crisis, inflation was maintained below ten per cent and in fact, there were two months in the first half of 1997 when there was a fall in the consumer price index (CPI) or a deflation. The rise in prices was already evident in the second half of 1997, with the CPI increasing by 8.51 per cent, causing the inflation for 1997 to reach 11 per cent. Inflation rates continued to rise rapidly in the first half of 1998, reaching a record 12.8 per cent in February alone. Cumulative inflation reached more than 40 per cent for the first five months of 1998, and then reached 70 per cent in September 1998. Because of the increasing monetary stability in October and November 1998, the inflation was under control in the fourth quarter of 1998 so that the final cumulative inflation in 1998 was 77.6 per cent.

Table 5.1 The Growth of the Gross Domestic Product, 1996-98

Classification	1996	1997	1998
By Sector			
Agriculture, Forestry and Fishery	3.0	0.9	0.2
Mining and Quarrying	5.8	2.2	-4.2
Manufacturing Industry	11.6	6.4	-12.9
Electricity, Gas, and Water Supply	12.8	13.6	3.7
Construction	12.8	6.4	-39.7
Trade, Hotel, and Restaurant	8.0	6.0	-19.0
Transport and Communication	8.7	8.3	-12.8
Financial, Ownership, and Buss. Services	8.8	3.6	-26.7
Services	3.4	2.8	-4.7
By Expenditure			
Private Consumption	10.9	5.5	-2.9
Government Consumption	2.7	0.1	-14.4
Gross Domestic Fixed Capital Formation	14.5	8.6	-40.9
Change in Stock	-76.1	94.9	-137.1
Export of Goods and Services	7.6	7.8	10.6
Less : Import of Goods and Services	6.9	14.7	-5.4
Gross Domestic Product	8.0	4.7	-13.7

Source: Central Board of Statistics.

The increase in prices of traded commodities, especially food, dominated the increase in Consumer Price Indexes in 1998. The prices of foodstuff, including cereals and roots, preserved fish, bean, and nuts increased by more than 118 per cent. Clothing prices increased by 98.7 per cent in 1998, followed by health commodities and services that increased by 86.1 per cent. Housing prices increased by 47.5 per cent and housing equipment increased by more than 126 per cent. This means that the prices of non-traded components of housing, such as land have decreased very substantially.

The growth rates of liquidity and money supply increased very dramatically in the first half of 1998. It was precisely during this period that the rush on banks forced Bank Indonesia as the lender of the last resort to inject liquidity support to prevent a collapse of the banking system. As a result, money in circulation increased by around 60 per cent in the first six months of 1998 (100 per cent growth from November 1997). The growth rate of M1 (currency and demand deposits) also continued to be high at 40 per cent and the growth rate of M2 (M1 and time deposits) at around 60 per cent. Despite the fact that Indonesia is on an International Monetary Fund (IMF) program, reserve money growth continued to be high at 47 per cent indicating that there continued to be a lot of liquidity in the economy.

Table 5.2 Selected Monetary Indicators

	1996	1997	1998
Inflation (per cent year-on-year)			
General CPI	5.9	11.6	77.6
Food	6.1	19.9	118.4
Housing	4.8	6.2	47.5
Clothing	5.9	7.9	98.7
Interest rate (per cent)			
1 M0. SBI (highest rate)	13.4	17.7	69.5
1 M0. SBI (lowest rate)	12.3	8.2	35.4
Growth of money supply (per cent year-on-year)			
M0	33.1	34.0	63.0
M1	21.7	22.2	29.2
M2	30.5	23.2	62.3
Exchange rate (average level) Rp/US$)			
July	2,334	2,506	14,230
December	2,355	4,628	7,485

Source: Bank of Indonesia, various publications.

The central bank and the IMF continued to maintain a high interest rate environment to prevent the money supply from exploding in 1998. The peak of the interest rate was in August 1998 when the interest of Bank Indonesia Certificate was up to around 70 per cent. Without any significant move in banking restructuring, the central bank had to pump liquidity into the nearly collapsed banks and to provide blanket guarantee to all depositors to prevent a bank run. The money then flowed from the bad banks to the good ones and then went back to the central bank.[5] This circulation of money would continue without any asset liquidation mechanism in place to separate bad and good assets, as well as good and bad banks. The establishment of such mechanism, which should consist of special court settlements, bankruptcy laws, independent auditing processes, and other mechanisms is crucial in breaking and escaping from this vicious circle. This mechanism requires a massive amount of work that is not only very technical and difficult, but also requires a supportive political climate. Unfortunately, the required political support would be hard to find during the year of political uncertainty in 1998 and 1999.

The high interest rate environment had killed the stock market by declining both stock prices and volume of transaction. The volume of transaction dropped from around US$5 billion in July 1997 to slightly more than US$100 million in August 1998. The Jakarta Composite Stock Price index decreased by around 50 per cent 721 in July 1997 to around 350 in August 1998. The stock price index remained at around the 400 level in early 1999.

The prolonged economic crisis, especially the high interest rate environment and the severe crisis of confidence has damaged the banking sector. The non-performing loan levels had shot up to around 50 per cent by mid 1998[6] with lending rates kept at above 35 per cent. Banks with a high proportion of US$ loans on their loan portfolio had feared the worst as most of those bank customers borrowed unhedged in US dollars. Banks had not only been hit on their asset side, but also on the liability side. Deposits were also under pressure as concerns over the health of national private banks had led to sporadic bank runs causing a large amount of deposits to shift from national private banks to either state or government banks or foreign banks. As a result, banks were under considerable pressure to maintain high deposit rates to keep their third-party liabilities while struggling to keep earnings on loans flowing. On the income statement side, this translates into negative interest spreads and a larger loan loss provision that further resulted in operating losses. The bottom line is a slowly depleting capital adequacy ratio.

Since December 1997 many foreign suppliers no longer trust most banks in Indonesia, including some of the state banks to open and honor the letter of credit (L/C). Suppliers are asking foreign banks to 'confirm' such L/C from domestic banks. Foreign banks are reluctant to take L/C issued by Indonesian banks fearing that the latter will be unable to service their commitments. The number of non-credible banks has also grown from a few private banks at the beginning of the crisis to most private banks including large state banks as the crisis unfolded. But with the provision of a blanket guarantee by the central bank for all depositors in all amounts in all domestic banks, the banking system became practically centralized, with the central bank functioning both as the central bank and as a commercial bank.

The exchange rates depreciated from Rp2,400/US$ before the crisis in July 1997 to Rp15,000/US$ in July 1998 and around Rp9,000/US$ in September 1998. The depreciation of the exchange rates (up to 600 per cent at the bottom) was mainly caused by the excessive monetary expansion to save the banking system from collapsing. Up to December 1997, the depreciation of the Rupiah was comparable to the movement of other currencies in Southeast Asia. But because of the excessive printing of money in January and February 1998 and again in May 1998 after the riots, the depreciation of the Rupiah has dramatically deviated from the common patterns of the other Southeast Asian currencies. Monetary stabilization, especially the stable growth of the base money in the third and fourth quarter of 1998 led to a stronger Rupiah at around Rp7,500/US$. But again, the strengthening of the Rupiah seems to be a temporary phenomenon because of the relatively weak and uncertain economic fundamentals throughout 1998-99. In early 1999, the Rupiah seemed to stabilize at around Rp7,500-8,000/US$.

In summary, the Indonesian economic collapse is characterized by sharp contraction in the real sector of the economy, the movement of resource from non-traded to traded sectors, from import dependent to export oriented industries, and from modern to traditional sectors. On the monetary side, excessive monetary expansion to bail out banks led to hyperinflation and drastic currency depreciation. With the lack of confidence in the economy, partly because of a non-supportive political climate, the interest rate was high. This led to a further deterioration of the bank balance sheet and to corporate and economic insolvency. The collapse of the financial system eventually led to the fall in real sectors leading to the fall in output, the decrease in employment, and a large government budget deficit. While Indonesia shares similar problems with other Asian countries in crisis such as in the problem of credit crunch and huge foreign debt, there are other problems that made the Indonesian case worse. In addition to the political turmoil, the explosive monetary expansion, high inflation, and massive Rupiah depreciation have characterized the Indonesian case that unfortunately made its crisis the worst among those experienced by other Asian countries in crisis.

Labor Force, Employment, and Unemployment

The Indonesian labor market from 1990 to 1996 was characterized by rapid labor market transformation followed by labor market tightening and increasing real wages. Labor moved from informal to formal sectors, from rural to urban, from primary sectors such as agriculture to modern sectors such as construction, manufacturing, and services. The engine of growth for labor market tightening was broad based growth in all sectors, especially the labor intensive manufacturing sector.[7] The number of working age population increased by 2.2 per cent annually from 136 million in 1990 to 154 million in 1996. A strong pattern of urbanization can be seen by the 5.8 per cent annual growth of urban working age population from 1986 to 1996, compared with 0.7 per cent in rural areas. During the boom period 1990-96, the number of labor force in urban areas increased by 7.5 per cent annually, compared to 0.8 per cent in rural areas. The labor force participation rate (LFPR)[8] has also been relatively constant at around 60 per cent in rural areas and has been generally higher than that in urban areas.

The crisis has increased the growth of the female labor force and employment. Before the crisis, from 1990 to 1996, the female labor force grew at around 2.3 per cent annually. During the crisis in 1997-98 it grew by 4.8 per cent. The growth of female employment also increased from 1.8 annually before the crisis to 4.2 per cent during 1997-98. The number of the male labor force, however, has been relatively constant before and during the crisis. The fact that the crisis has increased the labor force participation rates for women suggests an increasing employment opportunity for women. But it could also mean that the crisis has forced women to involuntarily participate and work in the labor market to provide an additional income for the houschold.

The labor market in Indonesia is dominated by the informal sector where there is no precise measure for reduction in employment. Measuring employment reduction in the informal sector is almost impossible because self-employed, temporary, and family workers dominate this sector. The formal sector accounted for only around 35 per cent of the total employment in 1996, but there is no reliable data to measure the reduction in employment or layoffs during the crisis. This is so because firms are not strictly required to report to the Department of Manpower in the case of layoffs. One quick but rather dirty way to predict the number of employment reduction is by using employment elasticity. Feridhanusetyawan estimated that the reduction in economic growth by minus 13 per cent in 1998 would lead to around three million reduction in the total employment and four million reduction in formal employment. This implicitly means that around one million of the workers who lost their jobs in the formal sector went to the informal sector.[9] Based on a similar methodology, International Labor Organization (ILO) predicted that around 5.4 million workers would lose their jobs in 1998.[10]

Table 5.3 Labor Force in Indonesia, 1990-98

	Number (million)					Growth (%)	
	1990	1997[b]	1998[b]	1997[b]	1998[b]	1990-96	1997-98
Working age population	135.7	135.1	138.6	100.0	100.0	2.2	2.6
Rural	94.2	81.7	82.5	60.5	59.5	0.4	0.9
Urban	41.5	53.4	56.1	39.5	40.5	5.6	5.1
Labor Force	77.8	89.6	92.7	100.0	100.0	2.4	3.5
Rural	58.3	57.7	59.3	64.4	64.0	0.5	2.9
Urban	19.5	31.9	33.4	35.6	36.0	7.3	4.7
Female	30.2	34.3	36.0	100.0	100.0	2.3	4.8
Male	47.6	55.3	56.8	100.0	100.0	2.5	2.7
Employment (Working population)							
Total	75.9	85.4	87.7	95.3	94.5	2.0	2.7
Rural	57.6	56.1	57.4	97.2	96.7	0.1	2.3
Urban	18.3	29.4	30.3	92.0	90.7	6.9	3.2
Female	29.4	32.4	33.8	94.4	93.9	1.8	4.2
Male	46.4	53.0	53.9	95.9	95.0	2.2	1.7
People looking for work[a]	2.0	4.2	5.1	4.7	5.5	13.6	20.6
People not in the labor force	57.9	45.5	41.7	33.7	33.1	1.8	0.8

[a]Open unemployment, some changes in definition in 1994.
[b]Population of age 15 and above.

Source: Central Board of Statistics, *Sakernas*, various years.

Another estimate of employment reduction involves the decrease in the formal sector wage employment. The results of the *Sakernas* 1998 data show that the formal employment decreased by 4.7 per cent from 1997 to 1998, while it grew by 5.5 per cent annually during 1990-96 before the crisis.[11] The number of employment in the formal sector—this includes both employees and employers with permanent employees—decreased from 31.7 million in 1997 to 30.3 million in 1998, suggesting that around 1.4 million people left the formal sector during the crisis. At the same time, the number of informal sector employment increased from 53.7 million in 1997 to 57.3 million in 1998, suggesting that the informal sector absorbed an additional 3.6 million people during the crisis.

The data from the national labor market show that the crisis has affected male workers more than females. More than 90 per cent of the total 1.4 million people who were displaced from the formal sector in 1998 were in fact male. Such is not surprising since the economic sector that suffered the most from the crisis had been the male-dominated construction sector. On the contrary, sectors that had survived well during the crisis were the female-dominated labor-intensive export-oriented sectors such as textile, garment, and footwear industries.

However, the decrease in employment is clearly an underestimate of the number of worker displacement, because some displaced workers would soon find other jobs and accounted as fully employed. The *Sakernas* data indicated that there were around 4.2 million cases of worker displacement in August 1997-98, and the fact that employment reduction was only 1.4 million suggests that around 2.8 million workers found other jobs after being displaced. Among the 4.2 million displaced workers in 1997-98, around 1.2 million workers were recorded as quitting their jobs. It is also estimated that among 4.2 million workers who lost their jobs, around one million people were accounted from the informal sector.

Unemployment rate is generally low in Indonesia because people are considered employed even when they work only for one hour a week. In 1996, open unemployment was almost five per cent and was dominated by the unemployed young people. The unemployment rate was the highest among the age group 15-24 (around 13 per cent) when secondary school graduates enter the job market. Unemployment among those who are 30 years or older is generally not significant in Indonesia. Another characteristic of unemployment in Indonesia is urban unemployment. While urban areas accounted for only 30 per cent of the total employment, urban unemployment accounted for almost 60 per cent of unemployment.[12] Manning and Jayasuriya[13] indicated that there has been increasing urban unemployment among the youth in the 1990s. According to Agrawal, however, unemployment in Indonesia is not a serious problem.[14] First, those unemployed are mainly young people who enter the job market for the first time. Second, the duration of unemployment is usually short – an indication of a relatively flexible labor market in Indonesia. While unemployment might not be significant, the under-employment is severe. The definition of under-employment in Indonesia is working for less than 35 hours a week. Under this definition, 35 per cent of Indonesian workers were under-employed in 1996. Under-employment in rural areas has been much higher than in urban areas. Because of the seasonal nature of agricultural work, around 45 per cent of workers in the rural areas worked less than 35 hours a week compared with around 21 per cent in the urban areas.

The crisis has increased the number of unemployed, but the increase is smaller than originally predicted. Results from the *Sakernas* data show that total unemployment rate increased from 4.7 per cent in 1997, to 5.5 per cent in 1998. The preliminary result of the *Susenas* data shows a similar result – unemployment increased from 5.0 in 1997 to 6.8 in 1998.[15] The government, through the Minister of Manpower, cautioned several times that unemployment was expected to reach around 15 to 20 million people in 1998, but this was clearly an overestimate.[16] The more reliable official estimates of unemployment in 1998 by the Ministry of Manpower and National Planning Agency (BAPPENAS) put it at around 14.8 per cent (13.7 million) and 13.6 per cent (12.4 million), respectively. The special task force of the ILO[17] estimated that open unemployment rate in 1998 would be around ten per cent, or 9.3 million people.

Table 5.4 Unemployment Rates: Before and After the Crisis

Classification	August 97		August 98		%
	Number	%	Number	%	Change
	(million)		(million)		
Urban	2.6	8.1	3.1	9.3	15.0
Rural	1.7	2.8	2.1	3.3	16.9
Male	2.3	4.1	2.9	5.0	22.5
Female	2.0	5.6	2.2	6.1	8.5
Total	4.3	4.7	5.1	5.4	16.2

Source: Central Board of Statistics, *Sakernas,* 1997-98.

The *Sakernas* data results show that overall open unemployment rate increased by 16 per cent, from around 4.7 per cent in 1997, to 5.4 per cent in 1998. Moreover, the crisis had hurt the male more than the female worker. The unemployment rate among males increased from 4.1 per cent in 1997 to 5.0 per cent (22.5 per cent increase) while that of the females increased from 5.6 to 6.1 (or 8.5 per cent increase). This result was previously predicted because the economic sectors that have suffered the most from the crisis, especially construction have a larger number of male workers. On the contrary, labor intensive and export-oriented industries that have survived the crisis due to their export orientation employ more female workers.

In Indonesia's statistics, open unemployment is defined as 'working for less than one hour a week and at the same time looking for a job'. When real income is shrinking as a result of stagflation in a country where there is no unemployment insurance and social security, people cannot afford to be unemployed. So, when some people work for more than an hour a week – for two hours for example, either in the formal or informal sector a week before the survey was conducted – these people were not counted as unemployed.

While the number of unemployed is likely to be smaller than the previously expected number, it does not mean that there are no serious layoffs or employment reductions in the labor market. Small increases in unemployment rates at the aggregate or average level clearly show that those who lost their jobs in one sector have found another job or have been absorbed by other sectors' employment. Economic adjustments caused by the crisis have led to both booming and shrinking sectors and industries. Many displaced workers from the shrinking sectors have been forced to work in other industries or in the informal sector. Because the labor market in Indonesia has been flexible, real wages would easily adjust to the changing supply and demand conditions. These smaller-than-expected unemployment figures once again show the flexibility of the Indonesian labor market and the large reduction in real wages that it has to bear as a result of the crisis. In other words, the price of this smaller-than-expected unemployment rate is a sharp correction in real wages.

Preliminary results of the *Susenas* data show that the majority of the unemployed labor force consists of those who just recently entered the job market. Around 79 per cent of female and 68 per cent of male unemployed consist of those who had never worked before. There is no significant difference between rural and urban areas on this issue and these data confirm the reality that young people have dominated the composition of unemployment in Indonesia. In terms of education, preliminary *Susenas* data suggest that the increase in unemployment is among those with higher education. The percentage of unemployed people with high school education or above increased from 1997 to 1998, while those with education lower than high school in fact decreased at the same period. These results support the notion that only those who have higher income could survive and afford to be unemployed and their unemployment spell could be longer.

The results from the *Sakernas* data show that the number of underemployed increased from 21 per cent to 24 per cent in urban areas and from 44 per cent to 47 per cent in rural areas. The larger increase in the urban areas (20 per cent) compared with that in the rural areas (10 per cent) reflects the fact that urban areas have been hit harder during the crisis. But this is also due to the fact that formal employment is much larger in urban areas and the decrease in formal employment would force those who lost their jobs to work less than 35 hours a week in the informal sector. The increasing number of underemployed during the crisis appeared for both male and female workers. But it is important to note that similar to other countries, the Indonesian labor market is characterized by a high underemployment rate even during the economic boom period in the early 1990s. During the last decade of this period, the relation between economic growth and underemployment was not really clear. While high economic growth in 1990-96 significantly reduced unemployment especially in the formal sector, the underemployment rate had always been high. Therefore, the increase in underemployment from around 35 per cent before the crisis, to around 39 per cent overall during the crisis can not be seen as a large adjustment.

Because of the seasonal nature of agricultural work, underemployment in rural areas is generally much larger than in urban areas. Around 45 per cent of workers in rural areas work less than 35 hours a week, compared with around 21 per cent in urban areas in 1996. After the crisis, reduction in employment opportunities might have reduced the number of working hours and increased underemployment. However, a sharp reduction in real wages and income might have forced people to work more hours, and therefore, could even reduce the number of underemployment.

The Changing Structure of the Labor Market

The crisis has reversed the formalization of the labor market from 1990 to 1996 into the process of informalization during the crisis period from 1997 to 1998. The share of the informal sector in general increased from 63.3 per cent to 65.4 per cent. This 6.9 per cent annual increase during the crisis was much larger than the annual growth of the informal sector at around half a per cent for the last decade. At the same time, the growth of formal sector employment declined by 4.4 per cent. The fact that total employment grew by 2.7 per cent from 1997-98, higher than the annual rate at around 2.0 per cent before the crisis, was in fact due to the sharp increase in informal employment.

The informalization of labor has been very strong both in the urban and rural areas, although stronger in the urban areas. Prior to the crisis, during 1990-96, people were leaving the informal sectors at the rate of 2.9 per cent in the urban areas. The trend shifted sharply during 1997-98, where there was a substantial growth of 10.3 per cent going into informal sectors. A similar trend happened in the rural areas, not as salient but nevertheless, quite significant. During 1990-96, informal sector employment declined by around one per cent annually. Following the crisis, the growth of the informal sector in the rural areas increased to 5.8 per cent. Meanwhile, formal sector employment in both urban and rural areas contracted by 2.0 per cent and 7.2 per cent, respectively. In the urban sector, the increase is more salient where the informal sector employment grew by 10.3 per cent from 1997 to 1998.

Table 5.5 Employment Status of Indonesian Workers, 1990-98

	Number(million)			%			Growth (%)	
	1990	1997*	1998*	1990	1997*	1998*	1990-96	1997-98
Total	75.9	85.4	87.7	100	100	100	2	2.7
Formal	21.7	31.7	30.3	28.6	37.2	34.6	5.5	-4.4
Employer with permanent employee	0.6	1.5	1.5	0.8	1.7	1.7	11.7	4.1
Employee	21.1	30.3	28.8	27.8	35.5	32.9	5.3	-4.9
Informal	54.2	53.7	57.3	71.4	62.8	65.4	0.4	6.9
Self-employed with no employee	14.9	19.9	20.5	19.7	23.3	23.4	3.4	3.3
Self-employed with temporary or family worker	17.9	18	19.7	23.6	21.1	22.5	2.9	9.5
Family worker	21.3	15.8	17.1	28.1	18.5	19.5	-4.9	8.3
Female	29.4	32.4	33.8	100	100	100	1.8	4.2
Formal	6.7	9.7	9.6	22.8	29.8	28.5	5.1	-0.4
Informal	22.7	22.7	24.2	77.2	70.2	71.5	0.6	6.2
Male	46.4	53	53.9	100	100	100	2.2	1.7
Formal	14.9	22.1	20.7	32.2	41.7	38.4	5.7	-6.2
Informal	31.5	30.9	33.2	67.8	58.3	61.6	0.3	7.3
Rural	57.6	56.1	57.4	100	100	100	0.1	2.3
Formal	11.5	14.9	13.9	20.0	26.7	24.2	3.7	-7.2
Informal	46.1	41.1	43.5	80.0	73.3	75.8	-0.9	5.8
Urban	18.3	29.4	30.3	100	100	100	6.9	3.2
Formal	10.2	16.8	16.5	55.6	57.2	54.3	7.4	-2
Informal	8.1	12.6	13.9	44.4	42.8	45.7	-2.9	10.3

*Population of age 15 and above

Source: Central Board of Statistics, *Sakernas*, various years.

By looking at employment status within the informal sector, the crisis has reduced the proportion of the self-employed with no employee and increased the share of family workers. The increasing number of employment in the informal sectors is expected, but the fact that the number of family workers increased significantly during the crisis suggests that people look for jobs within their family unit as part of the coping mechanism to survive the crisis. It is worth mentioning that the number of women working as family workers increased more significantly than that of the men during the crisis. From 1986 to 1996 before the crisis, the number of female family workers decreased by 1.8 per cent annually. This reflects greater opportunities for women working in the labor market outside the family. But from 1997 to 1998, the number of female family workers increased by 6.5 per cent.

There has been a rapid movement of labor out of the agricultural sector for the last seven years from 1990 to 1996 before the crisis hit. Agricultural employment declined rapidly from 56 per cent of total employment in 1990 to around 44 per cent in 1996. The number of employment in the manufacturing sector increased from around eight per cent in 1990 to almost 13 per cent in 1996. The construction sector has absorbed a large proportion of unskilled labor moving out from the agricultural sector as employment in the construction sector grew by almost 11 per cent a year from 1990 to 1996. The share of the trade, restaurant, and hotel sectors increased sharply from almost 15 per cent in 1990 to almost 19 per cent in 1996 and became the second largest sector (after agriculture) in absorbing labor.

The economic crisis has seriously affected the non-tradable sectors especially construction, the inefficient financial sector, and the highly import-dependent manufacturing sectors. Labor from these sectors have been laid off and moved to other sectors—especially the surviving agricultural sector and other natural resource-dependent sectors. Through the terms of trade effects, sharp currency depreciation led to the collapse of highly import dependent sectors. In contrast, some export-oriented manufacturing such as textile, shoes, and garment have largely benefited from the crisis.

Sakernas data showed that during the crisis in 1998, employment in the utility (electricity, gas, and water) sector decreased by 37 per cent, followed by mining (23 per cent), construction (16 per cent), and manufacturing (ten per cent). These reductions represent drastic changes from, for example, the 10.7 per cent annual growth of employment in the construction sector and the 6.6 per cent annual growth in the manufacturing sector from 1990 to 1996. The collapse of the financial sector during the crisis also created employment reduction by minus 5.8 per cent in 1997-98. Again, during the economic slow down, agriculture turned out to be the savior of the economy in labor absorption with an increase of 13 per cent employment during the crisis period. After decreasing from 56 per cent in 1990 to 41 per cent in 1997, the share of employment in the agricultural sector increased to 45 per cent in 1998. The movement of labor to the informal sector and to the traditional and natural resource-based sectors such as agriculture, forestry, and fisheries was accompanied by the movement of employment opportunities to rural areas. The crisis has reduced the growth of urban employment from around 5.2 per cent per annum during the boom years in 1990-96 to around 3.1 per cent from 1997-98. But the annual growth of rural employment increased from 0.6 per cent before the crisis to 2.3 per cent after the crisis.

Table 5.6 The Changing Patterns of Sectoral Employment, 1990-98

	Number (million)			%			Growth (%)	
	1990	1997*	1998*	1990	1997*	1998*	1990-96	1997-98
Total	75.85	85.41	87.67	100.0	100.0	100.0	2.1	2.7
Agriculture, Forestry, Hunting, Fisheries	42.38	34.79	39.41	55.9	40.7	45.0	-1.9	13.3
Mining and Quarrying	0.53	0.88	0.67	0.7	1.0	0.8	6.6	-23.0
Manufacturing	7.69	11.01	9.93	10.1	12.9	11.3	5.8	-9.8
Electricity, Gas, Water	0.14	0.23	0.15	0.2	0.3	0.2	3.3	-36.9
Construction	2.06	4.19	3.52	2.7	4.9	4.0	10.7	-15.9
Trade, Restaurant, Hotel	11.07	16.95	16.81	14.6	19.9	19.2	6.5	-0.8
Finance, Insurance, Real Estate, Business Services	0.48	0.66	0.62	0.6	0.8	0.7	6.3	-5.8
Community, Social, Personal Services	9.07	12.57	12.39	12.0	14.7	14.1	4.4	-1.4
Others	0.13	0.00	0.00	0.2	0.0	0.0	-34.6	-100.0

*Population of age 15 and above

Source: Cental Board of Statistics, *Sakernas* Data, various years.

The Decline in Labor Income and Productivity

Nominal and real wages have generally moved along the same pattern for the last ten years before the crisis, with inflation at around eight to ten per cent as the difference. But it is clear that with more than 77 per cent inflation in 1998, the economic crisis has sharply reduced real wages from 1997 to 1998. The 1998 *Sakernas* data show that nominal monthly wages, measured as the monthly earning[18] in the formal sector, increased by 16 per cent from 1996 to 1997, and by 17 per cent from 1997 to 1998. Having been corrected by inflation, real wages still increased by around 4 per cent in 1997, but then sharply decreased by 34 per cent from 1997 to 1998. The new level of real wage in 1998 was comparable to the level in the late 1980s. This means that the increase in real wage during the last ten years disappeared only within one year during the crisis.

The largest decline in real wages occurred in the public utilities, manufacturing, and construction sectors at more than 35 per cent from 1997 to 1998. These sharp reductions were expected given the shrinking employment in those three sectors during the crisis. Compared with the decline in sectoral employment that shows large variations between sectors, the decline in real wage seems to be more even in distribution. The smallest decline in real wages took place in the mining sector, even though employment contraction in the mining sector was sharp in 1998. Declining real wages and employment contraction in some sectors, especially property, financial, banking, and insurance are expected to continue, because the needed adjustment in those sectors has been very slow due to the slow process of banking restructuring in Indonesia.

Table 5.7 Growth of Real Wages 1997-98

Classification	Growth of Real Wages*
Sectors	
Electricity, Gas & Water	-39.1
Manufacturing	-37.7
Construction	-35.3
Services	-33.5
Trade	-32.8
Transport etc.	-31.1
Finance & Insurance	-31.0
Agriculture	-26.6
Mining	-21.4
Gender and Urban-Rural	
Urban	-35.9
Male	-36.2
Female	-34.4
Rural	-31.6
Male	-30.4
Female	-33.0
Education level	
Tertiary Education	-35.7
Secondary Education	-35.0
Elementary Education	-34.5
No Education	-33.2

* Deflated by 77.6 per cent inflation in 1998.

Source: Central Board of Statistics, *Sakernas, 1997-1998.*

A look at the monthly wage in the formal sector further confirms that this crisis is a crisis for urban workers. The decline in real wages in urban areas from 1997 to 1998 was around 36 per cent compared with around 32 per cent in rural areas. In urban areas, the decline in real wages for male workers is larger than that for females. Classified by the level of worker's education, those with higher education suffered a larger real wage decline compared with those with less education. Those who have university and diploma education suffered the largest decrease in real wage, at about minus 35.7 per cent. Workers with secondary education experienced a 35 per cent decline in real wage and those with primary education suffered from a 34.5 per cent real wage reduction. Finally, those with no education suffered a 33.2 per cent decrease.

Table 5.8 Annual Growth of Real Wages versus Labor Productivity

	1990	1991	1992	1993	1994	1995	1996	1997	1998
All Sectors									
Nominal Wage	16.2	13.4	14.1	23.8	9.7	13.7	15.7	16.2	17.2
Real Wage	5.7	3.1	8.6	12.4	0.0	4.4	8.5	4.2	-34.1
Labor Productivity	2.3	4.7	5.9	14.0	1.7	6.6	7.3	3.2	-16.6
Agriculture									
Nominal Wage	13.5	23.5	2.7	29.2	17.9	12.3	13.8	11.5	30.7
Real Wage	3.2	12.4	-2.3	17.3	7.5	3.1	6.8	-0.1	-26.6
Labor Productivity	-6.4	-1.2	6.0	10.7	7.8	8.2	6.0	7.2	-15.2
Manufacturing									
Nominal Wage	29.5	4.5	8.4	34.8	4.1	15.2	17.7	18.4	11.0
Real Wage	17.8	-4.9	3.2	22.4	-5.0	5.8	10.3	6.1	-37.7
Labor Productivity	10.1	7.8	8.5	11.0	-10.6	12.9	16.0	1.4	0.1
Services									
Nominal Wage	22.1	12.0	8.9	20.1	8.0	15.5	18.1	8.4	20.8
Real Wage	11.1	1.9	3.6	9.1	-1.5	6.0	10.7	-2.9	-32.2
Labor Productivity	3.8	1.5	8.2	13.0	-3.1	0.3	1.1	-2.2	-20.2

Source: Calculated based on data from Central Board of Statistics, *Sakernas*, various years.

Labor productivity, measured as the real GDP divided by the number of employment also declined sharply in 1998 due to economic contraction. During the early period of the crisis in 1997, labor productivity still increased by 3.2 per cent, but then sharply declined by 16.6 per cent in 1998. It is expected that the decrease in labor productivity is less than the decline in real wage because of the large shock in inflation, but the 16.6 per cent decrease has brought back the productivity to the 1993 level, five years before the crisis.

The adjustment in the manufacturing sectors has been larger than in other sectors, reflected by larger correction in real wages. Real wages in the manufacturing sectors declined by 37.7 per cent in 1998, compared with 32.2 per cent in services and 26.6 per cent in the agricultural sectors. A sharp reduction in employment had also taken place in the manufacturing sectors, so that real labor productivity remained relatively constant. Labor productivity in the agriculture and services sectors declined by 14.2 and 20.9 per cent, respectively. Again, the sharp reduction in employment and real wages in the manufacturing sectors shows that the biggest labor market adjustment in 1998 took place in the manufacturing sectors.

In summary, labor market adjustment in Indonesia had been taking place in the form of price or wage reduction (30-40 per cent decline) rather than the increase in unemployment (16 per cent increase). Because of labor market flexibility and the absence of any unemployment benefit or other forms of social security, displaced workers would have to find other jobs mostly with lower wage rates in order to survive. This form of adjustment is slightly different from that in other Asian countries in crisis. In South Korea and Thailand, the adjustments have been taking place in the forms of more employment reduction. While real wages have been stable due to single digit inflation rates, the unemployment rate increased from 2.6 per cent in 1997 to 7.5 per cent in 1998 in South Korea and doubled from 2.2 to 4.6 per cent in Thailand.[19]

There are several contributing factors to the specific nature of labor market adjustment in Indonesia. The first is the flexible nature of the labor market itself, where labor turnover rate is generally high. Combined with the labor surplus nature of the economy, weak labor unions, and low reservation wage,[20] the flexible nature of the labor market led to flexible real wages. The second factor that also played a major role in sharp wage adjustment is the specific overall macroeconomic condition, where excessive monetary expansion led to high inflation and sharp depreciation. This specific macroeconomic condition has characterized the Indonesian crisis and in turn led to different adjustments in the labor market compared with that in Thailand or South Korea. In these two countries, inflation was still in single digit and real wage was relatively stable, which means that the adjustment would be in the form of rising unemployment rates.

The Lack of Social Safety Net

The social safety net programs in Indonesia have not been effective and have become the major factor contributing to workers' insecurity during the crisis.[21] Successful and effective implementation of social safety nets would clearly prevent the crisis-induced social and economic problems from becoming a threat or becoming a security problem for the society. When public works programs were available in urban areas, for example, displaced construction workers would not have to turn to informal activities or to go back to rural areas to survive the crisis. An effective food relief program would also be another mechanism to prevent food insecurity and malnutrition during the crisis.

While the need for social safety net programs was realized in early 1998, especially when the Indonesian crisis moved to a worsening path compared with other countries in crisis, it was only in June 1998 when the social safety net programs were spelled explicitly in the IMF reform package. So to begin with, the plan to have a social safety net program was formalized very late, almost one full year since the crisis started in August 1997. The plan to have social safety net programs was first mentioned in the revised government budget drafted in late June 1998.[22] According to the budget plan, around 7.4 per cent of GDP or Rp70.5 trillion were allocated for the social safety net program. This amount was significant compared with the budget deficit that was calculated at around 8.5 per cent of the GDP. But out of the Rp70.5 trillion budget, around 83.5 per cent or Rp58.8 trillion was allocated for various subsidies – mainly fuel subsidies. The remainder or around 16.5 per cent of the total allocated budget (Rp11.7 trillion) was planned for employment generation programs, support for education in the form of block grants and scholarships, and other expenditure for health-related services.

But before any implementation of this plan was reported anywhere, in September 1998 BAPPENAS announced that a nationwide social safety net program was being developed. This program consisted of four elements. The first was a food security program to guarantee the availability and affordability of food across society. This included the promotion of local food production, as well as the development of a reliable distribution system. The second was a public works program, especially labor-intensive activities to provide employment. The third was a social protection program to protect health and education facilities, and the fourth was the promotion of small and medium enterprises. The total cost was estimated at around Rp17 trillion (or 6.5 per cent of government budget).[23] But this was clearly a smaller figure compared with the total amount of food subsidy, employment generation programs, supports for health and education services, which amounted to around Rp25.5 trillion combined and based on the government budget drafted in June 1998.

Three months after the announcement of the social safety net program, however, there arose widespread criticism that the safety net program was a failure. It was reported in various media that the program did not work, did not reach the poor, and was suspected that the money ended in the pockets of corrupt government officials. In fact the World Bank (WB) had to delay the disbursement of the loan to Indonesia, partly because of some concern that the fund for the safety net was not properly used.

In early 1999, BAPPENAS admitted that the disbursement of the Social Safety Net fund had been very slow, and that the program had not run smoothly. It was also reported that only around 30 per cent of the fund was actually used. One problem is related to the design of the program itself. Another problem is related to budgetary constraints. The government budget for 1998/99 was revised several times before the final draft was finally formulated during the worst time of the crisis in July 1998. When the budget was formulated, it was actually unclear how the government would finance its daily operation, not to mention the social safety net programs. Soon, however, various foreign donors pledged their commitments to help. The total amount that foreign donors committed to fund the public spending on social sectors was around US$2.78 billion, or more than Rp22 trillion at Rp8,000/US$. While the money was going to be available from overseas, another problem was that BAPPENAS did not have full control and authority to channel the fund. Each department received its limited and partial budget from the Ministry of Finance, and there was no guarantee that the fund they received would be spent on social safety net activities. This uncoordinated and badly designed social safety net program was just one example of how the government did not function well during the crisis. There was a similar disarray of uncoordinated programs and policies in other crucial areas, such as trade financing, debt rescheduling, and banking restructuring. These bad responses of the government during the crisis were in fact one major factor that had worsened the crisis.

An independent committee was finally asked to review and evaluate the social safety net program. In February the committee reported that out of the total budget at more than Rp17 trillion, the core or the real social safety net program was only around Rp9.3 trillion, or slightly more than half of the total budget (United Nation Support Facility for Indonesian Recovery.[24] The remainder of the budget (48 per cent) was allocated for the so-called 'supplementary program' – a softer expression to refer to misallocation. However, it remains unclear how much of the already disbursed fund was actually part of the misallocated budget. While the design was bad and the coordination was even worse, the implementation was actually the worst. Concerned with the bad implementation of the program in the field, several NGOs have asked foreign donors to stop their assistance for the social safety net programs.[25] In protest of the various leakage and abuses that have been found in the field, they also requested the WB to delay its social safety net adjustment loan. Their argument was clear: the Indonesian people should not pay the foreign debt that was misspent by the corrupt government.

A recent WB report on Indonesia noted that the school scholarship program was found to be the most impressive of the social safety net programs because it targeted poor households effectively and provided tangible assistance. The cheap-rice distribution program was also found to be effective even though there had been some complaints published by the media. The employment generation and public works programs were found to be less effective in reaching the poor and unemployed. The provision of free medical assistance through the Health Card program was largely limited to the elderly poor.[26]

The Increase in Poverty Incidence

During the economic boom years of the last two decades, the incidence of poverty in Indonesia had declined significantly from around 40 per cent in the mid 1970s to around 22 per cent in 1984 and just around 11 per cent in 1996. According to official figures, urban poverty declined faster than rural poverty, where the share of people living below the poverty line declined from 23 per cent to ten per cent from 1994 to 1996. In rural areas, the number declined from 21 per cent to 12 per cent during the same period. More than 60 per cent, or around two thirds of the population in Indonesia live in rural areas.[27]

The estimated poverty, however, should be interpreted with caution. Because a large section of the population lives in the neighborhood of the poverty line (skewed income distribution), the measurement of the number of population below the poverty line is very sensitive to the poverty standard. In other words, the increase in the poverty line by Rp2,000 or US$25 cents, for example, would lead to additional millions of people living below the poverty line. It is not surprising, therefore, that the estimates of poverty incidence in Indonesia varied in 1998. ILO estimated that around 48 per cent of the population (98 million) lived below the poverty line in 1998.[28] At the same time, *Badan Pusat Statistik* (BPS or Central Board of Statistics) estimated that around 39 per cent of the population (79 million) lived under the poverty line in June 1998.[29] The incidence of poverty in rural areas increased faster than in urban areas. The WB came out with a more controversial but much smaller figure. It reported that poverty increased by three per cent from 11 per cent in 1996 to around 14 to 19 per cent in 1998.[30] While it is tempting to compare these results with those done by the BPS or ILO, it is important to note that they are based on different data samples and poverty measurements. The poverty measurement by the WB was based on the expenditure data of the Indonesian Family Life Survey (IFLS)[31] with a much smaller sample size compared with other large data such as those of *Susenas*. Another estimate using *Susenas* data by the BPS, however, supports the finding from the IFLS data and estimates that the poverty incidence in 1998 was around 18 per cent. It is important to note, however, that the *Susenas* data for 1998 was collected early in the year, so that the data might not capture the worst impact of the crisis in the latter part of 1998. By using different methodologies and deflators, other preliminary estimates by M.Ikhsan as reported in UNSFIR (1999) show that the poverty incidence increased from around 20 per cent in 1996 to 33 per cent in 1998.[32]

On 9 July 1999, the Central Board of Statistics announced the new official poverty figures based on the core *Susenas* data taken in December 1998. It came up with 24.2 per cent of overall poverty incidence, 21.9 per cent in the urban areas, and 25.7 per cent in the rural areas. It reported that urban poverty increased more rapidly than rural poverty showing that the urban areas had been hardest hit by the crisis. This official BPS report noted that poverty increased from 11.3 per cent (using the old standard) to 24.2 per cent (using the new standard). But unfortunately, the report did not present the revised poverty figure in 1996, so that it was actually not methodologically sound to compare these two figures. When the old poverty standard that was used in 1996 was then used to calculate the poverty incidence in 1998, the result showed that poverty increased from 11.3 per cent in 1996 to 16.7 per cent in 1998. Therefore, the poverty incidence in general increased by around five to six per cent.

All of these findings clearly suggest that the crisis has increased the poverty incidence in Indonesia. Depending on the methodology, price deflators, and sources of data that were being used, the precise measure of the increasing number of population below the poverty line is hard to obtain. When one has to make some conclusion about the number of poverty incidence, based on all the findings, it seems fair to conclude that the number of people living below the poverty line, or the incidence of poverty increased by around 65 per cent from 1996 to 1998. For example, the poverty incidence could increase from 11 per cent in 1996 to 17 per cent in 1998, or based on a different methodology, it could also increase from 19 per cent in 1996 to 24 per cent in 1998.

This generalization, however, should be treated with caution. The different results from various studies on poverty show the sensitivity of poverty incidence to the methodology, price deflators, and source of data used in the survey. The measurement of poverty incidence based on expenditure data, for example, has several important implications. First, the measurement does not capture the case of consumption smoothing, when people spend their savings or 'dissavings' to maintain their previous level of consumption. Second, the expenditure data do not capture the changes in the quantity and quality of consumption as a result of price changes. Another point worth mentioning is the limitation of the aggregated poverty number in uncovering the complex regional and distributional dimensions of poverty.

Table 5.9 The Number of Population Living Below the Poverty Line in Indonesia

	As a per cent of the population			In million people		
Year	Urban	Rural	Total	Urban	Rural	Total
1976	38.8	40.4	40.1	10.0	44.2	54.2
1996	9.7	12.3	11.3	7.2	15.3	22.5
1998 BPS, 1996 poverty standard BPS, 1996 poverty standard	-	-	16.7	-	-	34.1
1998 BPS, 1996 poverty standard (officially published) BPS, 1998 poverty standard (officially published)	21.9	25.7	24.2	17.6	31.9	49.5

Sources: Badan Pusat Statistik, various reports.

Food Insecurity

Indonesia was considered to be a food secure nation just before the crisis, so that the United Nation World Food Program (UNWFP) closed its office in Indonesia in 1996. But due to the economic crisis that led to a plummeting Rupiah combined with serious drought in 1997 due to El Niño, the problem of food security emerged once again in 1998. The UNWFP reopened its office in April 1998 and continued its program in providing food relief for Indonesians during the crisis.

Similar to the security issue in the labor market where price adjustment hurts more than quantity adjustment, the issue of food insecurity is not about the food availability but the skyrocketing food prices and declining workers' purchasing power for food items. The Food and Agriculture Organization (FAO) estimated that because of the drought and other factors, rice production was around 45 million tons in 1997-98, so that the demand for rice import was around 5.1 million tons. In fact the rice import for 1998 was actually around 5.9 million tons, higher than the regular annual rice import at around 2-3 million tons. The estimated total basic food availability has been estimated at around 2,100 kcal/day/person, close to the international standard for minimum nutrition intake, even though it was lower than the 2,700 kcal/day/person in Indonesia in 1995.[33]

In spite of food supply availability, the concern at the national level is the fiscal burden of the exchange rate subsidy to import rice in 1998.[34] Perhaps the more serious concern related to this policy is that the large exchange rate subsidy has not led to lower domestic price of rice compared with the international market price. The

UNSFIR report (1999) indicated that in late 1998 and early 1999, the price of domestic rice in the market was around 20-25 per cent higher than the international price. This suggests various problems, ranging from possible serious distortions in the domestic market, to problems related to distribution, or even the possibility that the subsidy went to someone's pocket instead.

While food availability in terms of quantity has not been a problem at the national level, food security remains a crucial issue at the household level. Food prices increased by more than 118 per cent in 1998, compared with 78 per cent increase in general inflation, and 17 per cent increase in nominal wages on average. Data on rice prices are even more shocking. The average price of rice increased from around Rp1,000/kg just before the crisis in 1997 to around Rp2,750 (275 per cent increase) by early 1999.[35] The collapse of real earnings forced families to reduce their food consumption in both quantity and quality. The micro-level analysis that is presented in the next section shows significant evidence of this pattern.

This aggregate picture of food security, however, has hidden heterogeneous aspects related to food security at the regional level, especially the urban and rural division. Some early findings suggest that the urban poor living in slum areas have suffered the most food insecurity.[36] Those who were laid off from the collapsing urban and modern sectors such as construction and utilities would be those who suffered the most from the declining purchasing power for food. In fact before the crisis, even the poorest in the urban areas were considered less vulnerable to food insecurity compared with their rural counterparts. During the urban boom years, the growth of their real income was generally higher than the increase in inflation, and certainly much more than the food inflation, making it possible for them to accumulate some savings. But the fact that they are 100 per cent food consumers relying on a fixed salary, they become vulnerable to food insecurity once they are unemployed and their savings are depleted.

The fact that the urban poor suffered the most, however, does not mean that rural food insecurity is less serious compared with the urban case. More than 25 per cent of rural households in Indonesia are landless and even in West Java the proportion is more than 50 per cent. This being the case, the proportion of the net consumers of food in the rural areas is large, and sooner or later, when coping mechanisms in rural areas are exhausted food insecurity becomes a serious problem both in urban and rural areas. Food security problem in urban areas would soon be transmitted to the rural areas along with the reverse migration to rural areas. This would stretch the rural resources and capacity to produce food.

To cope with the skyrocketing food prices, as part of the social safety net program, the government has conducted a special market operation by distributing rice at the subsidized price of Rp1,000/kg mainly to the urban poor since July 1998. From August 1998 to February 1999, around 700 thousand tons of rice were distributed to around nine million households or about 40 per cent of the 17 million targeted recipients. However, poor targeting made the program less effective in alleviating food insecurity in the rural areas. An independent survey conducted at the end of 1998 revealed that households received less than the amount that they were supposed to receive, or in other cases, they had to pay for the rice at inflated prices.[37]

International Labor Migration

The changing structure of the economy and the distressed labor market has led to an increase in the number of Indonesians working overseas. Unfortunately, the data on labor migration out of the country are limited. The currently available data are the number of Indonesians working overseas (or the TKI = *Tenaga Kerja Indonesia* /Indonesian Laborers) recorded by the Department of Manpower. The data on TKI in the Department of Manpower might also be underestimated considering the fact that many cases went unrecorded.

The crisis significantly increased the number of TKI because the reduction of employment opportunities in the country has forced many Indonesians to look for jobs overseas. Other data from the Department of Industry and Trade show a significant increase in the number of TKI working abroad from 1995 to 1998. The number of TKI in 1998 tremendously increased from 255,275 in 1997 to 1,256,725 in 1998, or five times that in 1997. While the government has been promoting the program of sending Indonesian workers overseas, the 1998 figure was slightly above the government's target of around 1.25 million for 1998/1999.

Malaysia is the number one country that receives the TKI, with 423,000 workers as of May 1998. Saudi Arabia is the second most popular destination with 418,000 workers as of June 1998. But it seems that there are differences in the type of the TKI working in those two countries. In Malaysia, around 70 per cent of the TKI work in the formal sector while in Saudi Arabia 70 per cent of the workers are women, most only have primary education, and work in the informal sector. The majority of Indonesian workers in Saudi Arabia are working as domestic helpers. The next popular destinations are Singapore and Hong Kong, but most of the TKI that work in these two countries are the better educated. On average, they have a high school education.[38]

The number of the TKI, however, decreased significantly from 1996 to 1998. The decrease was due to the fact that many of the TKI were sent home from Malaysia due to the economic crisis in that country. This is one example of how labor migration could become a serious regional security issue when the immediate reaction to the economic crisis is to push migrant workers out of the country to protect local workers and the sharp decline in real wages. The previously 'acceptable' illegal immigrant suddenly became unacceptable and was pushed out first, even though many employers and firms complained about the rising wage cost as a result.

While there are not many available data on illegal migration, it is generally understood that most illegal workers from Indonesia choose to go to Malaysia because of the distance and the similarities in language and religion. The Ministry of Manpower in Malaysia estimated that until November 1998 there were 72,191 illegal workers from Indonesia working in Malaysia.[39] It was also reported that in 1997, Malaysia deported 38,153 illegal Indonesian workers. Since then until October 1998, Malaysia once again deported 52,000 workers from Indonesia.[40] This shows that there has been an increasing number of Indonesians crossing the border and working illegally in Malaysia following the crisis. It is estimated that there were around 1,700 illegal Indonesian workers entering Malaysia from Sarawak (in Kalimantan Island) every month.[41] Illegal workers crossing the Malacca Straits border by boat

(*Pongpong*) is estimated to be around 6,000 people monthly[42] – see also Tigno's chapter in this volume.

The Delayed Labor Market Transformation

Labor market transformation in Indonesia in the early 1990s followed the common pattern of many developing countries in which the economy moves from a labor surplus to a labor scarce economy following industrial development. This transition from a labor surplus to a labor scarce economy is accompanied by an increase in wages and productivity as a result of labor market tightening.

It is expected that the process of labor market transformation in Indonesia would slow down, stop, or even reverse as the economic performance deteriorated during the crisis. There has been a massive reverse movement of labor from the manufacturing and construction sectors to the agricultural sector since the crisis. This process is expected to continue as the contraction in the construction and financial sectors would take place throughout 1999. Workers have moved to the rural areas because of the crisis, and it is expected that the process of urbanization would slow down in the near future even though the problems of urban poverty would continue. Another sign of the reverse process of labor market transformation is the rapid movement back to the informal sector, especially in the urban areas. Combined with the sharp reduction in real wages—up to 30 per cent in general—all of these signs show the reversal or delayed labor market transformation in Indonesia as a result of the crisis.

The reversal of labor market transformation means that Indonesia is moving back to a labor surplus economy as in the late 1908s at least for some time in the near future. The new level of real wage in 1998 that was similar to the level in the late 1980s, and the new level of labor productivity that was comparable to that in the early 1990s reflected this process of reversal. While workers in neighboring countries have successfully graduated from labor intensive to more capital-intensive industries, Indonesian workers would still work in the labor-intensive industries with lower technology and lower wages for some time in the future. The process of labor market transformation and turning point has been a longer process compared with that in other Asian countries. The crisis would not only further delay the labor market tightening, but also lengthen the process of catching up with other neighboring countries. Another factor that can potentially lead to a slower transformation process is the lower level of education of Indonesian workers compared with that in other Asian countries. This would hinder the process of industrial transformation because people are not flexible to change jobs into the more modern sectors.

However, the slower process of labor market tightening would increase the competitiveness of Indonesia's labor intensive manufacturing in the international market, at least in the short run, because of two forces. The first is in nominal terms from the terms of trade effect, when currency depreciation suddenly makes Indonesian wage standards very cheap compared with international standards. The second is from the adjustment in real terms when the growth of labor productivity becomes higher than the growth of real wages. The market will make some readjustment and the real wages will surely rise in the near future. However, as long as labor productivity can keep up with the increase in wages, Indonesia will remain competitive.

The Micro-Perspective

Having discussed the impact of the economic crisis on the security of Indonesian workers at the macro level, this section analyzes the crisis-induced adjustments at the micro level, by focusing on the changes in hours of work, income, and expenditure pattern of an individual worker. This section presents the result of the field surveys that recorded data on the changing pattern of worker's income and expenditure before and after the crisis. The real data would provide realistic empirical evidence to reveal how the crisis has changed the well being of the Indonesian worker. By gathering quantitative and qualitative data systematically collected at the individual level the study could also capture the workers' perception on job and income security during the crisis and how they cope with the crisis. The field surveys collected data from 150 production workers in labor-intensive industries, mostly export oriented in the greater Jakarta areas (Jakarta-Bogor-Tangerang-Bekasi) and Surabaya. The survey was conducted during the worst time of the crisis in Indonesia, in August–October 1998.[43]

Hours of Work and Employment Status

The result from the field surveys confirmed the presumption that an adjustment in the labor market has taken place more in the form of reduction in real income or wages rather than in employment or the number of hours of work. The total weekly working hours declined by around 5.7 per cent, from 53.7 hours a week in August 1997 to 50.6 hours a week a year later. The number of regular working hours was stable over the period at around 45 hours a week, so that the adjustment took place mostly in the overtime hours that declined by around 31 per cent on average.

The data also suggest that the reduction in overtime working hours was more for workers with lower education. That confirms the theory that the demand for lower-skilled employment would be more elastic compared with the more-skilled. In other words, any shock in the labor market would create bigger adjustments in the demand for the lower skilled labor. The fact that the decrease in overtime hours for male workers was larger than that of the females is similar to the national trend that male suffered more in terms of employment reduction compared to female workers. The data also suggest that among those labor-intensive industries, the textile industry suffered the most from the crisis in the reduction in working hours. This fact also matched the general trend that among other labor-intensive industries, the textile industry was hurt the worst during the crisis because of its highest dependence on import components.

The data also reveal that the crisis has reduced the proportion of permanent workers in the factories covered in the surveys. The proportion of permanent workers was around 65 per cent on average. Most workers on temporary status were actually being put out, which means that they either work at home or still work in the factory but paid on piece rate or hourly basis. Those put out during the crisis were 32 per cent of permanent workers compared to 10 to 15 per cent during the boom period in 1995.[44] This suggests that another crisis-induced adjustment was in the form of reduction in the permanent status of employment. The number of hours of work in total could be stable or declined slightly during the crisis, but more workers were under temporary status indicating an increase in job insecurity. The survey results also show that the proportion of male workers under temporary status was larger (54 per cent) than the females (22 per cent) in 1998, similar to that experienced at the national labor market. The proportion of workers being put out was also consistently higher in the textile industry at around 48 per cent.

Interviews with several factory managers revealed that the employment adjustment at the factory level during the crisis varies from one firm to another, ranging from reduction in overtime hours to layoffs. In general, higher dependence on export markets would increase the chance of survival during the crisis and reduced the necessity to displace workers. It was also hard to determine precisely how many workers have been laid off during the crisis because of the high labor turnover rates in these industries. One firm reported that it had laid off around 30 per cent of its workers, which was much higher than the average national rate of ten per cent. But the majority of this 30 per cent was due to the termination of contract workers once their contract ended.

Table 5.10 Adjustments in Workers' Working Hours, Before and After the Crisis

	Regular working hours			Overtime hours			Total working hours		
	1997	1998	% Change	1997	1998	% Change	1997	1998	% Change
By Education									
Primary school or less	45.7	44.9	-1.7	7.3	3.3	-54.5	53.0	48.2	-8.9
Junior High School	45.0	44.6	-0.8	8.5	5.9	-30.7	53.5	50.6	-5.5
High School and others	44.5	44.4	-0.4	9.5	7.2	-24.1	54.1	51.6	-4.6
By Gender									
Female	44.9	44.7	-0.5	9.3	7.3	-21.8	54.2	52.0	-4.2
Male	44.9	44.3	-1.3	7.7	3.5	-54.5	52.6	47.8	-9.1
By Industry									
Electronics	43.0	44.2	2.8	8.2	5.5	-32.9	51.2	49.7	-2.9
Garment	44.3	44.2	-0.2	9.5	7.2	-24.5	53.8	51.4	-4.5
Shoes	45.7	44.9	-1.8	12.6	9.0	-28.9	58.3	53.9	-7.6
Textile	45.3	44.7	-1.2	5.1	2.8	-46.3	50.4	47.5	-5.8
Total	44.9	44.6	-0.8	8.8	6.1	-31.0	53.7	50.6	-5.7

Source: Data from field surveys.

However, these labor intensive industries in the survey had no problems in raising wages by 15 per cent or more in compliance with the increase in minimum wages in August 1998. In fact, before the crisis these large firms were paying wages well above the minimum wage rate. Their biggest concern during the crisis was financial, related to the collapse of the financial sectors in the country, such as high interest rate cost and the unavailability of L/C facilities because of the collapse of the banking system. Most of these large exporters had been using financial services offered by foreign banks overseas due to a dysfunctional domestic banking system. The volatility of the exchange rate had also made it difficult to make business plans for the future.

Some firms that have relied heavily on overseas purchase orders were concerned about the fall of foreign orders due to riots and other mass violence throughout 1998. The amount of foreign order had declined significantly since the crisis because foreign buyers were not certain whether Indonesian suppliers could deliver their finished products on time. Foreign buyers had moved some of their purchase orders to foreign competitors in Thailand and China for more certainty even though they had to pay higher prices. This case is one example and one contributing factor to the general problem at the national level that the sharp currency depreciation during the crisis had not increased the value of Indonesian exports.

The Changing Patterns of Workers' Income

Similar to the adjustment in the national labor market, the monthly earning of workers in the survey decreased by around 33 per cent in real terms on average from August 1997 to August 1998. Average monthly earning actually increased by eight per cent from Rp286,000 in 1997 to Rp309,000 in 1998. Because of sharp currency depreciation, labor earning declined from around US$115/month in 1997 to US$31/month in 1998.[45] During the same period, overtime earnings in Rupiah slightly declined by two per cent mostly due to the significant reduction in overtime hours during the crisis. In terms of hourly wages, worker's wage increased by 12 per cent in nominal terms and decreased by 30 per cent in real terms. The composition of total earning did not change significantly between 1997 and 1998, where basic wages or salary from regular hours of work accounted for around 60 per cent, overtime salary eight to nine per cent, and bonuses 31-32 per cent.

Table 5.11 Workers' Monthly Earning, Before and After the Crisis

Earning	Before crisis (1997)		During crisis (1998)		% Change	% Change
	Rp.000	% Share	Rp.000	% Share	Nominal	Real*
Basic wages	168.1	58.7	186.7	60.3	11.1	-31.2
Overtime	26.5	9.2	26.0	8.4	-2.0	-39.3
Bonuses	91.8	32.1	96.7	31.3	5.3	-34.8
Total Earning	286.4	100.0	309.4	100.0	8.0	-33.1
Hourly Wages	3.8	-	4.2	-	12.3	-30.4

*Deflated by increase in CPI by 61.5 per cent in August 1997-August 1998

Source: Data from field surveys.

Income data from the field survey show the general stylized fact in the labor market where workers with higher education received higher wages and bonuses. Workers with primary school or lower education received a total monthly earnings of around Rp268,000, those with senior high school or higher education received

Rp330,000. In terms of hourly wages, workers with at least a high school education received around Rp4,500/hour, while those with a primary school or lower education received Rp3,900/hour. When bonuses and overtime salary were added, the hourly wages ranged from Rp6,200/hour to Rp7,200/hour, or at the prevailing exchange rate in 1998 was US$70 cent/hour on average. The hourly wage rate also shows how education and technology mattered in determining wages. Industries with higher technology such as electronics paid wages at up to 20 per cent higher than those in textile and garment industries.

These wage figures were well above the standard of minimum monthly wage at around Rp172,500 up to July 1998, and increased to Rp198,500 for greater Jakarta in August 1998 mainly because of the large component of bonuses that accounted for about 30 per cent of total worker's earnings. In general, the basic wages were at about the same level as the minimum wage, but the total of worker's take home pay was around 30 to 40 per cent higher. The monthly earnings from the surveys were also higher than the national average for unskilled workers. For example, the *Sakernas* data show that the national average monthly earning for workers with primary education was Rp200,000 in 1998, lower than Rp268,000 found in the survey. This is expected, however, because the survey was limited to labor-intensive manufacturing, mostly export oriented that turned out to be one of the surviving sectors during the crisis.

The data from the field surveys also reveal the dynamic changes in the pattern of worker's income during the crisis. While total earnings increased in nominal terms by around eight per cent on average, the increase was not the same among workers. Those with higher education, the female workers, and workers in the electronic and garment industries in fact received a larger increase in their incomes compared with other workers. Workers with high school education, for example, experienced a 9.6 per cent increase in their monthly earnings, while those with primary or lower education only got a 3.8 per cent increase. The larger increase in earnings for those with higher education was due to the large increase in wage component, where hourly wages increased by more than 15 per cent compared with less than ten per cent for workers with lower education.

It is noteworthy that the increase in average total earnings during the crisis was in fact due to the increase in the earnings of female workers. Female workers seemed to be consistently better off than the males as their total earnings increased by more than 12 per cent compared with only 0.3 per cent for the males. In terms of hourly wages, again female wages increased by more than 15.2 per cent, larger than the increase in male wages at around 7.6 per cent. The ratio of total monthly earnings between female and male workers was around 0.94 in 1998, larger than the ratio before the crisis at 0.84, and was much larger than the general ratio at the national level at around 0.7 in 1998. Hence, the field survey in these labor-intensive industries shows that the ratio between female and male wages was in fact improving during the crisis.

Table 5.12 Changes in Workers' Monthly Earning, 1997-98

	Wages		Overtime		Bonuses		Total Earning		Wages/hour	
	in 1998	% Change	In 1998	% Change	In 1998	% Change	In 1998	% Change	in 1998	% Change
Classified by	Rp.000	1997-98	Rp.000	1997-98	Rp.000	1997-98	Rp.000	1997-98	Rp.000	1997-98
Education										
Primary school or less	172.8	7.0	12.5	-6.2	82.8	-0.9	268.2	3.8	3.90	9.6
Jr. high school	179.0	7.1	36.9	5.0	85.2	10.7	301.1	7.8	4.01	8.5
Sr. high school or others	197.0	15.0	24.3	-7.1	109.5	4.8	330.8	9.6	4.48	15.6
Gender										
Female	175.9	13.9	29.5	0.5	97.7	13.8	303.1	12.4	3.97	15.2
Male	209.6	6.5	18.5	-9.5	94.6	-9.5	322.7	0.3	4.76	7.6
Industry										
Electronics	221.9	18.0	14.8	1.0	99.7	3.8	336.4	12.6	4.81	13.9
Garment	172.9	10.8	18.6	-19.6	122.5	23.5	313.9	12.8	3.98	12.2
Shoes	194.7	14.5	24.9	7.0	97.2	-1.4	316.9	8.5	4.38	17.7
Textile	187.1	7.1	36.4	4.6	70.0	-10.5	293.4	2.0	4.22	8.1
Total	186.7	11.1	26.0	-2.0	96.7	5.3	309.4	8.0	4.22	12.3

Source: Data from field surveys.

There are several possible explanations for the larger increase in female wages. The first is what is called 'the natural selection process' where larger numbers of female workers that were laid off during the crisis would lead to larger increase in wages for female workers who survive and stay. In fact, various reports show that more female workers were laid off in the labor-intensive industries during the crisis compared with males.[46] Interviews with managers of factories also suggested a similar trend. The larger number of female workers being laid off in the labor-intensive industries, however, is not surprising. First, female workers dominate the labor-intensive industries so that the numbers of women workers being displaced would be larger. Second, female workers have lower education and skill in general compared with the males, and those with lower skills generally are more likely to be laid off during the crisis. This being the case, female workers in labor industries are generally more vulnerable than male workers. This suggests that the higher increase in wages and earnings for female workers (who survive) does not mean that they have suffered less compared with their male counterparts. Another explanation for the higher increase in female wage is due to the decrease in bonuses for male workers by 9.5 per cent, compared with 13.8 per cent increase for the females. Because of generally higher skill and longer job tenure, male workers tend to receive a larger component of bonus in their earnings. The fact that these bonuses were reduced during the crisis would logically hurt male workers more than the females.

Workers in the textile and garment industries in the surveys suffered more than in other industries in terms of wage adjustment. Overtime earnings generally declined by almost 20 per cent in the garment factory and bonuses decreased by more than ten per cent in nominal terms. In the garment and textile industries, many workers had been paid on per piece basis and working under the 'put-out' status. Higher bonuses and lower overtime earnings of garment workers during the crisis reflected this tendency. It is noteworthy that garment workers had the biggest component of bonuses (around 40 per cent) in their total income, reflecting the higher tendency of employing workers on a part time bases.

The Changing Patterns of Workers' Expenditure

The data from the field surveys show that total consumption increased by around 12.4 per cent in nominal terms or decreased by 30.4 per cent in real terms from 1997 to 1998 during the crisis. The decrease in expenditure in real terms clearly shows the lower quality and quantity of goods and services consumed by workers in adjusting to the crisis. Compared with total earnings that increased by around eight per cent overall, the higher increase in consumption also shows the reduction in workers' savings. In fact, the expenditure component for savings decreased by 34.4 per cent in nominal terms. These figures show how workers have adjusted their expenditure patterns as part of consumption smoothing during the crisis.

Workers have reduced their consumption on durable goods and other secondary items and increased their spending on basic items such as food. Due to the crisis, food expenditure in nominal terms increased by 14 per cent on average, while clothing decreased by 13 per cent. The share of food out of total expenditures increased from 50 per cent to 53 per cent, while the share of savings decreased from around nine per cent to six per cent. The expenditures on health services also increased by 29 per cent in nominal terms, even though the share of health spending was only around 1.5 to 1.7 per cent of total expenditures.

While this pattern of consumption and expenditures switching is similar to the findings of other studies, as for example in the IFLS data, the proportion of food expenditure in this study was slightly smaller, mainly because of the higher level of workers' education in the sample. Comparable IFLS data show that the share of expenditure on food items was generally around 60 per cent of total expenditures and increased by eight per cent in urban households and six per cent in rural households from 1997 to 1998.[47] Among the food items, the proportion of expenditure on staples such as rice and cereals increased by 59 per cent in urban areas and 29 per cent in rural areas. The expenditure on more expensive food especially meat decreased by around 20 per cent on average. Using preliminary results from the 100 hundred village survey data, the proportion of expenditure for food increased by around ten per cent, from 66 per cent to 76 per cent from 1997 to 1998.

The decomposition of the changing patterns of expenditure based on education and gender reveals some interesting results. The increase in food expenditure turned out to be larger for female workers, while the decline in savings was higher for the males. Part of the explanation was the fact that most female workers in the survey were single, generally saving more than their male counterpart. For the mostly married and better-paid male workers, on the one hand their savings were depleted at a faster rate to meet the increasing family expenditures, while on the other hand, their food expenditure was smaller than that of the female workers. The increase in food expenditure and the decrease in savings for less educated workers were also larger, clearly showing that the changes in expenditure patterns were more drastic for those with lower education and lower earnings.

Table 5.13 Workers' Monthly Expenditure, Before and After the Crisis

Expenditure	Before crisis (1997)		During crisis (1998)		% Change	% Change
	Rp.000	% Share	Rp.000	% Share	Nominal	Real[a]
Total Consumption	259.6	90.6	291.8	94.3	12.4	-30.4
Food[b]	143.4	50.1	163.3	52.8	13.9	-29.5
Clothing	21.0	7.3	18.2	5.9	-13.2	-46.2
Housing	25.7	9.0	27.2	8.8	5.9	-34.4
Health	4.2	1.5	5.4	1.7	28.6	-20.4
Others	65.3	22.8	77.7	25.1	19.0	-26.3
Savings	26.7	9.3	17.6	5.7	-34.4	-59.4
Total Exp. = Income	286.4	100.0	309.4	100.0	8.0	-33.1

[a]Deflated by increase in CPI by 61.5 per cent in August 1997-August 1998.
[b]Including some unrecorded residual expenditure assumed as unrecorded food spending.

Source: Data from field surveys.

Workers' Perception of Job Security

More than 58 per cent of all workers in the survey felt that they would continue working in the same factory in spite of the crisis. It was clear from the survey that workers with higher education felt more confident about their job security compared with those with lower education. More than 17 per cent of workers with primary or lower education thought that they were about to be fired, while more than 51 per cent felt that they would remain at work. But workers with senior high school education, for example, felt more secure during the crisis, as the proportion of those who thought they would be fired soon was only five per cent.

Female workers and garment workers also seemed to feel more confident than the male and the other workers in other industries. More than 60 per cent of female workers said that they would continue working during the crisis, while 54 per cent of male workers had the same perception. Around 15 per cent of all workers in the shoes and textile industries thought that they were about to be fired soon, compared with only two per cent in the garment industries.

When workers were asked about company survival, around 57 per cent of them felt that the company would survive the crisis. This result is consistent with their perception on their job security. The results also consistently show that workers with higher education and female workers were generally more optimistic about their perception on job security. More than 63 per cent of those with high school education thought that the company would survive during the crisis, compared with around 48 per cent of those with primary school or lower education. The proportion of female workers who believed that the company would survive was around 59 per cent, compared with 54 per cent of the males. Those who work in the electronics industry also were more optimistic about their job security as 70 per cent of them thought that the company would survive the crisis.

Table 5.14 Workers' Perception of Job Security During the Crisis

	About to be fired	About to be put out	About to work on shifts	Not sure	Will continue working	No answer	Total
By Education							
Primary school or less	17.2	0.0	3.4	17.2	51.7	10.3	100.0
Jr.high school	10.6	0.0	0.0	17.0	59.6	12.8	100.0
Sr.high school or others	5.4	2.7	5.4	25.7	60.8	0.0	100.0
By Gender							
Female	9.8	0.0	3.9	17.6	60.8	7.8	100.0
Male	8.3	4.2	2.1	29.2	54.2	2.1	100.0
By Industry							
Electronics	0.0	0.0	10.0	30.0	60.0	0.0	100.0
Garment	1.9	1.9	1.9	15.4	73.1	5.8	100.0
Shoes	15.0	0.0	7.5	22.5	47.5	7.5	100.0
Textile	14.6	2.1	0.0	25.0	52.1	6.3	100.0
Total	9.3	1.3	3.3	21.3	58.7	6.0	100.0

Source: Data from field surveys.

Workers' Perception of Income Security

Related to workers' perception of income security, about two-thirds of workers in the survey said that their income in 1998 was sufficient to satisfy their needs - see Table 5.16. The fact that there has been drastic adjustment in the pattern of expenditure during the crisis, however, suggested a different reality. In other words, workers' income was not really enough to meet the increase in expenditure, but they felt that reducing their expenditure in real terms was a more viable option than looking for other jobs with higher income, which in fact were either very hard to find or unavailable. Workers had no other choice but to stay working in the same place. This argument is supported by the data on worker's reasons for staying and working in the same factory even though their income was not sufficient. When workers were asked why they stayed in the firm, the most common response (78 per cent) was 'difficult to find other jobs', while the next common answer (11 per cent) was 'receiving assistance from relatives'.

Table 5.15 Workers' Perception of the Survival of the Firm during the Crisis

	Don't know	No guarantee	Will not survive	Will survive	Grand Total
By Education					
Primary school or less	13.8	31.0	6.9	48.3	100.0
Jr.high school	14.9	25.5	6.4	53.2	100.0
Sr.high school or others	13.5	20.3	2.7	63.5	100.0
By Gender					
Female	17.6	18.6	4.9	58.8	100.0
Male	6.3	35.4	4.2	54.2	100.0
By Industry					
Electronics	10.0	10.0	10.0	70.0	100.0
Garment	19.2	19.2	3.8	57.7	100.0
Shoes	20.0	17.5	0.0	62.5	100.0
Textile	4.2	37.5	8.3	50.0	100.0
Total	14.0	24.0	4.7	57.3	100.0

Source: Data from field surveys.

Table 5.16 Workers' Perception of their Income Sufficiency

	Not Sufficient	Sufficient	Total
By Education			
Primary school or less	41.4	58.6	100.0
Jr high school	46.8	53.2	100.0
Sr high school or others	20.3	79.7	100.0
By Gender			
Female	30.4	69.6	100.0
Male	37.5	62.5	100.0
Total	32.7	67.3	100.0

Source: Data from field surveys.

When workers were asked about their willingness to have their wages cut if necessary in order to help the firm survive the crisis, the majority or 84 per cent of workers said that they would not accept a wage cut and only ten per cent said they would. To provide a more realistic and precise measure on their perception of income sufficiency, workers were then asked about the reservation wage or the minimum wage that they were willing to accept to work in the firm. The average value calculated based on the answers of 118 workers suggests that worker's reservation wage was significantly less than their actual wage in 1998. The average value of reservation wage was only 66 per cent of the actual average wage – see Table 5.17. This suggests that most workers would work for less income if necessary to keep their job in the firm. In general, the reservation wage for male workers was higher

(Rp206,000) than the females (Rp191,000). Similarly, the reservation wage for willingness to work for the highly educated was also higher than the less educated.

Table 5.17 Workers' Reservation Wage*

	Reservation Wage (Rp.000)	As % of Actual wage
By Education		
Primary school or less	190.5	71.0
Jr high school	207.7	69.0
Sr high school or others	206.0	62.3
By Gender		
Female	192.2	63.4
Male	224.3	69.5
Total	203.9	65.9

*Minimum wage that worker is willing to accept and to start working, or the minimum wage for willingness to work.

Source: Data from field surveys.

In summary, while workers in the survey felt that they would keep their job during the crisis, they did not feel the urgency to ask for higher wages in order to meet the sharp increase in their expenditure due to high inflation. In other words, their main coping strategy during the crisis was in the form of expenditure adjustments.

Workers' Coping Strategy

For a developing country like Indonesia where social security and unemployment insurance are not available, there are several types of workers' coping strategy during the crisis. The first strategy is to adjust their expenditure or spending in response to their lower income. The second strategy is to seek additional income by working part time, selling assets, and engaging in other livelihood activities. The third type is to rely on relatives and friends for assistance. Finally, the fourth type is a more drastic adjustment such as to move to another place and to seek new opportunities, including going back to the rural areas when they lose their jobs in urban areas.

When workers in the surveys were asked about their coping strategy in responding to insufficient income, the most common answers were: 'work part time' (30 per cent), 'do nothing' (28 per cent), and 'owe money from friends and relatives' (23 per cent) – see Table 5.18. Working part time is clearly in search of additional income. Owing money from friends and relatives means relying on the family and friend's safety net. The other type of coping strategy, namely 'doing nothing' basically means adjusting their expenditure to their lower real income.

Table 5.18 Workers' Coping Strategy for Insufficient Income

Coping Strategy	% of Respondents
Work part time	29.8
Owe money	22.8
Sell assets	1.8
Receive assistance from relatives	17.5
Do nothing	28.1

Source: Data from field surveys.

The first type of coping strategy, namely the drastic adjustment of expenditure to a lower real income and purchasing power was discussed more extensively in the previous section. There were basically several clear patterns of expenditure adjustments: to reduce savings and even to sell assets in order to cope with increasing overall expenditure, to reduce the quality and quantity of overall consumption, and to switch from the durable and tertiary goods to basic items such as food. These adjustments were clearly seen in the surveys, where workers' common strategies were reducing their meals from thrice to twice or even once a day, buying cheaper and lower quality food, and reducing expenditure for tertiary items such as recreation.

Another common strategy of expenditure reduction was to reduce their savings and remittances to relatives. There has been a dominant pattern of income transfer from workers in the urban areas to their relatives in the rural areas. This income transfer was generally a significant source of income for rural areas during the economic boom years in the early 1990s. Around 60 to 70 per cent of the workers in the surveys have stopped sending remittances to their relatives in rural areas, which meant that rural families who have relied on this transfer would soon find themselves in financial trouble. Therefore, while the urban areas have been hardest hit by the crisis, the reduction of income transfers from urban to rural areas would transmit the negative impact from urban to rural areas leading to the decline in the welfare of the rural population as well.

The second type of coping strategy (to seek additional income) was also a common response in the surveys. This was supported by the data on workers' plan once they were fired for their jobs. More than 45 per cent of the respondents said that they would seek other jobs, including part time jobs in the informal sectors to survive. It is important to note that the proportion of 'looking for new job' was a higher for workers with a higher level of education, suggesting again that education makes people more confident about their employment prospects.

Going back to rural areas and farms, however, was not very popular among these urban workers. This suggests that most of them have lost their ties with their rural origin, even though the higher level of education among workers in the sample also contributed to their unwillingness to go back to agriculture. The choice for alternative sources of income obviously varies between male and female workers. The males job preferences range from becoming a driver to setting up a small business such as going into motorcycle repair, selling cigarettes, collecting garbage, and opening a barber shop. The females job preferences were dominated by selling food, such as snacks, providing clothes washing services, and becoming a housemaid.

Table 5.19 Workers' Plan in Anticipation of Possible Layoff

	Don't know yet what to do	Farm	Look for a new job	Others	Temporarily unemployed	Total
By Education						
Primary school or less	24.1	3.4	31.0	20.7	20.7	100.0
Jr high school	14.9	19.1	40.4	17.0	8.5	100.0
Sr high school or others	20.3	4.1	54.1	13.5	8.1	100.0
By Gender						
Female	17.6	10.8	42.2	15.7	13.7	100.0
Male	22.9	4.2	52.1	16.7	4.2	100.0
Total	19.3	8.7	45.3	16.0	10.7	100.0

Source: Data from field surveys.

The third coping strategy in the form of reliance on support from family and relative is dominated by borrowing money, which in fact could only be a short-term solution. Depending on relatives and friends would be a worse strategy if workers' expectation of a better future were not realized. Workers who had borrowed money from relatives, for example, found themselves in a difficult position because their falling income lasted longer than they anticipated. In fact, the crisis has lasted for over two years with little sign of recovery at the macro level, so that borrowing money from friends and relatives can turn out to be an unsustainable strategy.

While this last coping strategy might not be sustainable when the crisis lasted longer than expected, this shows how social capital played a major role in forming workers' coping strategies during the crisis. The role of social capital is even more clear and important when, for example, due to the unfortunate developments workers do not have to repay their loan to their relatives.

Summary and Policy Implications

The Macro-Perspective

The survey data suggest that the labor market has been flexible in adjusting to the crisis and that the adjustment has been in the area of declining real income, rather than in increasing unemployment and underemployment. The small increase in unemployment does not mean a small number of layoffs; rather, it means that people could not afford to be unemployed. It is estimated that around one out of ten workers in the formal sector lost their jobs in 1998, but most of them took other jobs at a relatively lower income.

The real effect of the crisis is felt by the decline in purchasing power, higher labor turnover rate, and greater uncertainty in the labor market, as well as in the need among laborers to work more hours and to find alternative sources of income to meet the increase in expenditures. The crisis is also seen in the higher competition in the informal sector, increasing child labor and street children, increasing number of family workers especially women, and increasing number of workers unprotected by labor laws.

The crisis has seriously affected the non-tradable sectors, particularly the construction, public utilities, inefficient financial sector, and domestic-oriented manufacturing sectors. It has increased the share of the informal sector in the labor market as people who were laid off in the formal sector turned into informal activities. The movement of labor to the informal and the traditional and natural resource-based sectors, such as agriculture, forestry, and fisheries, had been accompanied by the movement of labor and employment opportunities into the rural areas.

The number of people living below the poverty line has increased since the crisis, even though the poverty estimates varied in 1998. Various data suggest that the distribution of expenditure is more even after the crisis, partly because of the sharp decline in income of those who were extremely rich before the crisis. But these do not suggest that the poor had suffered less than the rich because there had been drastic adjustments in the composition of income and expenditures in the family during the crisis that are not captured by the available data. In order to meet the increasing level of expenditures, the wealthy could consume their savings while the poor had to work longer hours or make other family members participate in the labor market. Therefore, those who suffered the most from the crisis were the ones with no savings and could not participate in the labor market, especially disadvantaged groups such as the elderly, single women with children, people with disabilities, and others.

The increasing number of female labor participation in Indonesia and the smaller number of layoffs for female workers relative to males, do not suggest that the depressed labor market has led to greater negative impacts for women. But it does not mean that women have suffered less than men considering the fact that the declining real income in many households, especially the poor ones, has forced women to work to obtain additional income for the family. The increasing number of family workers in the labor market shows that pooling human resources within the family is part of the coping mechanisms during the crisis.

While food availability at the national level was not an issue, the drastic increase in food prices during the crisis created some concern over food insecurity at the household level. Some data suggest that food insecurity was more serious in urban-poor communities, while others suggest that sooner or later the problem would be transmitted to rural areas considering the high proportion of landless farmers in rural areas and the movement of people back to the rural areas.

The Micro-Perspective

The data from the field surveys at the micro-individual worker in labor-intensive industries revealed how the crisis has changed the well being of Indonesian workers. The data on workers' income show that consistent with the trend at the macro-national level, workers' earnings had increased by around eight per cent in nominal terms but decreased by more than 30 per cent in real terms.

The total number of working hours had been relatively stable, with some decline in overtime hours. The data shows that the decline in earnings for female workers was less compared with those of the male. Workers in the textile and garment industries in the surveys had suffered more than workers in other industries in terms of wage adjustment.

The data on expenditures show that the crisis had increased workers' expenditures on basic items such as food and reduced their spending on tertiary needs such as clothing. The data also show how workers had been smoothing their consumption level by reducing and consuming their savings.

In terms of workers' perceptions on job security, majority of the workers felt that they would continue working in the same factory in spite of the crisis, and workers with higher education felt more confident about their job security. Female workers and garment workers also seemed to feel more confident than the males and those that work in other industries. It is important to note that the sample of workers in the survey is taken from labor export-oriented intensive industries, one of the surviving sectors during the crisis.

Related to workers' perception of income security, about two-thirds of workers in the survey said that their income in 1998 was sufficient to satisfy their needs, mainly because workers had no other choice but to keep working in the same place. The minimum wage for which workers would be willing to continue working was estimated at around 66 per cent of their actual average wage. This suggests that most workers would work for less income if necessary to keep their job in the firm. The survey data reveal three major types of workers' coping strategies during the crisis: adjusting their expenditures, seeking additional income, and relying on assistance from family and friends.

Policy Implications

Maintaining the flexibility of the labor market is very important during the crisis because it will lead to faster economic recovery as a whole. However, since real income adjustment is so severe in some areas, such as in the poor urban areas in Java, it is crucial that the provision of safety nets for those who need them and those that could not help themselves should be available.

Considering the nature of the impact of the crisis, employment creation programs should not be targeted only at certain individuals such those who were laid off. Instead, these programs should promote employment creation in general. Meanwhile, targeting should be done in areas or sectors with the most severe employment reductions.

The crisis has created a natural selection in the economy, where the inefficient and protected sectors are collapsing and the competitive sectors are booming. As such, employment creation programs should facilitate labor mobility from the shrinking sectors to the booming ones. Policies should not prevent the collapsing sector from laying off workers, but should provide incentives for the newly booming sectors, such as labor-intensive, natural-resource based, and export-oriented industries to expand and employ more workers.

Noting that the real effect of the crisis is in the decline in real income, it is important that the government provide general income support programs for safety nets. Attempts at securing food security, however, should avoid creating distortions in the market. Providing food subsidies might possibly be the only choice in the short run, but it must be targeted to the most needy—in the case of the present crisis, the urban poor. Meanwhile, from the supply side, instead of subsidizing farmers, they should be allowed to sell rice at market price to provide an incentive to produce.

The decentralization of the social safety net program should be encouraged. Here, the participation of NGOs in the implementation and monitoring of the program is crucial to provide a control mechanism that ensures that the social safety nets are applied without much leakage and corruption.

In any case, further research is needed to uncover the dynamic adjustment in family income and expenditures during the crisis to measure more precisely the impact of the crisis. Considering the complex adjustment in the patterns of income and expenditures of households during the crisis, a better indicator for a change in the quality of life, other than the level of poverty is needed.

The social safety net program should not overemphasize the short-run impact of the crisis such as problems associated with unemployment and income reduction. The flexibility of the labor market has basically absorbed the needed short-run adjustment to the crisis. The data suggest that the longer-term impacts of the crisis, such as education and health related issues could be more serious. Therefore, the social safety net program should also provide the required support for education and health services for the long run.

The major challenge in the longer run for Indonesia is the lower level of workers' education compared with neighboring countries. An increase in public investment in education is badly needed because public spending in education has been very low compared to other neighboring countries for several decades.

Appendix 1

The Field Surveys

Objectives

The field survey was designed before the economic crisis started in mid-1997, and the focus was on the conditions of labor in labor-intensive export-oriented industries such as textile, garment, and shoes. These labor-intensive industries became a very important segment of the labor market in Indonesia because of the dynamic changes and developments in the labor market in the last decade, especially during the economic boom times in the early 1990s that took place within these sectors. During these boom years, these labor-intensive export-oriented industries were the leading sectors in the economy in terms of creating employment, absorbing unskilled workers from agriculture, increasing real wages, and earning foreign exchange. The rapid increase in female labor force participation in Indonesia during the last decade was also due to the rapid development of these labor-intensive industries. Various forms of labor unrest and demonstrations in the early 1990s were also related to workers' dissatisfaction in these sectors.

The original objective of the field research or surveys was to uncover the perception of workers in these labor-intensive industries on security issues, especially related to their income and job security. But as the economic crisis took place and worsened, the survey was used to uncover adjustments in worker's income and expenditures during the crisis. It is important to note that this survey might not be the best survey to study the impact of the crisis, because these export-oriented industries in the survey turned out to be the biggest winner during the crisis. Workers in export-oriented industries that used to represent the average unskilled workers in the manufacturing industries became the workers who survived well during the crisis.

The field research consists of two types of field surveys: questionnaire survey and interview survey. The first is the collection of data from Indonesian workers by distributing questionnaires to workers, while the second is in-depth interviews, mainly of labor activists and union leaders, government officials, and members of the business community. The questionnaire survey is more quantitative in nature because it collects quantitative data on workers' income, expenditures, and perception on security. It turned out that this questionnaire surveys also involved an in-depth interview for each worker to precisely measure his/her income and expenditures before and during crisis. The second form of field research was in-depth interviews that were more qualitative in nature. These in-depth interviews were conducted to capture the perception of union leaders, government officials, and firm managers on employment problems and workers' security in general. Integrating those two methodologies would certainly lead to more precise and complete results. The data collection for the survey was conducted mostly in August, September, and October 1998. The locations for the surveys were Jakarta, Bogor, Tangerang, Bekasi, and Surabaya. These areas were chosen for their concentration of the selected labor-intensive industries.

Sampling Procedure

The sample was limited to 150 workers, mainly because of budgetary and time constraints. Because of the limited sample, the survey adopted a proportional sampling technique, rather than random sampling, to increase the efficiency and precision in deriving the sample. In addition, random sampling would be difficult in practice when the characteristic and the size of the population (low-skilled Indonesian workers) are hard to define and to locate more accurately. This proportional sampling technique, however, has some limitations. One of them is selection bias, which would lead to potential problems when the data are used for analysis involving statistical inference. For example, those workers in the sample were actually workers who have been surviving the crisis. In other words, the sample would not represent the condition of all Indonesian workers in all sectors. Therefore, any conclusion from this data should be interpreted carefully. Given this limitation, the data will only be reliable for descriptive analysis in uncovering economic conditions and perception on security of those unskilled workers in the labor-intensive sectors during the crisis.

The survey also adopted the stratification of sampling procedure, as there are many relevant factors in controlling the sample selection (regions, type of industries, company size, and also gender). The first step is the selection of four labor-intensive industries: textiles, garments, footwear, and electronics. These industries are characterized by relatively simple technology, high labor intensity, and absorption of massive numbers of unskilled workers during the last seven years. Because of the availability of the companies in the selected areas, certain types of products from each industry were selected for sampling. In the footwear industry, the selected products are sport shoes and footwear for daily use (ISIC 32412, 32411). The garment industry consists of mostly clothing apparel made of textiles (ISIC 32210), while the textile industry consists of weaving mills, finished textiles, printed textiles, and other finished textile articles except clothing apparels (ISIC 32114, 32115, 32116, 32121). Electronic industries cover radio, television, consumer electronics, computer software, and household electronic appliances (ISIC 38321, 38325, 38330).

The next step was to allocate a proportionate number of interviews to each industry. The distribution of respondents among four industries is based on the relative number of workers working in the four industries. For practical purposes, several firms were then selected from each industry and a sample of workers was chosen in each firm. To increase the variety of the companies selected, only five workers in every firm were taken for the questionnaire survey. The number of the targeted firms or companies, therefore, is 30, and these firms were then divided according to their economies of scale determined by the number of workers. This survey concentrated on the medium scale (20-100 workers) and large scale (more than 100 workers) companies. The respondents were distributed purposively in large scale (75-80 per cent) and medium scale (20-25 per cent) companies. In order to compare the impact of the economic crisis across gender and to see the different perceptions on security between male and female workers, it was important to look at both the female and male respondents. The application of this technique is to make sure that different types of respondent were adequately represented in the samples. Only production workers[48] were sampled because the focus of this study is on low-skilled workers.

Sampling Distribution

As indicated earlier, the distribution of respondents among industries was based on the relative number of total workers in the four industries (with certain types of products). The breakdown is 33 per cent in the textile industry, 33 per cent in garments, 27 per cent in shoes, and seven per cent in electronics.[49] Based on these percentages the number of respondents from each industry could be calculated proportionately. In addition, the respondents from each industry were distributed purposively according to the scale of the company. The distribution of the respondents according to the type of industry, the size of the company, and gender is presented in Tables 5.20 and 5.22.

The information related to companies was gathered from factory managers or owners, labor supervisors, and labor union representatives (mainly for qualitative data). The data from workers were collected directly from workers in the residential areas (*kampung* or village) near the selected company. To find respondents in the nearby *kampung*, this survey used a 'snowballing' technique. This technique involves asking a key informant, or one chosen respondent, to name other people who should be contacted by the investigator. This technique has some limitations, such as a certain bias since the people chosen as the next respondent may have the same characteristic as the previous one. Another limitation is that the companies or workers chosen in the surveys are the ones who survived during the crisis. Those unemployed workers who were laid off during the crisis were not in the sample because they were no longer in the factories. Additional respondents, especially those who lost their jobs during the crisis were also surveyed, but the result was not presented here. Finally, since the selected industries mostly employed women workers, most respondents were also women workers.

The Questionnaire

Each questionnaire that was distributed to workers consisted of 76 questions, which targeted the following information:

1. Firm Characteristics

This is on the respondent's general knowledge of the firm: what is the firm output, in which section the respondent works, how long the respondent has worked there, etc.

2. Personal Characteristics

This is mainly on the respondent's personal profile such as: age, sex, education, marital status, living arrangement, and others.

3. Employment and Income Conditions

The first information is about working status (part time, full time), job tenure, and experience. Then data on detailed income and expenditures, before and after the crisis, were collected to determine the respondent's economic condition.

4. Perceptions of Job Security

The respondent's perceptions on job and income security were investigated through several questions such as: Will your company survive in facing the economic crisis? Do you think you can continue to work in your company? Has there been any lay-off in the company? Did the company tell the worker why he/she was laid off? Do you agree with the reason?

5. Perceptions of Welfare and Benefits

The perception of workers on their quality of life and welfare was captured through several questions such as: Is your income sufficient? If not, how do you overcome that? What kind of benefits do you receive from your company?

The targeted respondents for the in-depth interviews were government officials, labor union activists, businessmen, or firm managers who were selected purposively on the basis of their special knowledge and experience in the area of interest. This qualitative approach is adopted to collect qualitative data, mainly related to more subjective issues such as government policy, feelings about future economic prospects, general security issues, and others. Data collected from this qualitative survey were used to support and to verify the quantitative data from the questionnaire survey.

The Characteristics of the Respondents

Tables 5.20 to 5.22 present the characteristics of the respondents in the sample and show that in terms of industry composition, the distribution is: 33 per cent from garments, 33 per cent from textiles, 27 per cent from footwear and seven per cent from electronics. In terms of gender, 68 per cent of the sample were female workers and the remaining 32 per cent were males. The gender composition reflects the actual proportion between men and women in the four selected industries where 70 -75 per cent are women and 25-30 per cent are men.[50] In terms of age, the minimum age of workers is 17 years, the maximum is 47 years, and the average is 25.7 years. This result shows that workers are relatively still young and in their most productive cycle. Another study reports that workers in the labor-intensive industries are mostly fresh graduates or new entrants.[51] It is not surprising, therefore, that most (65.3 per cent) workers are single, 32.67 per cent are married, and two per cent are widowed or divorced. This fact is in line with findings of several previous studies that the combination of social characteristics determines the stage of life cycle which in turn affect labor participation.[52] Almost 68 per cent of the respondents live in rented rooms or houses shared with friends, while the remaining 33 per cent live with their parents, relatives, or spouses, or live in the company's dormitory. The rented rooms are usually in close proximity to the factory. For independent workers with only one source of income, the place they can afford is generally sub-standard.

The education level of the respondent turns out to be generally higher than the education level of most workers in Indonesia. Around 18 per cent of the respondents are primary school graduates, 31 per cent are junior high school graduates, and 39 per cent are senior high school graduates. This level of schooling is high compared with the national standard in which more than 50 per cent of workers have primary school or less education.

The level of education of the respondents is also higher compared with a similar survey, which was conducted in 1997.[53] The previous survey, which focused on women workers in the textile, garment, and footwear industries, indicates that 70 per cent out of 300 respondents have only up to junior high school education. It might be true that the lower level of education in the previous survey is due to the fact that its sample consists of only female workers, who generally hâve a lower education level than males. But this finding is also in line with the fact that these labor-intensive industries have been very progressive in improving their technology, requiring a higher level of education for the new employees. It could also be the firm's reaction to the progressive increase in minimum wages during the last seven years. The government has tripled the minimum wages since 1990, forcing the firm to use more capital-intensive technology, to employ less number of workers but with higher levels of education and productivity.

Table 5.20 Distribution of the Sample

	Textiles (32114, 32115, 32116, 32121)	Garments (32210)	Footwear (32412, 32411)	Electronics (38321, 38325, 38330)
Number of Respondents	34 % x 150= 50 respondents taken from 10 companies	33 % x 150= 50 respondents taken from 10 companies	27 & x150 = 40 respondents taken from 8 companies	6 % x 150 = 10 respondents taken from 2 companies
Large Companies	80 % x 50 = 40 respondents	80 % x 50 = 40 respondents	75 % x 40 = 30 respondents	80 % x 10 = 8 respondents
Medium Companies	20 % X 50 = 10 respondents	20 % x 50 = 10 respondents	25 % x 40 = 10 respondents	20 % x 40 = 2

Survey population:
- Workers in Textiles (32114, 32115, 32116, 32121),
- Workers in Garments (32210),
- Workers in Footwear (32412, 32411), and
- Workers in Electronics (38321, 38325, 38330).

Research Areas:
- Jakarta,
- Bogor,
- Tangerang, and
- Bekasi dan Bandung.

Total respondents:
- 150 workers (maximum of 5 respondents per company).

Table 5.21 The Structure of the Sample

Area	Textile	Garment	Footwear	Electronic	Total
Jakarta	12	18	5		35
Bogor	10	10	5		25
Tangerang	13	2	15		30
Bekasi	5	5			10
Surabaya	10	15	15	10	50
Total	50	50	40		150

Table 5.22 Characteristics of the Respondents

Total % of Respondents Employed According to Industry Type	(%)	Sex	(%)	Age	Years
Textile	33	Male	32	Minimum	17
Garment	33	Female	68	Maximum	46
Footwear	27			Average	25.7
Electronic	7				
Education Level	(%)	Marital Status	(%)	Living Arrangement	(%)
Below primary	1	Single	65.3	Company dormitory	3
Primary school	18	Married	32.7	Rental	68
Junior high school	31	Divorce/Widow	2.0	With Parents/Family	16
High school	39			Own house	12
Others	11			Others	1

Notes

1 See Mitchel, P. T., Quadir, F., Shaw, T. M. and van der Westhuizen, J. (1997), 'Report of the Task Force on Development and Security Discourse', *Development and Security in Southeast Asia: Task Force Reports*, Canadian Consortium on Asia Pacific Security, Toronto.

2 United Nations Development Programme (UNDP) (1999), *Human Development Report 1999*, Oxford University Press, New York.

3 Mitchel, *et. al.*, 'Report of the Task Force on Development and Security Discourse', 1997.

4 The discussion on the causes of the crisis and the deteriorating confidence in the economy, and the transmission from the economic collapse to the social impact, can be seen in Feridhanusetyawan, T. (1988), 'The Social Impact of the Indonesian Economic Crisis', *The Indonesian Quarterly*, vol.XXVI, no.4, December.

5 The interest rate offered by the central bank is higher than the deposit rate offered by commercial banks.

6 Some banks have up to 90 per cent non performing loan.

7 The impact of rapid economic growth on labor market is discussed for example in Agrawal, N. (1996), *The Benefit of Growth for Indonesian Workers*, World Bank Policy Research Working Paper no.1637, Washington DC. See also Manning, C. (1998), *Indonesian Labour in Transition: An East Asian Success Story?*, Cambridge University Press.

8 Labor Force Participation Rate is the ratio of people in the labor force and the total working age population in per cent.
9 See Feridhanusetyawan, 'Social Impact of the Indonesian Economic Crisis', 1998, pp.4.
10 See International Labor Organization (ILO) (1998), *Employment Challenges of the Indonesian Economic Crisis*, ILO Report.
11 *Sakernas* (Survey Angkatan Kerja Nasional – National Labor Force Survey) is a major data source of data about the labor market in Indonesia used in this study. The survey is conducted annually in August, and the result is usually published in February of the following year. The latest data available is for August 1998, which already capture some impact on the crisis.
12 See Manning, C. and Jayasuriya, S. (1996), 'Survey of Recent Development', *Bulletin of Indonesian Economic Studies*, August, and also Manning, C. and Junankar, P.N. (1998), 'Choosy Youth or Unwanted Youth? A survey of Unemployment', *Bulletin of Indonesian Economic Studies*, vol.34, no.1, April.
13 Manning and Jayasuriya, 'Survey of Recent Development', 1996.
14 See Agrawal, *The Benefit of Growth for Indonesian Workers*, 1996.
15 *Susenas* (Survey Sosial Economi Nasional – National Social Economic Survey) is another source of data that covers wider range of information such as expenditure. The survey is conducted annually in February, but the result is usually available for public in very late – sometimes more than one year later. The sample size of *Susenas* is four times larger than *Sakernas* and they are generally not comparable.
16 From February – May 1998, Minister of Manpower, Representatives of Labor Unions, and others observers announced large and overestimated unemployment figures, ranging from 13 to 20 million people unemployed. They might use these large numbers to show the seriousness of employment problems in Indonesia. See for example, *Jakarta Post*, 14 April 1998, *Suara Karya*, 14 May 1998.
17 ILO, *Employment Challenges of the Indonesian Economic Crisis*, 1998.
18 Monthly earning consists of monthly wage plus other benefit.
19 To compare the social impacts of the financial crisis in various Asian countries, See Manning, C. (1999), 'Labour Markets in the ASEAN-4 and the NIEs', *Asian Pacific Economic Literature*, vol.13, no.1, May; and also Lee, E. (1998), *The Asian Financial Crisis: The Challenge of Social Policy*, ILO, Geneva.
20 Minimum value of wage offer that is accepted by someone to take the job and to start working.
21 The role of social safety net is crucial during the economic crisis to provide some protection for those who have to suffer from painful economic adjustments. The general objectives of the social safety net programs are to protect the poor against sharp reduction in consumption and to prevent losses in human capital as a result of the sharp decline in real income.
22 This was released before the final version of government budget announced in July 1998.
23 *Kompas*, 20 September 1998.
24 United Nation Support Facility for Indonesian Recovery (UNSFIR) (1999), *The Social Implications of the Indonesian Economic Crisis: Perception and Policy*, Discussion Paper No.1, April.
25 Reported in various newspapers in the second week of February 1999.
26 World Bank (1999), *Indonesia: From Crisis to Opportunity*, World Bank Report, July.
27 The benefit of economic development for the poor can be seen in for example in Mason, A. D. and Baptist, J. (1996), *How Important Ares Labor Markets to the Welfare of Indonesia's Poor?* World Bank Policy Research Paper no.1665, Washington DC.
28 ILO defines poverty standard in 1998 as the poverty standard in 1996 x 16.5 per cent increase in median consumption x 80 per cent inflation rate.

29 The poverty standard according to BPS is equal to 2100 calorie per day plus other basic needs, which was translated to Rp52,470/month/capita in urban areas, and Rp41,588/month/capita in rural areas.
30 Poppele, J., Sumarto, S. and Pritchett, L. (1999), 'Social Impact of the Indonesian Economic Crisis: New Data and Policy Implication', *Smeru Report*, February.
31 The Indonesian Family Life Survey (IFLS) is an ongoing longitudinal household and community survey conducted as a collaborative effort between RAND, Lembaga Demografi-UI and UCLA. The most recent of the survey is the IFLS 2+, a detailed resurvey of almost 2,000 households in seven provinces following the economic crisis (between August and December 1998). For the complete report see Frankenberg, E., Thomas, D. and Beegle, K. (1999), *The Real Cost of Indonesia's Economic Crisis: Preliminary Findings from the Indonesian Family Life Surveys*, Labor and Population Program Working Paper Series 99-04, March, Rand Corporation.
32 UNSFIR, *The Social Implications of the Indonesian Economic Crisis: Perception and Policy*, 1999.
33 *Ibid.*
34 The government provided exchange rate subsidy at around 50 per cent of the market rate for the National Logistic Agency (BULOG) to import rice in late 1997 and early 1998. By assuming that the rice imported was around six million tons in 1998, the international market price at around US$300/ton, the cost of import could easily reach US$1.8 billion. With subsidy at around 50 per cent, and the exchange rate at Rp10,000/US$, the subsidy was estimated at around Rp9 trillion or around 3.5 per cent of the total government budget.
35 BULOG (National Logistic Agency), various reports.
36 Popple, *et. al.*, 'Social Impact of the Indonesian Economic Crisis: New Data and Policy Implication', 1998.
37 UNSFIR, *The Social Implications of the Indonesian Economic Crisis: Perception and Policy*, 1999.
38 Data are from Depnaker, quoted from 'Permintaan TKI meningkat', *Suara Pembaruan*, 11 July 1998.
39 'Calo Puas Memeras, Pekerja Memelas', *Bisnis Indonesia*, 6 November 1998.
40 'Malaysia Mendeportasi 10.000 TKI Ilegal', *Republika*, 21 March 1998.
41 '1700 per bulan, TKI Masuk Sarawak', *Kompas*, 23 April 1998.
42 'Steps to protect workers 'slow compared to promotion'', *The Jakarta Post*, 18 December 1998.
43 The description of the field survey including its objective and methodology is presented in more detail in Appendix 1.
44 Pangestu, M. and Hendytio, M. K. (1997), *'Survey Responses from Women Workers in Indonesia's Textile, Garment and Footwear Industry'*, World Bank Policy Research Paper.
45 Using exchange rates at Rp2,500/US$ in 1997 and Rp10,000/US$ in 1998.
46 One study for example Hendityo, M. K. (1999), *Workers Coping Strategies: Ways to Survive the Crisis in Indonesia*, unpublished report for the World Bank, May.
47 See Frankenberg, Thomas, and Beegle, *The Real Cost of Indonesia's Economic Crisis: Preliminary Findings from the Indonesian Family Life Surveys*, 1999.
48 Industrial statistics in Indonesia classified workers into two broad categories separated by the supervisor level. Those below the supervisor are classified as production workers, while the supervisor and above are classified as non production workers.
49 This classification is based on Industrial Statistics, BPS, 1995.
50 See Industrial Statistics, BPS, 1995.
51 Pangestu, and Hendytio, *Survey Responses from Women Workers in Indonesia's Textile, Garment and Footwear Industry*, 1997.

52 See Singarimbun, M. and Sairin, S. (1995), *Liku-liku Kehidupan Buruh Perempuan*, Pustaka Pelajar, Jogyakarta. And see also Lok, HP. (no date), 'Labor in Garment Industry: an Employer's Perspective' in C. Manning and J. Hardjono (eds), *Indonesia Assessment 1993: Labor Sharing in the Benefit of Growth, Political and Social Change*, Monograph No.20, Research School of Pacific Studies, Australian National University, Canberra.

53 Pangestu, and Hendytio, *Survey Responses from Women Workers in Indonesia's Textile, Garment and Footwear Industry*, 1997.

References

Agrawal, N. (1996), *The Benefit of Growth for Indonesian Workers*, World Bank Policy Research Working Paper no. 1637, Washington, DC.

'Calo Puas Memeras, Pekerja Memelas', *Bisnis Indonesia*, 6 November 1998.

Feridhanusetyawan, T. (1988), 'The Social Impact of the Indonesian Economic Crisis', *The Indonesian Quarterly*, vol. XXVI, no. 4, December.

Frankenberg, E., Thomas, D. and Beegle, K. (1999), 'The Real Cost of Indonesia's Economic Crisis: Preliminary Findings from the Indonesian Family Life Surveys', *Labor and Population Program Working Paper Series* 99-04, March, Rand Corporation.

Hendityo, M. K. (1999), *Workers Coping Strategies: Ways to Survive the Crisis in Indonesia*, unpublished report for the World Bank, May.

Lee, E. (1998), *The Asian Financial Crisis: The Challenge of Social Policy*, ILO, Geneva.

Lok, HP. (no date), 'Labor in Garment Industry: an Employer's Perspective' in C. Manning and J. Hardjono (eds), *Indonesia Assessment 1993: Labor Sharing in the Benefit of Growth, Political and Social Change*, Monograph No. 20, Research School of Pacific Studies, Australian National University, Canberra.

Manning, C. (1999), 'Labour Markets in the ASEAN-4 and the NIEs', *Asian Pacific Economic Literature*, vol. 13, no. 1, May.

Manning, C. and Jayasuriya, S. (1996), 'Survey of Recent Development', *Bulletin of Indonesian Economic Studies*, August.

Manning, C. and Junankar, P.N. (1998), 'Choosy Youth or Unwanted Youth? A survey of Unemployment', *Bulletin of Indonesian Economic Studies*, vol. 34, no. 1, April.

'Malaysia Mendeportasi 10.000 TKI Ilegal', *Republika*, 21 March 1998.

Mason, A. D. and Baptist, J. (1996), *How Important Are Labor Markets to the Welfare of Indonesia's Poor?*, World Bank Policy Research Paper no. 1665, Washington DC.

Mitchel, P. T., Quadir, F., Shaw, T. M. and van der Westhuizen, J. (1997), 'Report of the Task Force on Development and Security Discourse', in *Development and Security in Southeast Asia: Task Force Reports*, Canadian Consortium on Asia Pacific Security, Toronto.

'1700 per bulan, TKI Masuk Sarawak', *Kompas*, 23 April 1998.

Pangestu, M. and Hendytio, M. K. (1997), *Survey Responses from Women Workers in Indonesia's Textile, Garment and Footwear Industry*, World Bank Policy Research Paper.

Poppele, J., Sumarto, S. and Pritchett, L. (1999), 'Social Impact of the Indonesian Economic Crisis: New Data and Policy Implication', *Smeru Report*, February.

Singarimbun, M. and Sairin, S. (1995), *Liku-liku Kehidupan Buruh Perempuan*, Pustaka Pelajar, Yogyakarta.

'Steps to protect workers 'slow compared to promotion'', *The Jakarta Post*, 18 December 1998.

United Nations Development Programme (UNDP) (1999), *Human Development Report 1999*, Oxford University Press, New York.

United Nation Support Facility for Indonesian Recovery (UNSFIR) (1999), *The Social Implications of the Indonesian Economic Crisis: Perception and Policy*, Discussion Paper No.1, April.

World Bank (1999), *Indonesia: From Crisis to Opportunity*, World Bank Report, July.

Chapter 6

Industrialization and Workers' Security: A Political Perspective

Muhammad AS Hikam

Background

Indonesia experienced a rapid industrialization process for more than three decades under the New Order government. From the vantage point of economic development, Indonesia's experience is considered as one of the most successful in Asia. Indeed, many studies have shown that the growth of the industrial sectors, especially the manufacturing industries reached 12.5 per cent annually during the period 1965-91.[1] This record achievement is quite substantial considering that when growth started in the 1960s, Indonesia had the lowest industrial output in the Association of Southeast Asian Nations (ASEAN). But beginning in the mid-1980s, especially following the switch from Import Substitution Industrialization (ISI) to Export Oriented Industrialization (EOI), Indonesia had attained the largest industrial output in the region representing 30 per cent of total industrial production.

The above success story has not, however, been followed by a similar trend in the realm of labor relations. Quite the contrary, labor relations under the New Order were exploitative in nature, especially when seen from the workers' point of view. Until recently, the national policy on labor relations that has been known as the *Pancasila Industrial Relations* (HIP) tended to disregard or at least neglect the basic rights as well as interests of the workers. As a result, the latter has remained at the lowest level in terms of wages compared with other industrializing ASEAN countries. The workers' political bargaining position *vis-a-vis* both the companies and the state is also probably the weakest, due in large part to the weakness of the existing Indonesian workers unions. It is not an exaggeration to say that Indonesian workers are still 'prisoners of progress' in their own country.

To be fair, the New Order government had attempted to improve its policy from time to time, including the setting of wage standards in order to meet the Food and Agriculture Organization's (FAO) standard of minimum physical needs that in Indonesia is known as *Kebutuhan Fisik Minimum* (the Minimum Physical Needs, KFM) and later *Kebutuhan Hidup Minimum* (the Minimum Living Needs, KHM). Politically, the workers had been allowed to form unions as long as they are under the umbrella of *Federasi Serikat Pekerja Seluruh Indonesia* (the All Indonesian Labor Union Federation, (FSPSI)), a state-sponsored organization established in 1973. There are also some regulations aimed at providing a set of rules governing labor relations in the country. The most recent, and by and large also controversial, is the Labor Law No.25, 1997.

Yet, it is precisely those three sets of government policy on labor relations that have mainly been responsible for the seemingly unending workers' protests, particularly in the end of the 1980s and early 1990s up to the downfall of Soeharto in the late 1990s. The issue of minimum wage has continuously become the main cause of worker strikes and other protests in industrial cities of Indonesia. The failure of the FSPSI in protecting its members and defending their basic rights in the workplace has made it a target of sharp criticism among worker activists which, in turn, causes a widespread distrust among the workers in general regarding its role as a labor organization. With the downfall of the New Order in May 1998, there emerged a window opportunity for Indonesian workers to realize their dream of having strong and independent worker unions. Existing labor regulations have been incapable of improving the workers' standard of living and protecting them from the vicissitudes of the market economy and political changes. If anything, they have served as instruments for maintaining the political and economic *status quo* in which workers would remain in subordinated position *vis-à-vis* the state and the companies.[2]

It is in the context of uncertain sociopolitical and economic conditions in Indonesia that this chapter attempts to examine the issue of workers' security in the country. In this respect, the notion of security will be understood in its broad definition that stresses the workers' sociopolitical situation. Thus, security includes the capacity of the workers to attain their goals in terms of basic needs, participation in the decision-making process related to their lives, in addition to the notion of the absence of internal and external threats to their well being. This definition will enable us to examine the political aspect of labor policies in Indonesia whose impacts are also felt in the entire body politic.

This chapter will be divided into three parts. First, an examination of the issue of labor wage and its impacts on workers' security. Second, an examination of labor unionization and its impacts on workers' security, and finally, an examination of labor policy, especially the existing labor law and its impacts on labor relations particularly those related to security. Attempts will be made to provide not only a general picture about existing labor conditions, especially in the post-Soeharto era, but also a detailed account of the existing workers' living conditions. The latter is based on the findings of fieldwork in Jakarta and Surabaya that had been conducted for the purpose of this study.[3]

Wage and Workers' Security

Wage Policy under the New Order

Wage has always been one of the most contentious problems and a major political issue in Indonesian labor relations. Its impacts not only affect the process of industrialization but also the issue of national security. Under the New Order, the government regarded wage as an important issue that should be addressed specifically within its industrial and labor relations policies. In fact, from the late 1980s, the problem of labor wage has been addressed specifically in the *Garis-garis Besar Haluan Negara* (the State's Broad Guidelines, GBHN), upon which any government in Indonesia would base its policies, including labor relations and industrialization.

Starting from 1989, through the Ministry of Workforce Decision No. 05/1989, the government had begun to implement the so-called regional minimum wage standard (*Upah Minimum Regional, UMR*). Through this policy, labor wage is regionally determined based on the following measurements: (1) KFM and later changed into KHM, (2) the existing Consumer Price Index (CPI), (3) the Regional Wage Base, (4) the existing national and regional economic development and performance, (5) the companies' capability and continuity, and (6) the current development in the labor market.

According to the government, through incremental increase of the UMR, the Indonesian workers' wage standard would gradually be competitive in the international labor market, while their living standard and condition would also be improved. Arguably, Indonesian industrial workers are the recipient of the lowest wage compared to such countries in Southeast Asia as Thailand and the Philippines, never mind Singapore and Malaysia. In order to support the regulation, the government reactivated the old *Dewan Penelitian Pengupahan Nasional* (the National Council for Wage Studies, DPPN) at the central government level and *Dewan Penelitian Pengupahan Daerah* (the Regional Council for Wage Studies, DPPD) at the provincial government level whose task is to give recommendations to the Ministry of Workforce regarding the UMR.

From the government's vantage point, there has been a significant improvement in terms of meeting the KFM standard ever since the wage policy was implemented.[4] According to official data, in 1989 the minimum wage standard only met 38 per cent of the KFM, while in 1994 it already reached 78 per cent – see Table 6.1. An official report in 1995 also maintained that the minimum wage reached 108 per cent of the KFM and, therefore, the government started to use the KHM standard, which in 1998 was expected to reach 100 per cent.[5] Unfortunately, with the onset of the economic crisis in 1997 it was impossible for the government to meet such a target and the existing wage policy had to be readjusted accordingly.[6]

From a close investigation in the field, however, the implementation of the UMR has been plagued with inconsistencies that led to its failure to meet its original objective. There are reasons for this problem. First of all, the nature of the UMR regulation itself is such that it is open to different interpretations in the field. Many companies, for instance, have distorted the notion of minimum wage standard into the maximum wage for their workers. This means that when the companies meet the requirement of minimum wage, they would use it as a benchmark for all of their workers regardless of their working experience and duration of employment.

Also the regulation opens the door for the companies to postpone the implementation of the UMR, because it contains a provision that allows the companies to do so. Therefore, it became common practice among companies to request a permit from the Ministry of Manpower in order to delay the payment of minimum wage according to the existing regulation. For example, the companies would send a letter asking for a grace period of up to three years in the implementation of the UMR on the grounds that they are not yet ready. However, by the time the UMR is implemented, the real value of the minimum wage would have already eroded substantially.

Table 6.1 Comparison between KFM and KHM (1988-94)

No	Province	1988	1989	1990	1991	1992	1993	1994
1	DI Aceh	54	51	77	75	75	91	Na
2	North Sumatra	44	42	67	62	80	91	Na
3	West Sumatera	44	41	64	62	65	66	87
4	Riau							
	a. Outside Batam	52	49	53	50	67	61	70
	b. Batam	Na	Na	Na	137	94	85	104
5	South Sumatera	39	37	53	50	44	63	Na
6	Jambi	48	45	44	64	69	40	Na
7	Bengkulu	52	47	46	43	62	55	82
8	Lampung	38	36	59	57	49	67	67
9	DKI Jakarta	63	57	73	77	72	81	82
10	West Java	30	28	44	63	58	68	78
11	Central Java	34	31	30	52	50	61	82
12	DI Yogyakarta	35	34	43	34	40	50	69
13	East Java	39	37	62	59	81	73	100
14	Bali	44	40	59	54	57	68	90
15	N T B	28	27	52	48	53	64	83
16	N T T	33	37	48	46	43	54	Na
17	West Kalimantan	52	47	43	54	51	61	Na
18	Central Kalimantan	32	29	30	40	38	75	Na
19	South Kalimantan	34	48	37	44	76	75	98
20	East Kalimantan	25	23	36	35	33	47	64
21	North Sulawesi	34	35	32	72	68	65	88
22	Central Sulawesi	27	25	30	37	35	53	69
23	South Sulawesi	35	33	33	37	48	48	63
24	Southeast Sulawesi	30	28	58	49	62	62	82
25	Maluku	31	31	51	49	46	56	56
26	Irian Jaya	39	42	41	54	50	66	66
27	East Timor	Na	Na	Na	46	44	43	64
	Average	42	38	49	55	57	64	79

Na: Not available.

Source: Simanjuntak, P. J. (1995).

Another point that frequently creates disputes between the companies and the workers is the interpretation of what constitutes the main wage (*upah pokok*). The regulation itself stipulates that there are two types of wages: the main wage (*upah pokok*) and the benefits (*tunjangan*). However, the regulation has opened a loophole because it fails to specify the elements that in turn can be distorted by the companies in order to avoid paying twice. Many labor disputes related to the UMR come from the disagreement between the companies and the workers because the latter would accuse the former of only paying the first category while according to the companies's interpretation it has fulfilled its duty.

Adding to the problem is the real value of the UMR that tends to fall below the rate of inflation and, therefore, affects the workers' purchasing power. A study by Indraswari and Thamrin on the real value of wage among workers in the tobacco processing industry demonstrated that the workers' purchasing power had diminished substantially from 1978 to 1993. In 1978, the daily wage was Rp225.00 and in 1993 there was an increase by a factor of ten, that is, Rp2,250. However, the workers were actually not better off due to the nominal wage increase. In 1978, with the existing wage they could buy more than five kilograms (kg) of rice, but in 1993 they could only get four kg for the same wage.[7]

The problem of the UMR is more pronounced when one also takes into account the earning ratios between the ordinary workers and the managers. A study of wage comparison in a shoe factory in Tangerang, West Java shows that the earning ratio between a director general and an ordinary worker was 150-220:1, a manager and an ordinary worker was 90-130:1, a section head and ordinary worker was 55-65:1, an operations manager and an ordinary worker was 13-22:1, a security guard and an ordinary worker was 3-6:1, and a foreman and an ordinary worker was 2-5:1.[8] The gap in earnings would affect not only the workers' welfare, but also their sense of justice. The workers would consider themselves exploited by both the companies and the managers and, therefore, they would always see the latter as exploiters and not as partners as suggested by the official principle of *Pancasila* labor relations.

Last, but certainly not the least is the fact that the implementation of the UMR has suffered from weak or inadequate law enforcement. It is common knowledge that the legal sanction for the failure of implementing the UMR is too weak. For example, a company that violates the regulation will only be fined a maximum of Rp100,000 (US$10.00), an amount that is not enough to deter such a practice. This inadequacy of law enforcement is also coupled with the practice of collusion between the government apparatus, especially in the district and provincial areas and the companies.

From the vantage point of the state, the wage policy is created to provide a guarantee of security for Indonesian workers, namely by improving their standard of living and of income. Politically, this policy is inseparable from the model of accelerated industrialization aimed at maintaining stability in the field of labor relations. By providing the minimum wage standard, the government could prevent the workers from being exploited in the workplace and gain their support as well as strengthen the state's political legitimacy. At the same time, however, the policy was created in such a way that it would not prevent the owners of capital and investors from being deeply involved in the process of industrialization in the country.

Yet as we will see from the fieldwork's findings, the impacts of the wage policy on workers' security have been generally negative. The Indonesian workers, primarily in the industrial sectors have remained in the circle of poverty and hopelessness due in large part to the lack of security in their daily life. In a study conducted in Manado and Surabaya, many light industrial workers expressed their feeling of insecurity because the UMR could not meet their basic needs.[9] Insecurity is also felt due to the uncertainty they experience in the urban environment that for most of them is relatively a new living environment. Although most of them had no intention to return to the agricultural sector in their village (because they would face similar problems anyway), they nevertheless acknowledged that working in the industrial sector was not so rewarding as they thought before they left their village.

Workers who have to take care of their dependents such as spouses and children also feel insecure. They have to be careful in spending their wages in order to live in the cities. Those who have better-off parents often ask for 'subsidies'. Earlier studies by Mather and Wolf in West Java province show that many workers in industrial towns such as Tangerang were subsidized by their village in the form of rice, clothes, others.[10] This is also consistent with findings in East Java and North Sulawesi provinces, in Surabaya and Manado cities, respectively where many workers, particularly women still depend on their families' support in their *kampongs* (villages).[11] However, those who have no such sources of support would have to depend on their own wages. Many of them have to work as peddlers or food sellers. Incidents such as illness or temporary unemployment could mean disaster for them and members of their family.

Insecurity caused by the uncertainty of wage has diminished the degree of independence among workers that in turn, affects their self-esteem as human beings. Most low skilled workers in light manufacturing industries are very dependent on the availability of job opportunities that are less demanding in terms of educational requirement and training or job experience. At the same time, they have to accept low wages, inadequate working conditions, and bad treatment from their supervisors in the workplace. Because of the abundant workforce in this particular position, unskilled workers have very little bargaining power *vis-à-vis* the companies. They are forced to accept the companies' regulations imposed by the management, including their wage and conditions of work. Many workers in this category work long hours and under very bad working conditions. Not only do they suffer physically from the lack of health provision but also psychologically from abuse and harassment by their supervisors. This is especially true for women workers who are mostly in light manufacturing industries such as textiles, shoes, and garments. They are prone to various abuse and harassment due to the lack of legal protection for them.

Another important factor that affects workers' security is the possibility of discriminatory treatment from the companies in terms of wage between the so-called permanent workers (*buruh harian tetap*) and non-permanent (*buruh harian lepas*) workers. The permanent workers receive much better treatment even if they violate some of the companys' rules such as absence from work for several days without reason. This will not be the case for non-permanent workers who will receive punishment from the companies according to existing rules such as deducting from their wages the monetary equivalent of the days of their absence from work.

In addition, it is well known in many companies that there is no clear policy on the procedure for changing one's status from a non-permanent to a permanent one. Some of the non-permanent workers have been in the companies for more than five years and have never been promoted to a permanent status. From the vantage point of the workers, a clear policy on promotions is very important because it means that they would have the security guarantee for their job in the future, while at the same time they enjoy some benefits such as retirement plans and housing programs. If they remained in the non-permanent status that means that they would be the first to go if their company considers downsizing its workforce.

Wage and Security in Industrial Sectors: Case Studies from Jakarta and Surabaya

The following case studies are based on a survey among low skilled workers in East Java Province, that is, Surabaya, and the *Jabotabek* (Jakarta, Bogor, Tangerang, and Bekasi) areas. They are purposively selected for their concentration of the selected industries whose products are for both domestic and export purposes. There are four labor-intensive industries that are selected for the purpose of this study, namely textile, garment, footwear, and electronic manufacturers. The reason for the selection is manifold, chief among which is the abundance of workers, particularly low skilled ones who are employed in these industries. Also they have similarities in the export orientation of their products. Lastly, these industries are characterized by low technologies and are highly labor intensive.

Profile of the Respondents The survey selected 30 companies, consisting of medium and large companies from which 150 workers were purposively selected and interviewed through a questionnaire. The medium scale companies are those that employ 20 to 100 workers, while the large scale companies are those that employ more than 100 workers.[12] In addition to the questionnaire, in-depth interviews were also conducted to obtain information from factory managers, worker union leaders, and government officers. These in-depth interviews were intended to collect data related to more subjective issues such as survival strategies, perceptions about the future, security, and so on. In this survey, the companies from the first category were represented by 75-80 per cent respondents, while those from the second category by 20-25 per cent respondents. Meanwhile, the respondents were chosen from the following industrial sectors: 34 per cent from the textile industries, 33 per cent from the garment industries, 27 per cent from shoe industries, and four per cent from the electronic industries – see Table 6.2.

The following is the profile of the respondents: in terms of gender, women constituted the majority (58 per cent) while the rest were men (32 per cent). This reflects the realities of the proportion of industrial workers where 70-75 per cent are women.[13] In terms of age, the youngest is 17 and the oldest is 47 years old. Furthermore, most of the respondents are also single (65.33 per cent) while 32.67 per cent are married and two per cent are either widowed or divorced. In terms of educational background, most are senior high school (SMU) graduates (42 per cent), followed by junior high school (SMP) graduates (28.66 per cent), elementary school (SD) graduates (18 per cent), and the remainder (10.67 per cent) are graduates from other schools such as vocational schools. The level of education of industrial workers in the two areas shows that industries now require a higher level of education, especially for the new entrants.[14] This also means that job opportunities for those who have a lower level of education are increasingly difficult in such a formal sector as the manufacturing industry – see Table 6.3.

Table 6.2 Structure of the Sample

Area	Textile	Garment	Footwear	Electronics	Total
Jakarta	12	18	5	-	35
Bogor	10	10	5	-	25
Tangerang	13	2	15	-	30
Bekasi	5	5	-	-	10
Surabaya	10	15	15	10	50
Total	50	50	40	-	150

Source: Fieldwork data.

Table 6.3 Characteristics of the Respondents

Total % of Respondents Employed according to Industry Type	**(%)**	**Sex**	**(%)**	**Age**	**Years**
Textile	34	Men	32	Minimum	17
Garment	33	Women	68	Maximum	46
Footwear	24			Average	25.7
Electronic	6				
Education Level	**(%)**	**Marital Status**	**(%)**	**Living Arrangement**	**(%)**
Primary School	18	Single	65.3 3	Company dormitory	3
Junior High	28.6 6	Married	32.6 7	Rental	68
High school	42.6 7	Divorce/Widow	2.00	With Parents/ Family	16
Beyond High School				Own house	12
Others	10.6 7			Others	1

Source: Fieldwork data.

In terms of their living conditions, the respondents mostly live in rented rooms (68 per cent) and the rest of them live with their parents, or in the companies' dormitory. Regarding their employment status, most of the respondents are daily workers (60.67 per cent) and permanent workers (32 per cent), while the rest are contract workers (two per cent), probationary workers (1.33 per cent), and put out workers (four per cent). Their working experience ranges from less than one year to 24 years, with an average of five years working experience.

In terms of income, before the crisis (July 1997) the respondents received an average amount of Rp237,670 that consisted of main wage, bonuses, and overtime pay. After the crisis, the respondents were receiving an average amount of Rp315,056. Their per-hour wage was a maximum of Rp17,500 and an average Rp4,038 before the crisis and Rp21,142 and Rp4,810, respectively after the crisis – see Table 6.4. In terms of working hours, 88.89 per cent of the respondents have stable working hours (seven hours daily), while those who experience decreasing working hours are 6.94 per cent and those who experience increasing working hours are 4.17 per cent. Their overtime schedule also tends to be stable. Most of the respondents (70.77per cent) have unchanged overtime schedules, while those who have decreasing overtime work are 18.46 per cent and those who have increasing overtime work are 10.77 per cent – see Table 6.5.

Table 6.4 Workers' Monthly Income, Before and After the Crisis (In Thousand Rupiah)

Income	Before Crisis			Crisis		
	Max (rp)	Min (rp)	Average (rp)	Max (rp)	Min (rp)	Average (rp)
Wages	5150	0	161302	424,0	0	185,548
Overtime*	1080	0	22679	148,0	0	31,302
Bonuses	5430	0	89689	509,0	0	98,206
Total			273670			315,056
Wages/hour	175	0	4038	21,142	0	4,810

*Overtime (per month) = 24 x first hour overtime wages + (Overtime B 24) x subsequent hour overtime wages

Source: Fieldwork data.

Wage Policy and Perception of Security among Industrial Workers Workers and factory managers in Jabotabek areas and Surabaya overwhelmingly support the establishment of minimum wage standard (81 per cent). Asked why they agree with this policy, most of the respondents said that it would provide workers a sense of income security and certainty. In addition, they believe that the UMR can gradually lead to wage equality. Some of the respondents also maintain that the exploitation of workers by their companies could be prevented through the UMR.

Among the factory managers, support for the UMR is also quite strong. A manager of a shoe factory in Surabaya, for example, says that the idea of establishing a wage standard such as the UMR is a noble one and from the business point of view would not reduce the productivity of his company. This is because the UMR is intended to establish a wage standard that is acceptable to all parties including the workers, managers, and the labor market. He also maintains that in the Indonesian context, if the wage were determined solely by market mechanism, it would tend to create unhealthy competition (*persaingan tak sehat*) among companies. The abundance of workers in the market, especially low skilled workers would have favored the companies at the expense of the workers. The policy of minimum wage, according to him, is especially sound for political reasons because it will contribute to stability in labor relations. By implementing such a policy in his company, he would be able to avoid political risks from the government, workers, and the labor union.[15]

Table 6.5 Employment Status

Working hours/week	Before Crisis	During Crisis	Overtime/week (hours)	Before Crisis	During Crisis
Minimum	7	7	Minimum	2	0
Maximum			Maximum	80	80
Average	45.10	44.61	Average	14.88	12.89

Changes in working hours/ Overtime	Working hours (%)	Over-time (%)	Working experience	Years	Work Status	(%)
Increase	4.17	10.77	Minimum	2	Probationary	1.33
Stable	88.89	70.77	Maximum	24	Contract	2.00
Decrease	6.94	18.46	Average	5	Monthly	32
					Daily	60.67
					Putting Out	4.00

Source: Fieldwork data.

When asked about the implementation of the UMR in their companies, most of the respondents (76 per cent) said that they have received the wage according to the existing standard. The majority of the respondents (67 per cent) also confirm that with the existing wage, they can meet their daily needs – see Table 6.6.

However, this finding is not consistent with the results of the in-depth interviews with some workers. The cases of Suyanti and Jaya (not real names), two workers in Surabaya can be used as an illustration.

> Suyanti, a woman worker at an electronics company in Surabaya had five years of working experience. As a daily worker, she received a monthly payment of Rp132,500, according to the existing regional wage standard (UMR). Yet, her monthly expenditures exceed her wage, which is approximately Rp199,000. This means that she has to find additional income to meet her monthly deficit. Added to this are various accidental expenses that she could not avoid such as helping her parents in the village or spending for medical care when she is sick. The latter happens because the health insurance program in her company only has a limited coverage. So if she could not earn additional income, she had to depend on her main wage. In this situation she has to force herself to 'make it enough' (*mencukup-cukupkan*) by lowering the quality of her food or delaying her purchase of non-essentials such as clothing or entertainment.

> Jaya, a single male that works in a textile factory in Surabaya is a little better off than Suyanti. He receives Rp144,150 monthly, consisting of his main wage of Rp141,000 and bonuses of Rp3,150. As a young and single man, he still lives with his parents in the nearby

kampong. Because of this he can maintain his monthly basic expenditures low at approximately Rp134,000. Yet, he says that there is no way for him to save the remaining Rp10,150 because, most of the time, he uses the money for accidental expenses, primarily entertainment. In short, the existing wage standard, according to him, is only barely enough to meet his basic needs as a single young man. Therefore, in his spare time he sometimes works as a pedicab driver or a night watchman (*Satpam*) in a shopping mall.

Table 6.6 Coping Strategies

Is income sufficient to cover living expenses	(%)	If income is insufficient why remain working in this company	(%)	If income is insufficient how do to cope?	(%)
Yes	67	Good relationship with employer	7	Working part time	33
No	33	Big bonuses	9	Owe money	23
		Difficult to find a job	91	Selling assets	4
		Receive assistance from relatives	7	Receive assistance from relatives	19
				Doing nothing	30

Source: Fieldwork data.

The above stories indicate that although the workers in general consider their wages insufficient for meeting their living cost and daily needs, in a deeper sense what they mean is that they actually have to make do whatever income they earn. This is especially true when we take into account the current crisis situation in which the rate of inflation is very high (approximately 90 per cent annually). The existing wage under the UMR is obviously far below the workers' basic needs. Therefore, it is not an exaggeration to say that they are forced to reduce their quality of life and accept the consequences, because for them the guarantee of job security is far more important.

Also, it is important to note that many workers like Suyanti and Jaya will attempt to look for other sources of income. The present survey finds that when asked abut this particular issue, 70 per cent of the respondents said that they tried to find such sources of income in part time jobs (33 per cent), borrowing money (23 per cent), or family assistance (four per cent). This finding is consistent with that of other studies on workers' income – see Table 6.6.[16] The availability of other sources of income has helped workers cope with income insecurity. It also explains why despite the decreasing value of their wage due to inflation workers tend to stay on in their jobs.

It is also noteworthy that in spite of these conditions, the workers seem to feel secure about their jobs. The majority of the respondents (62 per cent) said that they are quite sure that they will remain in their jobs regardless of the crisis. Only 32 per cent of the respondents said that they feel uncertain about their job security, while ten per cent were ready to be laid off – see Table 6.7. The reason for such confidence lies in the fact that most of the respondents were working with export-oriented manufacturing industries, especially textiles, garments, and shoes. According to a recent study on the UMR in the manufacturing industries,[17] these labor-intensive industries continue to grow because of their export orientation. As a consequence, they have no problem in meeting the demand for increasing the UMR standard.[18]

Table 6.7 Workers' Perceptions of Job Security

Are you working full time?	**(%)**	**Your position right now?**	**(%)**	**What do you think will happen to the firm in general?**	**(%)**
Full time	89.33	Work indefinitely	62.41	Will survive	57.33
On shift	5.33	About to be put at home	1.42	Will not survive	4.67
Temporary but at home	5.33	About to be fired	9.93	No guarantees	24.00
		About to work on shift	3.55	Don't know	14.00
		Not sure	22.70		
If you get fired, what is your future plan?	**(%)**	**Agree with wage cuts for company?**	**(%)**	**Minimum wage level you are willing to work at**	**(Rp)**
Temporary unemployment	10.67	Yes	10.00	Minimum	40.000
Farm	8.67	No	84.00	Maximum	400.000
Look for a new job	45.33	Don't know	6.00	Average	176,623
Don't know yet what to do	19.33				
Others	16				

Source: Fieldwork data.

This implies that the workers in non-export oriented manufacturing industries will be more vulnerable during the crisis. They will be less certain about job security because most of them are likely to be laid off sooner than later. The threat of being laid off is acknowledged by the respondents in this survey where the majority (51 per cent) tend to see that the number of workers' that were being laid off had been increasing in their companies lately. This means that despite the prevailing self-confidence among them regarding job security, the workers are also aware of the fact that their companies would be willing to take such a measure if they see it necessary.

How do the workers anticipate this prospect? Naturally, they will try their best to look for another job. However, they also seem to be aware that job opportunities are no longer abundant like before, particularly in the formal sector. The choice to return and work in the village is unattractive for most of them. Not only is the agricultural sector no longer interesting, but wages there are also low while the working conditions are equally bad. It is not surprising that recently the numbers of unemployed workers have increased in urban industrial areas such as Jabotabek and Surabaya as a result of the massive closure in the manufacturing industries. Some of them are now being absorbed by the informal sectors such as vendor peddlers (*pedagang kaki lima*) and pedicab drivers, but many also become scavengers (*pemulung*) or street beggars. A few of them attempt to become migrant workers in other ASEAN and East Asian countries or the Middle East but such an opportunity is also limited due to the restrictive policies by the host countries.

Policy Implications on Security The existing UMR policy should be better implemented in facing the crisis situation. Until recently, the implementation of the minimum wage standard was still inadequate because of internal and external constraints. Internally, the problem can be traced to the way in which companies interpret the regulation and the lack of bargaining power of the workers *vis-à-vis* the managers. According to a study on the implementation of the UMR conducted by the Legal Aid Foundation (LBH) Surabaya, the managers have manipulated the regulation in different ways. Chief among them are:[19]

1. The manipulation of the category of main wage and benefits in such a way that the workers will eventually receive less than the amount of the UMR.
2. The distortion of the application of the UMR standard.
3. The managers tend to ignore the workers' length of work experience, job risks, and the number of family members that are dependent on the workers.
4. The policy of not paying the wage of women workers who are absent from work because of their monthly cycle.
5. The policy of wage equalization between women workers who have a family and single male workers on the ground that women are not household heads.
6. Reducing the amount of bonuses and other fringe benefits for workers.
7. Manipulation in calculating the minimum wage. This has been done, for example, by giving no receipts or clear enumeration of wage components to the workers.

The lack of bargaining power of the workers has been due in large part to the weakness of the existing labor union, namely the FSPSI. This Federation, which until the downfall of the New Order was the recognized workers' union in the country has functioned, among others, supposedly to protect the workers from exploitative practices in labor relations. In the context of decision-making regarding wage regulation, the FSPSI is one of the permanent members of DPPN and DPPD representing the interests of workers.

In reality, the position of the FSPSI is quite marginal during the process of determining the minimum wage standard. In addition, the organization is also weak at the factory level, because it tends to be controlled by the management. This is due to the existing regulation regarding the establishment of the FSPSI at the company level (PUK-FSPSI). It is stipulated that the PUK cannot be established without the agreement of the management. This has made it possible for the management to intervene in the process of leadership selection. Most PUK leaders tend to be selected from workers who are close to the management.[20]

Because of such political weakness, it is only logical that PUK-FSPSI is incapable of fully supporting its members when they have wage disputes, including the implementation of the UMR. A former PUK leader in Surabaya maintains that the organization is rarely able to push the company to meet the workers' demands relating to wage. She also argues that so long as the organization is dependent on the management, there will be no hope for the workers to channel their interests through the PUK. The reason why she was leaving the PUK is because she felt that the organization had functioned more as the company's rather than the workers' instrument. If she remained in the organization, her credibility as a leader would be lost and she would no longer be trusted by her colleagues.[21]

In the meantime, the external constraint on policy implementation comes from the lack of enforcement in the field. It can be seen in the Ministry of Manpower's (*Depnaker*) lack of strong controls over companies that blatantly violate the regulation. This is particularly true in the case of the regional offices of the *Depnaker* who play the leading role in the enforcement of the UMR. In the view of workers, when there is a dispute regarding wage regulation most frequently the government would decide in favor of the company. This has resulted in the negative response by workers to the government's proposals. More often the workers choose to go to the NGOs such as the Institute of Legal Aid when they look for legal protection and advocacy *vis-à-vis* the companies.

Meanwhile, it is publicly known that the regional offices of the *Depnaker* also lack political leverage before the companies, especially the large ones. Thus, it is not unusual that the recommendation from the *Depnaker* would go unheeded. This has resulted in the increasing frustration among workers who felt betrayed by the government whom they regard as their ally. The feeling sometimes becomes too strong that when the workers go on strike, they not only direct their protest to the companies but also to the *Depnaker* offices.

The Wage Issue and Worker Protests On 4 June 1988 the workers of Maspion I in Sidoarjo, East Java went on strike. More than 12,000 workers of the company that manufactures electronic appliances stopped working and marched to the factory floor of Maspion II and Maspion III whose workers had already stopped working earlier. The combination of three divisions of Maspion industries had brought more than 15,000 workers on the street. The workers who organized themselves for several days before the strike demanded the increase of the UMR in addition to the increase in overtime, transportation, and daily meal allowances. After more than one week of struggle, the strike gained national prominence due to the electronic and printed media coverage. The management finally gave up and offered a deal to the workers. They would be given an increase in the UMR, but the extra money for transportation, daily meals, and overtime would not be given, at least for the time being. The workers were apparently satisfied with it and returned to work.[22]

The Maspion workers' strike is by no mean the only protest that occurred during the year. According to the Surabaya-based LBH, from January to July 1998 there were 132 cases of worker strikes more than 50 per cent of which were caused by the implementation of the UMR. Other cases related to workers' wage. This corresponds to the data presented by a Jakarta-based Yapusham (*Yayasan Pusat Studi HAM*, the Foundation for Human Right Studies) which reports that between October and December 1995, there were 173 cases of worker strikes in which 40.46 per cent were related to wage, 35.84 per cent related to forced lay off, 12.14 per cent related to working conditions, 6.36 per cent related to collective bargaining violations, and 5.20 per cent related to labor unions.[23]

The above data show that wage remains one of the most serious sources of dispute between the company and the workers. This will impact both on the process of production in the company and the wider dimension of security in society. The proliferation and continuation of worker strikes is likely to disturb the process of production and discourage investments in the industrial sectors in the future. It will also have wider political reverberations when work stoppage and other protest actions become widespread in industrial centers, especially in such regions as Jabotabek and Surabaya.

On the other hand, if both the government and the companies ignore the workers' demand for the improvement in the implementation of wage policy, it will only aggravate the tension in industrial relations. This is especially so during the crisis when the existing wage is barely able to meet the continued increase in the cost of the workers' daily needs. The policy of using repressive measures in dealing with workers' protests would only escalate the tension beyond the boundaries of labor relations. The latter has occurred when the workers' protest movements are eventually supported by other elements in the society such as the NGOs, students, and political activists. In several cases of worker protests such as the PT. Gadjah Tunggal (1991), the PT. Great River (1996), and PT. HASI (1997) the workers gained strong support from the outside, especially from human right watchdog organizations such as the *Yayasan Lembaga Bantuan Hukum Indonesia* (YLBHI) and the NGOs who work on labor issues.

Labor Unions and Workers' Security

Labor Unionization and State Control

Officially, the laws and the various governments in Indonesia have recognized labor unionization since independence. These always allowed workers to set up unions. However, following the transformation of the liberal-oriented regime in the fifties into the authoritarian regimes of Soekarno and Soeharto, there have been limitations in the freedom of association related to workers.[24] In fact, during the New Order era, workers unions had become an effective government instrument to control workers' activities to maintain stability and order in the realm of labor relations.[25]

The labor union policy under the New Order has been based on a development model that puts a strong emphasis on labor control in order to support the process of accelerated industrialization. As in many capitalist countries in the developing world, the Indonesian government saw it necessary to intervene in labor relations through a corporatist strategy.[26] Thus, since the early seventies the policy of a single labor union for Indonesian workers has been adopted through the establishment of the *Federasi Buruh Seluruh Indonesia* or All Indonesian Labor Federation (FBSI) that changed its name into *Serikat Pekerja Seluruh Indonesia* (SPSI) and FSPSI, respectively.[27]

Through this federation, the New Order government plays the role of a protector, guide, and arbitrator of labor relations and disputes, in addition to its role as the partner of production.[28] With such a title, the government indeed has a very broad range of powers of intervention in any aspect of labor relations. For instance, during labor disputes the state is crucial as a member of the tripartite body composed of the state, capital, and labor. In it, the state representative would play the role as a mediator among conflicting parties and usually it is the state representative which would have the final say in determining the outcome of the dispute.

It is, therefore, clear from the outset that the labor union in Indonesia does not fulfill the interests of the workers. This explains why the FSPSI has been unpopular among Indonesian workers hindering its expansion. In 1980 when the organization had its first congress, it was reported that its members numbered only 2,762,562 in 9,500 local units throughout the country. This was less than the number of industrial workers during this period. In 1985, when the FBSI was transformed into the SPSI, the total number of its members was only 2,963,716 in 9,761 local units. The data from 1991 also show that there had been no substantial increase of its membership. Out of 27,000 companies with more than 25 workers (a minimum requirement to establish a local unit or PUK), only 10,000 companies had formed the PUK.[29]

It is not surprising that workers have received the presence of alternative labor unions enthusiastically. Since the late eighties, such organizations as *Serikat Buruh Merdeka Setiakawan* or the Independent and Solidarity Labor Union (SBMSK), *Serikat Buruh Sejahtera Indonesia* or the Indonesian Prosperity Labor Union (SBSI), and others have emerged in the country. The SBSI under Mochtar Pakpahan has become the most well known due to its ability to obtain support from workers in urban areas such as Jakarta, Surabaya, Medan, Bandung, and Semarang, in addition to its activism in defending workers' interests. One of the most well known was the workers' strike in Medan in 1994 which resulted, among other things in the imprisonment of many SBSI activists including Mochtar himself.[30] After this case, SBSI was prohibited as an organization and only reemerged later when the New Order collapsed.[31]

The failure of FSPSI to become an effective channel for the workers has resulted in the lack of independence of the worker union *vis-à-vis* the state and the companies. It has constrained the workers to exercise their basic rights, especially the right to organize that is guaranteed by the constitution and existing labor laws. Furthermore, the weakness of the FSPSI at the local level has intensified the sense of insecurity among its members in the workplace because their support system does not work adequately. When a dispute between workers and management occurs, the presence of an independent labor union is very important because it represents the workers and thus, would be able to deal with the management effectively.

Labor Union and Workers' Security

Based on the survey in Jabotabek and Surabaya, it can be argued that the workers are less enthusiastic to join the local unit or PUK despite the fact that the companies where they work had already established the organization. Thus, when asked about their involvement in the PUK-FSPSI, 53 per cent of the respondents said that they were members while 47 per cent were not. The majority of the respondents (69 per cent) acknowledged the existence of the PUK in their workplace.

According to the workers, the weakness of the PUK lies primarily in its leadership. Most of the workers (53 per cent) maintain that it was the leadership of the PUK that was mainly responsible for the union's poor performance in defending its members. Another factor was the companies' intervention (43 per cent), which according to the workers have kept the union from performing its tasks. The attempt by government to motivate the workers who have no PUK to set up an organization through the so-called *Serikat Pekerja Tingkat Satuan Kerja* or the Unit-based Labor Union (SPTSK) has been seen by many SPSI leaders as creating dualism. According to a leader of FSPSI in Tangerang, the presence of SPTSK was not clear in terms of its goal and would only constrain the effort to establish a real workers' union.[32]

The weakness of the PUK has also created another problem, namely the feeling of antipathy among the workers about unionization. A woman worker in Surabaya argues that the PUK is actually a useless organization and, therefore, in her company the workers, who are mostly female refuse to have one. She said:

> In our company, where women constitute the majority of its workers, the PUK does not exist, because we refuse to have one. The reason is that we know from the experience of other companies in Surabaya that the existence of a PUK will only weaken the bargaining position of the workers, because the organization will always take the side of the company when there is a labor dispute. Meanwhile, the FSPSI leaders at the district or provincial level are mostly indifferent to our cause and, therefore, many of us have to protest against them through demonstrations.

When asked how they will face the company without a union, her response was:

> So far, we depend on our ability to unify our struggle. This is not very difficult to do because most of the workers here are women. I think in this company, the management could not push us around so much because of our unity and solidarity. So, we do not really need a PUK if there is no guarantee that the organization is able to channel our demands.[33]

Based on the survey, it seems that the policy of single unionization under the FSPSI will have to change in the post-Soeharto era. The workers, sooner or later, would prefer to have a say in the process of setting up a union in their workplace. Many regional leaders of the FSPSI now articulate this 'radical' view. According to the Jakarta regional head of FSPSI, the presence of other worker unions is no problem as long as they follow existing regulations. However, he cautioned that it is better not to have competing unions in a given company where a union already existed. This is to prevent conflicts between unions and their members that, according to him, would only benefit the other parties.[34]

Labor Regulations and Workers' Security

There are numerous labor regulations intended to protect the workers' position in labor relations in Indonesia. The most recent and also the most controversial regulation is Law No. 25/1998 that was passed by the Parliament during the end of Soeharto's rule. This law is supposed to take effect in October 1998, but the Habibie government postponed its implementation.[35]

The labor law, passed under heavy pressure from the government has attracted public attention from both inside and outside the country. Many labor activists and political observers argue that the law will further marginalize the workers and weaken their bargaining power. This is due to the fact that several provisions related to workers' rights are weak and inadequate. In fact, the law has been criticized heavily ever since its preparation and some of the labor activists even went so far as to say that the past labor regulations were more progressive compared to the current one.[36] The following section discusses some of the most crucial issues in the law that are likely to have a direct impact on the security of Indonesian workers.

Labor Law and the Right to Organize

Although basically Law No. 25/1998 guarantees the right of workers to organize, there are limitations that in effect can be used by the authorities to constrain its implementation. Chief among them is the provision that the workers who intend to establish a union must first report to the government.[37] The latter has the power to determine the ways in which any worker union shall be registered. In addition, the Law also says that there will be a *Peraturan Pemerintah* (Government Regulation) that will provide specific implementing rules on the issue of unionization.

From a political point of view, the above provision is clearly biased toward both the state and the company while giving only a little room for maneuver to the workers. This strategy is consistent with the model of development that has been applied for more than three decades, in which political order and stability are seen as the primary requirement in order to achieve and maintain a high degree of economic growth. In this respect, the workers' right to organize needs to be regulated in such a way that even if the workers' union may be legitimate, it will not become an effective means for channeling the workers' demands.

From a human rights perspective, the provision on workers union is clearly against the existing ILO Convention No. 98/1949 on the rights of workers to organize and to collective bargaining. This convention, ratified by the Indonesian government through Law No. 18/1956 stipulates that workers organizations should be protected and free from both company and government intervention. In addition, the Convention also clearly states that workers do not have to ask permission from nor report to the government in order to establish their union. Also, there is another ILO Convention, No. 87/1948, which stipulates that workers have the right to organize themselves in order to attain their interests and in this respect, there should be no intervention from the government and the company.

The Indonesian government under the New Order seems to disregard the above ILO conventions and continues to put political limitations on the workers. This means that under the new law, Indonesian workers would be politically vulnerable due to the weakness of their organizations that will become prone to state control. It remains to be seen whether in the post-New Order era there will be fundamental changes in the existing labor law. The transitional government under Habibie only suspended its implementation while the government of former President Wahid promised that a further review by Parliament would be made.

Labor Law and the Right to Strike

The right to strike is fundamental in the realm of labor relations for it enables the workers to bargain with the company or management when labor disputes can no longer be solved through dialogues. Unfortunately, in the new labor law the workers' right to strike is also limited by procedural requirements. Chief among them is the obligation for workers to limit their strike only to attain the so-called 'normative' aspects and the location is restricted only around the company's premises.[38] Under this requirement, it is impossible for the workers to go on strike through a rally or a mass demonstration outside the work place. In addition, the law also prohibits the workers from striking in protest of government policies related to workers' interests. Solidarity strikes with workers from other companies are also prohibited. Workers are only permitted to strike in protest of existing job-related issues in their own company.

The implication of such a limitation is obvious, namely that the workers are prevented from creating a network of solidarity among their peers outside their company, not to mention solidarity with other groups such as NGOs, students, others. The prohibition against staging a rally also means that the workers will no longer be able to bring their case directly and openly to such institutions as the parliament at both the central and regional levels, the national commission for human rights (*Komnas HAM*), the legal aid institutions, others, which may be interested in mediating or resolving the conflict. As a consequence, the workers' strike will not have substantive political impacts, and instead, will remain part of a company's internal affairs. From the state's interest, a limited strike would be easily controlled by its security apparatus and prevent non-worker elements from getting involved in the process. However, from the point of view of the workers, the limitation means that they would not be able to develop strategies through which they could expand their struggles beyond the boundaries given by the state and the company.

Another limitation imposed by the present labor law pertaining to the right to strike is the stipulation that the strikers will not be paid during their absence in the job. This is based on the principle 'no work no pay' that should be implemented for the strikers. Such a principle is obviously against the ILO convention that prohibits such a practice, because striking is one of the workers' rights that have to be respected by the company owners. The workers should not be penalized by not paying their wages.

If this stipulation is implemented, the workers will become insecure because they can be easily intimidated by the company.[39]

Labor Law and Conflict Resolution

Concerning the issue of conflict resolution, the new law is also weak in defending the interests of the workers. This is due to the fact that the workers are again in a marginal position as in the past. Under the new law it is proposed that industrial conflicts be resolved through (1) deliberation, (2) mediation, (3) arbitration, (4) conciliation, and (5) judicial decision. The conciliation process will be carried out through an institution called the *Majelis Penyelesaian Perselisihan Industrial* (the Board of Industrial Conflict Resolution, MPPHI).[40] Yet the Law does not specify the kinds of conflict that can or cannot be resolved under specific laws. This will result in confusion and lack of certainty among the workers who are mostly unfamiliar with the legal process.

Furthermore, the MPPHI is far from independent. According to Article 65, the government will determine the qualifications of the arbitrators by a specific government regulation. This is also applicable to mediators as stipulated in Article 70. Under such a condition, it is impossible for the workers to have independent arbitration and mediation bodies through which they can have legal protection.

Labor Law and Women Workers

There is still strong discriminatory treatment of women workers in this new legislation. For example, in Article 98, certain jobs are declared off limits to women. They are prohibited to work at night without a clear reason for doing so. The principle of 'no work no pay' will also put women workers at a disadvantage, especially for those whose absence is due to causes peculiar to women such as during menstruation or pregnancy.

Women workers are given very limited authorized leave due to menstruation, childbirth, or suckling their babies. The new law does not stipulate fixed periods allowing workers to rest. There are only stipulations that women workers have the right to a leave of absence because of menstruation, pregnancy, and childbirth. The failure to specify the duration of such leaves opens the possibility for the company to exploit the women workers.

Industrialization and Worker Security: Towards a New Approach

Based on the discussion so far, it is clear that the model of development and industrialization adopted by the New Order failed to deliver its promises, particularly in bringing security to the population including the security of workers both at the work place and in the community. The model's obsession with growth ultimately neglected the objective of development, namely, increasing the capacity of human beings to be hopeful about their future.[41] The workers as the stakeholders of development and industrialization have been denied control over their own affairs by the state and the company, thus keeping them in a state of insecurity. Hence, the workers have remained dependent on the mercy of outside forces that do not allow them to determine their own future.

Therefore, a fundamental reorientation in the model of development is required, particularly when an opportunity for change has arisen. The fall of the New Order and the demand for comprehensive reform can be used as an important steppingstone for such a transformation. There are some agenda of reform related to development and security that are relevant to the notion of security. They include reorienting the model of development from a top-down, state-oriented to a bottom-up, citizen-centered model; the restructuring of state-society relations in favor of society; and building social capital within Indonesian civil society, especially among the workers as an avenue of their empowerment and security in the future.

Reorienting the Model of Development

As in many developing countries in Asia and Latin America, Indonesia had adopted the model of developmentalism or the modernization paradigm since the early seventies. This growth-oriented model has been accompanied by political stabilization imposed by an authoritarian regime under President Soeharto. For more than three decades, the model has been unchanged although many criticisms against it have been raised, particularly on its failure to alleviate social and economic injustice among the people as well as the underdevelopment of the democratic process in the country.[42]

With the collapse of the New Order, it seems that this model of development can no longer be maintained and a new one should be introduced that can address the fundamental problems which have so far been neglected. The new model should view development in a transformative sense, namely building the capacity of human beings to shape their future. This will include such notions as capacity-building, equity, empowerment, and sustainability.[43] The notion of capacity-building involves improving the economic capacity such as growth and productivity of the people as well as the capacity of the nation and the community to develop political and social institutions responsible for production and allocation.[44]

The notion of equity particularly involves the issue of distribution of the fruits of development for the population. Development is only meaningful if it is capable of benefiting all of the population and not only a small segment of the people. The notion of equity also encompasses the capability of the nation and the community to provide equal access to economic, political, and social resources. On the other hand, the notion of empowerment includes 'acquiring leverage for the poor'.[45] In this respect, the capability of the population at the lower level to access political, economic, and social resources is enhanced when they are allowed to participate in the process of decision making and organize themselves in order to eliminate their powerlessness. Building social capital is part of the people's leverage to improve themselves particularly the poor.

The notion of sustainability involves the view that development should be future-oriented. The important question here is whether development policy includes the future in its calculation. The extraction of natural resources for industrialization should take the interest of future generations seriously, in addition to the importance of environmental effects resulting from it. The problem of sustainable development is particularly important for a developing country like Indonesia that is trying to catch up with the already advanced industrialized countries. Many regimes in developing countries, Indonesia included, have rejected the warning from outside about the danger of exploiting their natural resources such as rainforests, oil, natural gas, and others with impunity. They are suspicious that such a warning is nothing but a political tactic of developed countries to keep the developing countries lagging behind in the name of environmental protection and sustainable development. However, by ignoring and neglecting environmental problems, rapidly developing countries have run the risk of creating a time bomb that will affect the future generation that is not responsible for it.

By reorienting the development model through the inclusion of the above normative foundation, the possibility of improving the quality of development and industrialization is greater. For instance, by improving the workers' capacity to organize themselves and guaranteeing their economic and social rights, one can expect that labor relations in Indonesia will be less uncertain in the future. Workers would become an integral part of development and industrialization policy. They would no longer face uncertainty and insecurity. They would no longer be treated merely as a means of production, but as human beings and citizens.

Restructuring State-Society Relations

The reorientation of the development model necessitates the restructuring of state and society relations that have been uneven for the past three decades in Indonesia. The New Order de-politicized the society to maintain the dominant power of the state.[46] This process was carried out through the corporatization strategy in which all social and political organizations were put under state control and surveillance.[47] In the realm of labor relations, as discussed earlier, such corporatization was implemented through the single union policy and tight labor regulations.

The ongoing reform beyond the New Order has to focus on the empowerment of civil society through reorganizing its elements, including the workers. The empowerment of civil society in the long run could lead to the support the establishment of 'citizen politics' as an alternative paradigm to state-oriented politics. 'Citizen politics' that was actually advocated by the founders of the Republic has disappeared from Indonesian political discourse and practices ever since the establishment of Guided Democracy under President Soekarno in 1959 and continued by Soeharto in 1967. Both Soekarno and Soeharto believed that a strong state is more compatible with Indonesian society because it will provide a strong sense of unity and leadership. What they failed to see is that such an idea is not viable for a heterogeneous nation as Indonesia in which the sense of unity can only be achieved by active participation of the citizens in public life and not through political mobilization by the ruling elite or party.

The empowerment of civil society is an important step for the revitalization of 'citizen politics' in Indonesia by (1) developing a sense of autonomy in the individuals and the collectivity; (2) promoting public trust and responsibility, and; (3) providing an arena in which people can engage themselves actively in public life. Thus, the empowerment of workers' organizations and the community, for instance, will ultimately result in the revival of workers as a significant force in Indonesian politics as in the fifties. Workers are capable of gradually strengthening workers' solidarity and cohesiveness that have been obliterated by state control and the company's strategy of divide and rule. It is mainly the absence of solidarity and cohesiveness of the workers that has made it difficult for the working class to have its presence felt in Indonesian politics in the past three decades.

Building Social Capital

In order to empower the currently weak civil society, it is imperative for its elements to build social capital. According to Robert D. Putnam, social capital refers to 'features of social organization, such as trust, norms, and networks, that can improve the efficiency of society by facilitating coordinated actions'.[48] Coleman argues that like other capital, social capital is 'productive, making possible the achievement of certain ends that would not be attainable in its absence'.[49] Trust is a very crucial element in the building of social capital because it becomes a 'moral resource' that will provide a sense of certainty and enhance law enforcement. Putnam maintains that trust also entails a prediction about the behavior of an independent actor. This is important because social order and stability would be much stronger when actors can act freely and autonomously.

Networking is important in social capital building in order to strengthen civil society because it will enhance the capability of a single actor in dealing with complex situations. In the Indonesian case, the networking of elements within civil society is still in its early stage because of the weakness of organizational capability and the lack of trust among its members. This is especially true under the New Order regime in which the culture of fear and suspicion was particularly widespread among social groups. The notion of *aliran*, the ideological stream along with religion, ethnicity, and race has been strong and remained an effective means for political manipulation.

In the case of Indonesian workers, it is important for the organizations or worker unions to expand their networks in order to strengthen their capacity. It is clear from the experience in the last three decades that workers could not build a strong movement without substantial support from other elements of civil society. Not only do they need to forge alliances with the existing political parties, but also establish networks with other social organizations such as NGOs, religious organizations, the intelligentsia, students, media, and others. In some cases of workers' protests in Indonesia, it is clear that the support from NGOs and the students has forced the state not to interfere and the companies to settle their disputes in favor of the workers' demands. The weakness of the workers can be overcome when they use the networks available in civil society.

In the future, the empowerment of Indonesian civil society will depend on the ability of its elements to cooperate in building social capital. If the elements of civil society remain divided due to ideological differences and political interests, then social capital building will be disrupted. In this regard, the need for continuous dialogues and communication among the leaders in civil society is great. So far, there have been some initiatives from a number of NGOs to promote dialogues among members and leaders of civil society. For example, some religious leaders have established inter-religious dialogues in order to bridge their different perceptions about the relationship between the state and religion. Also, pro-democracy activities have created public forums on such issues as gender and politics, indigenous rights, ethnic and religious conflicts, among other issues.

Conclusion

During the last three decades, the Indonesian people have experienced a process of modernization and development in which rapid industrialization was the main objective. Despite the success story of rapid growth in Indonesia's industrial sectors, the condition of its workers has not improved significantly. The existing policy on labor relations has tended to marginalize the workers, politically, economically, and socially. Indonesian workers are worse off compared to their counterparts in other ASEAN countries.

The model of development and industrialization adopted by the New Order regime has failed to provide a sense of security for the workers. Therefore, it is necessary for the future government of Indonesia to pursue a viable alternative of development that is capable of enhancing the capacity of the people, including the workers to shape their future. In terms of the policy on labor relations, the government should also revamp existing regulations that have clearly violated the workers' basic rights, including the rights to organize, to strike, and to equal treatment of women and child workers.

As an integral part of Indonesian civil society, the workers should strive to strengthen their position in the post-Soeharto era, by building organizational capacity and developing social capital. Together with other elements of civil society such as NGOs, religious organizations, students, the intelligentsia, and mass media the Indonesian workers can become strategic groups that are able to balance the power of the state and the companies in the future. This can be achieved through reorienting and restructuring Indonesian politics toward 'citizen politics' that has been absent since the late fifties.

Notes

1 Hill, H. (1994), 'The Economy', in H. Hill (ed.) *Indonesia's New Order: The Dynamics of Socio Economic Transformation*, Allen & Unwin, Sydney, pp.54-122; Szirmai, A. (1933), 'Comparative Productivity in Manufacturing: A Case Study of Indonesia', in A. Szirmai, B. van Ark and D. Pilats (eds), *Explaining Economic Growth: Essays in Honor of Angus Maddison*, Elsevier/North Holland, Amsterdam, pp.1-23; Wie, T. K. (1992), 'Indonesia's Manufactured Exports: Performance and Prospect', in N. Mihira (ed.), *Indonesia's Non-Oil Exports: Performance, Problems, and Prospects*, IDE, Tokyo.

2 Harris, D. (ed.) (1995), *Prisoners of Progress: A Review on the Current Indonesian Labor Situation*, INDOC, KC Meppel.

3 See the detail of the field work in section II.

4 The KFM standard was designed in 1956 which consists of various costs for food, drinks, clothing, and shelter for the physical sustenance of workers. The basis of KFM standard was the price of the nine basic food stuff and the calory intake needed by workers. Thus, for example, a single male worker is targeted to receive 2600 calory/capita/day, which is equal with 234 kg of rice annually. In retrospect, this calory intake is far too low compared with the well known Sayogyo's poverty line, in which 320 kg of rice per person annually is considered the lowest. The KHM standard, on the other hand, is an improvement of the KFM in which there will be 20 per cent increase of the minimum wage. See Departemen Tenaga Kerja Indonesia (1991), *Studi dan Analisa Perkembangan KFM*, Depnaker, Jakarta.

5 See *Suara Karya*, 9 July 1996.

6 See also Tubagus' Chapter in this volume.

7 Thamrin, J. (1995), 'Development Policy', in D. Harris (ed), *Prisoners of Progress: A Review on the Current Indonesian Labour Situation*, INDOC, KC Meppel, pp.1-22.

8 *Ibid.*

9 Soekarni, M. (1998), 'Kebijakan Upah Minimum Regional di Indonesia: Dimensi Ekonomi', in M. A. Hikam (ed.), *Strategi Kebijaksanaan Pemerintah dalam Masalah PengupahanTenaga Kerja*, PEP-LIPI, Jakarta, pp.27-58.

10 Mather, C. (1985), *Women, Work, and Ideology in the Third World*, Tavitstock, London; Wolf, D. (1986), *Factory Daughters, Their Families, and Rural Industries in Central Java*, Cornell University Press, Ithaca.

11 Soekarni, 'Kebijakan Upah Minimum Regional di Indonesia: Dimensi Ekonomi', 1998.

12 This definition is used by the Indonesian Central Bureau of Statistics (BPS) to determine small, medium and large scale industries.

13 Central Bureau of Statistics (1996), *Industrial Statistics 1995*, BPS, Jakarta.

14 Pangestu, M. and Hendityo, M. K. (1977), *Survey Responses from Women Workers in Indonesia's Textile, Garment, and Footwear Industry*, World Bank Policy Research Paper.

15 Interview, 31 September 1998.

16 Mather, *Women, Work, and Ideology in the Third World*, 1985; Wolf, *Factory Daughters, Their Families, and Rural Industries in Central Java*, 1986; Soekarni, 'Kebijakan Upah Minimum Regional di Indonesia: Dimensi Ekonomi', 1998. Also see Tubagus' Chapter in this volume.

17 Wiranta, S. (ed.) (1998), *Penanganan UMR dalam Sektor Industri Manufaktur*, PEP-LIPI, Jakarta.

18 Negara, S. D. and Suhadak (1998), 'Upah dari Perspektif Kemampuan Perusahaan', in *Ibid.*, pp.75.

19 See, *Sketsa Hak-hak Asasi Manusia di Jawa Timur*, LBH, Surabaya, 1997, pp.57.

20 Hadiz, V. R. (1997), *Workers and the State in the New Order Indonesia*, Routledge, London; Hikam, M. A. (1995), *The State, Grass-roots Politics and Civil Society*, Ph.D Dissertation, University of Hawaii, USA; Abdullah, F. and Etty, T. (1995), 'Would Be', and 'Make Believe' in Crisis, in D. Harris (ed.), *Prisoners of Progress: A Review on the Current Indonesian Labour Situation.*

21 Interview, 1 October 1998.

22 This short version of Maspion workers strike is based on the Surabaya-based Institute for Legal Aid (LBH) report.

23 See *INDEX Magazine*, vol.II, no.7, 1996, pp.2.

24 For detailed discussions on the history of Indonesian labor union prior to the New Order, see Tedjasukmana, I. (1959), *The Political Character of the Indonesian Trade Union Movement*, Monograph Series, Cornell Modern Indonesia Project, Ithaca; Aidit, DN. (1952), *Sedjarah Gerakan Buruh Indonesia*, Yayasan Pembaruan, Jakarta; Semaun (1966), 'An Early Account of the Independent Movement', trans. by R. McVey, *Indonesia*, vol.1,

April, pp.46-75; Hawkins, E. (1971), 'Labor in Developing Countries: Indonesia', in B. Glassburner (ed.), *The Indonesian Economy: Selected Readings*, Cornell University Press, Ithaca; and Ingleson, J. (1986), *In Search of Justice: Workers and Unions in Colonial Java 1908-1926*, Oxford University Press, Singapore.

25 For recent studies on Indonesian labor union, see Hadiz, *Workers and the State in the New Order Indonesia*, 1997; 'Workers and Working Class Politics in the 1990s', in C. Manning (ed.) (1994), *Indonesia Assessment 1993*, RSPacS, ANU, Canberra; Hikam, *The State, Grass-roots Politics and Civil Society*, 1995; Rinakit, S. (forthcoming), 'Labor Union and Labor Unrest', in R.J. Baker, *et al.* (eds), *Riding the Miracle: Indonesian Institutions and Economic Growth*, ISEAS, Singapore.

26 For a discussion on labor control in the developing countries, see Southall, R. (ed.) (1988), *Trade Union and the New Industrialization of the Third World*, Zed Press, London.

27 See Sudono, A. (1984), *FBSI: Dahulu, Sekarang, dan Yang Akan Datang*, DPP FBSI, Jakarta.

28 These roles are spelled out in the principles of Pancasila industrial relations (HIP). See Ministry of Manpower (1985), *Manual on the Implementation of the Pancasila Industrial Relations*, Depnaker, Jakarta. For the discussion on the origin of the HIP, see Moertopo, A. (1975), *Buruh dan Tani dalam Pembangunan*, CSIS, Jakarta; Soekarno (1979), *Pembaharuan gerakan Buruh di Indonesia dan Hubungan Industrial Pancasila*, Alumni, Bandung; and Djumialdji, FX. and Soedjono, W. (1982), *Perjanjian Perburuhan dan Hubungan Perburuhan Pancasila*, Bina Aksara, Jakarta.

29 The data of 1980 and 1985 were from Sudono, *FBSI: Dahulu, Sekarang, dan Yang Akan Datang*, 1984, pp. 49 and 90, while those of 1991 were cited from YLBHI (1991), 'Background Report: The Shackling of the Workers' Right to Organize', *Indonesian Human Rights Forum*, no.1, July-September, pp. 1.

30 Mochtar was subsequently imprisoned based on a different allegation, namely involvement in the 27 July 1996 Affair, when Megawati's PDI headquarters was attacked by her rival Soeryadi, supported by the military. He was released from the prison soon after Habibie replaced Suharto.

31 Some SBSI activists have formed a new labor party, the PBN (Partai Buruh Nasional). However, in the post Suharto election, this party gaining a very little votes which may not reach the threshold of 2 per cent in order to be eligible to participate in the next general election in 2004.

32 Interview, August 1998.

33 Interview, September 1998.

34 Interview, August 1998.

35 Under the present administration the Law is still under review and most probably amended.

36 Rudiono, D. (1997), 'Peradilan Khusus Perburuhan, Sebuah Alternatif Penyelesaian Konflik: Beberapa Catatan Tentang RUU Ketenagakerjaan', in Komisi Pembaharuan Hukum Perburuhan (1997), *RUU Ketenagakerjaan Pantas Meresahkan Buruh*, KPHP, Jakarta, pp.62-71.

37 See Article 33, point 1 and 2.

38 See Articles 76 and 77. Normative aspects means those elements that have direct relation to workers' well being such as wages, collective bargaining, others As a consequence, the workers are prohibited to strike in protest of certain government policies which have no direct relations with their job. They are also prohibited to stage a strike, for instance, for the purpose of showing their solidarity to other fellow workers.

39 In addition, according to Article 79, the strike is not allowed to 'disturb public order', a provision which will be open to broad interpretation, especially by the security apparatus. It is common practice that in the pretext of protecting the so-called 'public order', the military and police will use repressive measures to stop workers' striking.

40 Article 71.

41 Bryant, C. and White, L. G. (1982), *Managing Development in the Third World*, Westview, Boulder, pp.15.

42 Critical analyses on Indonesian development model have been addressed since the eighties by scholars, intellectuals, and NGOs' activists. See, for instance, Robison, R. (1986), *Indonesia: The Rise of Capital*, Allen & Unwinn, Sidney; Yoshihara, K. (1988), *The Rise of Ersatz Capitalism in Southeast Asia*, Oxford University Press, Singapore; Arief, S. (1997), *Pembangunanisme dan Ekonomi Indonesia: Pemberdayaan Rakyat dalam Arus Globalisasi*, CPSM-Zaman, Jakarta; and Baswir, R., *et al.* (1999), *Pembangunan Tanpa Perasaan: Evaluasi pemenuhan Hak Ekonomi Sosial Budatya Orde Baru*, Pustaka Pelajar, Yogyakarta.

43 Bryant and White, *Managing Development in the Third World*, 1982.

44 *Ibid.*

45 *Ibid.*, pp.17.

46 Budiman, A. (ed.) (1990), *State and Civil Society in Indonesia*, Monash Paper on Southeast Asia No.22, Monash University, Clayton; Hikam, M. A. (1999), 'Problems of Political Transition in Post-New Order Indonesia', *Indonesian Quarterly*, vol.XXVII. no.1, First Quarter, pp.65-82.

47 For theoretical discussions on corporatism and corporatist strategies in developing countries, see Schmitter, P. (1974), 'Still the Century of Corporatism?' in F. Pike and T. Stricht (eds), *The New Corporatism: Social and Political Structures in the Iberian World*, University of Notre Dame Press, Notre Dame, pp.85-131; O'Donnell, G. and Schmitter, P. (1986), *Transitions from Authoritarian Rule: Tentative Conclusion about Uncertain Democracies*, Johns Hokins University Press, Baltimore; and Linz, J. and Stepan, A. (1996), *Problems of Democratic Transition and Consolidation: Southern Europe, South America, and Post Communist Europe*, Johns Hopkins University, Baltimore. For Indonesian case, see Reeve, D. (1990), 'The Corporatist State: The Case of Golkar', in A. Budiman (ed.), *State and Civil Society in Indonesia*, pp.151-176; and Hikam, *The State, Grass-roots Politics and Civil Society*, 1995.

48 Putnam, R. D. (1993), *Making Democracy Work: Civic Traditions in Italy*, Princeton University Press, Princeton, pp.167.

49 Coleman, J. S. (1990), *Foundations of Social Theory*, Harvard University Press, Cambridge, pp.302.

References

Aidit, DN. (1952), *Sedjarah Gerakan Buruh Indonesia*, Yayasan Pembaruan, Jakarta.

Arief, S. (1997), *Pembangunanisme dan Ekonomi Indonesia: Pemberdayaan Rakyat dalam Arus Globalisasi*, CPSM-Zaman, Jakarta.

Baswir, R., *et al.* (1999), *Pembangunan Tanpa Perasaan: Evaluasi pemenuhan Hak Ekonomi Sosial Budatya Orde Baru*, Pustaka Pelajar, Yogyakarta.

Bryant, C. and White, L. G. (1982), *Managing Development in the Third World*, Westview, Boulder, pp. 15.

Budiman, A. (ed.) (1990), *State and Civil Society in Indonesia*, Monash Paper on Southeast Asia No. 22, Monash University, Clayton.

Central Bureau of Statistics (1996), *Industrial Statistics 1995*, BPS, Jakarta.

Coleman, J. S. (1990), *Foundations of Social Theory*, Harvard University Press, Cambridge, pp. 302.

Departemen Tenaga Kerja Indonesia (1991), *Studi dan Analisa Perkembangan KFM*, Depnaker, Jakarta.

Djumialdji, FX. and Soedjono, W. (1982), *Perjanjian Perburuhan dan Hubungan Perburuhan Pancasila*, Bina Aksara, Jakarta.

Hadiz, V. R. (1997), *Workers and the State in the New Order Indonesia*, Routledge, London.

Harris, D. (ed.) (1995), *Prisoners of Progress: A Review on the Current Indonesian Labor Situation*, INDOC, KC Meppel.

Hawkins, E. (1971), 'Labor in Developing Countries: Indonesia', in B. Glassburner (ed.), *The Indonesian Economy: Selected Readings*, Cornell University Press, Ithaca.

Hikam, M. A. (1995a), *The State, Grass-roots Politics and Civil Society*, Ph.D Dissertation, University of Hawaii, USA.

Hikam, M. A. (1999b), 'Problems of Political Transition in Post-New Order Indonesia', *Indonesian Quarterly*, vol. XXVII. no. 1, First Quarter, pp. 65-82.

Hill, H. (1994), 'The Economy', in H. Hill (ed.). *Indonesia's New Order: The Dynamics of Socio Economic Transformation*, Allen & Unwin, Sydney, pp. 54-122.

Ingleson, J. (1986), *In Search of Justice: Workers and Unions in Colonial Java 1908-1926*, Oxford University Press, Singapore.

Linz, J. and Stepan, A. (1996), *Problems of Democratic Transition and Consolidation: Southern Europe, South America, and Post Communist Europe*, Johns Hopkins University, Baltimore.

Mather, C. (1985), *Women, Work, and Ideology in the Third World*, Tavitstock, London.

Ministry of Manpower (1985), *Manual on the Implementation of the Pancasila Industrial Relations*, Depnaker, Jakarta.

Moertopo, A. (1975), *Buruh dan Tani dalam Pembangunan*, CSIS, Jakarta.

Negara, S. D. and Suhadak (1998), 'Upah dari Perspektif Kemampuan Perusahaan', in S. Wiranta (ed.), *Penanganan UMR dalam Sektor Industri Manufaktur*, PEP-LIPI, Jakarta.

O'Donnell, G. and Schmitter, P. (1986), *Transitions from Authoritarian Rule: Tentative Conclusion about Uncertain Democracies*, Johns Hokins University Press, Baltimore.

Pangestu, M. and Hendityo, M. K. (1977), *Survey Responses from Women Workers in Indonesia's Textile, Garment, and Footwear Industry*, World Bank Policy Research Paper.

Putnam, R. D. (1993), *Making Democracy Work: Civic Traditions in Italy*, Princeton University Press, Princeton, pp. 167.

Rinakit, S. (forthcoming), 'Labor Union and Labor Unrest', in R.J. Baker, *et al.* (eds), *Riding the Miracle: Indonesian Institutions and Economic Growth*, ISEAS, Singapore.

Robison, R. (1986), *Indonesia: The Rise of Capital*, Allen & Unwinn, Sydney.

Rudiono, D. (1997), 'Peradilan Khusus Perburuhan, Sebuah Alternatif Penyelesaian Konflik: Beberapa Catatan Tentang RUU Ketenagakerjaan', in Komisi Pembaharuan Hukum Perburuhan, *RUU Ketenagakerjaan Pantas Meresahkan Buruh*, KPHP, Jakarta, pp. 62-71.

Schmitter, P. (1974), 'Still the Century of Corporatism?', in F. Pike and T. Stricht (eds), *The New Corporatism: Social and Political Structures in the Iberian World*, University of Notre Dame Press, Notre Dame, pp.85-131.

Semaun (1966), 'An Early Account of the Independent Movement', trans. by R. McVey, *Indonesia*, vol. 1, April, pp. 46-75.

Soekarno (1979), *Pembaharuan gerakan Buruh di Indonesia dan Hubungan Industrial Pancasila*, Alumni, Bandung.

Soekarni, M. (1998), 'Kebijakan Upah Minimum Regional di Indonesia: Dimensi Ekonomi', in M. A. Hikam (ed.), *Strategi Kebijaksanaan Pemerintah dalam Masalah PengupahanTenaga Kerja*, PEP-LIPI, Jakarta, pp. 27-58.

Southall, R. (ed.) (1988), *Trade Union and the New Industrialization of the Third World*, Zed Press, London.

Sudono, A. (1984), *FBSI: Dahulu, Sekarang, dan Yang Akan Datang*, DPP FBSI, Jakarta.

Szirmai, A. (1933), 'Comparative Productivity in Manufacturing: A Case Study of Indonesia', in A. Szirmai, B. van Ark and D. Pilats (eds), *Explaining Economic Growth: Essays in Honor of Angus Maddison*, Elsevier/North Holland, Amsterdam, pp. 1-23.

Tedjasukmana, I. (1959), *The Political Character of the Indonesian Trade Union Movement*, Monograph Series, Cornell Modern Indonesia Project, Ithaca.

Thamrin, J. (1995), 'Development Policy', in D. Harris (ed), *Prisoners of Progress: A Review on the Current Indonesian Labour Situation*, INDOC, KC Meppel, pp. 1-22.

Wie, T. K. (1992), 'Indonesia's Manufactured Exports: Performance and Prospect', in N. Mihira (ed.), *Indonesia's Non-Oil Exports: Performance, Problems, and Prospects*, IDE, Tokyo.

Wiranta, S. (ed.) (1998), *Penanganan UMR dalam Sektor Industri Manufaktur*, PEP-LIPI, Jakarta.

Wolf, D. (1986), *Factory Daughters, Their Families, and Rural Industries in Central Java*, Cornell University Press, Ithaca.

Yayasan Lembaga Bantuan Hukum Indonesia (YLBHI) (1991), 'Background Report: The Shackling of the Workers' Right to Organize', *Indonesian Human Rights Forum*, no.1, July-September, pp. 1.

Yoshihara, K. (1988), *The Rise of Ersatz Capitalism in Southeast Asia*, Oxford University Press, Singapore.

Chapter 7

Stockbrokers-turned-Sandwich Vendors: The Economic Crisis and Small-Scale Food Retailing in Thailand and the Philippines

Gisèle Yasmeen[1]

Introduction: Of Sandwiches, Security, and Social Capital

> Thailand's Sirivat Voravetvuthikun...[t]he bankrupt stockbroker, who is 'hundreds of millions' in debt because of a 28-unit condominium project, now peddles sandwiches. 'I'm still trying to sell the condo units', he says, 'I can't give up, especially since I've had so much support from the media and the Thai people who buy my sandwiches. I was very depressed, but my morale is up now'. Sirivat, 48, has given about 40 TV and print interviews. To outsiders, he personifies Thailand's rise and fall—and possible redemption.[2]

This chapter examines self-employment in the food sector in light of the economic crisis that has ravaged Southeast and parts of East Asia. First, it highlights the crisis of development in the region and globally; and, second, it opens up the discussion on the role of the mis-named 'informal sector' in assuring the economic security of the victims of the crisis. Sirivat's story made the cover of numerous magazines and was the subject of television news reports around the world approximately in 1997 and continues to draw attention as a symbol of the financial crisis in the region.[3] The media has focused on this vignette for its shock value—forcing the public to scrutinize the 'Asian Miracle' discourse that permeated depictions of East and Southeast Asian booming economies in the 1980s and early 1990s. The 'sandwich man' vignette, however, contains three ironies.

1. First, most food vendors in Southeast Asia (SEA)—particularly in the Philippines and Thailand—are women and not men. This gendering of the food system is a distinctive feature of the region and has implications for intra-household resource allocation and the economic security of families.[4]
2. Secondly, most of the lore about vendors *vis-à-vis* the corporate world are 'rags-to-riches' type stories rather than this tale of downward mobility. There are sagas of both women and men—particularly the overseas Chinese—starting out in life

thirty years ago as vendors and ending up at the helm of conglomerates such as Central Pattana group and Charoen Pokhpand (CP).

3. Finally, most Southeast Asian street foods—despite outside influences—are local or Chinese specialties rather than an obviously Western food item such as sandwiches.[5] Locally available ingredients still overwhelmingly dominate local diets with rice as a staple. The devaluation of local currencies makes the importing of wheat and other foodstuffs used to make items such as sandwiches out of reach for the masses and (former?) middle classes.

A more appropriate vignette for the region might have been the depiction of an impoverished migrant woman in her forties selling noodle soup on the streets of Bangkok or Manila. Nevertheless, there is a reason for this inversion of imagery and representation which emphasizes the way in which the economic crisis has turned thinking about SEA upside down, questioning the conventional paradigm of development. Sirivat's tale also draws out attention to human security issues, particularly the role played by micro-entrepreneurship in keeping people afloat financially. Beyond the obvious reference to food and income security, the widespread availability of prepared food is another distinguishing feature of the region. The recent turn of events has pointed to the consumer trend of purchasing traditional fast foods to the detriment of Western-owned chains and restaurants formerly catering to the middle classes and elites.[6] Laid-off employees are opening eateries and vending operations to earn needed cash on a daily basis.[7] Policymakers and scholars need to take small-scale food retailing seriously as an important component of the economic security of the under-and unemployed.

The remainder of this chapter will begin by outlining the conceptual framework on which its analysis is based. The crises in thinking about development and security will set the scene in which the concept of social capital will be introduced as one of the crucial building blocks of development benefiting local communities and the 'Third Sector'. From an empirical standpoint, some background on the emergence of the present state of small-scale food retailing in the region will be provided and the chapter then delves into the importance of understanding the gendering of micro-entrepreneurship. Particular attention is paid to urban areas in the Philippines and Thailand where the author undertook field research – see Map 7.1. The relationship between the economic downturn and the growth of self-employment in the food sector is the subject of section four. Section five details a number of initiatives, mostly in the Philippines that organize and provide services such as micro-credit to micro-entrepreneurs. Certain approaches—by strengthening the fabric of community—build social capital, thereby enabling people to help themselves in the face of economic adversity. Finally, the conclusion sums up the information presented in this chapter and points to policy options, which can be considered in SEA and other regions affected by economic crises.

This chapter is a contribution toward addressing the impasse resulting from two crises: one concerning the discourse of development and the other emanating from debates about the meaning of 'security'. It begins by outlining these two crises and their complex and sometimes contradictory relationship. Following this, the so-called informal sector[8] is analyzed as a blurry category of income-generating activities that need to be situated with respect to recent economic developments in SEA and, more specifically to what some would argue is a failure of globalized capitalism.[9]

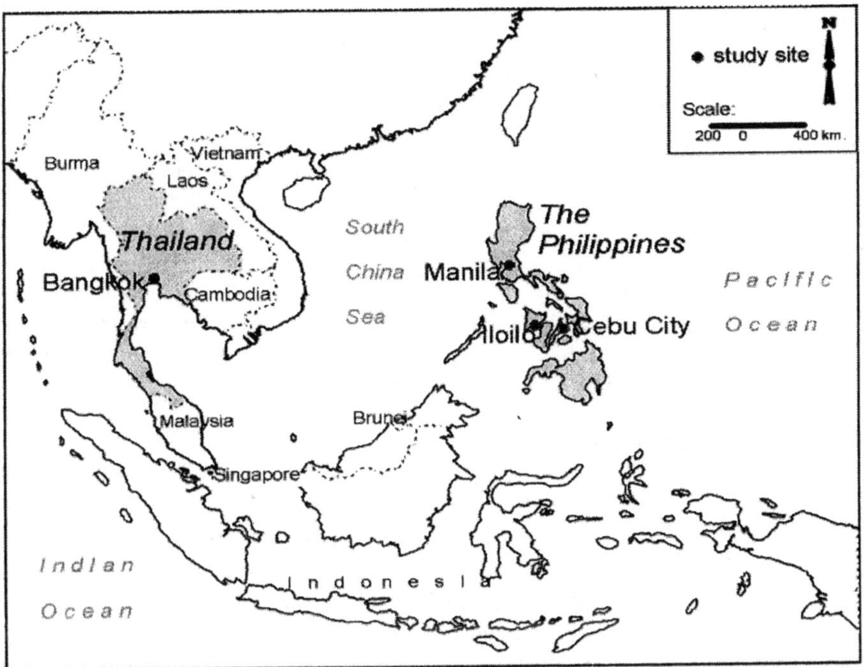

Conceptual Framework: Crises of Development and Security

Map 7.1 Map Showing Location of Study Areas

The Crisis of Development and in Development Studies

There is an irony associated with economic growth and decline in SEA which forces one to critically engage the concept of 'development'. More than 20 years of rapid growth in this region from the late 1970s until the early 1990s—though certainly increasing living standards as a whole—clearly has not resulted in the massive 'trickle down' movement cherished by neo-liberal economists. The benefits of double-digit growth in the 1980s did not accrue to the most vulnerable sectors of society in countries such as Thailand.[10] In fact, the gap between rich and poor widened during the boom period. Rapid growth predicated on both import substitution and the later trend of export-oriented industrialization has resulted in other nasty side effects such as environmental degradation and rapid over-urbanization. The 'overheating' of numerous Southeast Asian economies and overproduction in certain industrial sectors (such as automobile manufacturing) signalled the coming of an economic crisis several years ago.[11] The devaluation of the baht in July 1997 and accompanying financial turmoil came as no surprise to a number of economists and other observers such as Jeffrey Sachs.[12]

The 'market-triumphalism' so prevalent in development thinking in the latter part of the 1980s and early 1990s has been eclipsed due to numerous market failures elsewhere (such as Mexico) forcing us to question conventional development paradigms and the indicators used to measure 'development'. To come to terms with this conceptual crisis, larger issues of human well being have come to the forefront. These include social inequality, health, and control over resources.[13] Measures which foster community empowerment, gender equality, and development from the ground up—such as Grameen Bank models—have even been touted by traditionally conservative multilateral agencies such as the World Bank (WB) as examples of true development-promoting initiatives which develop local communities.[14] The discourse of development and poverty reduction has, therefore, shifted from one focused heavily on gross national product (GNP) and gross domestic product (GDP) growth to human development indicators and those of community empowerment. It is this perspective on development that is employed in this chapter.

New Discourses on Security

It became patently clear as of the late 1980s that traditional perspectives on security—that is, security defined as reducing interstate armed conflict and protecting the sovereignty of the nation-state—were, like conventional views on development unsatisfactory.[15] Discussions of security have shifted both in terms of scale of inquiry and the very definition of what it means to be secure.

First, the unit of analysis of the nation-state has expanded by looking at cross-border and international non-military sources of tension and disputes. Examples of foci include environmental degradation and resource management issues, refugee, worker, and illegal immigrant flows,[16] and contraband trade in illicit goods such as drugs and armaments. Second, various intra-state issues are now firmly on the security table such as inter-ethnic tensions[17] and labor unrest.[18] Human rights issues, the activities of 'third sector' institutions such as non-governmental organizations (NGOs) and people's organizations (POs), and the living conditions of individual communities—or subgroups such as women, youth, and so on—are now considered legitimate subjects of inquiry in security studies. The question of 'who's security and for what purpose' rather than an obstinate state-centered approach has broadened the debate.[19] Thus, food security, social security, and the gendering of security have come to the forefront in the 'post-statial' era.[20]

As Eero Carroll of the Swedish Institute for Social Research has argued, income and job security issues are at the forefront of the present-day debate. This chapter purports to explore the income security dimension of small-scale food retailing in Thailand and the Philippines post-crisis. Amartya Sen's concept of entitlements, with access to an adequate livelihood as a human right, fits into this perspective.[21] The state has an important role to play in eliminating barriers to the earning of an income as the primary means of acquiring food and other necessities of life in an urban context. Needless to say, a pool of disenfranchised, unemployed, hungry poor as recent events in Indonesia have shown are a threat to the state within the conventional discourse of security studies, as well as to the security of the affected individuals within the new discourse on security.

The Development and Security Nexus

The main focus of this volume and the two volumes that resulted from the Canadian International Development Agency (CIDA)-funded Development and Security in Southeast Asia (DSSEA) program is to investigate conceptual and empirical linkages between development and security. While development and security are themselves complex and contested concepts, the relationship between them is even more difficult to discern. Through examination of the 'bazaar economy', this chapter argues that the relationships between economic, urban-based development, and income (and therefore food) security are, in fact, contradictory.

The informal sector—contrary to many predictions—has **increased** as the economy boomed in SEA. The increase represented a growth in income-generating activities to guarantee or enhance the income and food-security of households that were marginalized by the development process. Ironically, however, informal sector employment has grown exponentially as a **result** of the economic crisis and the loss of formal sector employment. Again, the reasons for turning to this mode of income-generation are found in the need for income security and also in the fact that the pool of micro-entrepreneurs has increased drastically to include those who formerly benefited—at least somewhat—from rapid economic, industrial, urban-based growth. The economic downturn has not obliterated consumption altogether. Instead, it appears as though urbanites have 'down-shifted' their consumption habits away from places formerly patronized by the well-heeled classes to those which were more regularly frequented by the urban poor. Street restaurants, food stalls, and home-based catering businesses, therefore, have a much larger pool of customers from which to draw. However, as the remainder of this chapter will argue, more research is needed to fully understand the dynamics of development and security with respect to the informal sector—particularly the operation of food micro-enterprises.

The 'Informal Sector' and Small Scale Food Retailing

Prior to the collapse of several Asian economies in 1997, the reinforcement, rather than the disappearance, of the so-called informal or unorganized sector accompanied the boom period of industrial development in the region. The informal sector is customarily defined as small, usually family-run enterprises requiring low-skill levels, and characterized by an ease of entry and little interaction with state authorities.[22]

In fact, there have been many disputes as to whether or not this formal-informal sector dichotomy is even useful as there are numerous overlapping types of enterprises that straddle the formal/informal line. Indeed, the formal-informal sector model might be thought of as a conceptual continuum with many hybrid enterprises exhibiting features of both sectors. Within this analytical framework—rather than a strict empirical reality—it is clear that women's work tends to be located within the informal sphere. Eviota puts a feminist perspective on the relationship between the informal and formal sectors drawing from arguments on the 'bazaar' sector's ensconcement within capitalism well established in the 1970s and 1980s.

> The informal sector of subsistence trading, low-skilled services, and outwork has been far from a residual category of work for women: it is in fact an expanding category and appears to support export-led industrialization by providing complementary services to factory-based industrial enterprises, and low-cost services and goods to the laboring classes and low-paid middle class. These informal sector activities reveal undercurrents which connect the unpaid, low-productivity sector with the relatively higher-paid industrialized sectors.[23]

Eviota argues that the informal sector is dependent on and exploited by the formal sector and persists due to the lack of formal wage opportunities. The surplus pool of labor has no other choice but to 'service capital' by providing cheap goods and services, such as prepared food, to the masses.[24] In SEA, establishing a micro-enterprise becomes a matter of sheer survival:

> In economies such as the Philippines, the informal sector has been an important source of survival for the poor and the laboring classes, particularly in times of economic crises and government cutbacks. When neither the economy, nor the state are able to provide for basic needs, the casual or self-employed work of women from poor and low-income households is vital not only for their own and their household's survival but also for those formal-sector workers who are inadequately paid.[25]

The economic crisis has once again refocused attention on the economic security feature of micro-enterprise through attention paid to figures such as Sirivat, the sandwich man. Incomes in the region have plummeted due to plant closures and lay offs to the point that former workers are becoming self-employed. Furthermore, what was once a booming Southeast Asian middle class (as well as the very wealthy such as Sirivat) is forced to earn their living through peddling and small-scale business. However, it can no longer be argued that this sector is 'servicing' the formal sector. It has, instead, **replaced** much of the formal economy.

Self-employment, Food-systems, and Gender Relations in SEA

SEA is known for its high levels of female labor force participation – see Figure 7.1. This emerges from a history of female participation in agriculture and trade and is at least partly related to rapid industrialization over the past 10 to 20 years.[26] Industrial manufacturing in the region—particularly in fields such as textiles and electronics—was predicated on the hiring of large numbers of mostly young, single women from the 1970s onward. This phenomenon is familiar and has been studied extensively.[27]

Traditional and recent manifestations of women's self-employment is a subject that gained some attention in the 1970s and 1980s[28] though it did not extend to studies of industrial manufacturing. Female self-employment and the Southeast Asian woman's seeming zest for entrepreneurialism speaks to the distinctive gender relations in the region, stereotyped as those where women control small scale commerce, and the activities and occupational orientations of Southeast Asian men who have traditionally denigrated trading.

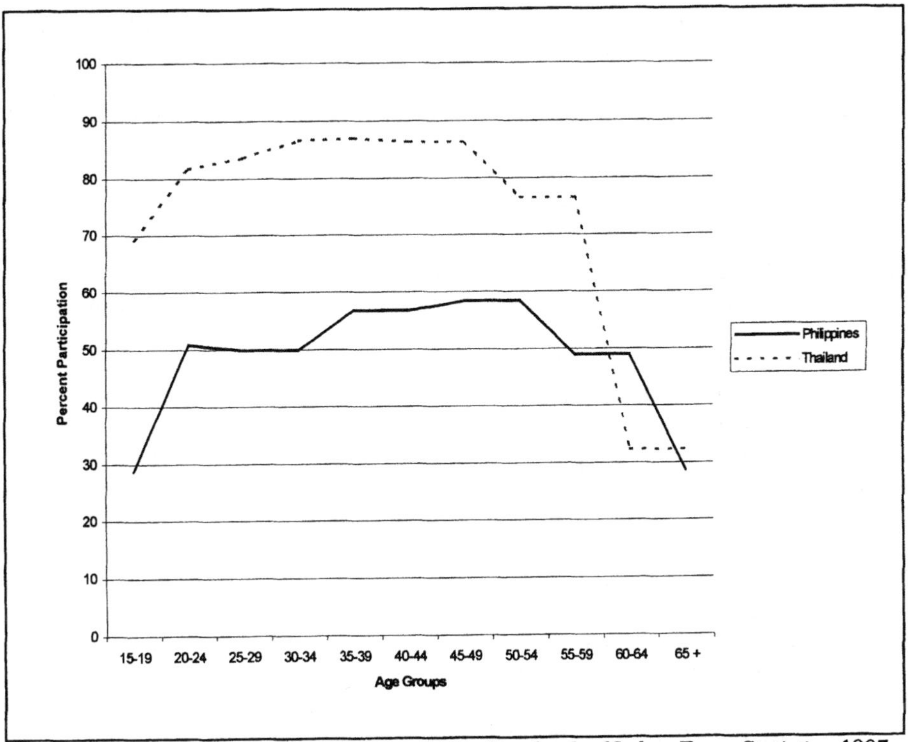

Source: International Labor Organization (ILO), *Yearbook of Labor Force Statistics*, 1997.

Figure 7.1 Female Labor Force Participation

Research on female micro-entrepreneurs was part of the 'Women in Development' (WID) framework of the 1980s where women's contributions were documented.[29] But research has tapered off in recent years because of a weakness in the analytical frames through which women's work may be approached. Interest in this topic waned in the 1990s despite accentuation of the phenomenon of self-employment of various types in light of rapid urbanization both in mega-urban regions (such as Manila – Cavite, Laguna, Batangas, Rizal, Quezon (CALABARZON), Jakarta – Jakarta, Bogor, Tangerang, Bekasih (JABOTABEK)) and other agglomerations of large, medium, and smaller scale in the region. However, with the financial crisis, an interest in economic security and a turn toward social capital issues has revived the topic with the benefit of fresh conceptual frameworks, such as hopefully that presented in this chapter.

Women's participation in the labor market is not a general, gender-wide process of exclusion and peripheralization, but instead, exhibits a range of locally specific processes of selective incorporation and segregation. Thus, in SEA, with its tradition of female involvement in trade women's entrepreneurial activities constitute both long and complex histories of gendering labor and innovative responses to new economic conditions brought about by the latest round of restructuring.[30]

As previously stated, the study of urban self-employment in small-scale food retailing and the link with issues of economic security is the specific topic of interest in the present research. The gendering of this economic activity is important and the task is now to explore the scope and nature of this activity in the Philippines and Thailand.

The Philippines and Thailand in Comparative Perspective

Earlier work has documented Thai urban *foodscapes* in some detail.[31] Generally, there are four patterns exhibited in urban Thailand within the sphere of small-scale retailing:

1. According to the Thai Department of Labor, 82 per cent of enterprises with less than four employees are owned and operated by women sometimes with the help of their husbands and children;
2. A number of informal enterprises are not included in government statistics because of the difficulty associated with gathering data from unregulated economic activities and a lack of recognition of this sector overall. It is certain, however, that at least 80 per cent are owned and operated by women;
3. The vast majority of the micro-entrepreneurs in Bangkok's foodscape are migrants from the poorest part of Thailand—the Northeast, or *Isan*;
4. Revenues accruing from the enterprise—which are often more generous than factory work and even some white collar occupations—are largely invested in human capital, particularly education of kin and supporting family members in rural areas. Profits are not typically reinvested in the enterprise. There is a similar trend in the Philippines – see Figure 7.2.

To get a clearer picture, there are a few factors distinctive to the Philippines that need to be enumerated. These have a bearing on the urban *foodscapes* under scrutiny.

1. To a far greater extent than Thais, Filipinos have the lucrative option of becoming Overseas Contract Workers (OCWs) in the Gulf States, wealthier Asian countries, and elsewhere. This has provided a source of investment capital for the creation of micro-enterprises. Quite commonly now, the quintessentially Filipino *sari-sari* store – or mixed, dry goods shop – is a small business that is in many cases created by overseas remittances or the savings of are turning OCWs.
2. Filipinos do not cherish the habit of eating outside the home as much as Thais, perhaps due to the Spanish and American influences. The range and availability of eating establishments, whether ambulant vendors or 'fixed-pitch' eateries are, therefore, quite limited compared to those in urban Thailand. The institutions that are more typical of the Filipino urban *foodscape* are the ubiquitous *sari-sari* stores – so many one cannot fathom how they survive[32] – as well as *carendarias* (small

Both personal communications and newspaper articles have made it clear that an important aspect of guaranteeing good life-chances for one's offspring in the Philippines is to find the money to send children to private schools. This is due to the generally poor quality of public schools in terms of quality of instruction, facilities and equipment. In an Iloilo newspaper article it was reported that 'A group of public market vendors here assailed on Monday the Commission on Higher Education (CHED) for endorsing the increase of tuition fees of up to 25 per cent by private colleges and universities... Teresita Galang, 48, a fish vendor, said the CHED should have regulated the tuition fee hike in order to spare parents earning minimum wage from getting severely affected. Education is therefore a policy issue related to livelihood concerns.

Figure 7.2 Sending Children to Private Schools

Field research in the Philippines was primarily concentrated in two secondary urban centers in the Visayas, namely Cebu and Iloilo. In data similar to those collected for Thailand, food vendors are typically female, middle-aged, and supporting a family. In 1991 in Iloilo, Concepcion and Braganza found that, for example, sidewalk vendors were predominantly female, married, Roman Catholics, between 40-49 years old.[33] Most had been selling for an average of 14 years. The authors found that a great number had finished high school (26 per cent) and some had even attended college (7.5 per cent). Most were living in nuclear or extended-type families and had interesting and varied employment histories. Most Ilongo food vendors reported low incomes, though this is consistent with other inquiries into the informal sector, where respondents fear tax officials and, therefore, sometimes underreport revenues. The ownership of many appliances, such as radios, motorcycles, and television sets, attested to a higher income than that which was reported. Most respondents (80 per cent) reported vending as the main source of household income.

In Cebu, the second largest urban agglomeration in the Philippines, Felisa Uy Etemadi recently estimated that half of the poor of Cebu City are self-employed.[34] Of the total self-employed population, a great number are working within the food system in small scale operations such as backyard pig-raising, *sari-sari* stores, *carendarias,* and snack sellers such as *bibingka* (native rice cakes):[35]

> Bensel and Remedio estimated the number of street food vendors in Cebu City at around 13,000 in 1992, 70 per cent of whom are household-based while 30 per cent, mostly barbecue vendors, operate outside the home.[36]

Barbecue vendors are particularly difficult for the government to monitor as they operate in the evenings and normally do not acquire a business license though they are technically required to do so.

It is not only important to understand the subtle differences between Thailand and the Philippines in the informal food sector but equally critical to understand how the economic crisis has differentially affected each country.

Coping with the Crisis

Though the Philippines has been somewhat cushioned from the economic crisis due to the remittances from OCWs and, some would argue, its earlier structural adjustments and more viable banking sector, a large number of poor and lower-middle class urbanites depend extensively on the revenues generated by the selling of food. In Thailand, by contrast, the economic downturn has made a huge impact on the small-scale food retailing system. Whereas a few years ago, some vendors were threatened with relocation due to the imminent construction of condominiums and office towers, the halt on construction post-crisis has left their selling spaces intact.[37]

Daeng, for example, a 33-year-old food shop owner near the Victory Monument thought she and her aunt Ying would be forced to vacate their selling space when she was interviewed in late 1994. Her business at present is doing well. Customers are regular and there are no threats of redevelopment. A letter Daeng sent in September 1999 informed the author that she has even acquired a cellular phone! Daeng is a member of one of the most vulnerable groups in Bangkok—rural migrants from the Northeast. She has the equivalent of a grade six education. Daeng perhaps possesses some advantages over those who have recently entered the field of selling prepared food on the street. She has over ten years of experience and can attract more customers. Those who are less experienced or who were higher placed on the Thai social ladder had more to lose.

Middle-class families such as the Chanpraserts, for example, have experienced some downward mobility in the past few years. Their travel agency rarely gets business any more and the informal residence for university students in their two shop houses is shabby and run down compared to 1994. In April 1999, they opened a food shop (or small eatery) in order to earn extra income for the household. There are several similar examples throughout the Victory Monument Area of central Bangkok. The presence of new eateries in nearly all parts of the city is overwhelming.

The most vulnerable victims of the downturn, however, have left Bangkok to return to their impoverished rural areas:

> Nouphen Chartsri is no poster child for the Asian crisis, no high-flying stockbroker who lost his Mercedes-Benz and is now selling sandwiches to survive... She's a far more average Asian, a farmwoman with a few years of education who had found a measure of the good life in Thailand's booming economy. The tropical sun has aged her beyond her 30 years.[38]

Nouphen is from the Northeast and worked in a factory on the outskirts of Bangkok where she earned twice her previous income from farming. When the financial crisis hit she did like many migrants and went back to the village. Nouphen is now cutting sugar cane for free to work off a family debt.[39] Recent articles in the

Far Eastern Economic Review, however, suggest that migrants are slowly trickling back to Bangkok.[40] Many of these returnees are living in slums and doing odd jobs to survive. They borrow from moneylenders and pay exorbitant interest to make ends meet from day to day.

Though the information on the social impacts of the economic crisis are somewhat anecdotal, the general observations and countless similar stories of individuals together are starting to paint a portrait of the emerging living and working conditions:

> The indications of mounting social problems are seen in growing unemployment and the need to turn to the informal sector for a living, as well as increased migration of displaced workers.[41]

To redress the information gap but more importantly, to quickly identify policy solutions organizations such as the International Labor Organization (ILO) and the United Nations Development Programme (UNDP) through the United Nations Development Fund for Women (UNIFEM) are beginning to examine ways in which to enhance coping strategies for micro-entrepreneurs, particularly women.

The Reversal of McDonaldization: Fast Foods and the Economic Downturn

Though several middle-class restaurants in Bangkok have closed following the devaluation of the baht (including the former world's largest restaurant, *Tom Nuk Thai*), Western fast-food chains are struggling to keep afloat and compete with the resurgent street food sector. Thai agri-food conglomerates such as Central Pattana Group (CP) license most of the large chains such as McDonald's and Kentucky Fried Chicken (KFC). Though a number of KFCs in the region laid off their staff or even closed due to reduced sales, spokespersons for these establishments insist that they still have a future. Suwanna Usanachitt, Marketing Manager of KFC International Thailand explains:

> 'We have not positioned KFC as a luxury restaurant but as a fast-food outlet affordable to middle to lower income earners...the parent company is still confident in Thailand's economic situation and is providing strong marketing and investment support...Fast-food chains that offer good products at reasonable and fair prices and benefit customers will survive'.[42]

Fast-food chains like McDonald's are introducing new products to compete with traditional fast foods such as those sold by small vendors. In Indonesia, McDonald's introduced the 'Rice Egg' sold for 2,000 Rupiah (24 cents) as opposed to the burger which jumped to 10,400 Rp (1.20) representing two days wages for most workers. Still, on the street, one can purchase a dish made of rice, meat, and eggs for 2,000 Rupiah or even less if one is not insistent about having a place to sit down.

> In Jakarta, the price of a Big Mac can buy you an eight-km cab ride, two cans of locally-produced Bintang beer, a big bag of good-quality rice or a ticket for the 112-km ride to the hill retreat of Bandung.[43]

One is tempted to applaud the tarnishing of the Golden Arches that are symbols of food imperialism and the converging of consumer tastes.[44] Whatever one's stand is on international fast-food chains, there are serious consequences for employment when these large, normally stable establishments decline or go out of business:

> Coca Holding International Co. Ltd. operator of the Coco sukiyaki restaurant chain, is suffering badly in cash-strapped Indonesia, Malaysia, and Thailand, where a heavy drop in spending power is keeping clients away... [Richard] Loo (executive director of Coca Restaurant Takashimaya) said the company has targeted a ten per cent reduction in staff this year by putting a freeze on hiring to fill vacancies. Pitaya [Phanphensophon, managing director of Coca Holding International Co. Ltd.] said the company is considering shutting down poor performing branches in Thailand and overseas, such as in Surabaya in Indonesia.[45]

Some of those who are laid off from formal employment, such as a fast-food chain or a factory are coping by opening their own micro-enterprises.[46] Those who turn to the food business appear to be the vast majority. Customers are assured as we all need to eat! Lack of kitchen space, the high price of cooking fuel, and the complexity of Thai food preparation assure small places offering good value for money of steady customers.

Table 7.1 indicates approximate investment costs and profit margins for micro-entrepreneurs in the *foodscapes* of urban Thailand, particularly Bangkok. However, the 'sandwich strategy' that requires less equipment and cooking experience/knowledge might be starting to spawn new micro-enterprises in the new economy. By August 1998, less than a year after making international news reports things had changed for Khun Sirivat.

> Siriwat Voravetvuthikhun, the former high-flying businessmen (sic) who set up a sandwich-making venture to keep staff a year ago is now finding lean pickings as rising costs have eaten into profits... His new line of business reflects trends towards natural products. 'Sandwiches do not make much profit any more. My staff and I are now offering fruit and vegetable juice, such as aloe juice. We also sell vegetable products from Doi Kham', he says.[47]

Sirivat's shift in business strategy may have more to do with the particular type of food he sells, his notoriety, spending habits, and general lifestyle than indicates a serious change in coping strategies for Thailand's urban poor and middle classes. Though Thailand has felt the crisis more deeply than the Philippines, it still appears as though well-entrenched patterns of micro-entrepreneurship, particularly in the prepared food sector have helped Thais survive the economic uncertainties. Even though the Philippines has been cushioned by OCW remittances economic survival has been enhanced by a strong civil society consisting of NGOs and POs. This social fabric contributes to the growth of social capital by strengthening community networks, organizing citizens and sub-groups such as vendors, and providing services such as micro-credit.

Table 7.1 What (Food) to Sell

Business	Investment (Baht)	Working Capital (Baht/day)	Profit (Baht/day)	Margin Rate (%)
Sandwich, Franchise	10,000	5-800	4-600	30-40
Sandwich, non-Franchise	n.a.	n.a.	4-500	n.a.
Rice Soup Stall	200,000	4-5,000	n.a.	n.a.
Grilled seafood	70,000–300,000	1-5,000	n.a.	n.a.
Mobile Noodle Stall	15,000	5-600	5-800	100
Juice	2,500	1-1,500	n.a.	15-20

Source: 'Retailers press government for more relief to ensure survival', *Bangkok Post*, 3 August 1998, pp.8.

Civil Society and the Fostering of Social Capital

This section will profile several initiatives in the Philippines that illustrate how social capital can be enhanced by the work of NGOs, POs, community-based organizations (CBOs) and other agents in the 'Third Sector' or civil society. Though Thailand does have a few similar initiatives, Thai social scientists argue that the social support mechanisms there are sorely lacking, particularly for women and their livelihood activities such as food vending.[48] First, a brief definition of what has become a ubiquitous term in development circles: social capital.

The Concept of Social Capital

When scholars such as James Coleman,[49] Caroline Moser,[50] and Patricia Wilson[51] invoke the term 'social capital' they refer to the intangible and complex set of social relationships, networks, trust, and co-operation that result in the creation of community. Others might add transparency and accountability as key ingredients in the recipe for social capital. It is this 'glue' that enables society to work smoothly and for authentic development, from the ground up or community development to take place. Though anthropologists and sociologists have known this for a long time, it is only recently that economists have latched onto the concept and dubbed it 'social capital'. Economic theory finally had come to terms with the fact that development is not fundamentally about growth rates, labor force structures, sites and services, and so on but is about people and their relationships to each other and how they can work within groups. At the same time, development theorists have had to acknowledge the effectiveness of innovative strategies, many emanating from the South rather than the North such as the Self-Employed Women's Association (SEWA) and Grameen-bank type micro-lending programs. These success stories have forced them to reevaluate their own frameworks of analysis, indicators, and policy recommendations.

This section will look at the community building and empowerment strategies employed in the Philippines where a strong civil society and its constituent organizations have thrived in the post-authoritarian era since 1986.[52] There are several examples beyond the ones focused on below. For example, several groups, such as the Urban Poor Associates[53] based in Manila and Cebu Labor Education, Advocacy and Research Center (CLEAR) in Cebu play the pivotal role of organizing the poor. They advocate ensuring that their collective rights are respected and disseminate information to make their constituency aware of the issues that affect them. These groups lay the groundwork for the more specific, targeted programs outlined below.

Community Organizing Strategies

Filipino civil society organizations can be classified as adhering to one of five approaches:

1. The Religious approach: such as the Christian Taytay Sa Kauswagan, Inc. (TSKI) and the Alliance of Philippine Partners in Enterprise Development, Inc. (APPEND) Network and smaller, Catholic organizations such as *Balay Ni Maria* (Iloilo). The commitment of leaders and workers in these groups are based on their values and beliefs and sense of duty and justice. *Lihok Pilipina* and the Urban Poor Associates also find their origin and inspiration in organized religion.
2. Trade unionists and left-leaning strategies: Cebu City United Vendors Asociation (CCUVA) and labor groups such as CLEAR are obvious examples. Some of these have or had links with various political parties on the left and are now struggling to have a wider appeal. They are doing so by moving away from a focus on industrial workers towards self-employed informal sector workers, women, and others.[54]
3. Local government initiatives: such as those undertaken by the City of Cebu and the City of Iloilo. Municipal policies, particularly the leadership of the Mayor play key roles in the formulation of these programs.
4. Corporate partnerships: the prime example being the Philippine Business for Social Progress (PBSP) where corporations donate ten per cent of their annual profits to reinvest in community building. The funds collected are generous and programs are numerous and are administered throughout the country.
5. UN approaches: though not discussed in this chapter, the ILO has published countless studies of the informal sector and made voluminous recommendations. However, they are accused by many grassroots organizations of not putting enough efforts toward the implementation of their policy suggestions through the establishment of pilot and demonstration projects.

Perhaps one of the most creative, successful, and impressive strategies to organize street food vendors is one in Cebu City where the micro-entrepreneurs have endeavored to organize themselves on their own terms. Here, vendors have formed associations, sometimes cooperatives and federated these associations to form the

CCUVA. CCUVA was founded in 1984 and includes 56 member organizations listed in Table 7.2. Most associations are those of vendors selling immediately outside public markets that specialize in both food and non-food items (such as *ukay-ukay* or second-hand clothing as well as other goods).

These vendors are clearly the most in need of being organized as they do not have formal access to stalls from which to sell their wares. They are, therefore, the most frequently harassed and displaced by police and municipal officials because they are defined as encroachers on public space. At the same time, however, many of the vendors occupying the footpaths pay a daily fee to the municipality for which they receive a receipt. This practice is known as *arklabay* in Cebuano, the local language, thus, making the status of sidewalk vendors as encroachers ambiguous—as they are, in a way, tenants. In Cebu, where the urban economy is still viable enough to sustain ongoing construction, and property is, therefore, a very valuable commodity **access to space** is the number one issue facing sidewalk vendors. Many of their mobilization efforts are geared towards securing access to space by employing a strategy of forming associations that have validity under Philippine law.

CCUVA, and many of its constituent organizations, is registered with the Securities and Exchange Commission (SEC) of the Philippines as of 1996. Unlike in Western countries, however, SEC registration in the Philippines is relatively straightforward and does not involve taking a company public or selling shares on the open market.[55] Registration with the commission is one of the first indicators of institutionalization, nevertheless, and does give a legal personality to the members of CCUVA. As evident in Table 7.2, many of the organizations affiliated with CCUVA are, like the federation itself, incorporated. The majority of the members of CCUVA's associations are women.[56] Seventeen of the 34 members of the Council of Presidents (or Board of Directors) of CCUVA are women. Women, therefore, occupy a prominent leadership position in the organization.

On the 29th of November 1998, CCUVA held its 7th Bi-Annual Convention and Election of Officers. This one-day event included special 'messages of solidarity' conferred by the Mayor, Alvin Garcia, as well as two city councilors and a representative of President Joseph Ejercito Estrada's staff. Though this is encouraging, it is clear that there are still many tensions between the objectives of the Cebu City municipal government and CCUVA with respect to the policies and procedures related to street vending. The city is at times seen as trying to reach compromises with vendors over the use of public space. Many vendors, however, accuse municipal officials of duplicity in still demolishing vendors' stalls (or threatening to do so) even after so-called compromises are reached.[57] Recent communications from Cebu suggest that there are more frequent dialogues between CCUVA and the Mayor.[58] Demolitions are, however, still taking place.[59]

CCUVA's future plans involve:

1. Engaging in policy development and advocacy activities to support legislative and executive measures to address street vendors' (SV) problems,
2. Organizing, strengthening and coalition-building among SVorganizations (including on a national level),

3. Facilitating access of SVs to credit and social security services, and
4. Developing support systems for child SVs.[60]

Table 7.2 Affiliate Organizations of CCUVA

Assorted Dried Fish Vendors Assn. Assorted Vendors Organization Calderon Dollar Association Calderon Watch & Jewelry Repair & Gold Plating Association Carcar Stall Owners Association Cebu Association of Laborers, Inc. Cebu Butcher's Association Cebu City Muslim Traders Vendors Association, Inc. Carbon Integrated Fish & Chicken Assn. City Central School, Abellana & Cebu College of Arts & Trade Association F. Escaño Vendors Association F. Gonsales Carton Vendors Association Fish & Meat Vendors Association Freedom Park United Vendors Assn. Fuente Osmeña Barbecue Vendors Assn. Guadelupe Livelihood Center, Inc. Juan Luna Sharpers Association Laborers Vendors Association Landing Area Vendors Organization Leon Kilat Ambulant Vendors Association Llorente Fruit Vendors Association Lower Salinas Vendors Association Mabolo Sidewalk Vendors Association Mabolo United Vendors Association Magallanes Leon Kilat Vendors Assn. Mandaue United Sidewalk Vendors Assn. Muslim Traders Vendors Association North Reclamation Sidewalk Vendors Association Osmeña Boulevard Vendors Sagangs Group	Pelaez & P. Del Rosario Vendors Assn. Pier Area Vendors Association B. Rodriquez Vendors Association Quezon Vendors Association Redemptorist Church Sidewalk Vendors Association Santo Niño Assorted Vendors Assn. Santo Niño Sidewalk Vendors Assn. Cebu Downtown Sidewalk Vendors Association, Inc. Sidewalk Vendors Association Zone I Sidewalk Vendors Association Zone II Sidewalk Vendors Association Zone III Sidewalk Vendors Association Zone IV Southern Island Medical Center Vendors Association SSS Sidewalk Vendors Association Tabako Vendors Association Tabo Sa Banay Vendors Association – II Tabunok Sidewalk Vendors Association Tobacco Sidewalk Vendors Association United Ambulant Vendors Association United Calderon & Progreso Vendors Association – A United Calderon & Progreso Vendors Association – B United Vendors Organization of Carbon Market Uptown Vendors Association Vegetables Ambulant Vendors Association Visayan Electric Ambulant Vendors Association Warwick Barracks Sidewalk Vendors Association Zamora Vendors Association

To what extent CCUVA will decide to work in conjunction with other types of organizations, such as those described below is as yet unclear. The group appears to be quite politicized and participates frequently and quite vociferously in mobilizations and with groups on the left. This approach is quite different than that advocated by more 'mainstream' NGOs dealt with in the next section.

Micro-credit Programs and Cooperatives

Several Filipino organizations, including some local governments have instituted micro-credit programs for small-scale entrepreneurs over the past several years. The Grameen bank model has inspired many. One example is the Cebu-based NGO, *Lihok Pilipina*. Though the credit program is still in its infancy as a pilot project, positive results are already evident. Participants have been able to buy and build homes, pay for their children's education, and reduce their traditional dependence on usurious moneylenders.

In the capital, Manila Community Services, Inc. has been carrying out similar programs with a high degree of success. Their micro-credit programs, like Grameen are group-based, involve developing leadership skills, and also provide training for members in financial and business management. A similar series of programs are being introduced by the PBSP, itself an innovative partnership between the corporate world and community building through a sub-program entitled Small and Medium Enterprise Credit (SMEC).

In Iloilo City, the TSKI is a Christian NGO that helps beneficiaries develop income-generating and job-creating small and medium enterprises. As part of the countrywide APPEND Network, it federates its efforts with like-minded organizations nationally and throughout the world as part of the Opportunity International movement which fosters self-reliance through micro-credit programs.

The City of Iloilo has also launched a number of micro-credit schemes, particularly targeted toward a number of 'depressed' *barangays* or poor quarters of the city. Municipal officials were frank in admitting that these are not as effective as programs launched by NGOs. Defaulting on loans has been prevalent, perhaps because recipients view themselves as entitled to government revenues rather than seeing themselves as borrowers.

A second set of refreshing examples from the Philippines concern the strong cooperative movement (there is, indeed, a Ministry for Cooperatives) and through local government policy, its outreach to groups of vendors, particularly in public markets. The idea to organize vendors into cooperatives is not new. As Concepcion and Braganza noted in 1991: 'When asked if they are willing to be organized into a cooperative, 77.81 per cent answered in the affirmative.'[61]

One particular pilot project is gaining a lot of attention in the Visayas. The City of Cebu, through the leadership of the mayor assisted by a former senior official of the Visayan cooperative federation (VICTO) is attempting to reorganize the formerly dilapidated public market in the center of the city. Where there were disputes with unlicensed street vendors in the market area a few years ago there are now extra spaces for fixed pitches thereby reducing tension over access to space. The vendors have organized themselves into cooperatives and are soon to manage the market on their own.[62] The city has helped with marketing campaigns to lure the public away from the many new shopping malls and back to the market. Current city employees will continue to play certain roles once the market is privatized to the cooperative and garnering their cooperation has proven to be one of the more challenging aspects of the new policy.

In these examples of micro-credit and enterprise support programs as well as the cooperative movement, gender relations are important. Women are the majority of beneficiaries of programs geared toward small-scale entrepreneurs. They are also pillars of the cooperative movement. At the same time, they are ensconced within households and economic pursuits where cooperation with men is essential.

Though the situation is improving, Thai NGOs and CBOs are not as numerous and well entrenched in society as their Filipino counterparts. The Filipino organizations acquired significant momentum after the fall of Marcos in 1986. This, overall, has strengthened civil society.

Thailand has also had a series of political upheavals, notably in the early 1970s and 1992 where student's groups, people's organizations, and intellectuals galvanized public support to voice protests against the authoritarian regime. These social movements were less successful and on both occasions, overt state criticism was met with brutal violence. However, there are a number of examples of successful civil society organizations both based in Thailand and having a pan-Asian membership, such as the Asian Coalition of Housing Rights as well as those more focused on the needs of the poor. Infamous slums, such as Khlong Toey have been the breeding grounds for the most well known organizations such as the Federation of Khlong Toey Slums. Prapapat Niyom explains:

> NGOs' roles have changed a lot during the past three decades. Initially they were instrumental in the formation of CBOs in urban poor communities. Through the years, however, aside from providing assistance, they have played the roles of trainer, advisor, and leader. With their assistance and support, the CBOs have developed and enhanced their self-confidence and capability in managing their own organizations, developing, and implementing appropriate projects in addressing urgent problems and in dealing with outside actors.[63]

Prapapat concludes, however, that better coordination and communication is needed to bridge the gap between government organizations and policies and those promulgated by civil society organizations. The Thai state, including at the local level has not been known historically to promote citizen's participation in governance.[64] Bangkok's present governor has at least stated that local governance ought to be more inclusive and is known to interact far more frequently and effectively with his constituents.[65]

Concluding Remarks and Policy Considerations

Concepcion and Braganza reported in 1991 that 90 per cent of sidewalk vendors in Iloilo City did not belong to any organization or association. The remaining ten per cent belonged to the small Iloilo Sidewalk Vendor's Association or the St. Vincent de Paul Foundation.[66] Since this time, throughout the Visayas and the Philippines as a whole there has been a tremendous growth of vendor's associations, NGOs, POs, and other civil society organizations that are starting to have a significant positive impact on the lives of the most vulnerable self-employed. In fact, as is the case in India, there are now so many NGOs in the Philippines that one has to tread carefully to separate the wheat from the chaff.[67] Some NGO executive directors, like in the sub-continent, are accused of using their organizations as a tax shelter, or, worse, as a means to get rich. This points to the need for transparency and accountability in **all** institutions involved in development, including civil society organizations.

Unemployment in the Central Visayas is on the rise. There is no need to repeat the fact that formal employment opportunities in Thailand have been decimated. Unemployment, as has been made clear here, is a security issue. The unemployment rate is predicted to be 3.3 per cent for Thailand in 1998. This represents 1.5 million people. Laksamana Sukardi of the Econit Research Centre observes, 'social unrest has become almost certain'.[68]

From a policy standpoint, civil society and some municipal governments in the Philippines appear to be moving in the right direction. The national government as well as public agencies and services (such as the police, tax authorities, and others) need to recognize these 'best practices', monitor and evaluate them, and try replicating them elsewhere in the country. At the same time, the corporate sector, perhaps under the leadership of the PBSP must put its full support behind micro-credit and cooperative development programs that strengthen small-scale industry and, thereby, reinforce the community fabric.

In Thailand, local strengths are in the field of food retailing and a general preponderance of entrepreneurship, especially of women. There are, however, serious lacunae when it comes to the protection of these workers and the existence of schemes to increase their access to credit and federate them as a group:

> The 7th Development Plan was more specific toward target groups in the informal sector by including plans for employment opportunities and welfare for the urban poor and underprivileged groups.[69]

Micro-enterprises have been targeted by the latest national development plan but there is no inclusion of welfare and social protection notes Napat. Instead, supporting these enterprises is seen as a way to ease the financial burden on government and social tensions surrounding unemployment. The notion of entitlements and the concept of social capital are not built into the plan and should be, particularly in light of the devastation of the recent financial crisis.

At present, unlike the Philippines, only a small number of NGOs in Thailand provide financial support such as credit and revolving funds to their beneficiaries, according to Napat.[70] Though agricultural co-operatives are strong, there is no indication that the co-operative movement is alive and well in urban areas.

Thailand is sorely lacking in the area of community building activities and can learn from some of the practices emerging in the neighboring Philippines. Due to many similarities in social structure and some cultural overlaps, the Philippines and Thailand are in a good position to engage in the types of 'South-South' exchanges and partnerships being fostered by groups such as Focus on the Global South.[71] Thailand's more well-developed indigenous food retailing system and creative entrepreneurship would benefit from experiences in the Philippines which aim to strengthen civil society through public policy and the work of community-based organizations. The policies of development agencies in the North should concentrate on fostering these types of horizontal linkages and using their vast networks in the South to facilitate the process.

Recommendations for Policy Makers and Further Research

1. **Micro-entrepreneurs in the food sector, often typified as 'vendors' need to be viewed both by policy makers and the research community as providing a crucial livelihood for households, especially in times of economic difficulty.** Food vendors in particular provide an opportunity to make a critical link between research and policy making in the areas of food security and income security. Their activities need to be understood and supported by local, regional, and national authorities. Contradictory process at the local level, such as municipal governments providing training for micro-entrepreneurship on the one hand, and then threatening vendors with eviction and demolition on the other need to be addressed and rectified. Local governments ought to support small-scale food vending across the board, from training through technical help with waste management.
2. **Micro-entrepreneurs also need to be included in the local and regional planning of their municipalities along with other members of society.** Devolution of central government power to the local level is currently taking place in the Philippines with indications that it is on the horizon in Thailand. This is an opportunity for vendors to have their voices heard on the condition that new forms of urban governance recognize the need for 'shared space'.[72] There is also a need for redistributive policies given the gross inequalities over resources at the local level.[73] Examples from India where the 74th Amendment to the Constitution has also recently devolved power to the local level and where street food vendors, through SEWA have concomitantly formed a national alliance would be worth looking into for comparison and policy options.
3. **The needs of micro-entrepreneurs need to be recognized and expanded to go beyond training and micro-credit to include *access to space*.** A link also needs to be made between this livelihood activity and other aspects of life including housing, education, and transportation. There is an urgent need to address the occupational health and safety needs of micro-entrepreneurs in the food sector including hazardous exposure to pollution, workplace injuries, and sleep deprivation among other concerns.
4. **In terms of development assistance more generally, there is a need to both support as well as critically engage the activities of NGOs, POs, and CBOs with respect to the activities of micro-entrepreneurs in the food sector (and other sectors).** All institutions in the development process including government agencies, private enterprises, and civil society organizations need to be transparent and accountable to their beneficiaries as well as their funding agencies. All organizations involved in aid toward micro-entrepreneurs need to be fully evaluated and audited by independent outside agencies.

5. **Canadian aid policy ought to foster 'South-South' exchanges and partnerships rather than replicate the typical formula of providing Northern expertise and solutions to Southern problems.**
This would, for example, include diffusing knowledge concerning innovative strategies employed in the Philippines to those working in other Southern countries that might replicate or modify these approaches. Workshops, conferences, publications, and other activities/outputs such as websites, video-documentaries, and other media should be supported by the North to put various Southern networks in touch with one another in order to share valuable information and experiences.

Notes

1 I would like to thank the Canadian International Development Agency for providing the funds for this study. I am particularly grateful to Drs. David Dewitt and Carolina Hernandez for guiding the research project on Development and Security in Southeast Asia and for selecting me as a member of the research team. My gratitude extends to Felisa Uy Etemadi, Zenaida Ligan, Terry McGee, Phoebe Zoë Sanchez, Jorge Tigno, and Leon Flores III for valuable comments on the paper. Also, Connie Del Rio, Pierre Fallavier, Deirdre McKay and Nadim Kara are thanked for their valuable research assistance. Ron Richardson must take credit for suggesting the case of the 'sandwich man'. Formatting help was provided by Judith Fairbairn. Most of all, I am in debt to the countless persons I interviewed – including those spoken to anonymously – who provided the most valuable insights into this topic.

2 Bacani, C.(1997), 'Surviving the Slump', *Asiaweek*, 28 November, pp.52-55.

3 *Ibid*; 'Retailers press government for more relief to ensure survival', *Bangkok Post*, 3 August 16 July, pp.F3; 'Pacific Rim Report, Report on effects of Asian financial crisis', *CBC Television*, November 1997 and June 1998.

4 Yasmeen, G. (1992), 'Bangkok's Restaurant Sector: Gender, Employment and Consumption', *Journal of Social Research*, vol.15, no.2, Chulalongkorn University, Bangkok, Thailand, pp.69-81; *Ibid.*, *Bangkok's Foodscape: Public Eating, Gender Relations and Urban Change*, unpublished Ph.D. dissertation, Department of Geography, University of British Columbia; Walker, M. and Yasmeen, G. (eds) (1996), '"From Scratch": Thai Food-Systems and Public Eating', *Contemporary Perspectives on Thai Foodways*, Monograph no.11, Centre for Southeast Asian Research, Vancouver, pp. 20-43.

5 There are, of course, many exceptions to this generalization, particularly due to colonial influences.

6 Rungfapaisarn, K. (1997), 'KFC plans big expansion in local market: Fast food chain still confident', *The Nation*, 11 November, pp.B3; Marshall, A. (1998), 'Indonesians toil 2 days for a Big Mac', *Vancouver Sun*, 16 July, pp.F3.

7 Sivasomboon, B. and Treerapongpichit, B. (1998), 'Laid off workers turn to small businesses', *Bangkok Post*, 23 March, pp.10.

8 Defining microenterprises as 'informal' is inaccurate which is why I cloak the term in speechmarks. There are several examples pointing to the formalization of enterprises we think of – at first glance – as informal. As this paper will illustrate, many vendors have formed organizations and some are even registered with the Security and Exchange commission! However, I continue to use the term informal for the sake of brevity.

9 Price, J. (1998), *Dissent and New Directions for Canada and the Asia Pacific*, 'Building on Canada's Year of Asia Pacific: Evaluation and Strategic Directions Conference', 7 March 1998.
10 'Two Thailands: Spreading Wealth Beyond Bangkok', *Far Eastern Economic Review*, 14 April 1994.
11 'Time for a Reality Check in Asia', *Business Week*, 2 December 1996, pp.59-66.
12 Sachs, J. (1997), 'International Monetary Failure?' *Time*, 8 December, pp.8.
13 McKibben, B. (1996), 'The Enigma of Kerala', *Utne Reader*, March-April, pp.103-112.
14 Khandker, S. R., Khalili, B. and Khan, Z. (1995), *Grameen Bank: Performance and Sustainability*, World Bank, Washington, DC; Carr, M., Chen, M. and Jhabvala, R. (1996), *Speaking Out: Women's Economic Empowerment in South Asia*, Aga Khan Foundation Canada and the United Nations Development Fund for Women (Unifem), IT Publications, London.
15 Kennedy, P. (1993), *Preparing for the 21st Century*, Fontana Press, London; Moran, T. (1990/1), 'International economics and security', *Foreign Affairs*, vol.5, Winter; Sorensen, T. (1995), 'What is international economic security?' *International Affairs*, vol.71, March, pp.305-24.
16 See, Lusterio, *Perceptions of Women Migrant Workers in the Philippines and Indonesia*, and Tigno, *Migration Security and Development: The Politics of Undocumented Labor Migration in Southeast Asia*, in this volume.
17 Bertrand, *'Good' Governance and the Security of Ethnic Communities in Indonesia and the Philippines*, in this volume.
18 See Tubagus Feridhanusetyawan, *Security Implications of the Economic Crisis for Indonesian Workers*, in this volume.
19 Carroll, E. (1998), 'Security, E-mail posting to Public Policy Network', Email, August 18.
20 Ahmad, E. (1991), 'Social Security and the Poor: Choices for Developing Countries', *World Bank Research Observer*, vol.6, no.1, January; Guhan, S. (1994), 'Social Security Options for Developing Countries', *International Labour Review*, vol.133, no.1, pp.35-53; Kara, N. (1997), *Transcending a historical legacy: sovereignty, the state and post-modernity*, unpublished paper, Spring, pp.1- 47; Maxwell, S. (1990), 'Food Security in Developing Countries: Issues and Options for the 1990's', *IDS Bulletin*, vol.21, no.3, July; Tweeten, L. (1997), 'Investing in People', and 'Food Security', *Promoting Third World Development and Food Security*, Praeger, Westport, CT, pp.183-204.
21 Sen, A. (1981), 'Poverty and Famines: An Essay on Entitlement and Deprivation', Clarendon Press, Oxford.
22 Amin, ATM N. (1991), *A Policy Agenda for the Informal Sector in Thailand*, Asian Employment Programme, International Labour Office, New Delhi; Sethuraman, S. V. (1992), *The Urban Informal Sector in Asia: an Annotated Bibliography Series: International labour bibliography*, International Labour Office, Geneva.
23 Eviota, E. (1992), 'The Political Economy of Gender', Zed Books, London, pp.132.
24 *Ibid.*, pp.132-133.
25 *Ibid.*, pp.13.
26 Jones, G. (ed.) (1984), *Women in the Urban and Industrial Workforce: Southeast and East Asia*, Australian National University, Canberra.
27 Angeles, *The Development and Security Implications of Global Restructuring in Export Manufacturing in Southeast Asia: The Case of Garments and Electronics Industries in the Philippines*, in this volume; Heyzer, N. (1986), *Working women in Southeast Asia*, Open University Press, Philadelphia; Ong, A.(1987), *Spirits of resistance and capitalist discipline*, SUNY Press, Albany; Salaff, J. (1981), *Working daughters of Hong Kong*,

Cambridge University Press, London; Wolf, D. (1992), *Factory Daughters*, University of California Press, Berkeley.

28 Dignard, L. and Havet, J. (eds) (1987), *Women in Micro- and Small-scale Enterprise Development*, Westview, Boulder; Hackenberg, B. and Barth, G. (1987), 'Growth of the bazaar economy and its significance for women's employment: Trends of the 1970s in Davao City, Philippines'; Jones, *Women in the Urban and Industrial Workforce: Southeast and East Asia*, 1984; Moser, C. (1998), 'The Asset Vulnerability Framework: Reassessing Urban Poverty Reduction Strategies', *World Development*, vol.26, no.1, pp.1-19; Tellis-Nayak, J. and Costa-Pinto, S. (1979), *Towards Self-Reliance ISI Program for Women's Development*, Divine Word Publications, N. Delhi Indore; Tinker, I. (1987), 'Street Foods: Testing Assumptions about Informal Sector Activity by Women and Men', *Current Sociology*, vol.35, no.3.

29 Rathgeber, E. (1989), 'Integrating Gender into Development', *Journal of Developing Societies*, vol.8; Rathgeber, E.(1989), 'WID, WAD, GAD', *Halifax Pearsonnotes*, vol.4, no.3, Summer.

30 Aslanbeigui, N. *et al.* (1994), *Women in the Age of Economic Transformation*, Routledge, London.

31 *Ibid.* Tinker, 'Street Foods: Testing Assumptions about Informal Sector Activity by Women and Men', 1987; and *Ibid.*, (1997), *Street Foods: Urban Food and Employment in Developing Countries*, Oxford University Press, Oxford and New York. Yasmeen, *Bangkok's Foodscape: Public Eating, Gender Relations and Urban Change*, 1996; *Ibid.*, 'Bangkok's Restaurant Sector: Gender, Employment and Consumption', 1992, pp.69-81; *Ibid.*, *Exploring a Foodscape: The Case of Bangkok*, proceedings of the 'Third International Conference on Geography of the ASEAN Region', Part I, and in *Malaysian Journal of Tropical Geography*, vol.26, no.1, 1995, pp.1-11; *Ibid.*, and Walker, '"From Scratch": Thai Food-Systems and Public Eating', 1996, pp.20-43.

32 According to Flores (personal communication, 1999) *sari-sari* stores grant credit easily, thus their popularity.

33 Concepcion, E. T. and Braganza, I. P. (1991), *Sidewalk Vending: An Alternative for the Urban Poor*, School of Development Management, Chancellor's Special Research & Writing Fund, UP Visayas, Iloilo City, April.

34 Etemadi, F. U. (1998), 'The Urban Poor in Cebu City: A Situationer', data links regional data from a regional perspective, University of the Philippines, Cebu College, also in *Cebu Data Bank*, vol.4, no.1, January, pp.4.

35 Numbers are difficult to estimate but there are 3,000 *registered* sari-sari stores in Lapu-Lapu City alone putting the total number closer to 5,000 or more for this suburb (Berame, 1998).

36 Etemadi, 'The Urban Poor in Cebu City: A Situationer', 1998, pp.5.

37 The halt on construction, however, also dampens prospects for some food vendors, as construction workers are a good source of revenue.

38 McDowell, P. (1998), 'Crisis drives migrants back to villages', *Vancouver Sun*, 16 July, pp.F3.

39 *Ibid.*

40 Crispin, S. W. (1999), 'Cycle of Despair', *Far Eastern Economic Review*, 23 September, pp.22, *http://www.feer.com/9909_23/p22thailand.html.*

41 Yuen-Pau, W. (1998), *Social Impacts of the Asian Crisis: The Unravelling of The Asian Miracle?*, Asia Pacific Papers Series, Asia Pacific Foundation of Canada, Vancouver, pp.3.

42 Rungfapaisarn, 'KFC plans big expansion in local market: Fast food chain still confident', 1997, pp.B3.

43 Marshall, 'Indonesians toil 2 days for a Big Mac', 1998, pp.F3.

44 Though the recent *Golden Arches East* (Watson *et.al.*, 1997) argues that McDonald's has

become culturally entrenched in the localities in which it is based in East Asia – taking on a distinct cultural meaning in those places rather than resulting in a standardization imposed on the periphery by the center.

45 Rungfapaisarn, 'KFC plans big expansion in local market: Fast food chain still confident', 1997, pp.B3.
46 Sivasomboon, B. and Treerapongpichit, B. (1998), 'Laid off workers turn to small businesses', *Bangkok Post*, 23 March, pp.10.
47 *Bangkok Post*, 3 August 1998, pp.8. (drawn from Thai Farmers Research Center).
48 Sirisambhand, N. (1994), *Hidden Producers in Bangkok Metropolis: Women in the Urban Informal Sector*, Friedrich Ebert Stiftung, Bangkok, November; Sirisambhand, N. (1996), *Social Security for Women in the Informal Sector in Thailand*, Friedrich Ebert Stiftung, Bangkok, January.
49 Coleman, J. (1988), 'Social Capital in the Creation of Human Capital', *American Journal of Sociology*, supplement, pp. 95-120; Coleman, J. S. (1990), *Foundations of Social Theory*, Harvard University Press, Cambridge.
50 Moser, C. (1998), 'The Asset Vulnerability Framework: Reassessing Urban Poverty Reduction Strategies', *World Development*, vol.26, no.1, pp.1-19.
51 Wilson, P. (1997), 'Building Social Capital: A Learning Agenda for the Twenty-First Century', *Urban Studies*, vol.34, no.5, pp.745-760.
52 These comments are made with knowledge of the growing critique of corruption and other problems related to transparency and accountability within NGOs and other organizations in the South. Though Sainath (1996/1998) has documented this extensively for the case of India, I am not aware of similar studies of the Philippines.
53 The Urban Poor Associates are part of a nation-wide coalition named Campaign for a Just and Humane City. The coalition went as far as to invite actor Martin Sheen for a four day tour of the slums of Manila drawing attention to poverty issues, local organizing and the response of the state. The story made international headlines and had the desired impact nationally (*Asiaweek*, 1997).
54 *Labour Force*, 1998 (publication of CLEAR, Cebu).
55 Stephen Heeney, Personal Communication, Vancouver, 1999.
56 Mr. Felicisimo C. 'Imok' Rupinta, Chairman, CCUVA, Inc. Personal Communication, 1998.
57 For example, near Gaisano City, a shopping complex in Cebu, vendors invested significant amounts of their own capital to renovate their stalls following a request by the municipal government. Subsequent to this improvement, however, they are still threatened with demolition on a regular basis.
58 Etemadi, Felisa Uy, Personal Communication (September 1999).
59 Ms. Phoebe Zoë Sanchez, Peronal Communication, 1999 (via e-mail).
60 Alolod, F. M. (1998), *Major Program Components for CCUVA*, unpublished document, Cebu, December, pp.1- 8.
61 Concepcion, and Braganza, *Sidewalk Vending: An Alternative for the Urban Poor*, 1991.
62 There is, apparently, some tension between the City's attempt to organize the vendors into co-ops. The city is accused of not recognizing existing organizations of vendors. This attempt to 'reorganize' is seen as co-optation.
63 Niyom, P. (1997), 'Critical Partnerships in Governance and Poverty Alleviation', in E. Porio (ed.), *Urban Governance and Poverty Alleviation in Southeast Asia*, Global Urban Research Initiative at Ateneo de Manila University, Manila, pp.149-164 and 155.
64 Porio, E. (1997), 'State, Civil Society and Urban Governance in Southeast Asia', in E. Porio (ed.), *Urban Governance and Poverty Alleviation in Southeast Asia*, pp.1-39.
65 Gearing, J. (1998), 'A Doer, Not a Speaker', *Far Eastern Economic Review*, vol.24, no.49, 11 December, pp.44.

66 Concepcion and Braganza, *Sidewalk Vending: An Alternative for the Urban Poor* 1991, pp.43.
67 For the case of India see, Sainath, P. (1998), *Everybody loves a good drought: Stories from India's Poorest Villages*, Review/Headline Book Publishing, London (previously published in New Delhi by Penguin Books, 1996.). The Philippines Center for Investigative Journalism has apparently recently conducted a study of corruption within Filipino NGOs but I have not yet accessed it.
68 *Asiaweek*, 28 November 1997, pp.53.
69 Sirisambhand, *Hidden Producers in Bangkok Metropolis: Women in the Urban Informal Sector*, 1994, pp.33.
70 *Ibid.*, pp.41-43.
71 Focus on the Global South (FOCUS) (1998), *Annual Report 1997*, Focus on the Global South, Bangkok.
72 For the classic exposé on shared space see Santos, M. (1975), *L'espace partagé*, editions M.-Th, Génin, Librairies Techniques, Paris. A shorter version was subsequently published in English by Methuen and Co. (London) entitled *The Shared Space – The two circuits of the urban economy in underdeveloped countries* in 1979.
73 Karaos, A. M. A. (1997), 'Urban Governance in the Philippines', E. Porio (ed.), *Urban Governance and Poverty Alleviation in Southeast Asia*, pp.63-86.

References

Ahmad, E. (1991), 'Social Security and the Poor: Choices for Developing Countries', *World Bank Research Observer*, vol. 6, no. 1, January.

Alolod, F. M. (1998), *Major Program Components for CCUVA*, unpublished document, Cebu, December, pp. 1-8.

Amin, ATM N. (1991), *A Policy Agenda for the Informal Sector in Thailand*, Asian Employment Programme, International Labour Office, New Delhi.

Aslanbeigui, N. *et al.* (1994), *Women in the Age of Economic Transformation*, Routledge, London.

Barth, G. A. (1983), *Street Foods: Informal Sector Food Preparation and Marketing*, Equity Policy Centre, Iloilo City.

Carr, M., Chen, M. and Jhabvala, R. (1996), *Speaking Out: Women's Economic Empowerment in South Asia*, Aga Khan Foundation Canada and the United Nations Development Fund for Women – Unifem, IT Publications, London.

Coleman, J. (1988a), 'Social Capital in the Creation of Human Capital', *American Journal of Sociology*, supplement, pp. 95-120.

Coleman, J. S. (1990b), *Foundations of Social Theory*, Harvard University Press, Cambridge.

Concepcion, E. T. and Braganza, I. P. (1991), *Sidewalk Vending: An Alternative for the Urban Poor*, School of Development Management, Chancellor's Special Research & Writing Fund, UP Visayas, Iloilo City, April.

Crispin, S. W. (1999), 'Cycle of Despair', *Far Eastern Economic Review*, 23 September, pp. 22.

Bacani, C.(1997), 'Surviving the Slump', *Asiaweek*, 28 November, pp. 52-55.

Dignard, L. and Havet, J. (eds) (1987), *Women in Micro- and Small-scale Enterprise Development*, Westview, Boulder.

Etemadi, F. U. (1998), 'The Urban Poor in Cebu City: A Situationer', *Cebu Data Bank*, vol. 4, no. 1, January, pp. 4.

Eviota, E. (1992), *The Political Economy of Gender*, Zed Books, London, pp. 132.

Eviota, E. (1992), *The Political Economy of Gender*, Zed Books, London, pp. 132.
Focus on the Global South (FOCUS) (1998), *Annual Report 1997*, Focus on the Global South, Bangkok.
Gearing, J. (1998), 'A Doer, Not a Speaker', *Far Eastern Economic Review*, vol. 24, no. 49, 11 December, pp. 44.
Guhan, S. (1994), 'Social Security Options for Developing Countries', *International Labour Review*, vol. 133, no. 1, pp. 35-53.
Heyzer, N. (1986), *Working Women in Southeast Asia*, Open University Press, Philadelphia.
Jones, G. (ed.) (1984), *Women in the Urban and Industrial Workforce: Southeast and East Asia*, Australian National University, Canberra.
Kara, N. (1997), *Transcending a historical legacy: sovereignty, the state and post-modernity*, unpublished paper, Spring, pp. 1-47.
Karaos, A. M. A. (1997), 'Urban Governance in the Philippines', E. Porio (ed.), E. Porio (ed.), *Urban Governance and Poverty Alleviation in Southeast Asia*, Global Urban Research Initiative at Ateneo de Manila University, Manila, pp. 63-86.
Kennedy, P. (1993), *Preparing for the 21st Century*, Fontana Press, London.
Khandker, S. R., Khalili, B. and Khan, Z. (1995), *Grameen Bank: Performance and Sustainability*, World Bank, Washington, DC.
Manila Community Services, Inc. (1993), *25 Years of Sharing in Development*, MCSI, Metro Manila.
Marshall, A. (1998), 'Indonesians toil 2 days for a Big Mac', *Vancouver Sun*, 16 July, pp. F3.
Maxwell, S. (1990), 'Food Security in Developing Countries: Issues and Options for the 1990's', *IDS Bulletin*, vol. 21, no. 3, July.
McKibben, B. (1996), 'The Enigma of Kerala', *Utne Reader*, March-April, pp. 103-112.
McDowell, P. (1998), 'Crisis drives migrants back to villages', *Vancouver Sun*, 16 July, pp. F3.
Moran, T. (1990/1), 'International economics and security', *Foreign Affairs*, vol. 5, Winter.
Moser, C. (1998), 'The Asset Vulnerability Framework: Reassessing Urban Poverty Reduction Strategies', *World Development*, vol. 26, no. 1, pp. 1-19.
Niyom, P. (1997), 'Critical Partnerships in Governance and Poverty Alleviation', in E. Porio (ed.), *Urban Governance and Poverty Alleviation in Southeast Asia*, Global Urban Research Initiative at Ateneo de Manila University, Manila, pp. 149-164 and 155.
Ong, A.(1987), *Spirits of resistance and capitalist discipline*, SUNY Press, Albany.
Porio, E. (1997), 'State, Civil Society and Urban Governance in Southeast Asia', in E. Porio (ed.), *Urban Governance and Poverty Alleviation in Southeast Asia*, Global Urban Research Initiative at Ateneo de Manila University, Manila, pp. 1-39.
Price, J. (1998), 'Dissent and New Directions for Canada and the Asia Pacific', *Building on Canada's Year of Asia Pacific: Evaluation and Strategic Directions*, Conference, 7 March.
Rathgeber, E. (1989), 'Integrating Gender into Development', *Journal of Developing Societies*, vol. 8.
Rathgeber, E. (1989), 'WID, WAD, GAD', *Halifax Pearsonnotes*, vol. 4, no. 3, Summer.
'Retailers press government for more relief to ensure survival', *Bangkok Post*, 3 August 16 July, pp. F3.
Rungfapaisarn, K. (1997), 'KFC plans big expansion in local market: Fast food chain still confident', *The Nation*, 11 November, pp. B3.
Sachs, J. (1997), 'International Monetary Failure?' *Time*, 8 December, pp. 8.
Sainath, P. (1998), *Everybody loves a good drought: Stories from India's Poorest Villages*, Review/Headline Book Publishing, London.
Salaff, J. (1981), *Working daughters of Hong Kong*, Cambridge University Press, London.
Santos, M. (1975), *L'espace partagé*, editions M.-Th, Génin, Librairies Techniques, Paris.
Sen, A. (1981), 'Poverty and Famines: An Essay on Entitlement and Deprivation', Clarendon Press, Oxford.

Sethuraman, S. V. (1992), *The Urban Informal Sector in Asia: an Annotated Bibliography Series: International labour bibliography*, International Labour Office, Geneva.

Sirisambhand, N. (1994a), *Hidden Producers in Bangkok Metropolis: Women in the Urban Informal Sector*, Friedrich Ebert Stiftung, Bangkok, November.

Sirisambhand, N. (1996b), *Social Security for Women in the Informal Sector in Thailand*, Friedrich Ebert Stiftung, Bangkok, January.

Sivasomboon, B. and Treerapongpichit, B. (1998), 'Laid off workers turn to small businesses', *Bangkok Post*, 23 March, pp. 10.

Sorensen, T. (1995), 'What is international economic security?' *International Affairs*, vol. 71, March, pp. 305-24.

Tellis-Nayak, J. and Costa-Pinto, S. (1979), *Towards Self-Reliance ISI Program for Women's Development*, Divine Word Publications, N. Delhi Indore.

'Time for a Reality Check in Asia', *Business Week*, 2 December 1996, pp. 59-66.

Tweeten, L. (1997), 'Investing in People', in *Promoting Third World Development and Food Security*, Praeger, Westport, pp. 183-204.

'Two Thailands: Spreading Wealth Beyond Bangkok', *Far Eastern Economic Review*, 14 April 1994.

Tinker, I. (1987a), 'Street Foods: Testing Assumptions about Informal Sector Activity by Women and Men', *Current Sociology*, vol. 35, no. 3.

Tinker, I. (1997b), *Street Foods: Urban Food and Employment in Developing Countries*, Oxford University Press, New York and Oxford.

Yasmeen, G. (1996a), *Bangkok's Foodscape: Public Eating, Gender Relations and Urban Change*, unpublished Ph.D. dissertation, Department of Geography, University of British Columbia.

Yasmeen, G. (1992b), 'Bangkok's Restaurant Sector: Gender, Employment and Consumption', *Journal of Social Research*, vol. 15, no. 2, Chulalongkorn University, Bangkok, Thailand, pp.69-81.

Yasmeen, G. (1995c), *Exploring a Foodscape: The Case of Bangkok*, proceedings of the 'Third International Conference on Geography of the ASEAN Region', Part I, and *in Malaysian Journal of Tropical Geography*, vol. 26, no. 1, pp. 1-11.

Yasmeen, G. and Walker, M. (eds), '"From Scratch": Thai Food-Systems and Public Eating', *Contemporary Perspectives on Thai Foodways*, Monograph no. 11, Centre for Southeast Asian Research, Vancouver, pp. 20-43.

Wilson, P. (1997), 'Building Social Capital: A Learning Agenda for the Twenty-First Century', *Urban Studies*, vol.34, no.5, pp.745-760.

Wolff, D. (1992), *Factory Daughters*, University of California Press, Berkeley.

Yuen-Pau, W. (1998), 'Social Impacts of the Asian Crisis: The Unravelling of The Asian Miracle?' *Asia Pacific Papers Series*, Asia Pacific Foundation of Canada, Vancouver, pp. 3.

Chapter 8

'Good' Governance and the Security of Ethnic Communities in Indonesia and the Philippines

Jacques Bertrand

The security of ethnic communities has become a major concern for policymakers worldwide. With the deaths of thousands of people because of ethnic strife in the last decade, new norms of intervention for conflict prevention are being created. International development assistance programs in Canada and other Organization for Economic Cooperation and Development (OECD) countries are devoting a larger portion of their resources to preventing and resolving these conflicts.

Development programs and policies constitute a set of instruments by which Canada and its international partners are seeking to reduce the incidence of ethnic conflict. In May 1997, the Development Assistance Committee (DAC) of the OECD adopted new guidelines for development agencies that add conflict prevention as a priority for development programming. 'Helping strengthen the capacity of a society to manage tensions and disputes without violence is a vital part of development work. [T]his 'peacebuilding' objective must form the cornerstone of all development co-operation strategies and programmes'.[1] If so, the policy community requires a better analysis of those development initiatives that will contribute to more peace and those that may exacerbate conflicts.

Governance and democratization constitute one area of development activity that requires more analysis of its impact on the security of ethnic communities. In its Asia programming, Canadian International Development Agency (CIDA) writes: 'Characteristics of "good" governance include effectiveness, transparency, accountability, predictability, integrity, equity, and participation'.[2] To what extent can support for these objectives, as well as democratization, contribute to a reduction of ethnic conflict?

This chapter argues that measures to improve governance and democratization are not necessarily conducive to an increase in security for ethnic communities. More specifically, in order to reduce the potential for conflict, measures to improve governance and democratization must first target the most severe perceptions of threat by the ethnic community. Only then can other values such as better transparency, individual representation, and equity be promoted to strengthen the sense of security and supersede ethnic affiliations. Sequentially, therefore, a recognition of security threats in ethnic terms and corresponding actions will contribute to a more rapid reduction in the potential for ethnic conflict than casting policy interventions in universalist terms, and thereby denying the specifically ethnic dimension of the perceived threat.

This argument can also be extended to recent initiatives to build 'social capital' in developing areas. Drawing insights from Robert Putnam's study of the conditions for effective democracy in Italy, policymakers have seized his central idea that effective democracy can be enhanced by the presence of 'networks of civic engagement'.[3] These networks are constituted by the myriad of associations, organizations, and clubs that foster more horizontal interaction among society, consequently contributing to the building of trust and cooperation. While recognizing the general benefits of social capital for democracy, this study argues that multiethnic societies pose a particular problem. There is a tendency to build networks of engagement that are defined by, and limited to, one's ethnic community. As a result, stronger social capital can lead to greater consolidation of ethnic identities and have no effect on the incidence of ethnic conflict. Social capital will only lead to a reduction of ethnic tensions if it is built across ethnic lines.

The empirical context for this study is Indonesia and the Philippines. The conflicts between Muslims and Christians in both countries are specifically analyzed as cases to draw more general insights on the impact of good governance strategies and the security of ethnic communities. Religious identity is one aspect of what is understood here by ethnicity, which is conceived broadly to include some sense of common origin and cultural distinctiveness. Aspects of development subsumed under the rubric 'good governance' are also focused on while recognizing that economic and social development also has important impacts on conflict. The principal sources of conflict between these ethnic communities are identified as well as the perceived sense of threat in these conflicts followed by an assessment of the potential responses in the area of governance and democratic development.

'Good' Governance and Ethnic Conflict

Policymakers often link 'good' governance to a reduction in conflict. 'Visible actions to address root causes of unrest are vitally important. Activities could be aimed at improving the allocation and management of natural resources, reducing poverty, targeting socio-political activities in support of participatory development, promoting good governance'.[4] These measures are based on implied assumptions about the causes of conflict and processes by which development actions respond to them.

The effects of good governance on ethnic conflict are related to the structure of the political system, its effectiveness of rule, its transparency and accountability, and issues of representation and recognition. By positing a positive relationship between these characteristics of good governance and ethnic conflict, we assume that the sources of the conflict lie in the presence of authoritarian rule, corrupt practices, and ineffective government. Provided with more transparency and a more democratic political system, ethnic groups are less likely to mobilize given the increased power of their respective groups.

Yet, better governance in itself does not necessarily lead to a diminution of conflict or ethnic tensions. When a particular ethnic group monopolizes the state, the removal of state dominance by this group may also trigger a conflictual response. Similarly, a government may be more effective at delivering programs and services but an increased capacity may have the unintended consequence of also greater incentives for various ethnic groups to compete for state power through peaceful or non-peaceful means.[5]

The literature on ethnic conflict has explored the effects of different political institutions on group representation and conflict. It has contributed many propositions on the extent to which democracy can help to reduce conflict or increase its incidence. Autonomy, federalism, and mechanisms that prevent ethnic majorities from monopolizing power have all been proposed, but the outcomes are not always conducive to greater stability. Scholars disagree, for example, on the positive effects of power-sharing arrangements such as coalitions, quotas, or formal representation of each ethnic group in government institutions. While some scholars argue in favor of giving equitable representation to each group, others argue that such arrangements institutionalize the ethnic divisions. Scholars such as Horowitz would argue that institutions should remain devoid of formal power sharing between ethnic groups. Instead, voting mechanisms should create incentives for building cross-ethnic electoral alliances.[6] 'There are alternative ways to view electoral systems that give priority to goals such as proportionality of seats to votes, or the accountability of representatives, or the mandate and durability of governments—all otherwise worthy goals that, in severely divided societies, ought to be subordinated to the lifesaving goal of making interethnic moderation rewarding'.[7]

Transitions to democracy are particularly unstable situations because a sudden expansion of popular participation can shift the balance of power between different ethnic groups. For example, an opening of the political system may allow a majority group to gain more power at the expense of minority groups, or vice-versa. A change in the status quo brings about a change in the relative security of different groups, by modifying perceptions of inclusion and exclusion from the polity.[8]

Autonomy and federalism are often prescribed as an alternative means to prevent ethnic conflict. They can give more power to each ethnic group and are generally favorable. Nevertheless, they can also be seen as concessions to secessionist movements and, therefore, unlikely to be adequately implemented in many countries.[9] No particular political system or set of institutions, therefore, can guarantee harmonious relations between conflicting groups.

Beyond institutional solutions that have been discussed above, theories of social capital argue that differences in governmental performance depend on the extent of cooperation and reciprocity found in a given social environment. The manifestation of this cooperation and reciprocity can be measured by the extent to which the society is constituted in webs of organizations and cooperative practices, which cut across civil society as well as in relation to the state.[10] It can be hypothesized that a greater number of social organizations would lead to a reduction of ethnic conflict. This would only be true, however, if they promote cross cutting cooperation that increase the levels of trust between ethnic communities. If social organizations are related to religious groups or remain divided along communal lines, a large web of social organizations is unlikely to reduce ethnic tensions.

If this is so, good governance, including building social capital must be prescribed with much caution before one could confidently argue that it would reduce the incidence of conflict. Efforts for greater democratic rule, accountability, and transparency may lead in the long run to stable ethnic relations but they must be assessed for their impact on the prior perception of threat.

The next two sections analyze the sources of conflict between Christians and Muslims in Indonesia and the Philippines in relation to problems of governance. In both cases, the analysis focuses on how political institutions influence popular participation, efficacy, transparency, and accountability, as well as how these impact on the structure of insecurities of Muslims and Christians. It also addresses the extent to which both societies encourage cross cutting [interlocking] organizations, as opposed to religiously defined organizations.

Indonesia

The governance structures of the New Order regime were largely responsible for the wave of religious violence and tensions in the last few years. Specifically, the New Order regime modified the balance of representation between Muslims and Christians while keeping severe restrictions on popular participation and transparency, especially with regard to expressing and advancing the grievances of religious groups. These measures contributed to an increase in suspicions and accompanying insecurities of both groups.

Democratization and good governance offer the best environment for an improvement in Muslim-Christian relations but not without some significant risks. They can both enhance the insecurities of both communities in the short-term and can lead to prolonged instability if not implemented concurrently with specific measures to recognize the grievances of each community. Similarly, measures to improve social capital as a means of fostering and strengthening the democratic process will only lead to a reduction of tensions between both communities if they specifically build bridges between them. Otherwise, stronger social capital may increase networks of engagement within ethnic communities while maintaining the divide along religious lines.

Religious relations have eroded dramatically in the last few years, leading to a significant change in perceptions of balance between the two communities. From 1996 to 1998, a series of violent incidents erupted across the island of Java. In June 1996, ten churches were burned down or ransacked in Surabaya. In October, several churches were burned down in localities around Situbondo in East Java during riots over an unrelated incident. In similar circumstances, churches were also damaged in Tasikmalaya in December 1996.

Christians remained generally silent despite a growing worry about the erosion of inter-religious tolerance. Christian leaders preferred discussions with the government behind closed doors rather than risk a backlash from either the government or the Muslim constituency if they publicly defended their interests. They obeyed the New

Order's approach against public discussions of religious and ethnic issues. Efforts were made to create various forums for inter-religious dialogue. On a few occasions, religious organizations issued public statements of concern.[11] Some Christian groups complained to the Indonesian Human Rights Commission after the burning of churches in Surabaya.[12] Except for these latter occasions, however, Christians appeared to accept the *status quo* despite the increasing tensions.

The tensions and violence increased after the resignation of President Soeharto. The May 1998 violence against the ethnic Chinese left more than 1,000 people dead. Although it was mainly a conflict against the Chinese, it reinforced the tensions between Christians and Muslims. The most violent conflict pitting Muslims and Christians occurred in January and February 1999 across Maluku. The conflict was first triggered by a violent incident between Muslim migrants and Ambonese Christians in the city of Ambon. The conflict, however, triggered a wave of violent responses. For several weeks, Muslims and Christians throughout Ambon and the surrounding islands attacked each other and burned down property in an unprecedented level of violence. The violence has continued throughout 1999 and hundreds of people have been killed.

How can we explain the sudden resurgence of religious tensions and conflict in the last few years? The apparent deterioration in Muslim-Christian relations is certainly not uniform across the archipelago. Church burnings have mainly occurred in Java, in places where Christians were a small minority. Predominantly Christian regions have not all been in conflict with the Muslim dominated state. While Irian Jaya and East Timor have had violent clashes with the state, and Ambon has seen violence between Christian and Muslim Ambonese, Flores, and North Sulawesi have been relatively peaceful.

The sources of the conflict are best understood through an analysis of their historical origins. Ethnic and religious stability had been disrupted on several occasions during the period of liberal democracy in the 1950s. Thereafter, Indonesia's first President, Soekarno, suspended liberal democracy in 1957 after the Constituent Assembly had failed to agree on a basis of the state. Political Islam was on the rise and several regions were disgruntled with the central government. When Soeharto came to power, he followed the authoritarian path laid out by his predecessor and intensified the central government's clamp on religious and ethnic claims. Soeharto's government used authoritarian means of governance to keep a lid on political mobilization, with significant impact on relations between Muslims and Christians.

Indonesia's struggle for political consolidation had been contested on several grounds during the first decade after independence. Many Christian Ambonese joined a movement that supported the creation of an independent state in the South Moluccas. This movement was defeated in 1950.[13] An islamist group, the *Darul Islam*, fought for the establishment of an Islamic state. Again, it was defeated by force. Finally, during the 1950s, regional rebellions in Sumatra and Sulawesi contested the increasing Javanization of the Indonesian Republic.

These rebellions occurred against a background of increasing political tensions at the national level. The campaign preceding the 1955 elections severely divided the proponents of an Islamic state and those who espoused a more secular orientation that included the nationalists and the communists. The Constituent Assembly that was formed after the elections failed to agree on a new constitution for the Indonesian state. The question of an Islamic state continued to divide the parties. Consequently, President Soekarno suspended democratic rule in 1957 and imposed a vision of Indonesia that had been created in the midst of the revolutionary struggle. He imposed a return to the constitution of 1945 and to *Pancasila* (five principles) as the basis of the state.[14]

The principles of *Pancasila* have been a stabilizing force in Indonesian politics. Its most important one recognizes the religious nature of Indonesian society but does not impose any official state religion. This historical compromise established a tradition of religious tolerance in Indonesian politics. It represented the nationalist struggle to build a united Indonesia where all religions would be given equal status. This compromise had been reached with Islamic groups before independence and was mainly a result of the recognition that Eastern Indonesia, where many areas are predominantly Christian would refuse to join an independent Indonesia where Islam would be the official religion.[15]

The New Order government reinforced its support for *Pancasila* and the original Constitution of 1945 while imposing further measures to ensure national unity. It significantly reduced the powers of regional governments, centralized economic and political authority in the capital, and imposed new restrictions on political parties. By 1974, all political parties were amalgamated into three. In subsequent years, *Pancasila* was imposed as the only permitted ideology for all organizations. Finally, ethnic and religious issues became increasingly barred from public discussion and from reports in the media.

In effect, the Soeharto government used authoritarian means of governance to project an image of ethnic and religious harmony. The political institutions became less democratic and political participation was severely curtailed. Freedoms were restricted, including some religious rights. Finally, the government imposed an ideology of tolerance rather than fostering it among religious communities. Ultimately, the regime relied on the use of physical force.

Tensions between Christians and Muslims began to rise in the early 1990s when Soeharto apparently turned to Islam for a new source of support. The New Order regime had denied Islamic interests a political space to advance their demands. The coalition of nationalists, *abangan* Javanese,[16] and Christians that long formed the core of the New Order's power base refused to allow political mobilization along ethnic, religious, or regional lines. For a long time, Islamic politics were seen as the greatest threat to a united Indonesia under *Pancasila*.

The creation in 1990 of the Association of Muslim Intellectuals of Indonesia (*Ikatan Cendekiawan Muslimin Indonesia,* ICMI) stirred many debates about the future orientation of the New Order regime. Under the leadership of B.J. Habibie, the Minister of Research and Technology, ICMI was accused of being the latest strategic twist of the regime to coopt frustrated interests.[17] ICMI did not represent a resurgence of the type of Islamic politics of the 1950s that aimed at the establishment of an Islamic state. It was an elite-based organization representing the interests of the Muslim community, but as a new vehicle for Muslim groups to counsel the government. Abdurrachman Wahid (Gus Dur), the vocal leader of the largest Muslim organization of Indonesia, *Nahdlatul Ulama* (NU), and several other prominent Muslims refused to join the organization that they saw as a ploy from the government to increase its political control. Nevertheless, the creation of ICMI brought together a wide spectrum of Muslims, from modernist Muslim leaders to bureaucrats and cabinet members. Muslim intellectuals of very different streams of thought chose to join, such as Amien Rais, the leader of *Muhammadiyah* and Nurcholish Madjid, a neo-modernist scholar. With the creation of ICMI, Soeharto hoped to coopt the modernist leaders who were the most vocal critics of his regime.[18]

Following the People's Consultative Assembly (MPR) meeting of 1993, ICMI members boasted a new sense of confidence. They gained a strong representation in the MPR session and subsequently obtained four cabinet positions under the patronage of Habibie. Although the modernists were excluded from the Cabinet, the strong support for ICMI members was interpreted as a significant gain. Christians, in turn, saw their Cabinet positions reduced from six to three.

At the same time, the military was undergoing an important transformation. After Soeharto had removed from power armed forces commander Benny Murdani, a Catholic, he gradually purged Murdani's followers, many of whom were Christians. Men who were perceived as devout Muslims, such as Feisal Tanjung and Hartono dominated the top leadership.[19] Within a few years, therefore, the balance of representation had tipped in favor of Muslim groups.

ICMI's increasing presence in the New Order's institutions, paralleled with the displacement of Christians left a sour taste among Christian communities. Their fears were intensified, as it became evident that the modernist Muslims dominated the organization and some even wanted an Islamic state.[20] Modernist leaders, such as Amien Rais, used their new platform to criticize the role of the Christians in government and business, and even directed their attacks on Soeharto.

The independence displayed by modernist ICMI members met with a strong response from Soeharto. After criticizing the Soeharto regime for its management of the Busang gold deposits, Amien Rais was forced to resign from his position as Chairman of the Experts Council of ICMI in February 1997.[21] A few months later, Parni Hadi, the editor-in-chief of the *Republika* newspaper, associated with ICMI was removed after the paper published a column by Amien Rais that criticized *Golkar* and the New Order regime.[22] These events marked a reversal of fortunes for ICMI that had gone too far in establishing its autonomy and allowing its members to openly challenge the regime and Soeharto. Prominent ICMI members were dropped from the list of members for the 1998 MPR session and the new cabinet saw a decline of ICMI members.[23]

With ICMI, Islam had gained a new vehicle and a new assertiveness. Reflecting a growing Islamization of Indonesian society, Islamic leaders were becoming bolder in their demands for a greater role for Islam. The Christians' relative position had continued to wane. In the last Soeharto cabinet, only one minister was Christian compared to three in the 1993-98 cabinet. Christians acknowledged that they were over-represented for some time but their subsequent marginalization created worries about the future prospects for religious tolerance. Christians were not only worried about the resurgence of Islam as a political force, but of a growing trend of intolerance and violence against them. In many areas of Indonesia with Muslim majorities, Christians repeatedly complained of local resistance to the establishment of churches or places of worship. In recent years, some of these cases have become violent. In June 1996, for example, youths in Kediri refused to accept a letter permitting Christians to use a local house as a place of worship and so they burned it down.[24] Controversies over places of worship and related violence occurred sufficiently often to provoke some Christian intellectuals, such as Franz Magnis-Suseno, to express their views in public. Magnis-Suseno warned that although inter-religious relations were still good, they were fragile. He particularly denounced the government's official policy on permits for places of worship that had shown signs of repressing religious freedom.[25]

In Eastern Indonesia, where many regions have a majority or near majority of Christians, these trends were interpreted as a growing repression and threat. In Ambon, where Muslims and Christians are almost equal in number, Christians were worried of policies designed to reduce their influence and role in the local government. The Muslim governor for the province of Maluku was accused of displacing Christians from the powerful positions in the provincial administration and systematically replacing them with Muslims. He also attacked positions in the local capital city of Ambon that has a majority of Christians. He attempted to prevent the nomination of a Christian rector for Pattimura University and was accused of trying to prevent the election of a Christian as mayor of Ambon city.[26]

Many Christian Ambonese were worried that the government adopted a deliberate policy to turn Christians into a minority in Maluku. In recent years, the transmigration program has chosen Maluku and Irian Jaya as priority areas of resettlement. For 1995/1996, 60 per cent of the 77,000 projected transmigrant families were to be relocated to Eastern Indonesia, especially Maluku and Irian Jaya.[27] In Ambon, people were growing worried that a rapid inflow of Muslim transmigrants would destabilize the balance between Christians and Muslims in the region.[28]

In Flores, religious intolerance also grew. After riots in 1995, for example, the local head of the police in Ende, a Muslim, reportedly accused Catholics of being fanatics and was suspected of unifying the local Muslims against Catholics. Some religious leaders in Flores were worried of the consequences of a diminishing representation of Catholics at the center. They even suspected that the central government might be systematically preventing local youths from entering the military academy, for example, and they cited in evidence the lack of high-level officials from Flores in almost every government institution. Frans Seda, a former minister in both the Soekarno and Soeharto cabinets, was reported to have reminded Soeharto of Soekarno's pledge to him at the time of the creation of the Republic, that the new state would be based on government and not on religion. Seda was reported to have said this to Soeharto as a result of the trends toward Islamization and policies hurting the interests of Christians, including Catholics.[29] These reports, although perhaps based on rumors, reflected a local discourse expressing a growing distress at the directions of the Indonesian polity and at the deterioration of relations between Christians and Muslims.

The New Order's approach to ethnic and religious conflict did not resolve the underlying tensions between Christians and Muslims. Its policies were directed toward resolving the problems behind closed doors with leaders of various religious communities and preventing their discussion in public forums. Despite this worthy attempt for dialogue between religious elites and their collaboration in encouraging tolerance among their followers, the levels of violence between religious communities continued to grow. These incidents were fueled by the use of Islam as a political vehicle for certain groups deemed marginalized in the past by the current political regime. The New Order's institutions failed to provide adequate channels for Islamic groups to advance their interests and so the latter increasingly challenged and criticized the regime in public. In these circumstances, the temptations were great to mobilize public support around Islamic ideology, with negative consequences on the relationships between Christians and Muslims.

The crisis of May 1998 marked the beginning of a wave of ethnic violence. The most dramatic event was the killing of more than 1,000 ethnic Chinese in the last days of Soeharto's rule. Afterwards, tensions remained high not only among ethnic Chinese but also between Christians and Muslims. In subsequent months, several incidents opposed Christians to Muslims in various parts of the country. On 22 November, 13 people were killed in Ketapang, Jakarta and 21 churches were burned down as a result of violent clashes between Christian and Muslim youths.[30] Partly as a response to the Ketapang incident, on 30 November, five mosques, several shops, and some houses of Muslim migrants from South Sulawesi were burned down by Christian rioters in Kupang (Eastern Indonesia).[31] A few days later, 11 stores were burned down on the island of Rote by Christian rioters when a bomb exploded close to a local church and migrant Muslims were rumored to be responsible.[32] Then in Ujung Pandang, the capital of South Sulawesi, a church was burned down on 5 December.[33] This series of Muslim-Christian violence reached its apex in January-February 1999 when riots erupted on Ambon Island and across the province of Maluku. The death toll reached more than 200 people while hundreds of places of worship, shops, and houses were destroyed.[34]

Several interpretations could be used to explain this rise in violence. One is that there are intrinsic differences in the beliefs of Christians and Muslims that are conflictual, but religious leaders themselves quickly dismissed this interpretation. 'The problem is not religious but political. Riots and disturbances are used for the interests of the political elite'.[35] Similarly, each case has its set of local explanations but these pale in comparison to the non-coincidental eruption of such violence across the archipelago in such a short period of time.

An alternative explanation focuses on economic inequality and migration. Large inequalities between the rich and the poor were created by Soeharto's economic policies. Since many of the richer Indonesians have been ethnic Chinese, frustrations against the middle class Chinese have been accumulating. The intensity of the violence against the ethnic Chinese is partly a result of these frustrations. The riots occurred, of course, as Indonesia was suffering from the worst pitfalls of the Asian economic crisis. With unemployment already high among the youth, the economic crisis made the situation extremely difficult. Combined with shortages of basic needs, the frustrations against the ethnic Chinese could easily be stirred.

A similar explanation can be used to analyze the violence against Muslim migrants in various Christian regions. Although the Muslim migrants have not been as successful as the Chinese, they have often held a very strong economic position in the local economies where they established themselves. They competed with local inhabitants for market control and have often been better off than many of the local inhabitants. As a result, many jealousies arose among the local population and created a terrain for conflict to emerge. The conflicts in Kupang, Rote, Ambon, and several others involved local Christians against Muslim migrants. Transmigrant areas have also been the sites of tensions during the course of the Soeharto years.

While economic inequality and migration may well be part of the explanation for these conflicts, they are insufficient in themselves to explain the unprecedented wave of violence in the last few years. Indeed, migrants have been present in all areas of Indonesia without such dramatic consequences. Economic inequalities have also been present. Although these inequalities have clearly been at the heart of repeated conflicts with the ethnic Chinese, they do not fully explain the sudden violence against Muslim migrants.

Instead, the violence needs to be understood as a result of the structure of insecurities among Muslims and Christians. Both the economic and migratory policies of the Indonesian government created tensions among local populations because the latter had no control over their content and their direction. Muslim migration only became a problem once it was perceived as a deliberate policy to assimilate the Christians and sideline their role in the polity. Similarly, past frustrations of the Muslims because of under-representation was only replaced by political maneuverings that did not diminish their suspicions against the Christians. Rather, the displacement of Christians was accompanied by a rhetoric that denounced their past control of New Order institutions and was perceived as a result of authoritarian and neo-colonial practices. The Soeharto government tried to use to its advantage a new resurgence of Islamic political confidence while trying to promote its imposed vision of national unity. It failed because of a lack of democratic process in the formation of this vision, as well as the tight noose held over ethnic and political relations in the country. '*Pancasila* under Suharto was forced...It was an instrument and symbol of rule. It was fed to bureaucrats and parliament, but it was a failure... It didn't touch the soul of the nation'.[36] The ideals of the unified nation under *Pancasila* were imposed rather than nurtured by the Soeharto regime.

The history of relations between Muslims and Christians under the New Order regime shows the delicate balance between the two communities because of a lack of reassurances and protection of each other's interests. In the earlier days of the Soeharto regime, Muslims were repressed because of the presumed threat of an Islamic state project. Later, Christians became side lined as Muslims were used to advance the regime's interests. During President Habibie's transition government, these insecurities continued. Christians still felt threatened in their freedom to practice and were uncertain about their future position in an increasingly Muslim country. Muslims continued to suspect alliances between Christians and anti-Muslim political agendas, so they reacted violently to acts of provocation.

At the societal level, the New Order regime discouraged the development of autonomous organizations and, therefore, social capital had not been nurtured. Under

Soeharto, civil society organizations were severely curtailed. Those that remained powerful and constituted sufficiently strong links between the political élite and the general population were religious organizations. Muslim organizations, such as *Nahdlatul Ulama* and *Muhammadiyah* remain the largest and strongest independent organizations in the post-Soeharto era. Not surprisingly, the leaders of two of the most important political parties in the last elections were Abdurrachman Wahid, the current leader of *Nahdlatul Ulama* and Amien Rais, the previous leader of *Muhammadiyah.* That Wahid became President and Amien Rais head of the People's Consulative Assembly shows the strength of their respective organizational bases. Similarly, the churches are the main foci for organizing Christians for social action. Non-governmental organizations (NGOs) operating outside of these religious groups often saw their activities restricted by the government. Therefore, whatever social capital was created under Soeharto reinforced religious identities instead of building stronger links across religious lines.

The transition to democracy in Indonesia makes the country particularly susceptible to violence. 'People are too strong, and the government too weak, so there is a tendency for anarchy'.[37] Most incidents of ethnic violence were blamed on 'provocateurs' seeking to create havoc and to disturb the first free elections of June 1999. Although there is much evidence to support the thesis about provocation, it does not explain the 'dynamite' of these conflicts. Indeed, if not for these provocateurs, such violence could still have erupted. Under conditions of transition, the repressive apparatus could no longer be used to quell incipient riots while channels to express grievances and resolve tensions peacefully had not yet been established. Once the electoral campaign began, many expected high levels of violence. Instead, the campaign was almost devoid of incidents and the 7 June elections produced a victory for the opposition Indonesian Democratic Party of Struggle (PDI-*Perjuangan*).

Yet, as soon as election results started to be published, there was a resurgence of the Muslim/non-Muslim issue. With the possibility that the PDI-*Perjuangan* could produce the next president and cabinet, Muslim parties began to mobilize for a coalition against the 'party of non-Muslims'. The PDI-*Perjuangan* fielded many Muslim candidates but its leader, Megawati Sukarnoputri and many in her team were perceived as over-representing non-Muslims.[38] Muslim parties formed an alliance with some members of *Golkar* to prevent Megawati's accession to the presidency. This alliance coalesced around a Muslim leader, Abdurrachman Wahid, as a compromise choice for President. The democratic process did not reduce Muslim suspicions toward non-Muslims but gave new institutional means for reinforcing the strength of Muslim representation relative to Christians.

Democratization will improve the capacity to resolve tensions peacefully, but it will need to address structural insecurities in religious relations before it can produce the expected benefits. It will be particularly important to recognize the rights to the freedom to practice one's religion and the protection of minorities. There are serious questions about the freedom to practice and to establish places of worship. 'Under the reform period, there are still limitations on rights to establish places of worship. Islamic ones are easier to establish or to be replaced if burned down, compared to Christian/Catholic ones'.[39] Some Christians feel threatened by the Islamization of

Indonesian society, which occasionally spills into the political realm. Muslims are still suspicious of the political role of Christians and fear that they will use a freer environment to expand their influence. Many religious leaders work to keep good relations between religious groups and moderation, but they are not always successful. While more democratic governance may help to ease tensions, they will only do so in combination with measures to reassure Christian minorities and preserve a central state that is representative of all religious communities. *Pancasila* has been discredited under Soeharto but it may offer the only symbolic means to preserve tolerance between religious communities. Islamic groups may have a legitimate claim to advancing Muslim interests by means of state instruments, but they risk creating much political instability if they do so at the expense of adequate representation and treatment of Christian minorities. If the latter become increasingly minoritized and given only 'special' rights in an overwhelmingly Islamic political society, they may sense that 'Indonesia' no longer represents their constituency. It will be a difficult balance to reach.

In civil society, there are many opportunities to expand the number of organizations that can build trust between Muslims and Christians. Although new organizations are rising with the democratic environment, there are still very few that self-consciously aim at bridging relations between Muslims and non-Muslims. Religiously defined organizations are still strongest. Social capital will only lead to less conflict between religious communities if it is nurtured across ethnic lines, rather than being expanded within each community. While democratization opens up opportunities to enhance social capital, it might also lead to missed opportunities for reducing conflicts.

The Philippines

The Muslim-Christian conflict in the Philippines differs from that in Indonesia because it is emerging from decades of armed struggle. Since the period of Spanish colonialism, the 'Moro' people have been resisting their integration with Christians into a single political entity. This struggle had been particularly violent after the rise of an armed rebellion in the 1970s under the leadership of the Moro National Liberation Front (MNLF). A peace agreement with the MNLF in September 1996 and a subsequent agreement to begin peace talks with its splinter group, the Moro Islamic Liberation Front (MILF) have come closest to resolving this long-lasting conflict.

With the peace agreement in place, the problem now is how to ensure that it will last. A democratic, efficient, and transparent autonomous government seems to be the best option to prevent a resurgence of violence. Yet, as the following section will show, these measures have been insufficient and inadequate to provide such lasting stability. What are the limits of governance strategies? How can they be modified to strengthen the peace agreement? Are they adequate responses to the sources of the conflict?

The Philippine case shows how a democratic environment and autonomy may not be sufficient to reduce conflict between religious communities. They will only do so if they are introduced with specific measures to address the grievances of both communities and serve to reduce, rather than enhance tensions. Democratic institutions and autonomy require sufficient economic resources and negotiations over crucial issues such as land ownership, religious rights, and adequate representation of Muslim minorities. At the societal level, years of civil war have prevented the development of sufficient social capital. Consequently, there is only a very weak network of civic engagement, mainly along religious lines, and almost no organizations that foster more interaction between Muslims and Christians.

Sources of the Conflict

There are multiple and complex causes to the conflict in Mindanao. From a historical perspective, the grievances of the Moro people date back to colonial and post-colonial policies. They gradually lost their land to Christian settlers and became a minority in their own territory. After independence, they were never given sufficient representation in the central government to advance their interests. Despite being granted autonomy in recent years, the latter did not seem to improve the problems of governance that have fueled the conflict. In part, this has been so because of a lack of efficacy of the new institutions, corruption, and lack of sufficient powers embedded in the new institutions.

The divisions between Christians and Muslims in the Philippines date back to colonial times. When the Spanish colony was ceded to the United States (US) in 1898, the colonial government had not established its control over the Moros. Although the American government was capable of establishing its rule in Mindanao and Sulu, Muslim-Christian tensions remained high. Christian Filipinos filled most of the positions in the colonial administration. There was a deliberate attempt in subsequent decades to integrate the Moros into the larger Christian Philippines especially after independence. In part as a solution to the problem of landless farmers in Luzon and the Visayas, large numbers of Christians were encouraged to migrate to Mindanao, as the Christians strengthened their control over the political and economic affairs of the region. By the 1960s, these policies had made the Moros a minority in their own territory.[40]

As a result, the Moros felt increasingly threatened. They began to engage in active resistance against the Philippine government. The MNLF was created in 1972 by an amalgamation of Muslim organizations that had sprung up in the previous few years. It chose armed resistance partly as a response to President Marcos' declaration of martial law in 1972. It was also due to the disenchantment by young Moro intellectuals with Muslim traditional politicians that they believed had compromised Moro interests. By 1973, the MNLF, under the leadership of Nur Misuari, demanded the withdrawal of government troops from Southern Philippines, a return of the lands taken away from the Moros, more autonomy, as well as the practice of Islamic law in Muslim areas. By 1974, the movement established the *Bangsa Moro Republik* with the stated goal of full independence.

Ironically, the government of President Marcos was actually more flexible towards the Moros than previous governments had been, but only after it used military force against them. Under his regime, there was less of a push for the assimilation of Moros into the larger Christian majority and certain gestures of recognition were made. The government allowed Muslim institutions to be established, such as the Institute for Islamic Studies at the University of the Philippines, the Mindanao State University's King Feisal Centre for Arabic and Islamic Studies, and the Amanah Bank, the first Islamic bank in the Philippines.[41] Yet, these were only few concessions that did not lead to a resolution of the armed conflict.

In 1976, the government met with the MNLF in Tripoli, under the auspices of the Organization of Islamic Conference (OIC). The Tripoli agreement signed by both parties provided for autonomy over a territory that covered 14 provinces and nine cities in Mindanao. The agreement was subsequently rejected by the MNLF that returned to its demands for independence. Nevertheless, Marcos moved forward with some of the elements of the agreement and established autonomous regional assemblies. Despite the failure of its implementation, the Tripoli agreement became the benchmark for future negotiations between the MNLF and the government.[42]

In subsequent years, internal squabbles and general fatigue significantly weakened the MNLF. After a leadership dispute in 1977, Hashim Salamat broke off from the MNLF and established the rival MILF. There were further defections of elite members of the MNLF who decided to cooperate with the government.

The violence continued for many years, but an improvement in the MNLF's relations with the government began to emerge after the return to democracy. Under Corazon Aquino, there were negotiations for autonomy provisions in the new constitution for the Muslims in Mindanao. The talks with all rebel groups eventually failed and the government then pursued separate talks with the MNLF, leading to a ceasefire agreement in 1986. The negotiations faltered and the MNLF abandoned talks in mid-1987, but the government went ahead with the creation of the Autonomous Region in Muslim Mindanao (ARMM). A plebiscite was organized to ratify the act but, because of the criticisms from the MNLF and some Christians, only four provinces were included in the autonomous region.[43]

During the administration of Fidel Ramos, a peace agreement was finally reached. Under a new ceasefire agreement and after two years of peace negotiations between the MNLF and the government, an agreement was signed on 2 September 1996, thereby ending a 24-year secessionist war. The peace agreement provided for a two-phase implementation of the 1976 Tripoli agreement and created a temporary administrative body, the Southern Philippine Council for Peace and Development (SPCPD). Some of its provisions include a Muslim autonomous region in Mindanao, the integration of 7,500 MNLF fighters to the Philippine armed forces and the police, and assistance programs to the rebels to reintegrate into society. The MNLF leader, Nur Misuari, was made chairman of the SPCPD and the government supported his candidacy as governor of the ARMM. Misuari was elected governor a few days after the peace agreement.[44]

The democratic context enabled the government and the MNLF to reach a mutually satisfactory agreement on the future of the Muslims in Mindanao. Autonomy was a cornerstone for achieving this compromise, as well as the reintegration of former rebels into the military and police. A crucial element of the agreement was the creation of an administrative body headed by the Moros with the instruments to implement the agreement. Given that it has been responsible directly to the President and it derives its powers from the President, the SPCPD would be able to avoid bureaucratic hurdles to implement the various points of the agreement. Following the agreement, the question would then become whether the new structures had the intended effect.

The pillars of governance in Muslim Mindanao are the ARMM and the SPCPD. The jurisdiction of the ARMM covers four provinces, with Muslim majorities, while the SPCPD includes 14 provinces and nine cities of Mindanao, most of which have Christian majorities. Christians in Mindanao have rejected both structures, while the Muslims are increasingly disillusioned with their performance. The problems reside with their ineffectiveness, the failure to combine these institutional changes with adequate representation and power in the national political system, and the imposition of these structures on a society where formal and informal authority were not captured by these institutions.

The ARMM was created to give more autonomy to Muslim Mindanao. It was added to the existing institutions of government in the region that already included provincial governments. The ARMM became an intermediary structure between four provincial governments and the national level. Citizens of these provinces would send representatives to provincial assemblies, the ARMM, and to the national congress and senate.

The SPCPD was designed as a temporary organization to implement the peace agreement. It reports directly to the President of the Philippines where its legal status resides. It has no independent power from the President. As such, it cannot initiate policies or implement them. It is a consultative body that monitors the various aspects of the peace process and the implementation of development programs in the area. Its jurisdiction corresponds to the territory that had been granted autonomy under the Tripoli agreement. Under the provisions of the peace agreement, a referendum is to be held after three years to create an autonomous region in Mindanao that will replace the ARMM and SPCPD.

In theory, the creation of the ARMM and the expanded autonomous region should respond to the long-standing grievances of the Muslims in Mindanao. The agreement falls short of providing independence for the Muslims, but it grants autonomy on all policy areas except foreign policy and defense. Autonomy should allow the Muslims to implement development programs for their population, reduce poverty, and repair the damages caused by 30 years of war.

In fact, the structures for greater autonomy were not capable of responding to the problems of Mindanao and the grievances of the Muslims. Observers have often cited problems of incompetence, lack of resources, or corruption. Yet, there are a number of other factors that have challenged the structures of autonomy. The peace process must still respond to the grievances of a significant proportion of Muslims who continue to follow the MILF and reject the option of autonomy. Furthermore, there are a number of obstacles internal to Muslim society, such as the power of clans that create problems of legitimization and authority of new political structures.

The ARMM and SPCPD have been criticized for the incompetence of their leaders, their ineffectiveness, and corruption. Nur Misuari and other officials in the ARMM and SPCPD were former guerilla fighters in the MNLF. Their leadership skills in combat were not easily transferable to political and administrative structures. As a result, they do not produce the results that were initially expected. There is a wide perception among the Muslim population that the ARMM does not address the needs of the people.[45] The SPCPD receives similar evaluations.

Corruption is part of the reason for the ARMM and SPCPD's failures. The payment of the salaries of ARMM employees has often been delayed. In May 1998, employees questioned a missing 625,000 pesos worth of amelioration benefits that were due to them and that were rumored to have gone to key high officials.[46] According to Father Eliseo Mercado, the President of Notre Dame University, a member of the SPCPD and a highly-respected figure in the peace movement among all communities, the SPCPD is currently an 'exclusive club of the MNLF' where members spend their time 'quarreling over the division of spoils of the peace agreement'. The ARMM is 'worse than the SPCPD'.[47] Monies devoted to the administration of the region and development programs are subject to graft from high officials and represent a lucrative source of income for the former MNLF leaders.

Underlying the corruption in the ARMM is a sense of lack of legitimacy and real autonomy. When the ARMM was originally created under the administration of Corazon Aquino, Nur Misuari and the MNLF rejected its establishment because it failed to provide sufficient autonomy for Muslim Mindanao. Once a peace agreement was reached, however, the MNLF had to work within existing structures before a new referendum could create a new autonomous region. According to Samuel Tan, the ARMM only provides a small space for autonomy. This fails to respond to the traditional Muslim demands for identity recognition, a shared political authority, and shared socio-economic resources. It is integrated to the bureaucracy and 'communicates national policy and programs with little autonomous options'. It is an 'implementing arm of the government'.[48] Finally, the fact that it will be replaced by another structure after the referendum on expanded autonomy undermines its capacity to strengthen its legitimacy and support among the population.

The SPCPD suffers from a lack of understanding about its mandate. Since the peace agreement, the population has been expecting the SPCPD to provide some peace dividends in the form of livelihood programs and an improvement in the region's living standards. The SPCPD, however, is only a temporary body with no power to implement policies and programs. A majority 'misunderstood the SPCPD as an implementing body that can improve economic conditions' while it can only make recommendations to various departments and agencies.[49] 'Most of our recommendations have not been answered by line agencies', complains the executive director of the SPCPD, Uttoh Salem. The SPCPD has no power to pressure these agencies and, as a result, the SPCPD is still waiting for the government to deliver the peace dividends.[50] Many people have not seen any change in their livelihood and are unaware of the implementation of any kind of development program in their area.[51] 'The majority are still waiting for an improvement in their living conditions…'.[52] The SPCPD, therefore, has been losing support among the population because of its lack of visibility and seeming incapacity to provide services and development programs.

Most of the economic investment in Muslim Mindanao has come from foreign donors. Several foreign countries have announced livelihood projects, support for local governments, and investments in infrastructure. Yet, foreign assistance has not produced sufficiently quick results to stimulate the local economy. Even if some groups have benefited from the programs, the majority are still waiting for assistance. They realize that the only changes occurring in Mindanao are a consequence of foreign assistance, while promised programs from the government have yet to appear. This contrast has only reaffirmed many Muslims' belief that the government is not truly committed to peace and is not ready to invest the necessary resources to ensure an improvement in living conditions among Muslims in Mindanao.

The Philippine government has little incentive either to inject more resources into existing structures or to use its power to curtail their ineffectiveness. The ARMM representatives ask for more funds to address the problems in their region, but the national government resists because of corrupt practices. At the same time, cynics argue, the government tolerates the existing corruption and waste of resources because it is still cheaper than waging war.[53]

Beyond its failures to properly govern the ARMM and the SPCPD, the MNLF and Nur Misuari suffer from a rapidly declining legitimacy among Muslims in Mindanao. During its early years, the MNLF was the only organization struggling for the independence of the *Bangsa Moro*. After Hashim Salamat and his supporters split from the MNLF and formed the MILF, the MNLF became increasingly associated with only a part of the Muslim population, especially Nur Misuari's ethnic group, the Tausugs. The Maranaw and Maguindanaoan, in turn, became supporters of the MILF. Also, it is widely argued that the MNLF reached a peace agreement with the government because of war fatigue, a weakening of its organization, and external pressures from the OIC. In effect, at the time of the peace agreement, the MNLF might no longer have been representing the Moro struggle, while the MILF was gaining more strength. The MNLF needed to regain its moral ascendancy among the Moro people and sought to do so through peace.[54]

The May 1998 elections in the Philippines have confirmed this trend. The MNLF fielded candidates in several gubernatorial and mayoral races across various provinces within the ARMM. Many of the prominent MNLF leaders were defeated. In a highly contested election, Muslimin Sema, the secretary of the MNLF and former executive director of the SPCPD won the position of mayor of Cotabato City by a small margin. He was the only MNLF leader to win a significant position.

Also, several governors began to think of withdrawing their provinces from the ARMM. The governor of Sulu, Abdusakur Tan, and 13 mayors were planning a plebiscite on the question of withdrawing Sulu from the ARMM. The immediate issue was the failure of Nur Misuari to discuss with the governors the problem of delays in the payment of salaries.[55] More generally, they were dissatisfied with the additional layer of bureaucracy with little visible benefits. The MNLF's paralysis has been compounded by the political culture of graft and corruption endemic in the Philippine political system and by traditional political authority. The corruption in the ARMM government is similar to the graft that exists at all levels of government, from the national to the local level. The ARMM is only one additional level where officials are trying to obtain a cut. Local politicians also expect to gain from their positions. With the establishment of an additional layer of government, they have seen a decline in potential sources of income.[56]

The competition is fiercer because it pits the MNLF leaders against traditional clan leaders. Many of the region's politicians are *datus*, traditional clan leaders, or are members of very influential families. The MNLF, the ARMM, and the SPCPD represent challenges to their established power base. This was an important factor in the defeat of MNLF candidates during the May 1998 elections. Many of them challenged the positions of clan leaders in gubernatorial and mayoral positions. That they failed partially indicates the continued strength of the clan structure and the political power of the *datus*.

Muslim society remains divided along clan lines and there is a very weak civil society. NGOs have multiplied rapidly since the end of the Marcos regime, but most have emerged in Christian areas including in Mindanao. Very few organizations were formed in Muslim Mindanao, in part because the decades of war still create obstacles for such organizations to emerge. Instead, guerilla organizations such as the MILF have been the strongest societal organizations. Islamic organizations are becoming more important in forging some alliances and cooperation among Moro groups, but there are still very few organizations bridging the gap between Christians and Muslims. As a result, social capital remains very weak, especially the kind that can forge networks of engagements between Christians and Muslims.

The MILF has been gaining popular support at the expense of the MNLF. Formerly divided among Tausugs, Maranao, and Maguindanao, the support of all groups is moving to the MILF.[57] '[With the] way the SPCPD is going..., [there will be] a phenomenal growth of the MILF, even among former MNLF combatants.'[58] Many MNLF field commanders, disgruntled by the little impact of the peace agreement on their lives, are thinking of returning to war.[59] Even some leaders of the MNLF, such as Dr. Farouq Hussein, MNLF vice chair for foreign affairs have expressed similar frustrations: 'I and our senior officials are still very much in the struggle and with the present situation, we may be forced to go to war because we still believe that it is the only recourse to achieve peace in our area.'[60] As the MNLF has seen itself paralyzed by a peace process that is functioning badly, therefore, the MILF has increased its support among the Muslim population.

The MILF's strength comes partly from its military, organizational, and ideological superiority over the MNLF. In contrast to the MNLF at the time of the peace agreement, the MILF is engaging the government of the Philippines from a position of military strength. It not only claims to have 100,000 fighters across Mindanao, but it is also producing some of its own weaponry.[61] Organizationally, it operates a shadow government that includes even an active Islamic court. Finally, Islam provides an ideological appeal that the nationalist ideology of the MNLF never commanded. Islam is a more entrenched form of identity that can unite the Muslims, whereas the concept of Moro nation often clashed with tribal distinctions among Tausugs, Maranao, and Maguindanao. Following its election, the administration of Joseph 'Erap' Estrada slowly advanced toward peace with the MILF while trying to safeguard the peace process with the MNLF. The administration retained many of the key advisors of the Ramos administration and pursued similar policies. Despite several armed clashes with the MILF, formal peace talks began on 25 October 1999. The government recognized 25 out of 48 MILF camps before the talks began, a territorial recognition that was one of the MILF's preconditions. Nevertheless, the fighting continued probably as a means for the MILF to strengthen its territorial position before the 31 December 1999 deadline for the Philippine government's recognition of MILF camps.[62] As these talks began, the government postponed the elections for the ARMM by one year, in order to give itself more time to organize the awaited plebiscite on expanded autonomy and attempt to raise more support for the new region.[63]

By the end of 1999, it appeared that the peace process with the MNLF was stagnating, at best, while only slow and piecemeal progress was made in talks with the MILF. The new governance structures under the ARMM and SPCPD have not sufficiently responded to the grievances of the Muslims in Mindanao. The structures have been incapable of increasing popular participation in a new political process that would lead to better living standards and a realization of the peace dividends. Instead, they became entangled in accusations of corruption and ineffectiveness that increased the popular perception that they only served the interests of the MNLF elite. Even among MNLF followers, the new structures have lost some support. These trends have boosted the popularity of the MILF that will be faced with similar dilemmas in negotiating a peace settlement with the government of the Philippines. One of the difficulties will be to resolve the perpetual problem of overlapping traditional and 'modern' authority, as well as the institutions of regional autonomy with the representative institutions of the government of the Philippines.

Conclusion

Efforts to implement 'good' governance are unlikely to reduce conflict if they do not address the perceptions of threat dividing ethnic groups. More democracy and better governance can create more trust among ethnic groups, and certainly do in the long run, but they can also create new sources of tension in the short term. Strategies to reduce ethnic conflict using instruments of governance need to be designed to improve the balance of representation between different ethnic groups, ensure that autonomous structures or powers are given on issues that differentiate ethnic groups (for example, language or religion), and institutions empowering different groups need to be efficacious in order to meet the expectations for which they were designed.

Authoritarian means of governance generally fail to address ethnic tensions in the long run. In the Indonesian case, decades of authoritarian governance did not remove the sources of tension between Muslims and Christians. Although *Pancasila* offers an ideology of the state that represents an ideal for religious balance and tolerance, it was imposed rather than nurtured under the New Order regime. With the opening of the political system, the questions of the role of Islam in the polity and the representation of minorities are resurfacing once again. Under Marcos, repression only increased the resolve of Muslims in Mindanao to use force against the Philippine government. The MNLF began fighting after the Marcos regime imposed martial law. Peace negotiations were favored when the democratic regime was installed.

Democracy creates an environment conducive to a reduction in conflict potential but it also carries its dangers. Democratic structures can increase the inclusiveness and participation of some groups while excluding others. The reforms in Indonesia have strengthened the resolve of many Muslim groups to strengthen their representation and advance their agenda, because of their status as an overwhelming majority. As the Christians gained a renewed representation with the victory of PDI-*Perjuangan*, the issue of Muslim-Christian representation has resurfaced in public debates. Democratic institutions in the Philippines have continued to marginalize the role of Muslims in Manila. They have been relegated to autonomous institutions whose power is not clear. In many ways, Muslims in Mindanao still feel the need for more power at the center, with increased autonomy at the regional level.

Regional autonomy became the cornerstone of governance in Muslim Mindanao. Nevertheless, while the existing institutions were promising they did not function well. They have increased the control of the MNLF over local and state resources without living up to the expectations of the local Muslim population. As a result, there are few chances that the disgruntled Muslims will support the plebiscite on expanding the autonomous area. If Muslims lose their autonomous institutions by a democratic process while failing to gain more representation at the center, they will find themselves increasingly marginalized and alienated, once again, from the Philippine Republic.

Furthermore, the new institutional structures do not adequately respond to the existing authority of traditional clans or to the representation of different Muslim groups. The clan wars across Muslim Mindanao continue to create major obstacles to any new political structure that is created. Without finding a solution to these wars, it is unlikely that these new structures will be able to perform as expected and be representative. Instead, they become new forums to fight out clan interests. Also, autonomous structures need to avoid competition with the *datus* in the meantime. Otherwise, it becomes even more difficult to gain legitimacy among the local population. Finally, it will be difficult to reconcile the divisions between supporters of the MNLF and the MILF, who have held separate talks with the government. If an agreement is reached with the MILF, how will it be integrated into the existing peace agreement with the MNLF? The separate nature of these talks may lead to renewed divisions among Muslims if they fail to agree on contentious issues in the reconciliation of the two peace agreements.

'Good' governance measures offer promising avenues for conflict prevention, but they are not sufficient in themselves. They must allow for the negotiation of grievances through peaceful means and for the protection of group rights. Both in Mindanao and in Indonesia, Muslims and Christians have developed suspicion toward the other group. In the case of Indonesia, these suspicions have led to violence. The rights of each group will need to be secured in the new political system and they will need measures to reduce suspicions between groups. Similarly, the Mindanao conflict still leaves Muslims suspicious of Christians and the Philippine state, while Christians in Mindanao fear greater autonomy that would give increased power to the Muslims. The mistrust is much higher than in Indonesia and will require much more effort to eliminate. No settlement will be successful if it does not reduce tensions between Christians and Muslims in Mindanao itself. Autonomy will need to lead to a greater representation of all groups in Mindanao before it can successfully be extended to several more provinces. Since both communities are present in most areas of

Mindanao, policies and programs for 'good' governance will work better if complemented by programs explicitly designed to protect the rights of all communities (Christian, Muslim, and tribal *Lumad*[64] groups). New structures will also need to provide the means to negotiate a settlement on major grievances such as land rights. Autonomous government may not be the best means to do so and Muslims have too little power in the institutions of central government to initiate a process at that level.

Increasing the transparency and efficacy of political institutions is conducive to a reduction in tensions. Part of the difficulties encountered by the autonomous government of Mindanao has been its own lack of efficacy. The corruption and inability to meet expectations undermined its own legitimacy, but it is not clear whether the autonomous government has had sufficient powers and representation to be efficacious. Similarly in Indonesia, the legitimacy of existing institutions has been severely shaken by the corruption of the New Order regime. The lack of transparency and the authoritarian means used to implement *Pancasila* and the constitution of 1945 have weakened Indonesian political institutions. As a result, there are tendencies to pursue struggles in the extra-institutional realm. The reform process needs to strengthen the general efficacy of central institutions and more important, their ability to provide peaceful channels to address grievances.

Building trust between communities is an important complement to the focus on political institutions. A greater amount of social capital is likely to increase cooperation and trust between ethnic groups, but only if the webs of cooperation cross ethnic lines are formed. A greater number of civil society organizations may increase tensions if they are organized along ethnic lines. Without recognition of the need to cross ethnic boundaries, the natural establishment of new organizations may well follow religious lines by building on existing institutional strengths. These are still very weak in Indonesia and the Philippines and, therefore, offer the greatest potential for constructive policy intervention.

'Good' governance may contribute to increasing the security of ethnic communities if the ethnic dimension of conflicts is recognized. Even if the root causes of conflict are not embedded in profound hatred between ethnic groups or fundamental differences in religious beliefs, the conflicts are expressed through ethnic means and create group insecurities. By recognizing the structure of these insecurities in ethnic terms, 'good' governance strategies can first address the perceived threats by improving channels to increase trust, cooperation, and peaceful negotiations. Afterwards, greater democratization, transparency, and efficacy can strengthen the balance of representation between ethnic groups and diminish the importance of ethnicity over time.

Notes

1 Organization for Economic Cooperation and Development (OECD) (1997), *DAC Guidelines on Conflict, Peace and Development Co-operation*, OECD, May.

2 Canadian International Development Agency (CIDA) (1998), *Rights, Democracy and Governance – Asia, an Overview*, September, *http://www.acdi-cida.gc.ca*, accessed 12 June 1999.
3 Putnam, R., Leonardi, R. and Nanetti, R. Y. (1993), *Making democracy work: civic traditions in modern Italy*, Princeton University Press, Princeton.
4 OECD, *DAC Guidelines on Conflict, Peace and Development Co-operation*, pp.14.
5 Brass, P. (1991), 'Ethnic Groups and the State', in P. Brass (ed.) (1991), *Ethnicity and Nationalism: Theory and Comparison*, Sage Publications, London and New Delhi, pp.247-299.
6 Horowitz, D. L. (1985), *Ethnic Groups in Conflict*, University of California Press, Berkeley; Lijphart, A. (1977), *Democracy in plural societies: a comparative exploration*, Yale University Press, New Haven.
7 *Ibid.*, (1993), 'Democracy in Divided Societies', *Journal of Democracy*, vol.4, no.4, pp.36.
8 *Ibid.*, pp.18-38. See also Gurr, T. R. (1993), *Minorities at risk: a global view of ethnopolitical conflicts*, United States Institute of Peace Press, Washington, DC.
9 Horowitz, *Ethnic Groups in Conflict*, 1985, pp.601-628.
10 Putnam, *Making democracy work: civic traditions in modern Italy*, 1993.
11 For example, see the Statement by the West Java Churches Collaborative Body (Badan Kerja Sama Gereja-Gerja se-Jawa Barat) in response to the Tasikmalaya riots, Bandung, 27 Desember 1996 and the Statement of Concern of the Three Christian-Protestant Communities of East Java and Surabaya. Surabaya, 11 October 1996.
12 *Suara Pembaruan*, 14 June 1996.
13 Chauvel, R. (1990), *Nationalists, Soldiers, and Separatists*, KITLV Press, Leiden.
14 Feith, H. (1962), *The decline of constitutional democracy in Indonesia*, Cornell University Press, Ithaca.
15 Kahin, G. M. (1963), *Nationalism and revolution in Indonesia*, Cornell University Press, Ithaca.
16 The *abangan* Javanese were those who followed a syncretic form of Islam. The *santri*, in turn, tended to be educated in Muslim schools and followed the precepts of Islam more closely. They were also the constituency supporting Muslim political parties. See Geertz, C. (1964), *The Religion of Java*, Free Press of Glencoe, New York.
17 See Liddle, R. W. (1995), *Islam and Politics in Late New Order Indonesia: The Use of Religion as a Political Resource by an Authoritarian Regime*, mimeo, Ohio State University; and Said, S. (1996), *Suharto's Armed Forces: Building a Power Base in New Order Indonesia, 1965-1995*, presented at the 'Annual Meeting of the Association of Asian Studies', Honolulu, Hawaii, 11-14 April 1996. Robert Hefner argues instead that the creation of ICMI reflects a change in Indonesian society that has become more devout in its practices of Islam. See Hefner, R. (1993), 'Islam, State, and Civil Society: ICMI and the Struggle for the Indonesian Middle Class', *Indonesia*, vol.56, October, pp.1-37.
18 Schwarz , A. (1994), *A Nation in Waiting: Indonesia in the 1990s*, Allen & Unwin, St. Leonards, Australia.
19 *Ibid.*, pp.175-183.
20 See quote by Abdurrachman Wahid in Schwarz, *A Nation in Waiting: Indonesia in the 1990s*, 1994, pp.186.
21 *Kompas*, 23 February 1997.
22 *Tempo Interaktif*, 5 June 1997.
23 The four prominent ICMI members that were excluded from the MPR list are Prof. Dr. Dawam Rahardjo, Dr. Watik Pratikya, Adi Sasono, and Jimly Assiddiqi. (*Tempo Interaktif*, 14 August 1997). On the last Suharto cabinet, see *Forum Keadilan*, 23 February 1998.
24 *Indonesia-L*, 22 July 1996.

25 Interview with Prof. Dr. Franz Magnis-Suseno SJ, published in *Mutiara Online*, 23 February 1997.
26 Confidential interviews with intellectuals and religious leaders, Ambon, April 1996.
27 *Kompas Online*, 29 February 1996.
28 Confidential interviews, Ambon, April 1996.
29 Confidential interviews with religious leaders, Flores, February 1996.
30 D&R (1999), *Dari Sabang sampai Merauke: Potensi kerusuhan*, special edition, Pemilu '99, Bom Waktu Kerusuhan, May-June.
31 *Ibid.*
32 *Nusantara*, 4 Desember 1998.
33 See Human Rights Watch Report (1998), *Human Rights Watch*, New York, 9 December.
34 D&R, *Dari Sabang sampai Merauke: Potensi kerusuhan*, 1999.
35 Interview with Cardinal Julius Darmaatmadja, Jakarta, 11 May 1999.
36 Interview with Dr Said Aqiel Siradj, a leader of Nahdlatul Ulama, Jakarta, 20 May 1999.
37 Interview with Dr Said Aqiel Siradj.
38 *Gatra*, No.30/V, 12 June 1999.
39 Interview with Cardinal Julius Darmaatmadja.
40 May, R.J. (1992), 'The Religious Factor in Three Minority Movements: The Moro of the Philippines, the Malays of Thailand, and Indonesia's West Papuans', *Contemporary Southeast Asia*, vol.13, no.4, pp.397-8.
41 *Far Eastern Economic Review*, 17 February 1994.
42 May, 'The Religious Factor in Three Minority Movements: The Moro of the Philippines, the Malays of Thailand, and Indonesia's West Papuans', 1992, pp.400.
43 *Ibid.*, pp.401-2.
44 *Manila Chronicle*, 9 September 1996; *Business World*, 9 September 1996; *Philippine Daily Inquirer*, 10 September 1996; *Asiaweek*, 13 September 1996; *Singapore Straights Times*, 12 May 1997.
45 Interview with Romy Elusea, Reporter of Today, Cotabato City, May 1998.
46 *Mindanao Trend*, 5 May 1998.
47 Interview with Father Eliseo Mercado, President of Notre-Dame University and Member of SPCPD, Cotabato City, May 1998.
48 Interview with Samuel Tan, Director of the National Historical Institute and author of numerous publications on Muslims in Mindanao, Manila, May 1998.
49 Datu Deng Ali, Joint Monitoring Committee (MNLF sector), Cotabato City, June 1998.
50 Interview with Uttoh Salem, executive director of the SPCPD, June 1998.
51 Focus group discussion with local NGOs and farmers' groups, North Cotabato.
52 Datu Deng Ali, June 1998.
53 Father Eliseo Mercado, June 1998.
54 This point was made by Chris Guerlin, Moro NGO activist, Manila, May 1998.
55 *Philippines Daily Inquirer*, 5 March, 1998.
56 For an interesting study relating to this issue, see Hutchcroft, P. D. (1998), *Booty Capitalism: The Politics of Banking in the Philippines*, Cornell University Press, Ithaca.
57 Interviews with Datu Deng Ali, Romy Elusea, and Abba Kuaman, Chair of the Board, Moro Human Rights Center, Cotabato City, June 1998.
58 Father Eliseo Mercado, June 1998.
59 Interviews with MNLF fighters and field commanders, North Cotabato, June 1998.
60 *Philippine Daily Inquirer*, 14 April 1999.
61 Interview with Gazhali Jaafer, Vice-chair for Political Affairs, Moro Islamic Liberation Front, June 1998.
62 *Philippine Daily Inquirer*, 7 September, 25 October, and 16 November, 1999.

63 *Philippine Daily Inquirer*, 9 September 1999.
64 Lumads are indigenous non-Muslim and non-Christian peoples in Mindanao.

References

Brass, P. (1991), 'Ethnic Groups and the State', in P. Brass (ed.) (1991), *Ethnicity and Nationalism: Theory and Comparison*, Sage Publications, London and New Delhi, pp. 247-299.

Chauvel, R. (1990), *Nationalists, Soldiers, and Separatists*, KITLV Press, Leiden.

D&R (1999), *Dari Sabang sampai Merauke: Potensi kerusuhan*, special edition, Pemilu '99, Bom Waktu Kerusuhan, May-June.

Feith, H. (1962), *The Decline of Constitutional democracy in Indonesia*, Cornell University Press, Ithaca, NY.

Geertz, C. (1964), *The Religion of Java*, Free Press of Glencoe, New York.

Gurr, T. R. (1993), *Minorities at risk: a global view of ethnopolitical conflicts*, United States Institute of Peace Press, Washington, DC.

Hefner, R. (1993), 'Islam, State, and Civil Society: ICMI and the Struggle for the Indonesian Middle Class', *Indonesia*, vol. 56, October, pp. 1-37.

Horowitz, D. L. (1985), *Ethnic Groups in Conflict*, University of California Press, Berkeley.

Horowitz, D. L. (1993), 'Democracy in Divided Societies', *Journal of Democracy*, vol. 4, no. 4, pp. 36.

Human Rights Watch Report (1998), *Human Rights Watch*, New York, 9 December.

Hutchcroft, P. D. (1998), *Booty Capitalism: The Politics of Banking in the Philippines*, Cornell University Press, Ithaca.

Kahin, G. M. (1963), *Nationalism and revolution in Indonesia*, Cornell University Press, Ithaca, NY.

Liddle, R. W. (1995), *Islam and Politics in Late New Order Indonesia: The Use of Religion as a Political Resource by an Authoritarian Regime*, mimeo, Ohio State University.

Lijphart, A. (1977), *Democracy in plural societies: a comparative exploration*, Yale University Press, New Haven.

May, R.J. (1992), 'The Religious Factor in Three Minority Movements: The Moro of the Philippines, the Malays of Thailand, and Indonesia's West Papuans', *Contemporary Southeast Asia*, vol. 13, no. 4, pp. 397-8.

Organization for Economic Cooperation and Development (OECD) (1997), *DAC Guidelines on Conflict, Peace and Development Co-operation*, OECD, May.

Putnam, R., Leonardi, R. and Nanetti, R. Y. (1993), *Making democracy work: civic traditions in modern Italy*, Princeton University Press, Princeton.

Said, S. (1996), *Suharto's Armed Forces: Building a Power Base in New Order Indonesia, 1965-1995*, presented at the 'Annual Meeting of the Association of Asian Studies', Honolulu, Hawaii, 11-14 April.

Schwarz, A. (1994), *A Nation in Waiting: Indonesia in the 1990s*, Allen & Unwin, St. Leonards, Australia.

Bibliography

Abdullah, A. and Chor Sooi, C. (1998), 'Security at Border Tightened to Stop Aliens', *New Straits Times*, 16 March, pp. 3.

Acharya, A., Dewitt, D. and Hernandez, C. (1995), 'Sustainable Development and Security in Southeast Asia: A Concept Paper', *CANCAPS Papier*, No. 6, August.

Agano, M. E. (1995), 'Migrant Labor and the Filipino Family', in A. E. Perez (ed.), *The Filipino Family: A Spectrum of Views and Issues*, University of the Philippines Office of Research Coordination, Quezon City, Philippines, pp. 79-96.

Agence France Press (AFP) (1997), 'Thai Labor Committee Wants to Send Back a Million Alien Workers', *Migration News*, 28 November.

Agence France Press (AFP) (1998a), 'Malaysia Relaxes Labor Rules to Woo Investment', *Migration News*, 29 November.

Agence France Press (AFP) (1998b), 'Go Where Jobs Beckon, Ramos Tells Filipinos Abroad', *Migration News*, 7 January.

Agrawal, N. (1996), *The Benefit of Growth for Indonesian Workers*, World Bank Policy Research Working Paper No. 1637, Washington, DC.

Ahmad, E. (1991), 'Social Security and the Poor: Choices for Developing Countries', *World Bank Research Observer*, Vol. 6(1), January.

Ahmad, R. (1998), 'Malaysia Dismisses Worries Over Indonesian Migrants', *Reuters*, 1 April.

Aidit, DN. (1952), *Sedjarah Gerakan Buruh Indonesia*, Yayasan Pembaruan, Jakarta.

Alaggapa, M. (1987), *National Security in Developing States*, Aubur House, Massachusetts, pp. 2.

Alolod, F. M. (1998), *Major Program Components for CCUVA*, unpublished document, Cebu, December, pp. 1-8.

Amin, ATM N. (1991), *A Policy Agenda for the Informal Sector in Thailand*, Asian Employment Programme, International Labour Office, New Delhi.

Arief, S. (1997), *Pembangunanisme dan Ekonomi Indonesia: Pemberdayaan Rakyat dalam Arus Globalisasi*, CPSM-Zaman, Jakarta.

Aslanbeigui, N. *et al.* (1994), *Women in the Age of Economic Transformation*, Routledge, London.

Associated Press (AP) (1998a), 'Malaysia Assures Neighbors It Won't Fire Foreign Workers', *Migration News*, 12 January.

Associated Press (AP) (1998b), 'Thai Minister Vows to Deport Illegal Workers in Three Months', *Migration News*, 16 January.

Associated Press (AP) (1998c), 'Jobless Rate Raises Fear of Social Unrest', *Bangkok Post*, 13 March, pp.4.

Associated Press (AP) (1998d), 'Indonesian Navy to Bring Home Workers From Malaysia: Antara', *Migration News*, 6 January 1998.

Associated Press (AP) (1998e), 'Indonesian Navy to Take Illegal Workers From Malaysia', *Migration News*, 20 March 1998.

Azar, E. and Moon, C. (eds) (1991), *National Security in the Third World: The Management of Internal and External Threats*, Center for International Development and Conflict Management, Maryland.

Bacani, C. (1997), 'Surviving the Slump', *Asiaweek*, 28 November, pp. 52-55.

Barth, G. A. (1983), *Street Foods: Informal Sector Food Preparation and Marketing*, Equity Policy Centre, Iloilo City.

Baswir, R., *et al.* (1999), *Pembangunan Tanpa Perasaan: Evaluasi pemenuhan Hak Ekonomi Sosial Budatya Orde Baru*, Pustaka Pelajar, Yogyakarta.

Battistella, G. (1996), 'Migration and APEC: Issues for Discussion', *Asian Migrant Forum*, November, pp.23.

'Be on Lookout for Illegals, says Shahidan', *New Straits Times*, 17 March 1998, pp. 3.

Beare, M. (1998), 'Illegal Migration', in C. G. Hernandez and G. R. Pattugalan (eds), *Transnational Crime and Regional Security in the Asia Pacific*, Institute for Strategic and Development Studies, Inc. (ISDS), Quezon City, Manila, Philippines, pp. 252, 256.

Beltran, R. P., Samonte, E. L. and Walker, Sr. L. (1996), 'Filipino Women Migrant Workers: Effect on Family Life and Challenges for Intervention', in R. P. Beltran and G. F. Rodriguez (eds), *Filipino Women Migrant Workers: At The Crossroads. Beyond Beijing*, Giraffe Books, Quezon City, Philippines, pp. 15-45.

Bernama (1998), 'Refugees' Free to go to Third Country', *The Star*, 6 May.

Bohning, W. R. (1996), *Employing Foreign Workers*, International Labor Office, Geneva.

Bohning, W. R. (1998), *SEAPAT Working Paper 1: The Impact of the Asian Crisis on Filipino Employment Prospects Abroad*, International Labor Organization Southeast Asia Multi-Disciplinary Advisory Team.

Bosniak, L. (no date), 'Human Rights, State Sovereignty and the Protection of Undocumented Migrants Under the International Migrant Workers Convention', *International Migration Review*, Vol. 25(4).

Brass, P. (1991), 'Ethnic Groups and the State', in P. Brass (ed.) (1991), *Ethnicity and Nationalism: Theory and Comparison*, Sage Publications, London and New Delhi, pp. 247-299.

Bryant, C. and White, L. G. (1982), *Managing Development in the Third World*, Westview, Boulder, pp. 15.

Budiman, A. (ed.) (1990), *State and Civil Society in Indonesia*, Monash Paper on Southeast Asia No. 22, Monash University, Clayton.

Cabilao, M. I. (1995), *Labor Migration: Issues for DFA Personnel in Servicing Filipino Migrant Workers*, Foreign Service Institute, Pasay City.

'Calo Puas Memeras, Pekerja Memelas', *Bisnis Indonesia*, 6 November 1998.

Carr, M., Chen, M. and Jhabvala, R. (1996), *Speaking Out: Women's Economic Empowerment in South Asia*, Aga Khan Foundation Canada and the United Nations Development Fund for Women – Unifem, IT Publications, London.

Central Bureau of Statistics (1996), *Industrial Statistics 1995*, BPS, Jakarta.

Chant and Radcliffe (1992), 'Migration and Development: The Importance of Gender', in S. Chant (ed.), *Gender and Migration in Developing Countries*, Belhaven Press, London, pp. 1-29.

Charoensutthipan, P. (1998a), 'Deadline on Aliens Put Off for Year; But Policy Will Not be Eased Further, Insists Bhichai', *Bangkok Post*, 16 July.

Charoensutthipan, P. (1998b), 'Plan to Let Aliens Work in Only 13 Provinces; Repatriation Centre Could be Established', *Bangkok Post*, 14 January.

Charoensutthipan, P. (1998c), 'Slump a Boom to Cheats', *Bangkok Post*, 14 April.

Chauvel, R. (1990), *Nationalists, Soldiers, and Separatists*, KITLV Press, Leiden.

Chintayananda, S. Risser, G. and Chantavanich, S. (1997), *The Monitoring of the Registration of Immigrant Workers From Myanmar, Cambodia and Laos in Thailand*, Institute of Asian Studies, Asian Research Center for Migration, Chulalongkorn University, Bangkok.

Coleman, J. (1988), 'Social Capital in the Creation of Human Capital', *American Journal of Sociology*, pp. 95-120.

Coleman, J. (1990), *Foundations of Social Theory*, Harvard University Press, Cambridge.

Concepcion, E. T. and Braganza, I. P. (1991), *Sidewalk Vending: An Alternative for the Urban Poor*, School of Development Management, Chancellor's Special Research & Writing Fund, UP Visayas, Iloilo City, April.

Crispin, S. W. (1999), 'Cycle of Despair' *Far Eastern Economic Review*, 23 September, pp. 22.

Cruz, V. P. and Paganoni, A. (1989), *Filipinas in Migration: Big Bills and Small Change*, Scalabrini Migration Center, Quezon City.

D&R (1999), *Dari Sabang sampai Merauke: Potensi kerusuhan*, special edition, Pemilu '99, Bom Waktu Kerusuhan, May-June.

Dancel, R. (1998a), 'OFWs Unfazed by Low Pay, Shrinking Marts', *Philippine Daily Inquirer*, 18 August, pp. B1.

Dancel, R. (1998b), 'Overseas Workers; Heroes in a Tragic Play', *Philippine Daily Inquirer*, 17 August, pp. B12.

Departemen Tenaga Kerja Indonesia (1991), *Studi dan Analisa Perkembangan KFM*, Depnaker, Jakarta.

Dignard, L. and Havet, J. (eds) (1987), *Women in Micro- and Small-scale Enterprise Development*, Westview, Boulder.

Djumialdji, F.X. and Soedjono, W. (1982), *Perjanjian Perburuhan dan Hubungan Perburuhan Pancasila*, Bina Aksara, Jakarta.

Duff-Brown, B. (1998a), 'Illegal Aliens to Enter Malaysia', *Migration News*, 30 March.

Duff-Brown, B. (1998b), 'Poverty Reaches Across Borders', *Bangkok Post*, 31 March, pp. 10.

Edmonston, B., Passel, J. and Bean, F. (1990), 'Perceptions and Estimates of Undocumented Migration to the United States', in F. Bean, B. Edmonston and J. Passel (eds), *Undocumented Migration to the United States; IRCA and the Experience of the 1980s*, The Rand Corporation, Santa Monica, pp. 11-31, 24-25.

Edwards, N. (1998), 'Fears Over Rising Illegal Immigration', *Bangkok Post*, 18 March.

Espenshade, T. and Hempstead, K. 'Contemporary American Attitudes Toward US Immigration', *International Migration Review*, Vol. 30(2), pp. 536.

Etemadi, F. U. (1998), 'The Urban Poor in Cebu City: A Situationer', *Cebu Data Bank*, Vol. 4(1), January, pp. 4.

Eviota, E. (1992), *The Political Economy of Gender*, Zed Books, London, pp. 132.

'Failed Policies Being Recycled; Buck-Passing Won't Solve Problem, Say Experts', *The Bangkok Post*, 19 July 1999.

Feith, H. (1962), *The Decline of Constitutional Democracy in Indonesia*, Cornell University Press, Ithaca.

Feridhanusetyawan, T. (1988), 'The Social Impact of the Indonesian Economic Crisis', *The Indonesian Quarterly*, Vol. XXVI(4), December.

'Firms Want Rules on Hiring Immigrants to be Eased; Need to Fill Positions Shunned by Thais', *Bangkok Post*, 22 May 1998.

Focus on the Global South (FOCUS) (1998), *Annual Report 1997*, Focus on the Global South, Bangkok.

Frankenberg, E., Thomas, D. and Beegle, K. (1999), *The Real Cost of Indonesia's Economic Crisis: Preliminary Findings from the Indonesian Family Life Surveys*, Labor and Population Program Working Paper Series 99-04, March, Rand Corporation.

Freeman, G. (1995), 'Modes of Immigration Politics in Liberal Democratic States', *International Migration Review*, No. 4, Winter, p. 883.

Gearing, J. (1998), 'A Doer, Not a Speaker', *Far Eastern Economic Review*, Vol.24(49), 11 December, pp. 44.

Gecker, J. (1998), 'Indonesians Ram Truck Into UN Base', *Migration News*, 30 March.

Geertz, C. (1964), *The Religion of Java*, Free Press of Glencoe, New York.

Go, S. (1998), 'Towards the 21st Century: Whither Philippine Labor Migration', in B. Carino (ed.), *Filipino Workers on the Move: Trends, Dilemmas and Policy Options*, Philippine Migration Research Network and Philippine Social Science Council, Quezon City, pp. 12.

Guhan, S. (1994), 'Social Security Options for Developing Countries', *International Labour Review*, Vol. 133(1), pp. 35-53.

Gurr, T. R. (1993), *Minorities at risk: a global view of ethnopolitical conflicts*, United States Institute of Peace Press, Washington, DC.

Hadiz, V. R. (1997), *Workers and the State in the New Order Indonesia*, Routledge, London.

Harris, D. (ed.) (1995), *Prisoners of Progress: A Review on the Current Indonesian Labor Situation*, INDOC, KC Meppel.

Hawkins, E. (1971), 'Labor in Developing Countries: Indonesia', in B. Glassburner (ed.), *The Indonesian Economy: Selected Readings*, Cornell University Press, Ithaca.

Hefner, R. (1993), 'Islam, State, and Civil Society: ICMI and the Struggle for the Indonesian Middle Class', *Indonesia*, Vol. 56, October, pp. 1-37.

Hendityo, M.K. (1999), *Workers Coping Strategies: Ways to Survive the Crisis in Indonesia*, unpublished report for the World Bank, May.

Hernandez, C. G. (1995), 'Philippine Foreign Policy in the Post-Cold War Era: Challenges, Opportunities and Prospects', *Philippine Foreign Policy and Regional Politics*, University of the Philippines Center for Integrative and Development Studies, Quezon City, pp. 40-41.

Hernandez, C. G. and Tigno, J. V. (1995), 'ASEAN Labor Migration: Implications for Regional Stability', *The Pacific Review*, Vol. 8(3), pp. 545.

Heyzer, N. (1986), *Working Women in Southeast Asia*, Open University Press, Philadelphia.

Hikam, M. A. (1995), *The State, Grass-roots Politics and Civil Society*, Ph.D. Dissertation, University of Hawaii, Hawaii.

Hikam, M. A. (1999), 'Problems of Political Transition in Post-New Order Indonesia', *Indonesian Quarterly*, Vol. XXVII. (1), First Quarter, pp. 65-82.

Hill, H. (1994), 'The Economy', in H. Hill (ed.), *Indonesia's New Order: The Dynamics of Socio Economic Transformation*, Allen & Unwin, Sydney, pp. 54-122.

Horowitz, D. L. (1985), *Ethnic Groups in Conflict*, University of California Press, Berkeley.

Horowitz, D. L. (1993), 'Democracy in Divided Societies', *Journal of Democracy*, Vol. 4(4), pp. 36.

Hugo, G. (1995), 'Illegal International Migration in Asia', in R. Cohen (ed.), *The Cambridge Survey of World Migration*, Cambridge University Press, Cambridge, pp. 398.

Human Development Network (1997), *Philippine Human Development Report*, Human Development Network and the United Nations Development Programme, Philippines, pp. 25.

Human Rights Watch Report (1998), *Human Rights Watch*, New York, 9 December.

Hutasingh, O. (1997a), 'Tough Fight Against Illegal Alien Workers', *Bangkok Post*, 15 December, pp. 2.

Hutasingh, O. (1997b), 'Studies Show Who Benefits From Alien Workers Here', *Bangkok Post*, 25 May.

Hutasingh, O. (1998), 'How to Stem the Flow', *Bangkok Post*, 8 February.

Hutchcroft, P. D. (1998), *Booty Capitalism: The Politics of Banking in the Philippines*, Cornell University Press, Ithaca.

Huysmans, J. (1995), 'Migrants as a Security Problem: Dangers of 'Securitizing' Societal Issues', in R. Miles and D. Thranhardt (eds), *Migration and European Integration; The Dynamics of Inclusion and Exclusion*, Pinter Publishers, London, pp. 59.

'In a Desperate Bid to Avoid Being Sent Home Foreign Workers Rush to Apply for Permanent Residence', *The Straits Times*, 7 January 1998.

Ingleson, J. (1986), *In Search of Justice: Workers and Unions in Colonial Java 1908-1926*, Oxford University Press, Singapore.

International Organization for Migration (IOM) (1994), *Trafficking in Migrants: Characteristics and Trends in Different Regions of the World*, unpublished discussion paper presented at the '11th IOM Seminar on Migration', Geneva, 26-28 October, pp. 2-3.

Jervis, R. (1997-98), 'Complexity and the Analysis of Political and Social Life', *Political Science Quarterly*, Vol. 112(4), pp. 569.

Jones, G. (ed.) (1984), *Women in the Urban and Industrial Workforce: Southeast and East Asia*, Australian National University, Canberra.

'Justice Ministry Postpones Plan to Expel Illegal Foreign Workers', *Korea Herald*, 8 January 1998.

Kahin, G. M. (1963), *Nationalism and Revolution in Indonesia*, Cornell University Press, Ithaca.

Kanlungan Centre Foundation (1997), *Destination: Middle East (A Handbook for Filipino Women Domestic Workers)*, Kanlungan Centre Foundation, Quezon City, pp. 9.

Kara, N. (1997), *Transcending a historical legacy: sovereignty, the state and post-modernity*, unpublished paper, Spring, pp. 1-47.

Kennedy, P. (1993), *Preparing for the 21st Century*, Fontana Press, London.

Khandker, S. R., Khalili, B. and Khan, Z. (1995), *Grameen Bank: Performance and Sustainability*, World Bank, Washington, DC.

Krishnamoorthy, M. (1998), 'Handsome Black Market Price for Our Passports', *The Star*, 28 July.

Krisnawaty, T. (1997), *The Role of Bilateral Agreements on Migrant Labor Issues: The Case of Indonesia and Malaysia*, paper presented at the 'Conference on Legal Protection for Women Migrant Workers: Strategy for Action', Manila, 8-12 September 1997, pp. 1.

Lee, E. (1998), *The Asian Financial Crisis: The Challenge of Social Policy*, International Labor Organization (ILO), Geneva.

Lee, K. H. and Sivananthiran, A. (1996), 'Contract Labor in Malaysia: Perspectives of Principal Employers, Contractors, and Workers', *International Labor Review*, Vol.135(1), pp. 75-91.

Liddle, R. W. (1995), *Islam and Politics in Late New Order Indonesia: The Use of Religion as a Political Resource by an Authoritarian Regime*, mimeo, Ohio State University.

Lijphart, A. (1977), *Democracy in plural societies: a comparative exploration*, Yale University Press, New Haven.

Lim, L. L. and Oishi, N. (1996), 'International Labor Migration of Asian Women: Distinctive Characteristics and Policy Concerns', *Asian and Pacific Migration Journal*, Vol. 5(1), pp. 85.

Link, M. and Oldendick, R. (1996), 'Social Construction and White Attitudes Toward Equal Opportunity and Multiculturalism', *The Journal of Politics*, Vol. 58(1), February, pp. 149-168.

Linz, J. and Stepan, A. (1996), *Problems of Democratic Transition and Consolidation: Southern Europe, South America, and Post Communist Europe*, Johns Hopkins University, Baltimore.

Lok, HP., 'Labor in Garment Industry: an Employer's Perspective' in C. Manning and J. Hardjono (eds), *Indonesia Assessment 1993: Labor Sharing in the Benefit of Growth, Political and Social Change*, Monograph No. 20, Research School of Pacific Studies, Australian National University, Canberra.

McDowell, P. (1998), 'Crisis drives migrants back to villages', *Vancouver Sun*, 16 July, pp. F3.

McKibben, B. (1996), 'The Enigma of Kerala', *Utne Reader*, March-April, pp. 103-112.

'Malaysia Mendeportasi 10.000 TKI Ilegal', *Republika*, 21 March 1998.

Manila Community Services, Inc. (1993), *25 Years of Sharing in Development*, MCSI, Metro Manila.

Manning, C. (1999), 'Labour Markets in the ASEAN-4 and the NIEs', *Asian Pacific Economic Literature*, Vol. 13(1), May.

Manning, C. and Jayasuriya, S. (1996), 'Survey of Recent Development', *Bulletin of Indonesian Economic Studies*, August.

Manning, C. and Junankar, P.N. (1998), 'Choosy Youth or Unwanted Youth? A survey of Unemployment', *Bulletin of Indonesian Economic Studies*, Vol. 34(1), April.

Marshall, A. (1998), 'Indonesians toil 2 days for a Big Mac', *Vancouver Sun*, 16 July, pp. F3.

Marukatat, S. (1998), 'Looking After Our Own in This Time of Crisis', *Bangkok Post*, 12 January, pp. 9.

Mason, A. D. and Baptist, J. (1996), *How Important Are Labor Markets to the Welfare of Indonesia's Poor?*, World Bank Policy Research Paper No. 1665, Washington, DC.

Mather, C. (1985), *Women, Work, and Ideology in the Third World*, Tavitstock, London.

Maxwell, S. (1990), 'Food Security in Developing Countries: Issues and Options for the 1990's, *IDS Bulletin*, Vol. 21(3), July.

May, R.J. (1992), 'The Religious Factor in Three Minority Movements: The Moro of the Philippines, the Malays of Thailand, and Indonesia's West Papuans', *Contemporary Southeast Asia*, Vol. 13(4), pp. 397-8.

Migrants Standing Committee (1996), *A Survey on Placement Fees Paid by Taiwan-Bound OFWs (Overseas Filipino Workers) to Philippine Agencies*, unpublished report by the St. Christopher's Parish Pastoral Council, October-December, Table 4, pp. 2.

'Ministry of Labor Tightens Work Permit Procedures', *The Straits Times*, 20 November 1997.

Ministry of Manpower (1985), *Manual on the Implementation of the Pancasila Industrial Relations*, Depnaker, Jakarta.

Mitchel, P. T., Quadir, F., Shaw, T. M. and van der Westhuizen, J. (1997), 'Report of the Task Force on Development and Security Discourse', *Development and Security in Southeast Asia: Task Force Reports*, Canadian Consortium on Asia Pacific Security, Toronto.

Moertopo, A. (1975), *Buruh dan Tani dalam Pembangunan*, CSIS, Jakarta.

Moran, T. (1990/1), 'International economics and security', *Foreign Affairs*, Vol. 5, Winter.

Moser, C. (1998), 'The Asset Vulnerability Framework: Reassessing Urban Poverty Reduction Strategies', *World Development*, Vol. 26(1), pp. 1-19.

Myint, N. (1998), *Myanmar Country Paper: Academic Aspects*, paper presented during the 'Regional Workshop on Transnational Migration and Development in ASEAN Countries', Institute for Population and Social Research, Mahidol University, International Organization for Migration, Bangkok and Hua Hin, 25-27 May 1998, pp. 3, Table 4.

Nafziger, J. and Bartel, B. (no date), 'The Migrant Workers Convention: Its Place in Human Rights Law', *International Migration Review*, Vol. 25 (4).

Nayyar, D. (1993), 'Statistics on International Labor Migration and Economic Analysis: Some Conceptual Issues', in ILO-ARTEP, *International Labor Migration Statistics and Information Networking in Asia*, International Labor Office, Geneva, pp. 41.

Niyom, P. (1997), 'Critical Partnerships in Governance and Poverty Alleviation', in E. Porio (ed.), *Urban Governance and Poverty Alleviation in Southeast Asia*, Global Urban Research Initiative at Ateneo de Manila University, Manila, pp. 149-164 and 155.

O'Donnell, G. and Schmitter, P. (1986), *Transitions from Authoritarian Rule: Tentative Conclusions about Uncertain Democracies*, Johns Hopkins University Press, Baltimore.

O'Neill, H. (1997), 'Globalisation, Competitiveness and Human Security: Challenges for Development Policy and Institutional Change', *The European Journal of Development Research*, Vol. 9(1), June, pp. 9.

'1700 per bulan, TKI Masuk Sarawak', *Kompas*, 23 April 1998.

Ong, A. (1987), *Spirits of resistance and capitalist discipline*, SUNY Press, Albany.

Organization for Economic Cooperation and Development (OECD) (1997), *DAC Guidelines on Conflict, Peace and Development Co-operation*, OECD, May.

Osborne, D. and Gaebler, T. (1992), *Reinventing Government; How the Entrepreneurial Spirit is Transforming the Public Sector*, Addison-Wesley Publishing Company, Inc. Massachusetts.

Pangestu, M. and Hendytio, M. K. (1997), *Survey Responses from Women Workers in Indonesia's Textile, Garment and Footwear Industry*, World Bank Policy Research Paper.

Perez, A. E. and Patacsil, P. C. (compilers) (1998), *Philippine Migration Studies: An Annotated Bibliography*, Philippine Migration Research Network, Quezon City.

Poppele, J., Sumarto, S. and Pritchett, L. (1999), 'Social Impact of the Indonesian Economic Crisis: New Data and Policy Implication', *Smeru Report*, February.

Price, J. (1998), 'Dissent and New Directions for Canada and the Asia Pacific', *Building on Canada's Year of Asia Pacific: Evaluation and Strategic Directions*, Conference, 7 March.

Putnam, R. (1993), 'The Prosperous Community: Social and Capital and Public Life', *The American Prospect*, Vol. 13, Spring, pp. 35-42.

Putnam, R. (1995), 'Bowling Alone: America's Declining Social Capital', *Journal of Democracy*, Vol. 6(1), January, pp. 65-78.

Putnam, R. (1996), 'The Strange Disappearance of Civic America', *The American Prospect*, Vol. 24, Winter.

Putnam, R., Leonardi, R. and Nanetti, R. Y. (1993), *Making democracy work: civic traditions in modern Italy*, Princeton University Press, Princeton.

Rathgeber, E. (1989a), 'Integrating Gender into Development', *Journal of Developing Societies*, Vol. 8.

Rathgeber, E. (1989b), 'WID, WAD, GAD', *Halifax Pearsonnotes*, Vol. 4(3), Summer.

'Retailers press government for more relief to ensure survival', *Bangkok Post*, 3 August 16 July, pp. F3.

Reuters (1998), 'Thais Among Immigrants Facing Cane', *Bangkok Post*, 23 March, pp.1.

Rinakit, S. (forthcoming), 'Labor Union and Labor Unrest', in R.J. Baker, *et al.* (eds), *Riding the Miracle: Indonesian Institutions and Economic Growth*, Institute of Southeast Asian Studies (ISEAS), Singapore.

Robison, R. (1986), *Indonesia: The Rise of Capital*, Allen & Unwin, Sydney.

Rudiono, D. (1997), 'Peradilan Khusus Perburuhan, Sebuah Alternatif Penyelesaian Konflik: Beberapa Catatan Tentang RUU Ketenagakerjaan', in Komisi Pembaharuan Hukum Perburuhan, *RUU Ketenagakerjaan Pantas Meresahkan Buruh*, KPHP, Jakarta, pp. 62-71.

Rungfapaisarn, K. (1997), 'KFC plans big expansion in local market: Fast food chain still confident', *The Nation*, 11 November, pp. B3.

Rungswasdisab, P. (1997), 'An Illegal Population Takes Root', *The Nation*, 2 June, pp. A9.

Sachs, J. (1997), 'International Monetary Failure?' *Time*, 8 December, pp. 8.

Said, S. (1996), *Suharto's Armed Forces: Building a Power Base in New Order Indonesia, 1965-1995*, presented at the 'Annual Meeting of the Association of Asian Studies', Honolulu, Hawaii, 11-14 April.

Sainath, P. (1998), *Everybody loves a good drought: Stories from India's Poorest Villages*, Review/Headline Book Publishing, London.

Salaff, J. (1981), *Working Daughters of Hong Kong*, Cambridge University Press, London.

Santos, M. (1975), *L'espace partagé*, editions M-Th, Génin, Librairies Techniques, Paris.

Scalabrini Migration Center (1992), *Pre-Employment and Pre-Departure Services for Filipina Migrant Workers*, La Trobe University Regional Social Development Centre and International Social Service for Migrant Women Project for the International Labor Organization, April.

Schmitter, P. (1974), 'Still the Century of Corporatism?', in F. Pike and T. Stricht (eds), *The New Corporatism: Social and Political Structures in the Iberian World*, University of Notre Dame Press, Notre Dame, pp. 85-131.

Schwarz, A. (1994), *A Nation in Waiting: Indonesia in the 1990s*, Allen and Unwin, St. Leonards, Australia.

Semaun (1966), 'An Early Account of the Independent Movement', translated by R. McVey, *Indonesia*, Vol. 1, April, pp. 46-75.

Sen, A. (1981), 'Poverty and Famines: An Essay on Entitlement and Deprivation', Clarendon Press, Oxford.

Sethuraman, S. V. (1992), *The Urban Informal Sector in Asia: An Annotated Bibliography Series: International Labor Bibliography*, International Labour Office, Geneva.

Shen-Li, L. (1998), 'Fighting to Keep Out Life-Threatening Ills', *New Sunday Times*, 18 January.

Singarimbun, M. and Sairin, S. (1995), *Liku-liku Kehidupan Buruh Perempuan*, Pustaka Pelajar, Yogyakarata.

Sirisambhand, N. (1994), *Hidden Producers in Bangkok Metropolis: Women in the Urban Informal Sector*, Friedrich Ebert Stiftung, Bangkok, November.

Sirisambhand, N. (1996), *Social Security for Women in the Informal Sector in Thailand*, Friedrich Ebert Stiftung, Bangkok, January.

Sivasomboon, B. and Treerapongpichit, B. (1998), 'Laid off workers turn to small businesses', *Bangkok Post*, 23 March, pp. 10.

'Slowdown May Send Foreign Workers in Malaysia Packing', *The Straits Times*, 24 November 1997.

Smith, P. (1995), *Asia's Economic Transformation and Its Impact on Intraregional Labor Migration*, unpublished, Council on Foreign Relations Asia Project Working Paper, New York, March, pp. 5.

Smith, P. (1997), 'The Military's Increasing Role in Immigration Enforcement', article reproduced by *CISNEWS@cis.org* from *Immigration Review*, No. 29, Summer.

Soekarni, M. (1998), 'Kebijakan Upah Minimum Regional di Indonesia: Dimensi Ekonomi', in M. A. Hikam (ed.), *Strategi Kebijaksanaan Pemerintah dalam Masalah Pengupahan Tenaga Kerja*, PEP-LIPI, Jakarta, pp. 27-58.

Soekarno (1979), *Pembaharuan gerakan Buruh di Indonesia dan Hubungan Industrial Pancasila*, Alumni, Bandung.

Sorensen, T. (1995), 'What is international economic security?' *International Affairs*, Vol. 71, March, pp. 305-24.

Southall, R. (ed.) (1988), *Trade Union and the New Industrialization of the Third World*, Zed Press, London.

Stephen, I. (1998), 'Tough Measures on Immigration Offenders', *Borneo Bulletin*, 1 April.

'Steps to protect workers "slow compared to promotion"', *The Jakarta Post*, 18 December 1998.

Sudono, A. (1984), *FBSI: Dahulu, Sekarang, dan Yang Akan Datang*, DPP FBSI, Jakarta.

Szirmai, A. (1933), 'Comparative Productivity in Manufacturing: A Case Study of Indonesia', in A. Szirmai, B. van Ark and D. Pilats (eds), *Explaining Economic Growth: Essays in Honor of Angus Maddison*, Elsevier/North Holland, Amsterdam, pp. 1-23.

Tedjasukmana, I. (1959), *The Political Character of the Indonesian Trade Union Movement*, Monograph Series, Cornell Modern Indonesia Project, Ithaca.

Tellis-Nayak, J. and Costa-Pinto, S. (1979), *Towards Self-Reliance ISI Program for Women's Development*, Divine Word Publications, N. Delhi Indore.

Tenaganita (1995), *A Memorandum on Abuse, Torture and Dehumanised Treatment of Migrant Workers at Detention Centres*, unpublished paper, August, pp. 1.

Tessier, K. (1995), 'The New Slave Trade: The International Crisis in Immigrant Smuggling', *Indiana Journal of Global Legal Studies*, Vol. 3(1), Fall, pp. 1.

Thamrin, J. (1995), 'Development Policy', in D. Harris (ed), *Prisoners of Progress: A Review on the Current Indonesian Labour Situation*, INDOC, KC Meppel, pp. 1-22.

'Time for a Reality Check in Asia', *Business Week*, 2 December 1996, pp. 59-66.

Tinker, I. (1987), 'Street Foods: Testing Assumptions about Informal Sector Activity by Women and Men', *Current Sociology*, Vol. 35(3).

Tinker, I. (1997), *Street Foods: Urban Food and Employment in Developing Countries*, Oxford University Press, New York and Oxford.

Torres, C. I. (1995), 'The New Overseas Employment Program: Effectively Managing the Labor Migration Process', *Development Research News*, Vol. XIII(3), May-June, pp. 10.

Tunyasiri, Y. and Charoenpo, A. (1998), 'Jobs Opened Up as 19,000 Foreign Workers Go Home', *Bangkok Post*, 17 February, pp. 1.

Tweeten, L. (1997), 'Investing in People', *Promoting Third World Development and Food Security*, Praeger, Westport, pp. 183-204.

'Two Thailands: Spreading Wealth Beyond Bangkok', *Far Eastern Economic Review*, 14 April 1994.

Unarat, S. (1998a), 'Alien Workers Issue to be Reviewed', *Bangkok Post*, 29 April, pp. 3.

Unarat, S. (1998b), 'Concern Among Rice and Rubber Operators', *Bangkok Post*, 29 April, pp. 3.

Ung, A. (1998), 'Malaysia May Expel One Million Workers', *The Straits Times*, 7 January.

United Nations (UN) (1994), *Report of the International Conference on Population and Development: Program of Action*, Cairo, 5-13 September.

United Nation Support Facility for Indonesian Recovery (UNSFIR) (1999), *The Social Implications of the Indonesian Economic Crisis: Perception and Policy*, Discussion Paper No. 1, April.

Vanaspong, C. (1997), 'Learning Lessons From a Neighbor', *Bangkok Post*, 9 March.

Vinesh, D. (1998), '200,000 Aliens to be Sent Back', *The Star*, 17 July.

Wie, T. K. (1992), 'Indonesia's Manufactured Exports: Performance and Prospect', in N. Mihira (ed.), *Indonesia's Non-Oil Exports: Performance, Problems, and Prospects*, IDE, Tokyo.

Wilson, P. (1997), 'Building Social Capital: A Learning Agenda for the Twenty-First Century', *Urban Studies*, Vol. 34(5), pp. 745-760.

Wiranta, S. (ed.) (1998), *Penanganan UMR dalam Sektor Industri Manufaktur*, PEP-LIPI, Jakarta.

Wolf, D. (1986), *Factory Daughters, Their Families, and Rural Industries in Central Java*, Cornell University Press, Ithaca.

Wolf, D. (1992), *Factory Daughters*, University of California Press, Berkeley.

Wong, J. (1998), 'Ethnic-Chinese Women Seek to Wed to Flee Fear, Violence in Indonesia', *The Wall Street Journal*, 21 July.

'Workers to be Classified; New Centre to Document Staff to Help Management of Labor Force', *The Bangkok Post*, 19 July 1999.

World Bank (1999), *Indonesia: From Crisis to Opportunity*, World Bank Report, July.

Yamamoto, T. (1999), *Deciding the Public Good; Governance and Civil Society in Japan*, Japan Center for International Exchange, Tokyo.

Yasmeen, G. (1992), 'Bangkok's Restaurant Sector: Gender, Employment and Consumption', *Journal of Social Research*, Vol. 15(2), Chulalongkorn University, Bangkok, Thailand, pp. 69-81.

Yasmeen, G. (1995), *Exploring a Foodscape: The Case of Bangkok*, proceedings of the 'Third International Conference on Geography of the ASEAN Region', Part I, and in *Malaysian Journal of Tropical Geography*, Vol. 26(1), pp. 1-11.

Yasmeen, G. (1996), *Bangkok's Foodscape: Public Eating, Gender Relations and Urban Change*, unpublished Ph.D. dissertation, Department of Geography, University of British Columbia.

Yasmeen, G. and Walker, M. (eds), '"From Scratch": Thai Food-Systems and Public Eating', *Contemporary Perspectives on Thai Foodways*, Monograph No. 11, Centre for Southeast Asian Research, Vancouver, pp. 20-43.

Yayasan Lembaga Bantuan Hukum Indonesia (YLBHI) (1991), 'Background Report: The Shackling of the Workers' Right to Organize', *Indonesian Human Rights Forum*, No. 1, July-September, pp. 1.

Yoshihara, K. (1988), *The Rise of Ersatz Capitalism in Southeast Asia*, Oxford University Press, Singapore.

Yuen-Pau, W. (1998), 'Social Impacts of the Asian Crisis: The Unravelling of The Asian Miracle?' *Asia Pacific Papers Series*, Asia Pacific Foundation of Canada, Vancouver, pp. 3.

Index

For Product Safety Concerns and Information please contact our EU representative GPSR@taylorandfrancis.com Taylor & Francis Verlag GmbH, Kaufingerstraße 24, 80331 München, Germany

Batch number: 10725941

Printed by Printforce, the Netherlands